ATTENTION AND MEMORY

OXFORD PSYCHOLOGY SERIES

1. *The neuropsychology of anxiety: an enquiry into the functions of the septohippocampal system*
Jeffrey A. Gray
2. *Elements of episodic memory*
Endel Tulving
3. *Conditioning and associative learning*
N. J. Mackintosh
4. *Visual masking: an integrative approach*
Bruno G. Breitmeyer
5. *The musical mind: the cognitive psychology of music*
John Sloboda
6. *Elements of psychophysical theory*
J. C. Falmagne
7. *Animal intelligence*
Edited by L. Weiskrantz
8. *Response times: their role in inferring elementary mental organization*
R. Duncan Luce
9. *Mental representations: a dual coding approach*
Allan Paivio
10. *Memory: imprinting, and the brain*
Gabriel Horn
11. *Working memory*
Alan Baddeley
12. *Blindsight: a case study and implications*
L. Weiskrantz
13. *Profile analysis*
D. M. Green
14. *Spatial vision*
R. L. DeValois and K. K. DeValois
15. *The neural and behavioural organization of goal-directed movements*
Marc Jeannerod
16. *Visual pattern analyzers*
Norma V. Graham
17. *Cognitive foundations of musical pitch analysis*
C. L. Krumhansl
18. *Perceptual and associative learning*
G. Hall
19. *Implicit learning and tacit knowledge: an essay on the cognitive unconscious*
Arthur S. Reber
20. *Neuromotor mechanisms in human communication*
Doreen Kimura
21. *The frontal lobes and voluntary action*
R. Passingham
22. *Classification and cognition*
William Estes
23. *Vowel perception and production*
B. S. Rosner and J. B. Pickering
24. *Visual Stress*
A. Wilkins
25. *Electrophysiology of mind*
Edited by M. Rugg and M. Coles
26. *Attention and memory: an integrated framework*
Nelson Cowan
27. *The visual brain in action*
A. D. Milner and M. A. Goodale

Attention and Memory
An Integrated Framework

Nelson Cowan
Department of Psychology
University of Missouri–Columbia

OXFORD PSYCHOLOGY SERIES
NO. 26

New York Oxford
OXFORD UNIVERSITY PRESS • CLARENDON PRESS
1995

Oxford University Press

Oxford New York Toronto
Delhi Bombay Calcutta Madras Karachi
Kuala Lumpur Singapore Hong Kong Tokyo
Nairobi Dar es Salaam Cape Town
Melbourne Auckland Madrid

and associated companies in
Berlin Ibaidan

Published by Oxford University Press, Inc.,
2100 Madison Avenue, New York, New York 10016

Oxford is a registered trademark of Oxford University Press

Library of Congress Cataloging-in-Publication Data
Cowan, Nelson.
Attention and memory: an integrated framework/Nelson Cowan.
p. cm. — (Oxford psychology series; no. 26)
Includes bibliographical references and index.
ISBN 0-19-506760-6
1. Human information processing. 2. Memory. 3. Attention
(Psychology) I. Title. II. Series.
BF444...C68 1995
153. 1—dc20
94–12555

1 3 5 7 9 8 6 4 2

Printed in the United States of America
on acid-free paper

In memory of Donald Broadbent
1926–1993

Preface

... writing is nothing more than a guided dream.

Jorg Luis Borges
in the preface of *Dr. Brodie's Report*
(1972: New York, E. P. Dutton)

The notion of writing a book was suggested to me by Donald Broadbent when he read my review article appearing in the *Psychological Bulletin* (Cowan, 1988) and sent two long letters full of helpful comments, ideas, and references. The purpose of my article had been to develop a model of the information processing system that captures what is fundamental about memory and attention and omits what we do not know. Developing such a model was, I felt, the best way to stay focused on learning how the components of the processing system affect one another, and on finding out what kinds of research would address the most general areas of ignorance. This also appears to have been the spirit of some previous models (e.g., Broadbent, 1958, 1984; Atkinson & Shiffrin, 1968), but they appeared to be in need of revision and modification.

Many other cognitive researchers have taken a different strategy. They have tried to model only a particular aspect of the processing system in great detail or have incorporated various untested assumptions into their models in order to derive more precise predictions from those models.

Although many of those efforts have indeed been fruitful, in my own work I have preferred the more general approach in which the emphasis is placed on resolving the most basic unsettled issues first, so as hopefully to minimize wrong turns.

The process that led me to the 1988 formulation in many ways turned out to be an interesting recapitulation of the processes that Broadbent (1958) followed in arriving at his seminal model. Again it was the interrelation between temporary memory and selective attention that was salient. Broadbent emphasized that subjects could recall only the last few seconds of an unattended channel in selective listening. Similarly, in the process of examining memory for unattended spoken syllables (Cowan, Lichty, & Grove, 1990), I began to rethink the role of selective filtering. I noticed that subjects required an irregularly timed set of syllables, with not too many seconds between syllables in order to allow them to habituate to the syllables and focus on a primary task, silent reading. During this work I realized that the habituation of orienting was an automatic mechanism that could play an essential part in the selective filtering of stimuli; and there was already research supporting that approach (e.g., Waters, McDonald, & Koresko, 1977).

There has been an explosion of new research since 1988 relevant to the points in my 1988 article. Perhaps that is indicative only of the maddening rate of research publications in general. There are over 50 journals in cognitive and neural sciences that are of direct relevance to memory and attention, and a wealth of books too. I doubt if anyone can keep up with this much new work on a regular basis, which is a problem that is leading to too much fractionation among researchers who logically should be talking. I do not know what the solution to this information exchange problem is going to be, but perhaps some highlights of the new research can be integrated in an intense effort that is limited in duration; and that has become a goal of this book. When I decided to write it, with a three-year fuse and some expert guidance and kind encouragement from my editor, Joan Bossert, I began organizing notes on research findings from these various sources.

My original intent was to consider the basic concepts discussed by Cowan (1988) as being already well-established, and strive primarily to elaborate upon those concepts. However, the recent literature caused me to revise my plans as I found that some of the fundamental hypotheses that I took for granted, other researchers questioned on reasonable grounds. For example, Crowder (1989*a*) has questioned the entire concept of transient memory storage (which, on the other hand, is very popular among psychophysiologists, at present), and Wickens (1984) and others questioned the notion of a central attentional capacity limitation. This book consequently takes a close look at such basic concepts. In the end, I reaffirm the foundations of my 1988 framework, although it is likely that someone else might reach different conclusions from these same data. I hope I have at least conveyed the scope of available evidence on the basic issues, which I have tried to consider with an open mind.

There are many important and theoretically related areas that I have had to omit, with regret. These include much of the research on memory and attention in animals, on life-span development, on individual differences within a normal range, and on social, emotional, and motivational factors.

One endeavor that I found especially helpful in bootstrapping the book was a three-week "whistle-stop tour" to seven cities in Great Britain in Fall 1990. During that trip I visited and received important input from Donald Broadbent, Clive Frankish, Charles Hulme, Graham Hitch, Susan Gathercole, Dylan Jones, and Alan Baddeley, among others. Broadbent looked over my list of these hosts and noted, clearly with some satisfaction, that all of them had worked for or with him. His influence has largely shaped Britain's strong program of research in basic memory and attentional processes, and I was quite fortunate to have taken my trip when I did because it was not long after that he passed away.

A large part of the recent research explosion has involved neurophysiological findings that are related to memory and attention, many of them using new techniques for imaging brain processes. I was fortunate to be able to spend March through May 1991 in Helsinki working with Risto Näätänen and his research group (with István Winkler as my closest collaborator), which allowed me to gain a better grasp of some of the psychophysiological literature. It also led to my presence at the International Conference on Event-Related Potentials of the Brain in Eger, Hungary in May 1992, during and after which I learned important information from Kimmo Alho, Diana Deacon, Riita Hari, Norman Loveless, Walter Ritter, Mikko Sams, and Hannu Tiitinen, among others. With their help I have been able to suggest neural counterparts to some basic cognitive concepts.

In the process of writing, I have learned from a number of other investigators. Dominic Massaro, who was an instructor and co-author of mine when I was in graduate school in Madison, Wisconsin, suggested the term "theoretical framework" for what it is that I have been investigating. My participation as a co-author on a review chapter (Massaro & Cowan, 1993) has also educated me a great deal. David Balota, Larry Jacoby, and Kristi Multhaup helped me understand some important issues regarding the role of attention in memory, as did a friend and public school teacher, Bill Roney, in 25 years of open-ended discussions.

Richard Schweickert, a leading cognitive psychologist, and Riita Hari, a leading neuroscientist, both read the entire manuscript and made invaluable, expert comments. From my own Department of Psychology at the University of Missouri, Steve Hackley, Peter Frensch, Michael Stadler, and Ines Stafford-Segert commented on parts of the manuscript, and David Geary and Ken Sher helped me locate important references. The book would not have been possible without the help of various people who have done excellent work as my research assistants, including Linda Day, Tim Keller, Scott Saults, and Noelle Wood. I am grateful also to my department chair, Tom DiLorenzo, for helping me find time to write.

In the process of writing I have become sensitized to the gradual flow of ideas from one generation to the next, and from one era to the next. For example, some of the seed concepts of Baddeley's (1986) articulatory loop theory of verbal short-term memory can be traced back to portions of Broadbent's (1958) book. When I visited the library in Baddeley's laboratory in Cambridge, I stumbled across his dissertation from the 1960s and found it to contain some interesting unpublished experiments that are quite relevant to his very recent work. It seems to me also that Crowder's (1989*a*) views are quite in line with what his mentor, Arthur Melton, had suggested (e.g., Melton, 1963).

These investigators probably are aware of their academic heritage. I hope I can give due credit to mine, as well. (It has been said, somewhere, that there is nothing new except what has been forgotten.) Some influences may have been indirect. Way before I began working at the University of Missouri, Melton was the chair here (in the 1930s) and taught and inspired a large number of people who later became important in experimental psychology.

Among them was Al Liberman, who in turn became a mentor for Philip Morse, my advisor in graduate school at Wisconsin. Morse and a close colleague, pediatrician Lewis Leavitt, with contributions also from Francis Graham, fostered an exciting atmosphere of inquiry into the nature of the mind and brain. My interests broadened in a postdoctoral fellowship with Martin Braine and three subsequent years at the University of Massachusetts.

I recall some formative early episodes, including a guest lecture by a graduate student named David Pisoni in my introductory psychology class. Reaching further back, my father, Arthur Cowan, is a retired optometrist and some of my interest stems from having played with spare lenses in his office as a child. Also, when I read the recent articles on the neural foundation of consciousness by Crick and Koch (1990, 1992), it brought to mind a discussion that occurred when I was a child in Wheaton, Maryland. The *Washington Post* reported that two men had just won the Nobel prize for discovering the molecular structure of DNA. (I have looked it up and found that Crick won the Nobel prize with Watson on 10 December 1962, when I was 11 years old.) I recall that when asked where he wanted to go from there, Crick stated that he wanted to find out "how the brain works." Reading this, I commented to my mother, Shirley Cowan, that this was awfully simple language for a Nobel prize winner to use, and she aptly replied that he didn't need to impress people anymore. This nicely alludes to the proper role of simplicity in research.

Finally, the work for this book has been made possible by two grants. One is NICHD grant HD-21338. The other is not financial in nature, but a grant of the large amount of time and support needed to write the book, from my wife Jean Ispa, a professor of Human Development and Family Studies, who generously delayed work on a book of her own, and from our understanding children, Simone, Zachary, and Alexander. I am extremely grateful to them.

Columbia, Missouri N. C.
10 March 1994

Contents

ATTENTION AND MEMORY

1. Introduction: modeling memory and attention

Everything should be made as simple as possible, but not simpler.

Albert Einstein
as quoted in *Reader's Digest*, October 1977

The purpose of this book is to examine some basic issues of memory and attention, in light of a burgeoning research literature including various factions that have remained unconnected. Originally, the plan was to interpret the phrase "memory and attention" as the *union* of these two concepts, but as I made my way through the literature, I found that the theme had to be reduced primarily to the *intersection* of memory and attention. This intersection is interesting because of the ways in which memory and attention interact, and this was also the basic theme of a review article (Cowan, 1988) that has served as the launching-off point for this book.

Chipman (1992) noted the following shortcoming in the state of the field of cognitive psychology:

> Read a textbook. Textbooks of cognitive psychology appear to have been organized by sorting a set of notecards describing experiments into a convenient number of chapter heaps.

I hope that the present emphasis on the interrelatedness of memory and attention, and the constraints that they consequently place upon one another within theories of information processing, will help to abolish the heap approach.

Sources from James (1890) onward have considered definitions of both memory (e.g., Crowder, 1976; Bower & Hilgard, 1981) and attention (e.g., Shiffrin, 1988; Näätänen, 1992). I believe that there would be little value in sifting through complex definitions of these intuitively obvious terms, except to caution that there are aspects of the definitions that can be tricky.

First consider Bower and Hilgard's (1981, p. 2) definition of memory as "the faculty of retaining and recalling past experiences." The definition is as good as any, but it must be kept in mind that the only evidence we have that retention has taken place is the nature of the recall. Not all change in behavior is adequate evidence of retention because it is possible for an event to affect a person's behavior without leaving a memory trace. For example, a drug slipped secretly and undetectably into one's drink might alter behavior relative to a no-drug control group, but that would not imply that a memory of the drug has been formed. We are always faced with the task of inferring that the change in behavior resulted from some sort of internal representation of information contained in the stimulus rather than from other mechanisms and, if it did, what kind of information was represented.

If anything, the concept of attention is even trickier. It is customary to refer to William James for an historical view and an intuitive bearing, and with good reason I think. James (1890, pp. 403–404) appealed to intuition when he stated the following:

> Every one knows what attention is. It is the taking possession of the mind, in clear and vivid form, of one out of what seem several simultaneously possible objects or trains of thought. Focalization, concentration of consciousness are of its essence. It implies withdrawal from some things in order to deal effectively with others . . .

Shiffrin's (1988, p. 739) definition, however, was more inclusive:

> *Attention* has been used to refer to all those aspects of human cognition that the subject can control . . . and to all aspects of cognition having to do with limited resources or capacity, and methods of dealing with such constraints.

Shiffrin's definition points out that voluntary control is not necessarily the same thing as conscious awareness in its limited capacity. In fact, it appears possible to control some actions, and even make some selections among stimuli, automatically. For example, one probably can walk around furniture without bumping into it and without interrupting an ongoing conversation. In this book, the term "selective attention" will be used in a sense closer to that of James, to refer to selections that can be accomplished only by committing a limited-capacity process to that selection. It need not be a voluntary selection; thus a loud explosion takes over the attentional system momentarily whether one wants it to or not.

James's definition implies that, at the very least, multiple concurrent stimuli must be used to infer selective attention. It must be found that experimental manipulations that enhance the response to one of those stimuli do so at the cost of a reduction in performance in other stimuli. Even if that is found, difficult questions remain. Was the total amount of available attention held constant between the two different task-priority conditions? Were the interference effects general, or were they specific to the particular tasks combined (e.g., two different perceptual tasks that logically would require simultaneously looking left and right, or would require making two different responses with the same effector, or, more subtly, would require conflicting uses of the same feature analysis system of the brain)? These difficulties must not be construed so as to rule out research on attention, but they must guide the interpretation of it. With these precautions in mind, we can advance to the main business at hand, which is to examine the relation between memory and attention, and their proper roles in a simple model of information processing.

1.1 The fundamental relation between memory and attention

Although one of the main charges of experimental psychology may be to specify the remarkable faculties and abilities of the human mind and brain, this must go hand in hand with a study of the limitations and inabilities. It is remarkable that we are able to concentrate on one topic for a fairly long period of time, shutting out distractions of both internal and external origins; but this can be accomplished only by sacrificing the ability to monitor what is going on elsewhere in the environment. It is also remarkable that we are able to keep in mind a set of important considerations as we wend our ways deftly through various physical and social situations; but the frequency with which required details are forgotten is also striking.

In the characterization of human abilities and limitations, the relationship between memory and attention has long been noted. James (1890, p. 405) addresses the question of how much can be attended at one time as follows:

> The number of *things* we may attend to is altogether indefinite, depending on the power of the individual intellect, on the form of the apprehension, and on what the things are. When apprehended conceptually as a connected system, their number may be very large. But however numerous the things, they can only be known in a single pulse of consciousness for which they form one complex 'object' . . . so that properly speaking there is before the mind at no time a plurality of *ideas* . . .

Components of this belief have been echoed in more recent theoretical statements on the severe limits of selective attention (e.g., Broadbent, 1958) and on the importance of integrated chunks of information in determining the limits of short-term memory (e.g., Miller, 1956).

James conceived of "primary memory" as the temporary memory that is associated with an initial encounter with a stimulus or a thought. He was aware of the intricacy of this memory in its relation to attention. He quotes Exner (James, 1890, p. 646) as follows:

> Impressions to which we are inattentive leave so brief an image in the memory that it is usually overlooked. When deeply absorbed, we do not hear the clock strike. But our attention may awake after the striking has ceased, and we may then count off the strokes. Such examples are often found in daily life. . . . This primary-memory image is, whether attention have been turned to the impression or not, an extremely lively one, but is subjectively quite distinct from every sort of after-image or hallucination . . . [James' ellipsis] . . . It vanishes, if not caught by attention, in the course of a few seconds. Even when the original impression is attended to, the liveliness of its image in memory fades fast.

One can discern in this and surrounding passages of James's book two aspects of primary memory: a sensory afterimage that automatically preserves the vividness of the experience for a short while, and a more abstract mental impression that encodes and captures some remnant of the experience if it is attended to soon enough.

1.2 The emergence of memory and attention in modern psychology

1.2.1 Behaviorist movement

It is well known that the status of memory representations and attention declined in importance in the field of psychology for many years after James. This decline can be attributed largely to the American behaviorist movement.

The behaviorists (e.g., Watson, 1919, 1924) reacted to the technique of introspection, which had provided the primary data for leading psychologists of the day such as James and Titchener, with the assertion that introspection had not led to replicable findings and could not do so because the data were not public. They advocated the exclusive use of objective techniques in which stimuli are administered to the subject and the responses are measured. This led to important advances in experimental psychology. However, the behaviorists also asserted that the terminology for internal representations and internal processes, including terms such as images, memories, percepts, and attention, were unscientific and should not be used in scientific discourse.

Watson's abolishment of mentalistic terms amounted to a requirement that all theoretical constructs must be directly observable. Unfortunately, though, this left out the possibility of indirectly observable constructs, which are commonplace in other domains of science. For example, astronomers infer that there are atoms in the sun, even though they cannot observe them directly.

At times, it must be acknowledged, Watson's statements have been ridiculed in an unfair manner. In the words of one defender (Malone, 1990), "Watson never denied that we see, hear, feel, and remember; but we see things, not images, and we feel things, not sensations." However, even acknowledging this typical misunderstanding, there are important justifications of mentalistic concepts that Watson seems to have overlooked. One need only consider the "double images" remarked upon by Helmholtz (Garrett, 1941, p. 360). For example, if you hold a finger close to your face while maintaining visual focus on a point across the room, you will see a double image of your finger. Given that you are not fooled into believing that you are seeing two fingers, it seems fair to say that you are seeing two images of a finger, not two fingers. If introspection alone can establish this much, certainly modern cognitive methods, including group studies of subjectively reported experiences, establish the usefulness of some mentalistic concepts.

1.2.2 Gestalt movement

Many European psychologists did not adhere to the behaviorist view, and many of those instead were Gestalt psychologists who would have been more friendly toward mentalistic terms and even introspection. However, Näätänen (1992, p. 3) maintained that the Gestalt psychologists were partly responsible for the decline in the concept of attention:

> Gestalt psychologists emphasized their intrinsic Gestalt laws as central determinants of our percepts, of course, leaving no role to attention in perceptual organization.

This point may be overstated, however. The Gestalt psychologists did not do much direct research on attention, but attention is implicit in favored concepts such as insight. One Gestalt psychologist defined attention as follows (Koffka, 1935/1963, p. 395):

> . . . it will be fitting to define what we mean by attitude and attention. From our previous discussions of both these concepts it is clear that we mean by them actual *forces* that participate in the total dynamic situation . . . It seems to conform to good usage if we attribute the more general meaning to the term attitude, the more special to the term attention. Attention would then be a special attitude, namely that of simple unspecific directedness towards an object, whereas other attitudes would be more specific, like expectation of something more or less definite . . .

That definition did not imply the limited capacity nature of attention, but consider this passage from Köhler (1947, p. 299):

> The self is virtually always directed toward something or away from it. The most striking instances are those of intense emotions and motivations. But attention in general may also serve as an example. In the case of vision, its direction tends to coincide with that of fixation; but this connection is by no means rigid. Actually, attention as a reference to particular things is experienced in its purest form when, while fixating a given point, we concentrate on one object after another in the periphery of the field.

It is true, however, that the Gestalt psychologists had not turned their preconceptions about attention into more convincing empirical demonstrations.

The Gestalt psychologists carried the torch even more steadily in the case of memory. They were interested in explaining their behavioral results in a way that incorporated physiology of the brain (unlike behaviorists, who felt that such an attempt was for the far future), so they were quite amenable to the concept of an internal memory representation. Note the definitive quality and sophistication of thought in the writing of Koffka (1935/1963, p. 51):

(c) MEMORY. There is memory. Now memory determines to a great extent our behavioural field . . . That I speak to A whom I met yesterday and not to B whom I never saw before is due to the fact that A is, in my behavioural environment, a familiar person, B a stranger. But there are other ways in which memory determines behaviour without the mediation of a behavioural field. The rapid and accurate activities of a trained typist are not explainable in terms of the actually present behavioural environment.

Not only has Koffka here essentially described declarative and procedural memory (cf. Squire, 1987), but he goes on, in a subsequent passage, to describe what is now termed the tip-of-the-tongue phenomenon (e.g., Brown, 1991). Notice also that the discussion of Strangers A and B involved selective attention as well as memory.

In summary, it can be argued that Gestalt psychology helped to keep alive mentalistic concepts, including memory and attention, through the behaviorist era in the United States. However, these concepts could not really contribute much to the rest of psychology until they could be translated into observable behavioral phenomena. That began to happen as part of the very beginning of cognitive psychology and information processing.

1.2.3 Empirical observations of capacity limits

In the case of both memory and attention, what was perhaps most striking in the approach of the information processing psychologists was the observation of capacity limits. Observations occurring not long after World War II provoked a great deal of advancement in the study of practical problems related to communication technology, such as the limitations in electronic sending and receiving channels, and the ability of people to select and retain critical information from a complex barrage of stimulation under stress, as when directions are relayed by radio to several airplane pilots simultaneously.

Broadbent (1952) and Cherry (1953) presented subjects with "dichotic" tape recordings, in which different spoken messages are presented to the subject's two ears at the same time. They found that subjects were able to attend to one message, provided that the messages were distinguished by physical cues and not merely by semantic cues; but if subjects selectively attended in this way, they recalled almost nothing of the unattended message. Thus, attentional capacity was limited.

Miller (1956) noticed that, across many domains, subjects could keep in mind no more than about seven "chunks," or psychological units, simultaneously. Thus, with a methodology very different from the one Cherry used, Miller also found that the capacity of the conscious mind was limited. Limitations of attention and short-term memory appear as two sides of the same coin because both refer to processes assumed to rely on the subject's conscious awareness. Most researchers in the early days of information processing research still did not dare use the term "consciousness" in scientific discourse, but that was the implicit assumption. These findings of processing capacity limits helped to spawn models of human information processing.

1.3 Modelling the processing of information

1.3.1 Broadbent's 1958 model

Broadbent (1958) assembled a great deal of information arising from his laboratory, and elsewhere, in order to suggest tentatively, as a footnote, a schematic model of how the human mind might operate as it receives stimuli, derives required information from them, and acts upon them. This model, which is redrawn in Fig. 1.1, incorporated the available findings of limitations in memory and attention. It was observed that, although subjects could not recall most of the unattended channel of a dichotic tape, they often could recall the most recent several seconds of that channel. This suggested that the brain temporarily retains information about all stimuli but that the information fades, and neither is admitted to the conscious mind nor is encoded in a way that would permit later recollection, unless attention is turned quickly to a particular memory trace.

The teleology of this arrangement presumably was that the large amount of information in the environment that potentially could be apprehended would overwhelm the severely limited ability of a limited-capacity system

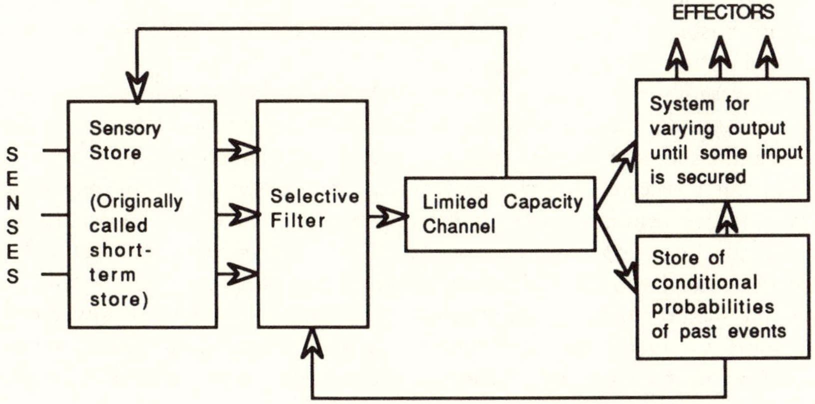

Fig. 1.1 An early model of information processing. (Redrawn from Broadbent, 1958 Fig. 7; p. 299.)

(which would include both conscious awareness and short-term memory) to deal with all of this information. The unattended information was said to be "filtered out" and lost without reaching awareness. (One exception to this is the rudimentary analysis of physical features of unattended stimuli. Cherry found that subjects easily and consistently noticed changes in the voice of an unattended channel, so it would have been evident that this information somehow occurred automatically and bypassed the attentional filter to affect the limited-capacity system.) Finally, because it was assumed that the limited-capacity system is needed to carry out the meaningful encoding of stimuli, the temporary, large-capacity store in which all stimuli were initially registered was thought to contain basically unanalyzed sensory information.

The model shown in Fig. 1.1 appears to have been inspired by the notion of a flow chart in computer science. Aside from the superficial similarity of boxes connected by lines or arrows, there are at least two substantive similarities. First, in both cases a complex program is broken down into logical modules in which particular tasks or processing steps are accomplished. Second, there are choice points where the routing of information must be decided. In the model, this occurs most notably when the setting of the attentional filter determines which information will be selected for further processing and which will be rejected.

In the early years of cognitive psychology, Broadbent's model was emulated and elaborated upon by other researchers. Most notable among these, Atkinson and Shiffrin (1968) concentrated a great deal more on the nature of the control processes that shuttled information from one type of information store to another. In their model, another choice point was considered. Specifically, decisions about how to process information in the limited-capacity system were said to determine the extent to which it would be saved in long-term memory.

One reason for the excitement about such models may have been that they seemed to take on an air of logical necessity. The brain system being modeled in fact resembled a digital computer, which also had a limitless supply of unprocessed data (e.g., punch cards) that had to be fed one channel at a time into a limited, temporary storage space ("read-and-access memory," or RAM) that received input also from a large-capacity, long-term storage device (tapes, drums, or disks) according to the instructions of a faculty that provided a set of control processes (the "central processing unit" or CPU). Newell and Simon (1972) showed that a digital computer could be programmed to solve logical problems that previously could be solved only by humans. Given similarities between the human and the computer in both structural organization and information processing, it was natural to suspect that there was something inevitable about that particular organization.

In recent years, though, Broadbent's (1958) model and others like it have been largely abandoned, except in introductory textbooks where they still serve as simple illustrations of the concept of an information processing model. Some of the most important reasons for the abandonment are clear, as explained, for example, by Lachman, Lachman, and Butterfield (1979). However, before considering the basis of this change in the field, it is useful to trace a progression in which the model was first amended in an attempt to preserve it.

1.3.2 Modifications of Broadbent's (1958) model

Broadbent's (1958) model assumed that sensory information that is unattended is filtered out without being analyzed. Subsequent experiments using selective listening procedures soon produced evidence contradicting that assumption. It was found that attention sometimes is attracted to an unattended channel in which the subject's own name is spoken (Moray, 1959), and that attention sometimes shifts involuntarily to the channel that is supposed to be unattended when the semantically coherent message is shifted to that channel (Gray & Wedderburn, 1960; Treisman, 1960).

Was the rejection of the model premature? There are reasons to question the validity of the early evidence of automatic semantic processing (e.g., Cowan, 1988), but a wealth of additional evidence was subsequently obtained, suggesting that at least some automatic analysis of semantic properties of unattended stimuli takes place. This evidence now includes priming effects from words that were so closely masked that they were undetected, semantic effects of words presented in an unattended channel, and words presented outside of the fovea (for a review see Holender, 1986).

Holender argued persuasively that, in the aforementioned procedures, it is quite difficult to prove that a particular channel of input that has been analyzed was actually completely unattended at the time, although his main point was that there is no evidence for semantic activation without conscious awareness either before *or after* the automatic analysis. Cowan (1988) did not take a definitive stand on the issue of automatic semantic activation, and the same indeterminate stance will be adopted here. We will see that it is possible to progress on other issues about processing and to arrive at a framework organizing more certain aspects of the findings, while leaving open the question of automatic semantic activation.

There were several important modifications of the model of Broadbent (1958) that preserved its basic flavor. To account for the early findings of automatic analysis of unattended input, Treisman (1960) proposed that the filter merely attenuated the input rather than totally eliminating it from further analysis. The attenuated input was said to have the potential to activate the relevant units in long-term memory. That way, it was possible to suggest that certain units (such as the subject's own name) had a low enough threshold to be activated to the point of recruiting attention automatically. The model still could account for the original findings described by Cherry (1953) and Broadbent (1958), such as the finding that attention is most easily directed at physically defined channels of stimulation.

Broadbent (1971) similarly modified his account by acknowledging that it is possible to select stimuli on the basis of semantic properties and not just on the basis of physical properties, as was implied by the original notion of an attentional filter. The seemingly effortless attending was still supposed to require physical cues, but it was possible to apply the limited-capacity system in a way that resulted in a semantically based selection, termed "pigeonholing." Subsequent research provided support for this amendment of the theory. For example, in experiments to be described later on, Greenwald (1972) found evidence for both a perceptual set (filtering) and response set (pigeonholing), and Johnston and Heinz (1978) found evidence that selection on the basis of physical cues is less effortful than selection on the basis of semantic cues, though both can be carried out.

One difference between the models of Broadbent (1958, 1971) and other, similar models, such as Atkinson and Shiffrin's (1968) model, has to do with restrictions on the transfer of information between stores. As shown in Fig. 1.1, Broadbent (1958) thought that the limited-capacity processor could pass coded information back to the large-capacity buffer store that occurred before the attentional filter, and Broadbent (1971, p. 398) continued tentatively to endorse that suggestion. In retrospect, the suggestion makes some sense because mental imagery can, to some extent, mimic sensory memory processes (e.g., Crowder, 1989*b*). On the other hand, there is a limit to what information can be passed back from memory to a temporary buffer and what information must come from the senses directly. For example, the ability to compare two tones declines as a function of the duration of a silent interval between the tones, even though the subject typically is left free to engage in auditory imagery processes during the interval (Cowan, 1984). Perhaps this type of consideration is why other theorists have not endorsed the idea of feedback from imagery to a transient, preattentive sensory memory buffer.

This last difference between Broadbent's model and other models in the field has proved unfortunate in one way: it has contributed to confusion in terminology. Where the prototypical model based on Atkinson and Shiffrin (1968) speaks of a "sensory store" followed by a filter and then a "categorical short-term store," Broadbent's (1958) model termed the initial buffer, before the attentional filter, a "short-term store", as shown in Fig. 1.1. Broadbent (1971) also used the term "echo box" to refer to phenomena that potentially encompassed categorical as well as sensory information, in contrast to the field's subsequent use of "echoic memory" to refer specifically to auditory sensory information (Neisser, 1967). Acceptance of concepts and the use of terminology interact.

1.3.3 Abandonment of Broadbent's (1958) model

On the basis of the noted breakthrough of information through the filter, some theorists (e.g., Deutsch & Deutsch, 1963) proposed that all information is completely analyzed automatically, with attention being used only to determine which of this analyzed information will enter into the subject's response. This has been termed a "late filter" theory of attention in contrast to the "early filter" of Broadbent (1958). However, one cannot represent this proposal graphically simply by moving the location of the filter in the theory. One would have to rearrange the boxes, or use other boxes, to show that the perceptual analysis of content occurs before the filter whereas the selection of responses occurs after it.

It is important to note that the early filter theory does not assert that attention operates only at an early level. Thus, Broadbent's (1971) "pigeonholing" is like a late filter that operates in combination with his early filter. In contrast, the late filter theory does deny that some filtering takes place at an early level.

Cowan (1988) reviewed considerable evidence against the late filter approach; it has become quite clear in the literature that attention modulates the extent of analysis of even the basic sensory properties of an event. I will not re-review that evidence in detail here, but it is worth noting that the evidence against a late filter theory has become stronger since 1988. For example, consider the electrophysiological evidence. The mismatch negativity, a component of the event-related brain potential that occurs to discriminable changes in a background auditory stimulus, was thought to occur automatically (Näätänen, 1990), but Woldorff, Hackley, and Hillyard (1991) showed that even this component depends upon the direction of attention toward vs. away from the auditory channel in which the change occurs. (For a more detailed analysis of possible attentional effects on the mismatch negativity and their limits, see Alho, Woods, Algazi, & Näätänen, 1992). Hackley (1993) reviewed other evidence for physiological effects of attention quite early in stimulus processing. In a recent study, Woldorff et al. (1993) observed attentional effects in neuromagnetic fields beginning about 20 milliseconds (ms) after the auditory stimulus. Perhaps the most extreme example of this sort is the observation that attention to one of two tone frequencies affects the magnitude of otoacoustic emissions produced in the cochlea of the human ear (Giard, Collet, Bouchet, & Pernier, 1994). Numerous neural fibers leading from the brain back to the ear may mediate this effect.

The behavioral evidence against a late-filter theory was already strong before 1988. For example, Treisman and Geffen (1967) presented dichotic tapes in which sentences within both channels contained target words. Subjects were to shadow (repeat) one channel and, at the same time, make a tapping response whenever there was a target word on either channel. The measure of target recognition sensitivity, *d'*, was 4.2 on the attended channel vs. 1.8 on the unattended channel. Moray and O'Brien (1967) obtained similar results and also obtained intermediate results for targets in a split-attention condition.

Johnston and Dark (1982) extended these results to an indirect measure, priming. State names were embedded in separate word lists in both auditory channels, and subjects were asked to detect names in one or both channels. This task was meant to direct attention. Meanwhile, subjects were to produce associations to visually presented words, and primes relevant to this task were presented in the spoken channels. The largest priming effect occurred when the primed channel was attended, the least priming occurred when the primed channel was unattended, and intermediate results were obtained with attention split between the auditory channels.

One might counter that the results of selective attention could have occurred in memory rather than perception. The attended information might be used immediately, whereas the unattended information might be allowed to decay before the subject got around to attending to it and using it. However, Treisman and Geffen (1967) obtained some evidence that argues against that interpretation. Response latencies were nearly identical for attended vs. unattended targets when they were detected, even though the rate of detecting unattended targets was much lower.

As mentioned above, an alternative account of the new evidence was to amend Broadbent's model (e.g., Treisman, 1960, 1964*b*). However, those amendments, especially the attenuating filter, still may have made the model seem somehow less convenient. The attenuation concept required that information go from the sensory store to make contact directly with the long-term store, automatically activating concepts there without passing through short-term storage. If one were to sketch the entire model, one would have to draw a line from the sensory store to the long-term store. Actually, a similar bypass might already have been needed to account for the fact that subjects notice gross physical changes in unattended stimuli, but the possibility of an automatic semantic triggering of attention expanded the need considerably. Of course, an initial bypass of the short-term store could also explain how stimuli are coded in short-term storage in the form of psychologically meaningful units derived from long-term memory.

Although the step of adding a direct bypass of short-term storage might have saved Broadbent's model, this step was not taken explicitly. Perhaps the reason was that other problems with this type of model, with separate serial stores, were emerging. As Lachman et al. (1979) explained, for example, different testing procedures led to vastly different estimates of the duration of both sensory storage and short-term storage. It is unacceptable to postulate structural stores if their properties are indeterminate. Other distinctions between stores, such as the suggestion that verbal material is coded phonetically in short-term storage but semantically in long-term storage, also failed to be supported. As Cowan (1988) noted, the actual basis of that distinction is likely to be that control processes used to retain verbal information in short-term memory, such as rehearsal, operate largely on phonetic bases, whereas processes used to retrieve verbal information from long-term memory are likely to operate primarily on semantic bases.

As Lachman et al. (1979) explained, the evidence began to look more as if the processing system had a great deal of flexibility not captured by the structural types of models like that of Broadbent (1958) or Atkinson and Shiffrin (1968). Those models were replaced in the field, not by other models, but by a diversity of approaches and more focus on specific research problems rather than an attempt to model the entire processing system.

1.3.4 A reconsideration of approaches to modeling: what is being modeled?

I believe that another major factor leading to the downfall of "Broadbentian" models in psychology was that the profligacy with which investigators drew models was contrasted by the usual failure to specify fully what the boxes were supposed to represent. Reconsider the possibility mentioned above: a direct line from sensory memory to long-term memory. If that is the main route of information through the stores, then why not simply draw sensory memory at the left of the flow diagram, long-term memory in the middle, and short-term memory at the right? Why does this possibility seem somehow aesthetically unpleasing?

One reason is that it leaves out something basic that was captured by the original model: the temporal sequence in which the stored information is used. It is clear that new information in sensory memory is used first (e.g., to facilitate recognition), information in a limited-capacity short-term memory typically is used later and for a longer period (e.g., to keep track of what one is doing), and information recorded in an unlimited long-term memory is used for a much longer period than that (e.g., to recognize familiar objects and people). However, the order in which stores typically are used (sensory, short, long) does not appear to match the order in which each of the stores is first involved in the processing of a stimulus (sensory, long, short). Old information is accessed from long-term memory in order to form a short-term memory representation, but the new sequence of these old elements, forming a new episodic memory, can be saved in long-term memory only after it is constructed in short-term memory.

A more recent, "Maltese cross" model proposed by Broadbent (1984) might be viewed in part as one attempt to solve this paradox of temporal order. That model consists of four different stores surrounding a central processing unit that receives and sends information from one store to another. The four stores are: a sensory store, a short-term store, a long-term store, and a motor output store. In this system, it becomes clear that the information must be traced back and forth through the stores; there is no one right order. One likely routing is that the input would first enter the system through the sensory store; some of it would be compared with information in long-term memory in order that the input could be identified; the identified information would be entered into short-term memory in order that recent information could be accumulated, arranged, and enhanced with other relevant information also supplied by long-term memory; and the result would be sent back to long-term memory to be filed away.

One problem with this kind of model is that it seems to be underspecified. For example, a great deal of recent research suggests that new information that is processed by the limited-capacity system and present in short-term memory should subsequently be stored in long-term memory, better than information that never made it to the limited-capacity, short-term-memory system (e.g., Posner & Snyder, 1975*a*, 1975*b*; Jacoby & Kelly, 1992). Yet, according to the Maltese-cross model, storage of the new information in long-term memory would be voluntary and up to the discretion of the central processing unit. Also in that model, there still is no definite indication that incoming stimuli must make contact with long-term memory in order to derive the categorical information to be placed in short-term storage. Finally, the clarity of the earlier approach of Broadbent (1971) regarding selective attention mechanisms may be lost here; it is not fully clear exactly how to work filtering and pigeonholing into the model.

Other investigators, such as Norman (1968) and Shiffrin and Schneider (1977), have emphasized the great extent to which short-term memory relies upon data structures in long-term memory for its essential coding (for a review, see Lachman et al., 1979). These investigators have re-conceptualized short-term memory in a way that is not found explicitly in the Maltese-cross model, namely as a temporarily activated subset of elements from long-term memory. As events occur and are coded, the relevant categories of long-term memory would be activated and linked together to form the perceived ongoing episodic sequence. This newly linked combination of units then could be re-stored in long-term memory as a new episodic memory record.

At any rate, in this progression of modeling concepts, an arbitrary choice has had to be made. One can have a flow chart in which each step represents a specific module of processing, the choice that was taken; or, alternatively, one can have a flow chart in which each step represents the processes that occur at a particular segment of the time spanning between a stimulus and the subject's response to it. For example, a simple model of this sort might include steps in which stimulus information is encoded, a response to it is selected, the response is retained until the conditions are right for it to be executed, and the response finally is executed.

It seems difficult to represent both modules and processes in the same graphic model because the modules probably are used recursively. For instance, in the simple example of a process model described above, long-term memory may be consulted during stimulus encoding, and then again during response selection. Short-term memory may come into play by providing a context in which the stimulus is encoded, and it is used again in response maintenance. In such a case, it is difficult to denote clearly both the lines of communication between processing modules and a recursive or convoluted temporal sequence in which the modules come into play.

A prime example of the process model is the one developed by Sternberg (1966, 1969, 1975) and supported by the "additive factor method" (see also Sanders, 1990). One assumes that the stimulus is first encoded; then a decision is reached concerning the response type that is appropriate for the stimulus as it has been encoded; and then a motor response is planned and executed. These three stages appear well justified on a priori grounds because each stage is logically dependent upon the previous stage.

In the additive factor method, it is assumed that factors that affect different stages should not interact. For example, stimulus clarity should affect the encoding stage, whereas the difficulty of the mapping between stimulus and response should affect the decision stage. Any effects on encoding speed should be independent of effects on decision speed, and vice versa. For a particular task, the three stages are subdivided into other stages suitable to the task, resulting in a model that serves as a hypothesis for empirical investigation. For example, in a memory search task (Sternberg, 1969), the subject must encode the target stimulus and then must search through the memory set to determine if the target stimulus was in that set. If the answer is "yes," then one response key must be selected; if "no," another key. The additive factor logic is used to verify the existence of the stages of processing that were hypothesized, and to characterize some of them. Thus, the number of items in the memory set affects the reaction time linearly, with an increase of about 40 ms per item in the memory set.

Various assumptions of the additive factor method have been questioned by different people for a variety of reasons (McClelland, 1979; Broadbent, 1984; Massaro & Cowan, 1993). However, what is relevant here is the fundamental purpose of such a model. The model is designed to account for subjects' reaction times by dividing them into sequential stages in which the time was taken up completing Process A, Process B, and so on.

Assuming that there are situations in which subjects engage in processing in sequential stages, such a purpose is quite useful. It seems clear that the analytic simplicity of the model is lost, on the other hand, if it is necessary to draw lines that can bypass a stage, or worse, if a recurrent loop must be drawn from one stage to a previous stage. Such situations occur in computer flow charts, but they greatly increase the difficulty of verifying the existence of each stage separately. One way to avoid this fate is to restrict the levels of analysis to those stages that do in fact occur in a linear sequence (Massaro & Cowan, 1993).

It should be clear that the aim of finding a linear sequence of stages for precise mathematical analysis in a particular task, which is in the Sternbergian tradition, is far different than the aim of depicting the main modules of the processing system and their connection to one another in general, which is in the Broadbentian tradition. Perhaps at the dawn of information processing research, it could have been hoped that one model could satisfy both aims. That hope would have begun to fade quickly, though, with the realization that a rich set of back-and-forth interactions between short- and long-term memory is needed in order to understand adequately the processes of short-term coding and long-term retention. There has been some minor convergence of approaches, such as models that deal with the limited channel concept mathematically and in combination with processing stages (see Schweickert, 1993), but on the whole the Broadbentian (module-oriented) and Sternbergian (stage-oriented) traditions have remained separate.

One unfortunate result of having conflicting traditions for modeling information processing was that some researchers operated under implicit assumptions that apply to one tradition but not the other. Not fully realizing that there are two distinct metatheories of information processing models, it would be easy for an investigator to assume that his or her working assumptions were shared by other investigators more than was actually the case. I suspect that this conflict in traditions has remained partly unresolved to the present time in cognitive psychology.

The kind of model one attempts to build also determines the types of evidence that one must obtain. From a Sternbergian tradition, what is needed is a small cluster of very powerful, elegant, and unconfounded experiments that make the distinctions between processing stages clear and incontrovertible. From a Broadbentian tradition, though, a wide variety of convergent data from vastly different tasks is needed because the model must be shown to be general across tasks. Neither tradition can be said to be exclusively right, but the distinction must be kept clear if progress is to be made.

There is a second important dimension on which modeling aims of investigators differ. Some researchers have attempted to pare down the features of their model until they reach the core assumptions in which they believe solidly on the basis of already-existing data. These models can serve as a framework for additional research because each new prediction should at least be understandable in terms of the model. However, these models in themselves are flexible enough not to make very many highly specific predictions. Certainly the models that Broadbent (1958, 1971, 1984) has developed over the years are of this type, as are the model of working memory proposed by Baddeley (1986) and the model of Cowan (1988). On rare occasions, stage models also have been used in this general sense. For example, a stage analysis has been useful in distinguishing between components of event-related potentials of the brain that reflect stimulus-encoding processes and others that reflect the subsequent decision and response preparation processes (Ritter, Simson, Vaughan, & Macht, 1982; Meyer, Osman, Irwin, & Yantis, 1988).

At other times theorists (certainly including Meyer) have had an aim different from these general models. They have attempted to go further, to model the possible rather than the necessary in information processing. The idea would be to state how a particular skill might be accomplished, in as much detail as possible, in fact completely enough so that precise predictions can be made. If the model fits the data obtained with that skill, then an attempt typically is made to see if the model can be adapted to other, slightly different abilities. In this way, evidence accumulates in favor of the model and makes it seem more likely. On the other hand, if another model can fit all of the same data better, or can fit it almost as well and fit additional data that the old model cannot fit, then the old model is considered to be disconfirmed and is discarded or modified. Models of that sort can attempt to account quantitatively for processes across time, as in the additive factor models of Sternberg (1969, 1975), the cascade model of McClelland (1979), and the fuzzy logical model of perception of Massaro and Friedman (1990).

To reiterate, two separate distinctions of modeling have been drawn. First, models can focus on a fixed sequence of processing stages (like Sternberg), or on processing modules that can be activated recursively (like Broadbent). Second, one can model just the general conclusions that appear necessary on the basis of past research, or those conclusions plus additional, more detailed, tentative suppositions that possibly could be true and that lead to a detailed mechanism to account for more aspects of the data.

So far we have discussed stage models of what is considered necessary (e.g., the interpretation of event-related potentials by Ritter et al., 1982, and Meyer et al., 1988); stage models of what is just possible (e.g., Sternberg, 1969; McClelland, 1979); and modular models of what is necessary (e.g., Broadbent, 1958, 1984; Baddeley, 1986; Cowan, 1988). There also are many examples of the fourth possible category, namely more detailed modular models of what is possible. One example is the interactive activation model of McClelland and Elman (1986). Different levels of analytic units (features, phonemes, words) can be viewed as separate but interactive modules. In other models of the "possible, modular" variety, the modular nature is more obvious, as in the system-wide computer models of Anderson (1983), Schneider and Detweiler (1987), and Newell (1990).

It is, however, quite difficult to be general across tasks and mathematically precise at the same time. For example, Newell's model has been criticized for not making very extensive contact with the psychological literature (Carlson & Detweiler, 1992). Approaches like that of Newell thus are in contrast to the present approach, which also will deal in modular concepts but will operate at a less precise, more empirical, data-intensive level of analysis to focus on the necessary.

Given these different aims of different information processing models, it is no wonder that there has been some confusion. It appears that any particular information processing model must be evaluated with respect to two separate questions. First, how valuable is the aim of the model? Second, how well does the particular modeling approach that was proposed further this aim?

1.3.5 On the role of models in scientific progress

Before settling upon a particular theoretical viewpoint in this book, it seems worthwhile to consider briefly the metatheory of scientific progress. A well-known article by Platt (1964) defined what has become the conventional view of how scientific progress can best be made. According to this view, the universe of possible scientific hypotheses about a topic might be organized according to a binary decision tree. By selecting fundamental hypotheses to test, one works near the trunk of the tree and therefore rules out the maximal number of possible hypotheses at once. The alternative, much less efficient method is said to be the one in which an investigator seeks support for a specific theory specified in detail. The problem is that two investigators might account for the same evidence with theories that occupy very different places on the decision tree, without fundamental differences between the assumptions of the theories having been tested. As Platt (1964, p. 350) more colorfully noted,

> . . . I think that there are . . . areas of science today that are sick . . . because they have forgotten the necessity for alternative hypotheses and disproof. Each man has only one branch—or none—on the logical tree, and it twists at random without ever coming to the need for a crucial decision at any point. We can see from the external symptoms that there is something scientifically wrong. The Frozen Method. The Eternal Surveyor. The Never Finished. The Great Man With a Single Hypothesis. The Little Club of Dependents. The Vendetta. The All-Encompassing Theory Which Can Never Be Falsified.

Although the wisdom of Platt's observations seem almost self-evident, perhaps there is more to be said. Newell (1973) likened the approach of basic hypothesis testing in cognitive psychology to a game of 20 questions, and doubted that one could "play 20 questions with nature and win." He suggested that behavior is so strategy-dependent that one might obtain different results in different test situations. Instead of just using the simplest test situations in which a mental process occurs and then attempting to collapse results across test situations to understand the process, Newell suggested that it is important to analyze complex behaviors to determine how the simple processes play a role. In opposition to Platt's strategy of strong inference, Newell appeared to favor a strategy of developing a detailed model that put all of the constraints together.

One basis of the difference between these investigators' prescriptions for science may be their differing conceptions of the possibilities. Where Platt (1964) spoke of a "logical tree" of hypotheses, Newell (1973, p. 306) spoke of an "inferential web." Whereas in a tree structure one knows which hypotheses are more fundamental than which others, such is not the case in a web. Given a web structure, one might have to proceed by examining at least several interrelated questions and the constraints that their answers logically place on one another.

It should be noted that Newell was not advocating a total overthrow of the conventional hypothesis-testing approach. In a comment that eerily presaged his death in July 1992, Newell (1973, p. 306) wrote:

> Maybe we should all simply continue playing our collective game of 20 questions. Maybe all is well, as my other half assures me, and when we arrive in 1992 (the retirement date I pick might as well be my own) we will have homed in to the essential structure of the mind.

Is there a way to resolve these views and plot a course? Perhaps the first step is to gain a better appreciation of what is more likely to be apt, the decision tree or the inferential net. In the field of memory and attention, it seems likely that the net is more apt. We already have discussed the fundamental interrelatedness of memory and attention, so it is clear that neither of these areas could be pursued in a linear, decision-tree-like fashion in isolation, without consideration of the findings for the other concept.

It will help to examine one partial inferential net more closely in order to appreciate where the field may stand. Consider the divisions of the memory system. Some investigators have divided long-term memory into multiple separate types of storage: either separate procedural and declarative modules (e.g., Schacter, 1989) or separate procedural, semantic, and episodic modules (Tulving, 1985). Other investigators have not divided long-term memory in this way (e.g., Shiffrin & Schneider, 1977), and some have explicitly suggested that different forms of memory can result from differential coding within a unified long-term memory system (e.g., Humphreys, Bain, & Pike, 1989). Other investigators have focused on a very different question, the nature of a temporary memory store that is used in immediate memory tasks. Some have proposed what appears to be a separate short-term or temporary memory module (e.g., Atkinson & Shiffrin, 1968; Broadbent, 1984). Others have proposed that temporary memory storage actually consists of the currently activated elements of long-term memory (e.g., Shiffrin & Schneider, 1977; Cowan, 1988). Still others have doubted if there is a temporary memory system at all, and have suggested instead that all memory performance can be accounted for on the basis of a single set of rules, such as the distinctiveness of items and interference between them (Wickelgren, 1965; Crowder, 1989*a*).

The inferential net comes into play when one tries to envision the combination of these possibilities into an overall description of the memory system. Fig.1.2 depicts the relevant hypothesis space. Letters A–F indicate what I believe to be the positions of various investigators on the hypothesis space. Notice first how little agreement there is; practically every conceivable space is occupied (although not every position is clear because not every investigator addressed both long-term and temporary memory). It should be

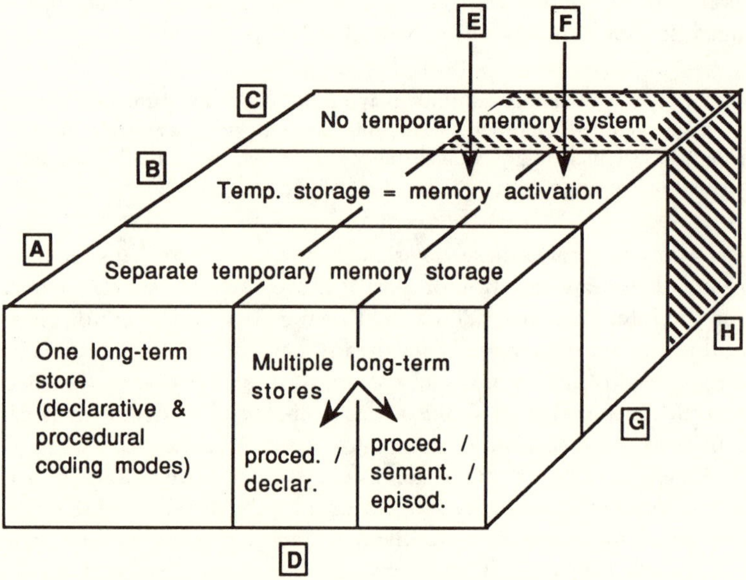

A Atkinson & Shiffrin (1968); Broadbent (1984)
B Shiffrin & Schneider (1977); Cowan (1988)
C Wickelgren (1975); Crowder (1989a)
D Schacter (1989) (Conscious system must have temp. copy)
E Anderson (1983)
F Tulving (1985)? (View of temporary memory unspecified.)
G Further question: which long-term stores activated?
H Infeasible? (Separate distinctiveness cues for each store?)

Fig. 1.2 One depiction of the hypothesis space for types of memory. The question mark for Tulving (1985) indicates that the classification of this theory in terms of short-term storage is uncertain.

a high priority to bring as much evidence as is possible to bear on these fundamental, competing hypotheses.

Second, notice that the questions that must be asked are sometimes dependent upon other decisions, but are sometimes independent. A competition between temporary memory storage as a separate module versus the activated portion of long-term memory can be pursued regardless of the nature of long-term memory. However, if there turn out to be separate long-term memory modules, the activation hypothesis would be complicated because it would be necessary to ask which long-term storage modules become activated (G). Finally, it seems likely that not all combinations of hypotheses are reasonable (H). In the proceduralist view (Crowder, 1989*a*), which includes the hypothesis that there is no separate temporary memory storage system to play a role in immediate memory tasks, as well as the hypothesis that a coherent set of rules predicts all of memory performance (Crowder, 1989*a*), it would appear to make little sense if one had to contend with multiple types of long-term memory module.

Because of the web of inferences, some of Platt's (1964) view must be amended; but not all of it. It still makes sense to focus on experiments that rule out large classes of hypotheses. However, we should not be lulled into believing that there is a linear course for us to follow if we just can find it. We will need integrative attempts that can account for a wide range of data, in addition to experiments that can resolve fundamental issues.

Some of the general models in our field, such as those of Broadbent and Baddeley, have stayed with basic issues, making simple assertions about the major processing components. The more specific models have taken a more fine-grained approach, but unfortunately have not reached that point by adequately proving each step along the way. Thus, even though we now have various classes of model that can account for a great deal of data in detail, there still is disagreement on basic issues. One such issue is whether there are separate declarative and procedural systems (e.g., Anderson, 1983) or one long-term memory system (e.g., Newell, 1990). Seemingly decisive data, such as the selective deficit in declarative memory that is caused by temporal lobe lesions (e.g., see Squire, 1987), might still be compatible with the view that there are simply "different ways to cue a coherent memory system" (Humphreys et al., 1989), with the temporal lobe areas involved in the cueing process rather than memory storage *per se*. Another unresolved issue is whether higher-level (e.g., lexical) units feed back to influence the encoding present in lower-level (e.g., phonetic) units as in the "interactive activation" account (McClelland & Elman, 1986), or not (Massaro & Cohen, 1991). The latter authors describe how contextual effects can be explained even without top-down feedback or interactive activation. For examples of other unresolved issues, see Massaro & Cowan, 1993.

It is sometimes easy to disprove individual detailed models, but it also is easy to modify a model to take a new piece of evidence into account.

Moreover, though the acceptance of one of these detailed models implies acceptance of fundamental assumptions leading up to the model, rejection of the specific model still leaves many of the fundamental assumptions viable.

It appears most efficient for the time being to try to stay near the most basic level of the hypothesis space until the fundamental issues are resolved, even though this results in a model too general to make specific predictions in many situations. With this rationale in mind, let us now proceed to examine the simple processing framework developed by Cowan (1988). It will be interesting to observe that some of the fundamental assumptions made even within this simple, general framework have been challenged.

1.4 The model of Cowan (1988)

1.4.1 The article and the book

One might think that, with an entire book to spare, considerable space would be spent elaborating on all of the various detailed points made in the seed paper (Cowan, 1988). This has not turned out to be the case. The book concentrates instead on just the most basic points made in the article. Considerable relevant, and sometimes controversial, evidence regarding those main points has emerged since 1988.

1.4.2 Background of the modeling framework

Cowan (1988) stressed that different aspects of the information processing framework constrain one another. To illustrate, consider the status of the popular hypothesis that short-term memory is formed from the subset of the elements in long-term memory that are in a temporarily heightened state of activation. This conception remains problematic until it can be reconciled with another hypothesis, carried down from James (1890): that short-term memory represents the information currently in conscious awareness, the extended present.

Activated memory and the focus of attention cannot be identical if one believes studies demonstrating unconscious semantic activation, such as the priming by undetected masked primes observed by Balota (1983), Marcel (1983), and others. Even if one does not believe such results, it is clear that the number of items that can be retained in the short term (e.g., Miller, 1956; Baddeley, 1986) is greater than the number of items that could be held in the focus of attention at one time, so that activated items must exist outside of the focus of attention. A unitary concept of "short-term memory" makes no distinction between activated information in vs. out of the focus of attention and awareness.

Cowan (1988) suggested that the focus of attention comprises just a subset of the information that currently is activated, and that the implicit concept of short-term memory in the research literature has sometimes been that of activated memory (like Hebb, 1949) and has sometimes been that of memory in the focus of attention (like James, 1890).

This nested description of memory also must be shown to be compatible with the attentional selection mechanism. To review some necessary requirements, first, the activation of long-term memory elements must be more complete for selected than for nonselected stimuli; that is to say, attention enhances the perceptual process (e.g., Posner & Snyder, 1975*a*, 1975*b*; Neely, 1977). Second, major changes in the physical properties of nonselected stimuli attract attention to those stimuli (Cherry, 1953). Third, special significance of the stimuli may also do this (e.g., Moray, 1959; Treisman, 1960) although this is not yet certain (Holender, 1986; Cowan, 1988). Fourth, only selected stimuli are admitted to the subject's awareness.

It is possible that Treisman's (1960, 1964*b*) attenuation hypothesis can do all of this and still be consistent with the nested description of memory. However, this is uncertain, because Treisman did not sketch out the entire processing system including all of the elements discussed above. There

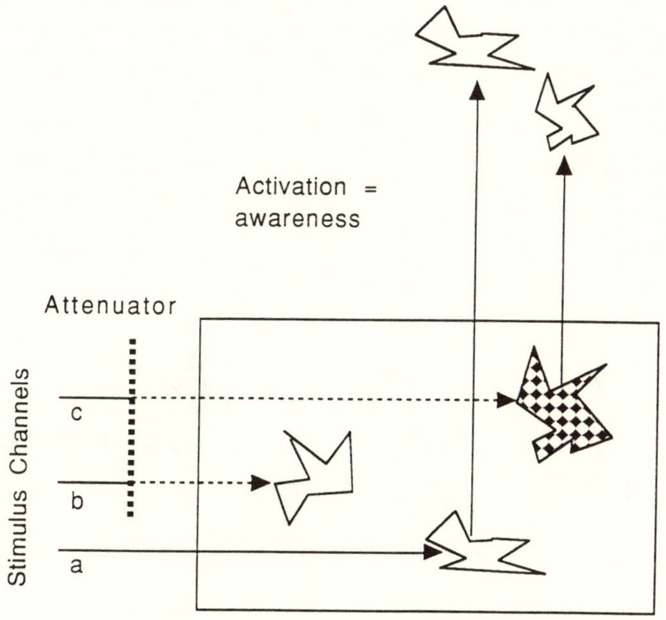

Fig. 1.3 One interpretation of Treisman's attenuating filter.

appears to be an important ambiguity in her proposal, regarding the possibility of unconscious memory activation.

Fig. 1.3 depicts one way to represent Treisman's attenuating filter. In this representation, incoming stimuli have the potential to activate elements in long-term memory (solid shapes) if the signal is strong enough, bringing them into awareness. The signal is attenuated in strength for all except the selected channel (a). However, the threshold for activation is lower for some memory elements (represented by the checked shape activated by channel (c) than for others (represented by unmarked shapes). The elements with especially low thresholds (checked shapes) would be items of temporary significance, a status based on the ongoing attended stimulation; or of permanent significance, such as one's own name. As shown, activation could occur either because the input was attended, and therefore not attenuated (a), or because the threshold was low enough to be activated even by attenuated input (c). In this figure, all activation leads to awareness.

In a different possible representation of Treisman's attenuation process, however, any input would be said to activate the relevant elements of memory to some extent, but some levels of activation would not be great enough to reach awareness. A revised depiction of the attenuation view, in

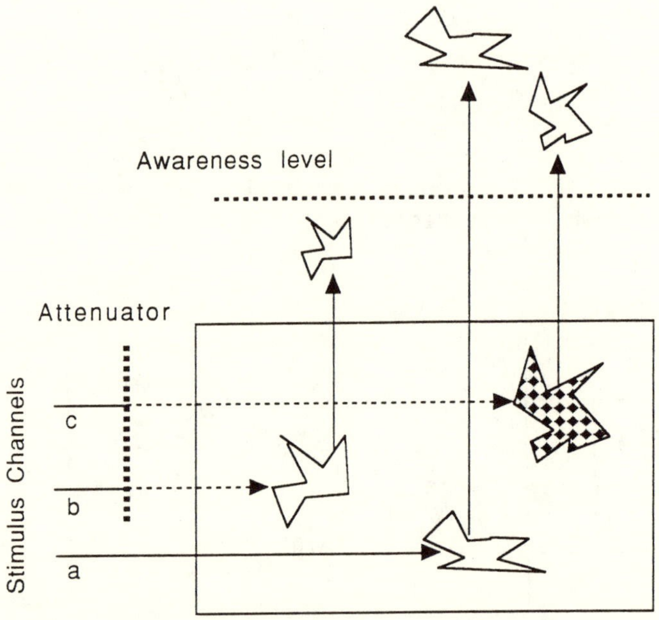

Fig. 1.4 A second interpretation of Treisman's attenuating filter.

which there are both sub- and supraliminal levels of activation, is shown in Fig. 1.4. If this representation is what was intended by Treisman, it is a clear precursor to the concept of short-term memory in the Cowan (1988) model (see also Shiffrin & Schneider, 1977, Fig. 11).

1.4.3 Cowan's (1988) formulation

The basic point of the review by Cowan (1988) was that there is an intricate relation between memory and attention in a model of processing. The organization of memory stores must be ascertained before it can be determined what attentional systems are possible.

One re-analysis of the memory system discussed by Cowan (1988) was in regard to sensory memory. The conventional account has been that visual sensory storage persists for a few hundred milliseconds (e.g., Sperling, 1960) whereas auditory sensory storage persists longer, for a matter of seconds (e.g., Broadbent, 1958; Crowder, 1982) or even up to 20–30 seconds (e.g., Norman, 1969), depending on the procedure used to examine it. However, Cowan (1984) had argued that there were two phases of auditory sensory memory, a brief phase lasting only a few hundred milliseconds, as revealed by tests of sensory persistence (e.g., those by Efron 1970*a*, 1970*b*, 1970*c*), and a longer phase of up to about 30 seconds. The alternative possibility, that the data actually reflected a continuum of estimates rather than two separate entities, was considered but ruled out in an examination of test conditions. Those procedures that had indicated an intermediate estimate of persistence (e.g., several seconds) turned out to be contaminated in each case. Such estimates were due to procedures that either permitted categorical recoding of the stimuli or provided acoustic interference with the target stimulus.

Cowan (1988) extended this review across modalities, and found evidence in the literature favoring the existence of the same two phases of sensory storage in the visual and tactile modalities. The conclusion was that the persistence of sensory storage does not appear to differ among modalities, although the features stored in it differ because of perceptual differences between modalities (with, for example, better temporal resolution in the auditory modality and better spatial resolution in the visual modality). In each modality, there is persistence of sensation for several hundred milliseconds after the onset of the stimulus, and there is a second phase of storage for a number of seconds after its offset that is perceived not as an afterimage, but as a vivid recollection of the stimulus. Neither type is limited to the peripheral nervous system; even the shorter type has a central locus and can be elicited by stimuli alternating between the two eyes or between the two ears (e.g., Haber & Standing, 1969, 1970; Kallman & Morris, 1984).

The postulation that there are two phases of sensory memory is similar to an earlier theory by Massaro (1975*a*). That earlier theory termed the second phase of sensory memory "synthesized" sensory memory. It was said to be followed by another form of memory that was modality-independent, termed "generated abstract memory," which would correspond closely to the information handled by the limited-capacity system of Broadbent (1958) or the short-term memory of Atkinson and Shiffrin (1968).

Cowan (1988) questioned the fundamental separation between the second phase of sensory memory and short-term memory. The distinctions that traditionally had been drawn between them did not appear to hold up here. First, they apparently had similar rates of decay, unlike the previous assumption (e.g., Atkinson & Shiffrin, 1968) that short-term memory lasts longer.

Another alleged distinction was that sensory memory was supposed to have an unlimited capacity, and short-term memory, a limited capacity. However, the suggestion of unlimited capacity never was supported for the longer type of sensory memory; it was demonstrated only for the brief sensory afterimage. Specifically, in Sperling's (1960) partial report procedure, an array of characters was presented and a partial report cue allowed one row of the array to be read off before the brief afterimage faded. Adaptations of Sperling's procedure with stimuli in the auditory modality (Darwin, Turvey, & Crowder, 1972; Treisman & Rostron, 1972; Rostron, 1974) ended up indexing the longer, more processed phase of sensory storage (see Massaro, 1976). They did so with a much smaller number of stimuli per array, and the level of performance that was attained does not necessarily indicate that an unlimited number of items can be contained in that longer phase of storage.

In short-term memory viewed as a linkage of currently active elements in long-term memory, it also is the case that multiple items can be held simultaneously; it is, at least, not as limited as the number of items that can be in the focus of attention at one time. Thus, for example, Baddeley (1986) viewed covert rehearsal as a mental trick that can be used to maintain the activation of more items than one can concentrate on at a particular moment.

Another difference between the second phase of sensory storage and short-term storage was said to be the type of coding. However, this distinction is not necessarily as fundamental as it might seem. A difference between the brief phase and the longer phase of sensory storage is stimulus encoding, as is made clear by studies of the backward masking of recognition. Those studies indicate that identification of a brief target stimulus is impaired by a second, masking stimulus presented in the same modality as the target if it is physically similar and follows within a few hundred milliseconds of the target (e.g., Massaro, 1972; Turvey, 1973). Presumably, the mask terminates encoding of the target. This encoding could very well occur through the activation of sensory feature detectors in the cortex (e.g., Hubel & Wiesel, 1963; Gersuni, 1971). Given that these features are tuned by early experience (Held & Hein, 1963; Werker & Tees,

1984), they might well be considered part of long-term memory. Thus, the second phase of sensory memory can be considered an activation of sensory features in long-term memory, in a manner similar to the activation of non-sensory features that is said to represent short-term memory storage.

Although both sensory and non-sensory activation would involve the same types of processes, this does not imply that there can be no modality-specific aspects of memory storage. It may well be that some of the features that are activated by sensory stimuli (e.g., exact pitch of a tone) cannot be activated by imagery processes alone, unlike other, non-sensory features (e.g., note category of a tone), which can be activated either by stimuli or by mental processes such as imagery.

Once the second phase of sensory storage is said to be a special case of memory activation, some of the impediments to understanding attentional selection have been removed. It is possible to conceive of a preliminary phase of perceptual encoding that is independent of attention and results in the activation primarily of simple physical features, but possibly with the activation of certain non-physical, abstract semantic features also. This would be followed by a second phase of perceptual encoding in which attention is used to activate a more coherent, connected set of features for selected objects (Posner & Snyder, 1975a, 1975*b*; Neely, 1977; Treisman, 1992*a*).

Cowan (1988) suggested that, in fact, what has been seen as the "selective filter" is actually intrinsic to the long-term memory activation process. It was viewed not as the active screening out of unselected stimuli, as in the filtering or attenuation concepts, but as habituation of the attentional orienting response for a repeated pattern of stimulation in a nonselected channel (Sokolov, 1963).

The orienting response occurs for novel stimuli and sometimes for particularly significant stimuli. It is a combination of transient physiological and motoric responses that include cessation of movement, slowing of the heart, and increased perceptual sensitivity (e.g., Kimmel, van Olst, & Orlebeke, 1979; Näätänen, 1992). Sokolov suggested that a neural model of a stimulus is developed with repeating presentations of the stimulus, and that incoming stimuli are compared to that neural model. As the neural model develops, the orienting response habituates. When a subsequent stimulus is found to differ from the current neural model, dishabituation of the orienting response occurs. Support for the hypothesized comparison process has included the finding that an orienting response results from a decrease or omission of stimuli that would be expected according to the ongoing stimulation, and not just an increase or onset.

Given this orienting and habituation process, the focus of attention then would be controlled in two fundamentally different ways. First, gross physical changes in the repeated pattern would elicit an orienting response; especially significant stimuli sometimes might also do this, but that is not yet proven beyond a reasonable doubt (Holender, 1986). Second, any stimulus or any features in long-term memory could be selected by a voluntary attentional focus or spotlight (Posner & Snyder, 1975*a*, 1975*b*).

The attentional focus presumably can find features in long-term memory only with the investment of some time and effort. Pre-existing activation of certain features would, however, make these features more easily and quickly reached by the focus of attention. This pre-existing activation would occur for features corresponding to recent stimuli, but also for some features stimulated only through internal events such as mental associations and recent thoughts.

All of this might be drawn into Treisman's attenuation model as depicted in Fig.1.4, but Cowan (1988) chose another notation, reproduced in Fig.1.5. That notation uses a nested relation to illustrate that, structurally speaking, the activated memory is a subset of long-term memory. The focus of attention is a subset of activated memory, because any elements of long-term memory that are entered into the focus of attention presumably become activated by that process if they were not already activated.

As shown in the figure, Cowan (1988) separately represented the brief, literal sensory storage process, as well as the central executive structures that we know so little about but assume to exist and to be involved in the control of the focus of attention (Norman & Shallice, 1985; Baddeley, 1986).

We should not be overly concerned with a particular graphic representation, but with what is represented. One shortcoming with the graphic representation of Cowan (1988) is that it does not reflect the possibly continuous nature of the distinction between items in vs. out of the focus of attention, and in vs. out of the activated area. It also appears to imply that all of the material that is activated is coherent, but in reality it might be represented by several disjunctive areas within long-term memory. The model also does not graphically represent the likely possibility that attention also acts by inhibiting elements of long-term memory, giving them a higher threshold of activation than they ordinarily would have in a neutral, resting level of background activity (Neill, 1977; Carr & Dagenbach, 1990; Neumann & DeSchepper, 1991; Tipper, 1992). Finally, the model appears to imply that processing progresses from left to right, from stimulus to response without feedback; but that would be an unfounded conclusion to draw with respect to this model. The components can transfer information in cyclic loops.

The second model representing Treisman's view (Fig. 1.4) is not preferred over Cowan's model for a more fundamental reason. That model assumes that the focus of attention is composed of the most active elements within the activated set. However, as discussed in several later chapters, it is quite possible that the neural counterpart of memory activation differs qualitatively from the neural counterpart of the focus of attention (e.g., for activated memory, cell assembly activity in diverse association areas of the

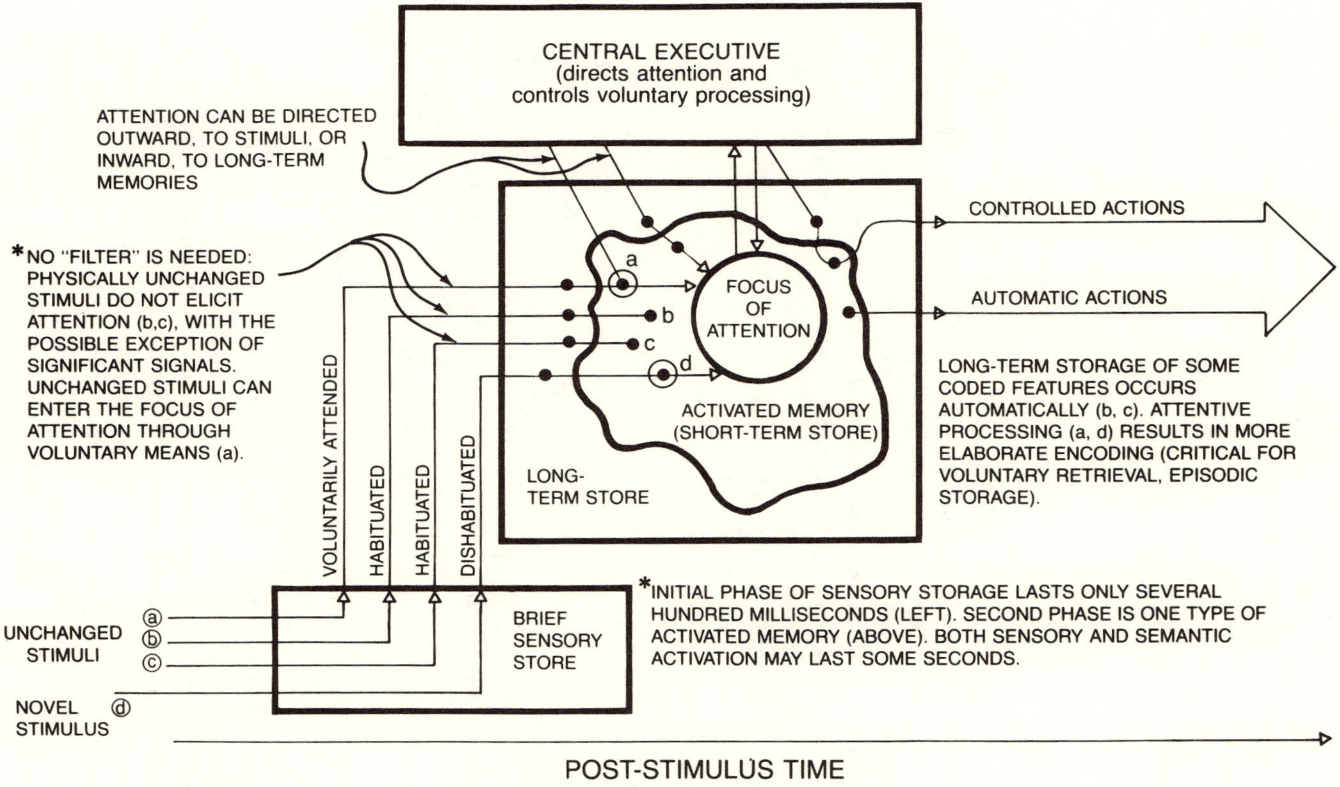

Fig. 1.5 A basic model of information processing. (From N. Cowan, Evolving conceptions of memory storage, selective attention, and their mutual constraints within the human information processing system. *Psychological Bulletin, 104*, p. 180, Fig. 1. Copyright © 1988 by the American Psychological Association. Reprinted by permission.)

cortex; for the focus of attention, that plus additional activity in the attentional structures of the frontal and parietal lobes and hippocampus and surrounding regions; see the concluding chapter of this book).

It is not clear if a perfect representation that incorporates all features could be found, but no attempt to do so will be made in this book. The representation shown in Fig. 1.5, from Cowan (1988), is adequate for the present purposes and has the virtue of simplicity.

1.5 A comparison of Cowan (1988) with other modeling approaches

There are many ways that one can react to a model of information processing. Should one accept it? Test it? Attack it? Ignore it? Modify it? Incorporate it into one's own model? The decision depends partly on how the model is interpreted and how well its motivations are understood. One might be well advised to determine the goals of a model first, and only then move on to evaluate the successes and failures of the model.

Cowan (1988) attempted to appraise approaches that might serve as alternatives to the approach that was adopted. However, that effort concentrated primarily on how well the models fit, mismatched, or failed to speak to particular empirical phenomena that were considered to be of special importance. There was little attempt to evaluate the goals of the models themselves.

In the discussion to follow, a primary focus will be on the goals of modeling, which allows the discussion to apply to classes of models rather than just specific models. The fit to particular empirical phenomena will be discussed also, as a secondary focus. However, in this broader context, it can be seen that certain goals may be problematic precisely because they fail to deal with phenomena that one assumes to be important. Different classes of approaches will be examined, starting with approaches most similar to Cowan (1988) and ending with the most dissimilar.

1.5.1 Alternative graphic representations of the assumptions of Cowan (1988)

A graphic representation of processing is useful for at least some investigators, on the basic premise that a picture is worth a thousand words. The graphic representation allows one to keep in mind a collection of premises that might be burdensome to remember as a list of propositions. However, there may be no one perfect, elegant manner to represent a model graphically. This case can be illustrated by comparing one interpretation of Treisman's attenuation hypothesis, shown in Fig. 1.4, with Cowan's (1988) model, shown in Fig.1.5. The models are similar in many ways, but they emphasize slightly different premises.

It is possible that the difference between activated information inside vs. outside of the focus of attention is a matter of the level of activation. In that case, it may also be that awareness is a continuum, and that the threshold of activation needed for awareness depends on a criterion set by the subject. That criterion might even be variable, depending on behavioral state. In a relaxed state, the threshold might be lowered to let more items into awareness (as in daydreaming), whereas in a state of concentration, the threshold might be raised to let in fewer items. Fig. 1.4 (after Treisman) represents this possibility well, whereas Fig. 1.5 (after Cowan) is vague on the point.

The model inspired by Treisman (Fig. 1.4) also easily permits the possibility that activation, the focus of attention, or both at certain times could exist as multiple, unconnected islands (e.g., in a split attention task) rather than being unitary. On the other hand, it may be that multiple foci, by the mere fact of being active concurrently, form an associative link to the same episodic context and therefore must be represented as unitary, as in the Cowan (1988) model.

Some advantages of Fig. 1.5 are the explicit presence of a central executive, the re-analysis of sensory memory, and the explicit reference to orienting and its habituation, although those features conceivably could be incorporated into the representation inspired by Treisman's model. There also are limitations inherent in both representations, such as the difficulty of graphically representing the finding that attention may be used not only to excite or activate, but also to inhibit elements of memory below the level of activity that they have in a neutral resting state (e.g., see Tipper, 1992). The bottom line is that, until a perfect representation is devised, the user can pick his vice and must keep the limitations of each model in mind. Graphic models are like complex machines in that they should come with operating manuals that are kept handy at all times.

1.5.2 More explicit theories of memory and attention

There are others who have produced models that do not directly conflict with the basic ideas promoted in Cowan (1988), but differ in the level of analysis. Schneider and Detweiler (1987) produced a model that is one possible instantiation of many of the ideas of Cowan (1988). It involves assumptions detailed enough to permit the system to work as a computer program, simulating much of the automatic and controlled (attention-directed) behavior that humans produce. The detailed assumptions could turn out to be wrong, but the model is useful at least in demonstrating that many of the basic ideas summarized in Cowan (1988) feasibly could form a processing system; they could work. Therefore, it is worth spending a little time appreciating the Schneider and Detweiler model.

The model includes eight separate modules: visual, auditory, speech, lexical, semantic, motor, mood, and context modules. Cowan (1988) was not committed to this particular breakdown, but it at least seems plausible.

The operation of each module was said to occur according to a connectionist network. Schneider (1987, p. 74) listed four defining properties of connectionist networks (e.g., the approach exemplified in detail in McClelland and Rumelhart, 1986) as follows:

> [1] processing is assumed to occur in populations of simple [neuron-like] elements . . . [2] all knowledge is stored in the connectionist weights between the elements . . . [3] all the units perform a simple combination of their inputs . . . [4] learning occurs via simple learning rules that are based on local information available within a unit. Learning involves modifying the connections to enable a later input pattern to evoke a new output pattern.

Schneider and Detweiler (1987) suggested that the modular arrangement consisted of a similar structure within each module, but vast differences in the input and output connections of the different modules. This basic structure was supported by neurophysiological evidence that cortical hypercolumns have this arrangement.

The architecture differed from most connectionist models in that it allowed a simulation of attentional control. The activity of populations of neuron-like units could be attenuated by a higher-level control, and the direction of attention could be affected by priority reports coming from lower levels.

In addition to the level of analysis, another main difference between the Schneider and Detweiler model and the framework of Cowan (1988) is the way in which the model was assessed. Cowan (1988) evaluated many experiments with an aim of questioning the soundness of the conclusions. Schneider and Detweiler (1987) discussed many studies also, but basically with the aim of showing that their model could duplicate many of the effects obtained in those studies. Thus, the assessment of the model was more heavily a confirmation rather than a disconfirmation process. If the model failed to duplicate a particular phenomenon, it seems likely that Schneider and Detweiler still would favor the belief that a failure of certain parameter values or minor assumptions was responsible for the mismatch between data and theory. I believe that it is quite useful to have this kind of detailed model, operating on a confirmatory bias, but that it must go hand in hand with a fundamental questioning of the main assumptions. That must be done with a strong disconfirmatory bias if it is to be useful (Platt, 1964). That type of attitude is hard to maintain, but I will try to do so in this book, at least in the sense that much of the space will be taken up with discussions of data that potentially threaten the basic approach of Cowan (1988).

1.5.3 More extensive unified theories of cognition

Both Anderson (1983) and Newell (1990) have designed theories of cognition that operate as computer programs and attempt to account for a wide range of complex cognitive phenomena. Like the model of Schneider and Detweiler (1987), the tests of these models have operated basically with a confirmation bias; they can duplicate the patterns of many interesting data sets. These "unified theories" have been extended to a much wider variety of tasks than has the Schneider and Detweiler model.

Unfortunately, and perhaps inevitably with efforts of this scope at this point in time, the models of Anderson and Newell rest on some fundamental assumptions that have not been tested. For example, the Anderson (1983) model involves separate storage of declarative and procedural information, whereas other investigators have just as reasonably proposed that the two types of memory involve different codes within a single common memory system (Humphreys et al., 1989). Many of the commentaries following the book précis by Newell (1992) criticized the fact that Newell (1990) incorporated a short-term memory system with no structural limits, in opposition to much of the psychological literature. Thus, the models may be too far in some of the wrong directions in a multidimensional hypothesis space concerning basic facts of human information processing.

The theories, though they are impressive achievements in artificial intelligence, may be neither as unified nor as well-specified as they would seem. Regarding the lack of true unity, some of the commentaries following Newell (1992) suggested that, because it contains numerous independent principles tacked together to solve separate problems, if one application of the theory failed it often could be corrected without damaging other applications of the theory. Regarding the lack of specificity, Hunt and Luce (1992) refuted a view, commonly heard in computer science, that the program is the theory and that if one wants to know the theory, one should simply run the program. Hunt and Luce pointed out that only part of the program is meant as theory and that other aspects are meant as conveniences to get the program to run. It is not always clear which parts of the program are meant as theory and which are meant as conveniences.

Finally, of most specific concern in the present context, these overarching theories based on work in computer science have not expended much effort examining the limitations imposed by attention. It seems reasonable that the aim of getting the computer to think *as well as* a human would take precedence over the aim of getting the computer to have the same *shortcomings* as a human (although those supposed shortcomings probably instill some advantages; e.g., the short-term memory limit may reduce the time it takes to respond to items that do remain in short-term memory). From the point of view of psychology, however, it is the pattern of abilities and limitations that is important. Mainly because of the large differences in method and emphasis between the present approach and that of the unified theories of cognition, the latter play little role in the discussion within this book.

1.5.4 Partial-system models

Unlike some models, the model of Cowan (1988) aimed not for completeness, but for "exhaustiveness." The meaning of exhaustiveness in this context is that there must be a place in the model for any kind of stimulus, task, process, or behavior that actually takes place. Although the model does not specify all such things (e.g., it does not specify exactly how problem-solving takes place, or even exactly which features are activated when a stimulus is presented), one presumably could add the relevant processes into the model by embellishing it, without contradicting its current structural divisions or mechanisms.

In contrast, for many models there is no attempt at either completeness or exhaustiveness; yet these still may be useful models for more narrowly defined purposes. A good example is the working memory model of Baddeley (1986). The model consists of a central executive plus two passive storage systems, the phonological store and the visuospatial sketch pad. It is obvious that, within this model, the passive storage component is not exhaustive. For example, it makes no provision for nonphonetic, nonspatial acoustic storage, nor does it allow for such things as the storage of recent or intended gross motor actions. The model does not completely consider attention in that there is no mention of the interruption of voluntary attention by novel or significant stimuli.

These points are not meant as criticisms of Baddeley's model, given that it does reasonably well at accounting for the types of memory that it was designed for. It is just that investigators might have a tendency to compare the Cowan (1988) approach to this model when, in fact, they appear to have different aims. Although both models work at a similar level of analysis, that of emphasis on necessary conclusions from the literature, they are different in scope and therefore are not directly comparable except where they might conflict with one another.

There is at least one place where the models do appear to conflict. Where Baddeley (1986) postulated two distinct passive stores (phonological and visuospatial), for Cowan (1988) these would be two instances of activated memory. The concept would be that every stimulus has the potential of activating a number of types of memory feature corresponding to that stimulus (e.g., modality-specific sensory, modality-related such as musical note category, phonetic, orthographic, lexical, spatial, and semantic features). Memory search through the focus of attention would have the capability of activating any of these features except, perhaps, modality-specific sensory, which might be stimulated only through the senses. Interference with activated features in memory would come from any subsequent stimulus or thought process that elicited the activation of similar types of features.

According to this analysis, the distinctness and noninterchangeability of phonetic and spatial information occurs because different types of features are being activated, not because of distinctly different storage modules. I assume (similar to Schneider and Detweiler, 1987) that all types of features share a common set of abstract dynamic properties, such as the neural mechanism of activation, the persistence of activation, and the neural mechanism of interference caused by similar features.

Most specific mathematical models, of necessity, are usually also are partial-system models. A good example is Massaro's "fuzzy logical model of perception" (Massaro & Friedman, 1990; Massaro & Cohen, 1991). That model does a reasonable job in describing a large number of perceptual phenomena. It consists of a stage at which the individual features of a stimulus are resolved, followed by a stage at which the features are weighted and combined to produce an overall judgment. However, there are many cognitive processes that are not part of perception, and for those the model cannot apply as it is currently stated.

It is interesting but perplexing when models of different levels of analysis are pitted against one another. Massaro has pitted his model against both the interactive activation models, with their top-down feedback assumption (e.g., Massaro & Cohen, 1991) and the connectionist approach, with its "superpowerful" use of hidden units (Massaro, 1988). However, at least the connectionist approach has been used to model processes that are not primarily perceptual in nature (e.g., learning and motoric processes). Unless the present connectionists saw nonconnectionist ways to mediate those nonperceptual processes, they would not be likely to drop the connectionist approach in favor of another approach like Massaro's, on the basis of moderate differences in the models' fits to perceptual processes.

To summarize the comparison of the present approach with unified-system and partial-system models, the present approach differs from all of them in various ways. The use of data is similar to Baddeley (1986), but the present model is an attempt to be able to accommodate all of the psychological research findings, although with many details necessarily missing. This "exhaustiveness" of the present approach is similar to the Schneider and Detweiler (1987) model, but they add untested assumptions in order to increase the level of specificity of the model. Some partial-system models, such as the fuzzy logical model of perception of Massaro, achieve even greater mathematical precision for a single, broad domain of behavior. Attempts to achieve exhaustiveness for all behavior without losing specificity (Anderson, 1983; McClelland & Rumelhart, 1986; Newell, 1990) require more untested assumptions.

1.5.5 Alternative arrangements of components

So far in this section on model comparisons, we have discussed models that differ from Cowan (1988) in emphasis, but do not positively contradict that model. If the model has meaningful content, it should conflict with certain other possible models.

We already have discussed one model that is in conflict with Cowan (1988), the model of Broadbent (1984). Another such model, which conflicts for similar reasons, is the model of Shallice and Warrington (1970). This model was designed to account for the finding that certain brain-lesioned patients have a normal long-term memory even though they have a deficient short-term memory. If short-term memory precedes long-term memory in series, as in the models of Broadbent (1958) and Atkinson and Shiffrin (1968), then a deficiency in short-term memory should imply a deficiency in long-term memory because the transmission to long-term memory should be deficient. To solve this paradox, Shallice and Warrington suggested that there are separate short- and long-term memory stores arranged in parallel.

There are problems with this solution. If one adheres to the notion of short-term memory's reliance on an activated set of features from long-term memory, then it is unreasonable to propose that information could reach a short-term store before any contact has been made with the information from long-term memory.

The paradox stated by Shallice and Warrington does not seem convincing because identical methods were not used to examine short- and long-term memory. It is quite possible that their subject had lost certain coding processes (e.g., some phonetic processes, possibly including rehearsal) that typically are used to maintain recently presented items for immediate recall, but did not lose the coding processes (e.g., visual and semantic processes) that may be used to retrieve items for long-term recall. This suggestion is reinforced by a subsequent study of the same patient (Warrington & Shallice, 1972), which indicated that the short-term memory deficit occurred primarily for verbal items, and also that visually presented, phonetically similar sets of verbal items did not produce acoustic confusions as they do in normal subjects. This type of interpretation seems to fit a larger sample of patients reviewed by Shallice and Vallar (1990).

From the point of view of the present Fig. 1.4 and 1.5, in which long-term memory is reached before short-term memory, the paradox occurs instead for patients in which short-term memory is normal but long-term memory is impaired (e.g., Scoville & Milner, 1957; Schacter, 1987). However, as will be explained in Chapter 6, the likely answer to this paradox is that short-term memory includes attention-demanding processes that, in normal people, permit attended information to be stored in long-term memory in a directly retrievable form. That use of attention is blocked in patients with a typical long-term memory deficit involving hippocampal or frontal brain lesions, even though in the case of isolated hippocampal lesions, attention itself appears normal (Schacter, 1989).

1.5.6 Strong modularity

Part of my discomfort with the approach of Shallice and Warrington (1970) may go beyond the specific model that they proposed. It may include the tendency to accept too quickly the notion that processing is based on a number of separate modules that operate independently (see Massaro & Cowan, 1993 for a more general critique of modularity). A comprehensive debate on this issue can be found in Shallice (1991).

As an illustration of the debate, consider that Shallice proposes separate speech and nonspeech short-term memory buffers, and in fact terms the short-term buffers "various and specific and lowly in function" (Shallice, 1988, p. 401). The problem with apparently separate storage modules is that they actually may result from a common storage medium fed by separate coding areas. Even for the coding processes, the notion of modularity may not be justified. For example, it seems likely that speech and nonspeech sounds are coded in slightly different areas (or congregations of areas) within the temporal lobe cortex, but then, the difference in the location of coding of two very different nonspeech sounds may be equally as great. If there are substantially different storage areas for different types of sounds, the basis of inferring a modular speech/nonspeech difference may be weakened.

In each allegedly different short-term memory buffer, the dynamics of memory processing, such as the persistence of activation and modification of synaptic connections, might occur in the same way regardless of the nature of the specific memory code. It also must be considered that not all functional differences imply storage differences; for example, even if speech and nonspeech memories were stored together, they still would differ functionally because only speech sounds can be rehearsed easily.

Even with these observations in mind, it is not always easy to determine how modular a model of processing is meant to be. For example, in Schneider and Detweiler's (1987) model, the modules were separate but with identical internal structures. One can view the presence of separate modules as a convenient simplification of a system in which the alleged modules actually blend into one another, or alternatively as a proposal that these boundaries are factual. Cowan (1988) left the issue open by omitting such dividing lines.

1.5.7 Summary remarks on model comparisons

The previous discussion appears to find fault with many of the modeling attempts in which very specific proposals were made, and to champion the approach in which the model is little more than descriptive of what is known. I believe that both approaches are valuable, but that much work can be wasted if models rest unduly on assumptions that have not been justified and therefore risk overdeveloping an infeasible model (cf. Massaro, 1987).

One could argue that, by now, enough basic assumptions have been settled (see Cowan, 1988) to permit more explicit modeling attempts (e.g., Schneider & Detweiler, 1987). There is some validity to this. Yet, in my reading of the current research literature, I find that even the basic points made by Cowan (1988) are more controversial than I had assumed at the time. This book concentrates primarily on summarizing and assessing the empirical research literature for certain fundamental issues. These issues, each forming the basis for a different chapter of the book, will now be described in turn.

1.6 Key issues regarding memory and attention

Consumer Reports (1993, p. 21) noted that a 1990 study from the American Psychiatric Association indicated that benzodiazepines, drugs commonly prescribed to control anxiety, "tend to impair memory". Dr. Robert J. Gladstone was quoted as stating that a new type of benzodiazepine, Xanax, "sort of wipes out people's attention to things." It is clear from this report that, in layman's discussions, a sharp distinction between memory and attention is not always drawn.

There is indeed a complex and intimate relationship between memory and attention. This relationship will be examined from many standpoints in the remainder of this book. Most of the chapters emphasize particular facets in the relationship and examine fundamental theoretical points that are at issue. When the suggested resolutions of the controversies are considered together, they amount to what I believe to be a strengthened framework for the joint consideration of memory and attention.

1.6.1 Chapter 2: sensory memory

The practical, operational definition of sensory memory has changed in the course of research in cognitive psychology. Originally it was taken to be indexed by memory for unattended input, which was assumed to be sensory in nature (e.g., Broadbent, 1958; Sperling, 1960; Eriksen & Johnson, 1964). The basic rationale was that a completely unanalyzed memory would have to consist of something similar to the original sensations that produced the memory; and this rationale was backed up by the observation that subjects became aware only of changes in the gross physical features of an unattended channel (Cherry, 1953). Later, researchers seemed more willing to admit the possibility that some categorical coding could take place automatically, so specific manipulations such as the physical similarity of target and interference stimuli were carried out to examine further the assumption that the memory trace in a particular test situation was sensory in nature (e.g., Eriksen & Collins, 1967, 1968; Morton, Crowder, & Prussin, 1971; Turvey, 1973; Phillips, 1974; Greenberg & Engle, 1983).

Most researchers in cognitive psychology probably hold the view that there is a sensory memory store that persists for a few seconds, or the view that it persists for a few hundred milliseconds in vision and a few seconds in audition. However, much of the evidence that might be cited in support of these views is known to be of questionable validity.

For the visual modality, the evidence most commonly cited in textbooks is the finding of a partial report superiority at short cue delays (Sperling, 1960), that is, the finding that subjects' ability to recite characters from a spatially determined subset of the array depends critically on the temporal delay between the array and a cue signalling the subset to be reported (Sperling, 1960). The evidence that has been cited most often in support of an auditory sensory memory is the existence of modality and suffix effects, both of which are found in procedures in which lists of verbal items are to be recalled. The "modality effect" refers to the finding that the most recently presented items in the list are recalled better if the list is spoken than if it is presented in printed form, even though there is little difference between modalities in the recall of earlier portions of the lists (see Penney, 1975, 1989 for reviews). This was thought to occur because auditory sensory memory lasts longer than visual sensory memory. The "suffix effect" (Crowder & Morton, 1969; Morton et al., 1971) refers to the finding that a sound placed after the last item in a spoken list (the so-called suffix item) greatly reduces this modality advantage, with little or no effect of a suffix item when either or both items are visually presented. The explanation of this effect was supposed to be simply that the suffix item interferes with the auditory sensory memory that otherwise would have allowed an auditory modality advantage.

The weight of these observations about visual and auditory sensory memory has been critically weakened in recent years. In the visual modality, the conclusions to be drawn from Sperling's partial report procedure have had to be amended because of subsequent research on the nature of errors subjects make in the partial report procedure. The degradation of an exact copy of the initial sensation through neural noise should result in random errors, but instead it has been found that, in most errors, the correct items are reported in incorrect locations (e.g., Mewhort, Campbell, Marchetti, & Campbell, 1981). This must lead to some complication in the theoretical account of the partial report procedure in which it is acknowledged that a partial coding of features has been incorporated into the memory available to subjects at the time of recall.

The logic for the auditory research started to fall apart when Bjork and Whitten (1974) observed that the ordinarily observed superiority of memory for items at the end of the list as compared with immediately prior items, termed the recency effect, can be obtained in a situation in which temporary memory storage would not be expected to contribute. Specifically, it was obtained with a distracting task inserted for a number of seconds between each two items and between the last item and the recall period. This was termed a "long-term recency effect." Other investigators (Gardiner and Gregg, 1979; Glenberg, 1984) subsequently found that "long-term modality effects" also can be obtained under similar circumstances, and Glenberg (1984) found that long-term suffix effects can be obtained. No account of modality and suffix effects that is based on an auditory sensory store that persists for only a few seconds could account for these data; they have been accounted for with theories that emphasize that temporal factors and modality affect the distinctiveness of the memory traces for various items.

If the case for the existence of a short-lived sensory store rested entirely on partial report, modality, and suffix procedures, then the concept of sensory memory would have died. However, there are many other procedures that have been used to demonstrate sensory memory. Some investigators who formerly placed considerable stock in sensory memory storage now believe that all of these phenomena will similarly turn out to be examples of distinctiveness and other principles that do not rely upon the notion of temporary storage (e.g, Crowder, 1989*a*, 1993). Chapter 2 therefore takes a close look at the evidence for sensory memory, tentatively concluding that the concept is alive and well.

1.6.2 Chapter 3: short-term storage

The fate of the concept of short-term storage in general has followed the fate of sensory storage. Some of the original evidence for short-term storage depended upon the existence of a recency effect in short-term verbal recall. The recency effect was thought to result from the availability of a temporary memory trace for the most recent items only (e.g., Waugh & Norman, 1965; Glanzer and Cunitz, 1966). Clearly, Bjork and Whitten's long-term recency effect weakens that argument.

An entirely separate type of evidence for a temporary memory trace comes from research on word-length effects in recall. Baddeley, Thomson, and Buchanan (1975) found that lists composed of words that take a relatively long time to pronounce cannot be recalled as well as lists composed of shorter words. In fact, subjects could recall about as many words of a particular type as they could pronounce in about 2 seconds (see also Schweickert and Boruff, 1986). Baddeley (1986) has accounted for this type of finding on the basis of a temporary phonetic memory trace that decays in about 2 seconds if it is not refreshed through a covert rehearsal process.

Given the qualifications of other procedures that have emerged, the word-length effect is perhaps the best remaining solid evidence in favor of temporary memory storage. Therefore, it is important to understand word length effects, and the related processes involved in verbal recall, in some detail. A considerable amount of recent work has been devoted to understanding this type of process, and that work will be reviewed.

In order to better understand short-term storage, various phenomena will be analyzed according to the view that short-term storage consists of both the activated information and the attended subset of that activated information. There are, however, a number of problems with the concept of short-term memory that were not stated clearly by Cowan (1988). For example, "activated elements from long-term memory" cannot fully describe short-term memory, because short-term memory must also include the specific new links between activated elements. These links represent the new episodic record that is not yet present in long-term memory. Such processes and their potential neural representation will be discussed in Chapter 3 with the aim of sketching out a fuller description of short-term memory processes.

1.6.3 Chapter 4: "virtual" short-term memory mechanisms

The term "short-term memory" has been used to refer both to performance in tasks in which there is little or no delay between the presentation and recall phases of a trial, and to the theoretical mechanisms underlying such performance. One type of theoretical mechanism involves temporary storage or activation of a memory trace but, as mentioned above, this type of mechanism does not account for all types of immediate memory phenomenon. For some of those phenomena, such as the long-term recency effect, the correct explanation is unclear but may involve only long-term storage along with factors, such as temporal distinctiveness, that make some memory representations more easily retrievable than others.

These phenomena are important in their own right and should not be overlooked or dismissed if a general model of processing is the aim. I have referred to these for convenience as "virtual", as opposed to real short-term memory phenomena. The implication is that they are not genuine indices of short-lived memory activation, but may appear similar on casual inspection.

The remaining, crucial question that is examined is whether or not, as Crowder (1989*a*, 1993) has implied, all short-term memory phenomena may be virtual short-term memory phenomena. I argue against this position on the basis that the virtual short-term memory phenomena differ from their conventional counterparts in some important details, suggesting that the concept of memory activation is an important one after all.

1.6.4 Chapter 5: habituation and dishabituation of orienting

The ability of orienting and the habituation of orienting to perform the work of an attentional filter (Cowan, 1988) depends on the correctness of key predictions. A great deal of work has been accomplished by other investigators since 1988, supporting the concepts of novelty and significance (e.g., Gati & Ben-Shakhar, 1990), their role in attentive processing (e.g., Johnston, Hawley, Plewe, Elliott, & DeWitt, 1990), and physiological processes that could reflect the formation and use of a neural model. Thus, Chapter 5 will not focus on conflicts with Cowan (1988), but on findings that help to resolve some of the uncertainties that remained about the concept of habituation of orienting and its suggested role as a selective attentional filter.

For a broad concept such as habituation of orienting, there may be questions about the breadth of the domain of application of the concept. Chapter 5 ends by considering phenomena (e.g., automaticity) that may or may not fit the pattern of orienting and habituation as selective attention devices.

1.6.5 Chapter 6: attention and long-term memory

A broad theme of Cowan (1988) was that attention plays a central role in memory phenomena. We have seen this already with respect to sensory memory and other types of short-term memory. The theme is made more extensive by recent work emphasizing the key role of attention in long-term memory retention and retrieval (e.g., Jacoby, 1991). The basic idea is that memory storage takes place automatically, but that explicit, direct recall of the stored material is possible only with the presence of attention both at the time of encoding and at the time of recall. Various behavioral and neurophysiological aspects of this hypothesis will be discussed and elaborated upon.

1.6.6 Chapter 7: attention and awareness

It could be argued that the two types of phenomena that have played the largest role in overall models of information processing are transient memory storage and selective attention. Both of these concepts reflect limitations in human information processing capacity. We have already seen that the concept of transient memory storage has been called into question. Similarly, the generality of the concept of selective attention also has been called into question.

The concept of attention is central to the way that information processing models are interpreted phenomenologically. Information that is attended is supposed to be the same as information that is in one's conscious awareness. However, this unitary concept of attention and awareness has been challenged on several very different grounds.

First, some cognitive psychologists (e.g., Allport, 1980; Wickens, 1984) have proposed that the concept of attention should be replaced with the concept of multiple limited processing resources, none of which would seem to possess any unique correspondence with awareness. If this were true, then the nature of information processing would have to be fundamentally different from what Cowan (1988) and others (e.g., Baars, 1988) have proposed.

Second, neurologists have shown that consciousness is divisible; patients whose corpus collosums have been severed demonstrate separate, non-communicating minds in the left and right hemispheres (e.g., Gazzaniga, 1985). It has not yet been determined what the implications of this are for the concepts of attention and awareness in normal individuals, but some possible implications will be discussed in Chapter 7.

Third, some psychologists who have examined dissociated states in neurologically normal individuals, such as hypnosis, have concluded that consciousness is divisible into parts that do not communicate with one another (e.g., Hilgard, 1986). This again has the potential of threatening the kind of account in which a basically unitary attention and awareness is proposed.

Fourth, and finally, some philosophers have proposed that the phenomenological impression of a unified awareness is an illusion, and that in reality there are a host of totally separate processes that work together to create that illusion.

There is an interesting commonality in the themes that emerge from all of these very different research endeavors. Whereas the traditional information processing psychologists have emphasized that attention and awareness can be treated as a unified entity, others have emphasized that attention and awareness can be dissected into parts. Resolution of this issue (like that of the existence or nonexistence of temporary memory storage) is probably one of the most fundamental goals that must be reached in narrowing down the processing hypothesis space. There may be little point in embellishing models of processing until such issues are settled.

Chapter 7 will argue in favor of the unified view. It will be argued that, in neurologically normal humans, although there are many separate cognitive processes, some conscious and some unconscious, there is a core interactive process that forms the backbone of conscious experience and cannot be divided except through neural lesions.

1.6.7 Chapter 8: summary discussion including neurophysiological underpinnings of memory and attention

The first part of this chapter summarizes a theme that has run throughout the book, that memory and attention are intricately linked. To clarify the point, effects of attention on memory and effects of memory on attention will be summarized separately. These effects amount to mutual constraints on the type of memory and attention concepts one can use in a model of information processing.

Many of the issues discussed in this book have been debated in cognitive psychology without much reference to neural sciences. In Chapter 8 it is argued that, given recent advances in neural sciences, there no longer is justification for separating the field into behavioral and neurophysiological methodologies because combining information from both methodologies is the best way to make progress. A speculative analysis will be offered in which neural counterparts to each of the components of the model proposed by Cowan (1988), as well as neural hypotheses about the concept of consciousness, will be suggested on the basis of recent evidence.

The last part of the chapter is rather reflective and asks how cognitive and neural theorizing might best continue in the face of problems such as the tendency to be satisfied with explanations that amount to no more than homunculi. A limited defense of homunculi will in fact be offered.

1.6.8 Strategies for reading this book

The chapters in this book might be understood independently. A reader well-versed in cognitive psychology might reasonably decide to skip to his or her favorite topics, or perhaps to the ones with the most controversial material: Chapters 4 ("virtual" short-term memory), 7 (attention and awareness), and 8 (summary discussion and neurophysiological speculations). If so, I hope that the reader will check the unread chapters at some point in the future if basic concepts of sensory memory, short-term memory, long-term memory, and selective attention have been brought into question.

Part I

Transient-Memory Phenomena

2. Sensory memory persistence

Broadbent (1958) and Sperling (1960) demonstrated, in different ways to be discussed later, that a wealth of sensory information about the environment is saved in the brain for a short time, even though only a small amount of it can be reported before the rest of the information is lost. On these grounds they drew a distinction between a sensory store of unlimited capacity and a categorical short-term store of limited capacity. Massaro (1975*a*) and Cowan (1988) questioned this distinction, arguing that many sensory memory phenomena may be, in principle, no different than non-sensory types of short-term memory. For those sensory memory phenomena, for example, Cowan (1988) questioned the unlimited capacity assumption, and the basis for those doubts will be explained in the next chapter.

Whether the distinction between sensory and non-sensory memory is considered to be fundamental or both types are thought of as varieties of a transient or "short-term" memory, the case can be made that the act of remembering sensation is still important in unique ways. Humans must extract, from everything in the environment, the most meaningful information. How is that to be accomplished? One way would be to extract all of the available information and then sift through it to find out what is relevant. That would be workable if it were possible to process all information at once, in parallel. However, this does not seem likely. Not only are there very many objects in the environment to be processed, but also there are multiple ways in which each object can be considered. For example, what at first appears to be a squadron of airplanes may prove to be a flock of geese. Sometimes the objects remain in view for as long as the perceptual systems need, but sometimes they do not (e.g., the geese fly out of view, perhaps behind some trees).

When continued perception is not possible, the perceptual system may still retain, for a short period, enough of the original sensory data for a reanalysis to be carried out when necessary. Then the processing system can hedge its bets. Some amount of processing might be carried out automatically, followed by more intensive analysis of objects that appear to contain potentially important information. The observer can go back to the sensory information to check if it has remained similar and could be interpreted as, say, a flock of geese instead of planes. Of course, this going back to the sensory information may be even more critical in the auditory modality, where the stimuli never linger. Thus, sensory memory has a special place in information processing. It is our protection against living in a fragmented present, dominated by our own arbitrary and abstract interpretations of the outside world on a moment-by-moment basis. We think about things at a finite pace, and sensory memory allows the memory of these things to linger while we think about them.

The basic premise of this chapter is that the phenomenon of sensory memory is important enough to serve as an essential basis from which to reason about information processing. I have not been able to find any recent reviews of sensory memory across different modalities (though see Coltheart, 1984; Cowan, 1988). The purpose of the chapter is to provide such a review, furthering an understanding of the sensory memory concept by considering its role in cognitive psychology, its distinguishing features, its types and their potential uses, and a bit about its neural representation. The concept of a distinct, temporary sensory memory has not gone unchallenged, however, and we will begin to deal with the challenges in this chapter, picking up that issue again in Chapters 3 and 4 after other transient memory phenomena have been discussed.

2.1 Sensory memory in current cognitive psychology

In the early days of cognitive psychology, there was quite an emphasis on sensory memory. Broadbent (1958) pointed out that subjects could not fully perceive more than one physically defined stream of stimuli at a time, but that they could recall the most recent few seconds of stimulation from an unattended stream. This was shown with separate streams that were both auditory (e.g., stimuli presented to the left and right ears, or presented to both ears in two different voices) or were visual and auditory (e.g., one spoken and one written message). Neisser and Becklen (1975) later demonstrated that the situation is comparable when two videotaped events are shown superimposed upon one another. Other early studies also emphasized the importance of sensory memory as the first source from which information processing proceeds. Sperling (1960) demonstrated that subjects have more information about a briefly presented visual character array than they can report before it fades, and that more of it can be accessed if a partial report cue is presented quickly after the array (within several hundred milliseconds). Other researchers similarly showed that subjects ordinarily extract information about a brief, isolated stimulus from a vivid sensory memory for a few hundred milliseconds, given that the recognition process can be aborted by a physically similar, second stimulus or "mask" that occurs in less than about 300 ms after the target stimulus, both in the visual (e.g., Turvey, 1973) and the auditory (e.g., Massaro, 1972) modalities. The perceptual result is that the subject can easily detect the backwardly masked stimulus but still cannot identify it. In contrast, there is much less effect of a mask that precedes instead of following the target. Still other researchers (Eriksen & Collins, 1967, 1968; Haber & Standing, 1969, 1970; Efron, 1970*a*, 1970*b*, 1970) showed that there is a period of up to several hundred milliseconds after the beginning of the stimulus for which the sensory memory is actually perceived as a continuation of the stimulus.

The studies cited above indicated that some sort of vivid sensory memory lasts for several hundred milliseconds. Additionally, a great deal of research in the auditory modality (e.g., Guttman & Julesz, 1963; Crowder & Morton, 1969; Morton et al., 1971; Darwin, Turvey, & Crowder, 1972; Treisman & Rostron, 1972; Pisoni, 1973; Rostron, 1974; Watkins & Todres, 1980; Crowder, 1982; Balota & Duchek, 1986) and a small amount of research in the visual modality (Phillips, 1974; Scarborough, 1972) suggested that sensory memory of some sort could be used for stimulus retrieval in memory tasks for a longer period, in some studies up to perhaps 20 seconds.

Though there is still some interest in sensory memory within the field of cognitive psychology, researchers lately have turned more toward an interest in how the semantic and lexical memory system is organized, as well as in imagery processes. This could be explained on the grounds that we now have a more solid basis for investigating complex mental representations (with, for example, the development of many interesting semantic priming techniques), whereas the research on sensory memory has reached a plateau at which it is difficult to know how to proceed. Although much has been learned and important questions remain, a muddle of alternative methods exists, each with accompanying methodological concerns.

The de-emphasis of sensory memory within cognitive psychology alternatively might be explained on the basis of the shifting goals of the field. It always has had at least two major objectives: to develop an understanding of the general mechanisms of information processing (e.g., Broadbent, 1958), which would be applicable for any processing domain; and to determine in more detail the representations and processes involved in specific domains of cognition, such as language processing, reasoning, and mental imagery. Sensory memory is relevant to the former goal, because it may be an early step in the processing of any stimulus. However, as Cowan (1988) argued, most researchers lately appear to have stepped back from the task of forming an overall processing model in order to be able to explore specific domains in more detail. As a result, there have been very few attempts to bring a model such as that of Broadbent (1958) up to date.

At least two attempts have been made to examine the processing system as a whole while maintaining the newer emphasis on the explication of the details of the model. However, these were made by computer scientists (Anderson, 1983; Newell, 1990). Although they are important efforts, they tend to take the initial coding and sensory storage of the stimulus for granted rather than discussing it as a critical research topic. That would appear to be more adequate in the case of computer input than in the case of human stimulus input. The connectionist approach (e.g., McClelland & Elman, 1986; McClelland, Rumelhart, & Hinton, 1986) also has strived for a general system architecture that will be applicable to any situation, but such a satisfactory solution has not yet been obtained, and again the question of the form of the initial coding and storage of stimuli has been largely bypassed rather than explored. Finally, studies that seek to describe processing in a restricted domain have also bypassed the study of sensory memory to focus on more sophisticated, meaning-laden representations of stimuli.

Cowan (1988) suggested that it is important to integrate recent research into a general model of processing, and sensory memory plays a critical role in any such model. There also are additional reasons why sensory memory is interesting. These have to do with our scientific understanding of how the mind uses time, and hence our understanding of cognition, perception, and phenomenology. Time is not conveniently divided into segments, but can be seen as an unending flow, on one hand, or as an infinite train of infinitely small moments, on the other hand. If *psychological* time were describable in either of these ways, though, it would be disastrous for perception. We need to be able to distinguish between events that are occurring in the present and those that occurred in the past. If the present moment were infinitely short, though, no event that unfolds over time could be totally in the present. Thus some researchers (e.g., Stroud, 1955; Lichtenstein, 1961; Allport, 1968; Creel, Boomsliter, & Powers, 1970; Robinson & Pollack, 1971) were inspired to investigate the "psychological moment," the period of time during which two or more successive events are perceived as simultaneous. For example, Lichtenstein found that series of visual stimuli presented in rapid enough succession appear to occur at the same time. The studies cited above suggest that the psychological moment might persist for about 100 ms, with the exact duration dependent on stimulus characteristics such as brightness. The concept of a psychological moment implies that events are retained in memory in a sensory form at least until some subsequent events are presented.

The specifics of the psychological moment concept can be challenged, however, on the basis of results suggesting that temporal discrimination in the auditory modality is very acute, with people able to distinguish the order of events only 10–20 ms apart (Hirsh, 1959; Penner, 1977). These results need to be reconciled with those that lead to an estimate of the psychological moment that is an order of magnitude larger. Thus, one philosophically important issue that has not been resolved is whether or not the concept of the psychological moment is valid and, if not, whether any other concept is needed to explain how events can be perceived in ongoing time.

A further puzzle is whether we need to distinguish between the "present" and the merely "current" in mental life. James (1890) advocated that short-term memory reflects the contents of what is perceived as current, the information that determines our present state of mind. If so, the portion of that short-term memory that consists of sensory information reflects one's direct link to the current environment. What does this direct link include?

We are ignorant of so basic a point as whether it can include a sequential series of images, a single image that incorporates movement (e.g., in space or frequency), or only a single static image (Cowan, 1984 reviewed this question). The difficulty has been in distinguishing between sensory memory and other varieties of memory.

There also is the question of what is saved by the brain and what it lets go. Clearly, we retain some permanent memory related to sensory images. For example, one can imagine the face or voice of an old friend without any new environmental input. However, this long-term sensory memory may include less information than one would think. One demonstration of this (Hinton, 1979) is as follows. Imagine a cube (say, 50 cm on each side) tilted so that it is standing on one corner, with another corner straight up. Now point to the remaining corners. Then check your answer against a real cube or a drawing of one. (Put the book down and try it now.) The task is surprisingly difficult; many people point out four corners around the equator of the figure, which is incorrect in number as well as placement. Clearly, mental imagery and sensory memory are not the same thing.

Below, questions about sensory memory will be addressed, and sometimes controversial stands will be taken, as findings in the field relevant to the definition of sensory memory, its distinguishing features and subtypes, its duration, and its neural representation are mentioned.

2.2 Definition and distinguishing features of sensory memory

There are two criteria that one can use to distinguish sensory memory from other types of memory, thereby defining sensory memory. First, only sensory memory should include information that is modality-specific and cannot be translated into another modality. Second, only sensory memory should include fine information that allows a distinction between two slightly different stimuli that fall within the same pre-existing conceptual category (e.g., two acoustically different versions of the vowel /a/).

As a counterexample to both of these criteria, consider the ability to tell apart two different piano notes. The first note must be retained in memory until the second note is perceived. Nevertheless, sensory memory theoretically would not be necessary. The first note could be retained in terms of its membership in a tone category within the conventional musical scale, and it might even be translated into a visual representation if the listener knows how to read and write music. On the other hand, auditory sensory memory could be used instead to retain the specific pitch of the first tone, no matter whether the two tones to be compared differed in category membership or not. A similar line of reasoning applies to any other modality. In vision, for example, sensory memory should not require that the visual field be divided into a number of known objects or known features.

It seems important to ask whether the concept of sensory memory makes any difference, speaking practically and theoretically. Does sensory memory have any properties that differ from other types of memory, or has it been distinguished from other types arbitrarily? One possible difference is that sensory memory of a stimulus is critically sensitive to interference from subsequent stimuli with similar physical features. Examples of this include both the backward masking of recognition of a brief, target item when it is followed quickly by a physically similar item or mask (Massaro, 1972; Turvey, 1973) and, with slower presentations, the "suffix effect," or poorer retention of items at the end of an auditory list obtained when the list is followed by a physically similar sound that is not to be recalled (Morton et al., 1971; Greene & Samuel, 1986).

In at least some cases, it appears that the amount of interference depends on a mental categorization of the stimuli instead of the physical characteristics of the stimuli directly. For example, although Morton et al. (1971) clearly found that the suffix effect depends on the acoustic similarity between the list and suffix, Ayres, Jonides, Reitman, Egan, and Howard (1979) found that it also depends on the perceived category of the suffix. Specifically, a musical sound that was made by a trumpet but sounded rather like the syllable "wa" interfered with recall of a spoken list of items much more when the sound was perceived as speech than when it was perceived as a musical sound. This basic finding was replicated and extended by Neath, Surprenant, and Crowder (1993).

Even if one can find cases in which the susceptibility of an apparent sensory memory is affected only by the physical similarity between stimuli, this difference between sensory memory and other types of memory may not be a fundamental one, for the following reason. For each variety of memory, the most effective interference involves the presentation of stimuli with like features of that variety. Just as there is interference with the sensory memory of a stimulus from subsequent stimuli with similar sensory features, there is evidence of interference with, for example, phonological memory from stimuli with similar phonological features. Thus, Conrad (1964) found that subjects did not recall lists of printed letters as well when the letters in a list had names that rhymed with one another. Similar evidence can be cited for the interference with semantic features. For example, there is a "release from proactive inhibition" when the items in a list to be recalled abruptly shift from one semantic category to another (Wickens, 1972). For a given stimulus, more than one type of memory code could be present, with codes used together to help retain the item in memory; and an intervening stimulus could interfere with more than one of these codes at once.

Perhaps a difference between sensory memory and other forms of memory coding is in the way in which the memory codes can be activated. Phonological, semantic, and even spatial codes can be activated through various types of covert mental processing, often termed "rehearsal", at least in the case of verbal materials (see Baddeley, 1986 for a review). For example, rehearsal is an important component of short-term memory for lists of words, and blocking rehearsal by requiring articulation of an irrelevant word or sequence severely impairs recall (Baddeley, Lewis, & Vallar, 1984; Cowan, Cartwright, Winterowd, & Sherk, 1987). In contrast, there is as yet no clear evidence as to whether or not truly sensory memory can be rehearsed in some way. Pechmann and Mohr (1992) recently reported that subjects cannot compare the pitches of two tones any more accurately when permitted to concentrate on the tones during a 5-second period of time between the tones than when required to attend to a silent, visual distracting task during that period. However, in a similar study with intertone intervals of up to 20 seconds, Keller, Cowan, and Saults (in press) found that attention to the tones did make a small but significant difference in delayed tone comparison (about 15% in the proportion correct). Thus, the question of whether subjects can rehearse sensory memory is an important one that remains unsettled.

In any case, it appears that subjects cannot rehearse sensory memory as easily as they rehearse more abstract forms of memory. With an abstract memory code, there is little memory decay when subjects' attention is not sufficiently engaged in a distracting task during the delay period (e.g., Vallar & Baddeley, 1982). This helps to explain an additional difference between sensory and nonsensory forms of transient memory code. The interference with the longer phase of sensory memory appears to be primarily retroactive in nature, whereas interference with other memory codes can be retroactive, proactive, or both (e.g., see Crowder, 1976). If a Stimulus A is followed by a Stimulus B but Stimulus A subsequently is rehearsed, then in terms of the activation of memory codes, it may be as if A follows B. Therefore, interference between transient memory codes could be primarily retroactive in principle, with the added assumption that nonsensory codes can be self-generated (or regenerated) through rehearsal more easily than sensory codes.

It should be emphasized that, because subjects can use multiple memory codes in a single task, it is usually the case that sensory memory cannot be equated with the raw result in any one task condition. For example, Merikle (1980) found that it is possible to obtain a partial-report cue advantage over the whole-report condition using categorical cues in a modified version of the procedure designed by Sperling (1960). However, this effect is much smaller than the effect of a location cue, and other research suggests that categorical information is used only in combination with sensory information. Pashler (1984) found that degrading the elements in an array affected partial-report performance regardless of the cue delay, which should not have been the case if subjects used *only* categorical information at longer delays (because stimulus quality is irrelevant to a categorical code once the latter has been formed). A similar case could be made regarding other tasks, such as the suffix effect in acoustic memory. The suffix effect can reveal influences of acoustic coding, but also higher-level coding (e.g., see Greenberg & Engle, 1983; Neath et al., 1993).

2.3 Types of sensory memory and their durations

Cowan (1984, 1988) discussed numerous studies suggesting that there are two phases of sensory storage with very different properties: a brief afterimage lasting up to several hundred milliseconds, and a more processed (i.e., perceptually resolved) memory preserving sensory features for up to 10 or 20 seconds. This is not, however, the same gospel found in many textbooks of cognitive psychology. The predominant view seems to be that there is a marked difference between the visual and auditory modalities, with visual sensory storage lasting several hundred milliseconds and auditory sensory storage lasting 10 to 20 seconds. On the other hand, there has been support for the view of two sensory storage phases in each modality (Massaro, 1975*a*; Cowan, 1984, 1988). How could such different interpretations of the same evidence arise?

The original evidence of visual sensory memory, Sperling's (1960) study using the partial report procedure, revealed a store of several hundred milliseconds. This estimate was reinforced by findings of a visual backward masking function (Turvey, 1973) and flash fusion (Haber & Standing, 1969, 1970) in the same time range. In contrast, observations of memory for speech sounds that were unattended at the time of their presentation (Cherry, 1953; Broadbent, 1957; Eriksen & Johnson, 1964; Cowan et al., 1990) led to an estimate for auditory sensory storage of at least several seconds. The attempt to adapt the partial report procedure to the auditory modality also led to estimates in this range, both for tones (Treisman & Rostron, 1972; Rostron, 1974) and for speech sounds (Darwin et al., 1972). This estimate was further reinforced by numerous studies in which subjects were asked to compare two sounds separated by a silent interstimulus interval, which also suggested that auditory memory persists over a period of some seconds (see Cowan, 1984).

Finally, there has been substantial evidence of an auditory modality superiority in list recall; for items at the end of the list to be recalled, performance is superior when the items are presented in the auditory modality (see Penney, 1975, 1989 for reviews). The common interpretation of this finding has been that, with visual presentation, sensory memory for the entire list is largely unusable by the time that the subject is to recall the list, but that auditory sensory memory for the last few items can persist long enough to be used in recall. This interpretation was strengthened by the finding (Crowder & Morton, 1969; Morton et al., 1971) that the auditory modality superiority could be all but eliminated by the presence of a list-final "suffix" item that was not to be recalled but was acoustically similar to the spoken list, with no comparable effect occurring for printed lists and suffixes (Crowder, 1976).

With the apparent strength of this interpretation in which the storage durations are said to differ drastically between the modalities, conflicting evidence went relatively unnoticed. Massaro (1970*a*, 1970*b*, 1972) observed auditory backward recognition masking functions comparable to what had been observed in the visual modality, with asymptotic performance occurring when the target and mask onsets were separated by about 250 ms. This occurred even when the target identification task was made so difficult that the asymptotic level of performance was well below ceiling level (Massaro, 1975*b*). The simplest account appeared to be that no masking took place after 250 ms because there was little or no sensory memory left to mask, although an alternative view (that the memory persisted but that the recognition process ran to completion in 250 ms; see Crowder, 1976) could not be dismissed.

There was, however, converging evidence from a procedure developed initially by Sperling (1967) in which brief stimuli from one modality are used as indicators to establish the times of the perceived onset and offset of stimuli presented in another modality. The subject's task was to adjust the time of the indicator (e.g., a brief light flash) so that it coincided with the onset of another, target stimulus (e.g., a tone) in one condition, and with its offset in another condition. The period between the perceived onset and offset times could be taken to reflect the perceived duration of the target stimulus. Efron (1970*a*, 1970*b*, 1970*c*) required subjects to judge the perceived onset and offset of brief target stimuli by saying if a marker stimulus, which was physically quite different from the target (e.g., a tone as a marker for a visual target), coincided with the onset or offset of the target. Whereas the perceived onset of the target was fairly accurate, perceived simultaneity of the target offset and marker onset occurred when the marker came about 150 ms after the target onset, provided that the target was shorter than that. Thus, the duration of brief targets was overestimated and the extent of overestimation decreased as the target's duration increased, so that targets longer than about 150 ms were not overestimated at all. Similar results were obtained for stimuli in both modalities, although the results did depend on stimulus intensity. One instance of this finding, for visual stimuli, is reproduced in Fig. 2.1. The results suggest that the minimal perceived duration of brief stimuli is about 150 ms.

Based on such evidence along with evidence from the backward masking of recognition, Massaro (1975*a*) proposed that the duration of sensory memory was about 250 ms in both the visual and auditory modalities. (Small differences in the time estimates probably are related to task demands; e.g., the perceptual recognition process may be able to continue for a brief time even when the sensory memory trace is too weak to permit any further sensory persistence.) Massaro suggested that the memory observed for

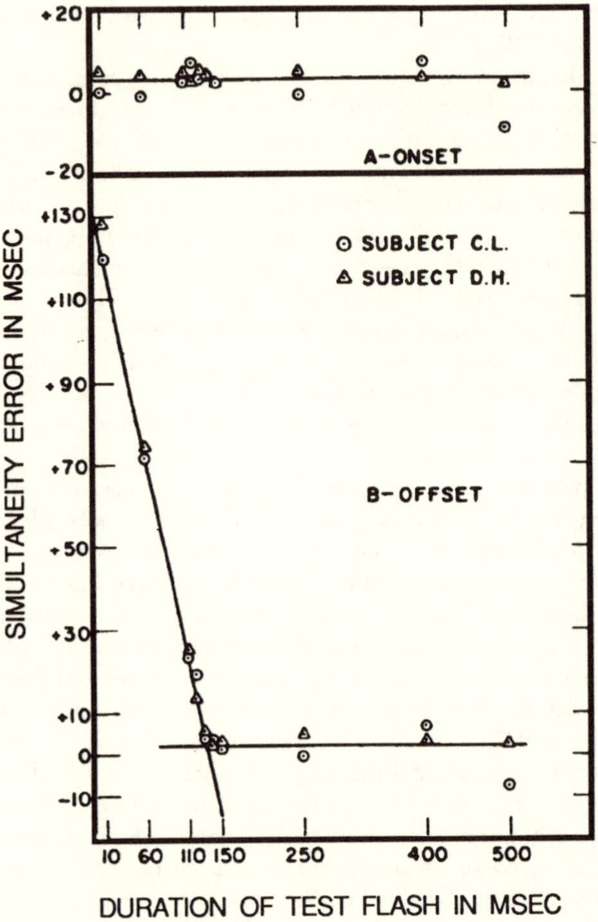

Fig. 2.1 Data on sensory persistence. (From R. Efron, 1970*c*), Effects of stimulus duration on perceptual onset and offset latencies. *Perception & Psychophysics, 8,* p. 232, Fig. 1. Adapted by permission of the Psychonomic Society.)

longer periods was not really literal in nature, but consisted of a set of coded acoustic features extracted from the sensory memory trace. These features differ from the literal sensory trace in that they are ready to be used in perceptual comparison and identification tasks.

Massaro (1976) argued, in the same vein, that the auditory partial-report procedure of Darwin et al. (1972) was not comparable to the visual procedure of Sperling (1960). Whereas subjects could not rapidly encode 12 or more visual items in Sperling's procedure, they might well encode many of the stimuli in the Darwin et al. procedure, which were presented as a spatiotemporal array in the form of three sounds at separate spatial locations, followed by three more sounds. (Given the limitation in the auditory system's spatial resolution, it might not be possible to present enough simultaneous stimuli to exceed the subject's processing rate in the auditory modality).

Kallman and Massaro (1979) carried out an auditory backward recognition masking study that demonstrated more directly that the shorter and longer auditory memories were functionally distinct. They proposed that a mask could interfere with a preceding target in two ways. First, the mask could prevent physical features from being fully extracted from the sensory memory trace within the first few hundred milliseconds, as previous studies had suggested. Second, even if the features were extracted so that a more persistent, more processed auditory memory representation of the stimulus could be formed, the mask still could interfere with that representation, in much the same way that a list-final, "suffix" sound interferes with memory of the last few items in a spoken list (Crowder & Morton, 1969). One ordinarily might not observe the latter type of interference unless the subject must postpone the use of auditory memory for a while after the representation is formed.

The procedure that Kallman and Massaro used to examine this hypothesis is illustrated in Fig. 2.2. Three tones were presented on each trial. Two of the tones (A and B) were presented 750 ms apart from one another, and the task was to compare their pitches. The third tone (C) was a masking tone presented at a variable stimulus onset asynchrony (SOA) after the first of the two comparison tones, in one condition (I), or after the second comparison tone, in the other condition (II). The similarity between the frequency of the target and the frequency of the mask were varied, and the level of performance was adjusted independently in each condition.

The rationale for this procedure was that, when the masking tone followed the first comparison tone, it intervened between the two tones to be compared to one another and therefore could interfere with retention of the memory of the first tone even after it was consolidated. When the mask followed the second comparison tone, this was not the case. It still could prevent the perceptual resolution of the second tone if the SOA was short enough, but the tone comparison could take place immediately after the second tone was perceived, making any subsequent interference by the mask unlikely. The results matched that rationale. When the first comparison tone was masked, effects of the mask (specifically, of target-mask similarity) were found regardless of the SOA between the masked and masking tones. On the other hand, when the second comparison tone was the one masked, effects of the mask were observed only at short SOAs. This pattern strongly implies that two forms of auditory memory are used at different points in subjects' performance.

A remaining weak point in the two-store account of auditory memory was that it actually appeared from the literature that one could obtain any

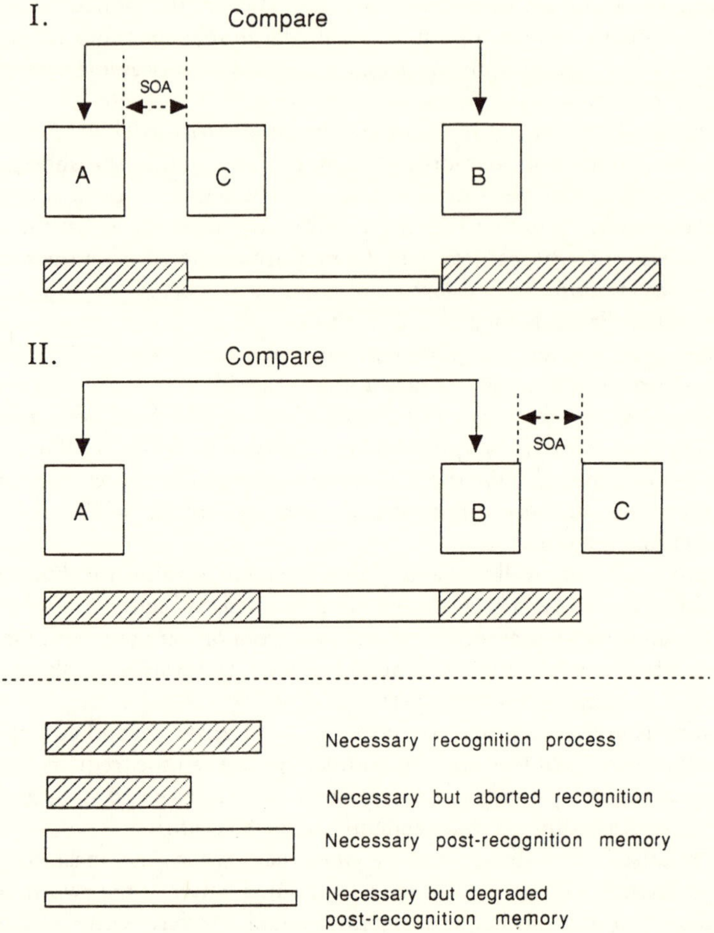

Fig. 2.2 The experimental logic of Kallman and Massaro (1979).

estimate of the duration of auditory sensory memory that one wanted between, say, 150 ms and 20 seconds, by varying the demands of the task. However, Cowan (1984) reviewed evidence that this is not the case. Many of the extant studies of auditory memory could have permitted the assignment of stimuli to conventional categories of various types (e.g., speech sound categories), or could have involved a nonsilent period between the item to be remembered and the time of the test (e.g., filled with the attended sounds and the speaker's voice in studies of selective listening with shadowing). These would alter the observed rate of loss of memory.

As mentioned above, an example of a study that could have permitted the assignment of stimuli to conventional categories is the auditory partial-report study of Darwin et al. (1972), using spatiotemporal arrays of spoken digits and letters. That study produced an estimate of auditory sensory memory persistence of about 4 seconds, but a similar study using tones instead of speech sounds produced a longer estimate, with an asymptotic level of performance still not reached when the report cue was delayed by 5 seconds after the array. In Rostron's tone study, it would have been much more difficult to assign categorical labels to many of the concurrently presented stimuli.

Examples of the detrimental effects of a nonsilent delay interval are not limited to studies of speech memory. An example with nonspeech sounds is the periodicity detection study of Guttman and Julesz (1963; for a review of followup studies, see Cowan, 1984, pp. 350–351). In this study, listeners heard a segment of random noise repeated over and over without pauses. Each point within such a segment has its own distinct sound quality because of the random fluctuations in spectral composition. Detection of the repetition requires that the beginning of the segment be remembered at least throughout the rest of the segment, so that successive iterations can be compared. It was found that the repetition could be detected only if the repeated segment was under about 2 seconds long. Presumably, with longer segments, the sensory memory of the beginning of the segment was forgotten by the time that the segment ended. However, that sensory memory had to be maintained during the continuation of the segment, not during a silent period.

When the large number of problematic cases were eliminated, the remaining "pure" studies suggested that there are, indeed, two types of auditory memory with distinct properties: a sensory afterimage lasting several hundred milliseconds after the stimulus onset, which is perceived as a continuation of the stimulus, and a longer form of memory lasting up to 10 or 20 seconds, which is perceived as a vivid recollection of the sound rather than as a continuation of the stimulus or afterimage. The best direct evidence for the shorter phase of auditory sensory memory is that subjects overestimate the time of offset of a brief sound by up to about 150 ms (Efron, 1970*a*, 1970*b*, 1970*c*), though there is a great deal of additional, more circumstantial evidence. Cowan (1984, Fig. 3) illustrated data from nine potentially relevant phenomena (e.g., forward and backward masking of detection, and backward recognition masking) with similar decay functions lasting several hundred milliseconds. The most direct evidence for the second, longer phase of auditory sensory memory may come from studies in which subjects were asked to compare two slightly different sounds separated by a silent interval of variable duration. Cowan (1984, Fig. 2) illustrated data from many such studies, with a similar course of memory loss lasting roughly 10 seconds.

It was also pointed out by Cowan (1984) that many basic properties of these stores remain unclear. For example, it is not clear if the afterimage is based totally on the stimulus onset (which seems improbable) or, if not, how the afterimage is supported or modified by later segments of the same sound. It is unclear if the secondary form of auditory memory should be considered truly "sensory" or not, and it is unclear how long a sequence of sounds it can represent at one time.

Hawkins and Presson (1977) discredited the backward recognition masking studies in a way that had a profound effect on the field, probably quelling researchers' interest in the procedure. They made the ear of presentation of the target and mask tones either the same or different, and also varied the similarity of the target and mask frequencies. They found that, with practice, masking effects could be eliminated provided that the subject knows that the target and mask are to be presented to opposite ears, and knows which ear will receive the target (which can be achieved by presenting separate blocks of trials for each stimulus condition). The interpretation was that masking occurs only when the subject is placed in a situation in which the target and mask cannot be segregated into separate streams so that the target is attended and the mask is ignored. This attentional account is in opposition to Massaro's (1972) account stating that the mask overwrites the sensory afterimage of the target, although it still is compatible with the more general view that processing of the stimulus outlasts the stimulus itself and is based on an auditory afterimage. In either account, the mask terminates processing of the target (by overwriting it vs. by shifting attention away from it).

In a less widely read paper, Kallman and Morris (1984) challenged the account offered by Hawkins and Presson (1977). They argued that the masking that was obtained in that study might have occurred primarily because of interference with the secondary form of auditory memory, and that the perceptual task may not have been difficult enough to observe an interruption of perceptual processing (because it could be completed much sooner than 250 ms). With a more difficult task and a three-tone procedure (Tone 1, then Tone 2 + mask) modeled after the Kallman and Massaro (1979) study, they obtained backward recognition masking even with consistent, contralateral presentation of the target and mask.

So far, the research that has been discussed establishes that there are two forms of transient auditory memory. However, only the briefer form was known to have a counterpart in the visual modality. Cowan (1988) argued that there was sufficient evidence pointing to a longer form of visual storage as well. That conclusion has been hard to come by, because it would appear to be especially difficult to distinguish between sensory and nonsensory representations of visually presented stimuli. However, for some of the results discussed by Cowan (1988), it is hard to believe that a categorical (nonsensory) coding could be used. For example, Phillips (1974) required subjects to compare spatial grids containing up to 64 squares per grid. About half of the squares were black and about half were white. Two grids were presented with an inter-grid interval varying from a fraction of a second to 9 seconds, and the two grids differed by at most one square. Performance declined gradually across 9 seconds, in a manner resembling two-stimulus comparison procedures that have been carried out in the auditory modality (see Cowan, 1984). Phillips' main result is reproduced in Fig. 2.3.

It seems unlikely that subjects would be able to use categorical representations for such complex visual stimuli. The results also support the existence of two phases of storage. At very short delays, performance was nearly perfect and was interrupted by a spatial displacement between the grids. At longer delays, performance dropped off steadily and was independent of spatial displacements. Cowan (1988) also reviewed evidence for short and long sensory stores in the tactile modality.

In a different line of research, some researchers appear to have confirmed the existence of two phases of visual sensory storage in another way. One basis for this distinction has been in the analysis of errors in partial report procedures. According to the original conception of visual sensory storage (Averbach & Coriell, 1961; Sperling, 1960), it should be a visible image that

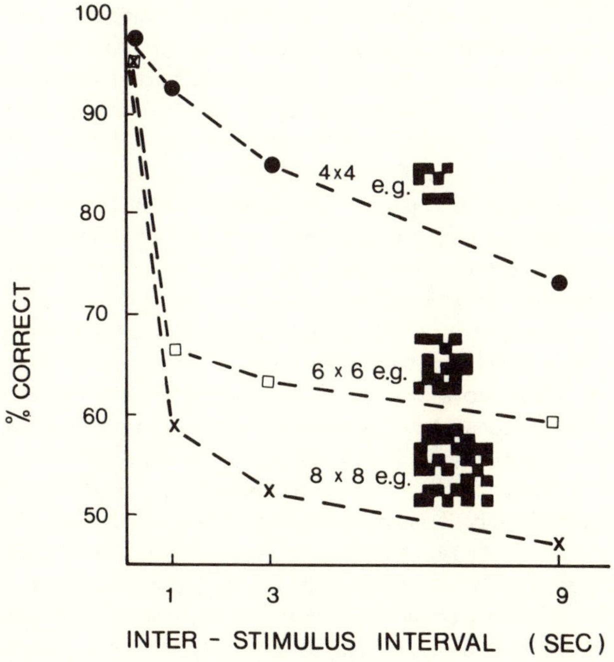

Fig. 2.3 Data on visual sensory memory. (From W. A. Phillips, 1974, On the distinction between sensory storage and short-term visual memory. *Perception & Psychophysics, 16,* p. 284, Fig. 1. Reprinted by permission of the Psychonomic Society.)

is rapidly degraded. If so, errors should occur because of the degraded image, in a way similar to viewing a television picture that has become blurry or speckled with visual "noise." Because the array contains only a minority of the letters present in the alphabet, the majority of errors in recall should be "intrusion" errors, in which an item not present in the array is reported instead of a correct item. Instead, though, several researchers (Townsend, 1973; Mewhort et al., 1981; Irwin & Yeomans, 1986) have found that most of the errors are "location errors," in which an item that actually did come from the array is reported, but in the wrong spatial location.

One way of accounting for the pattern of errors in partial report is to suggest that much information about the selected portion of the array is quickly transformed from the visual sensory afterimage, which is literal and "picture-like" in nature, to a secondary visual store, which contains character information but not much detailed information about where each character was seen. In further support of this hypothesis, Mewhort et al. (1981) found that intrusion errors could be increased markedly by presenting a masking stimulus along with the partial report cue (an arrow above one letter in a row of eight). Presumably, this prevented subjects from selectively transferring information about the targeted row of the array from the visual afterimage to a secondary store. Similar results were obtained by Irwin and Yeomans (1986) in a procedure modeled after Averbach and Coriell (1961). In Irwin and Yeomans' study, the partial report cue was a circle around the location of one of the letters in the row of the array to be selected, which thus also masked the corresponding letter from that row. This allowed masked and nonmasked items within a single trial to be compared. Intrusion errors appear to be limited to situations in which a mask forced subjects to rely directly on a brief sensory trace because there was an inadequate opportunity for it to be fully coded into a longer, secondary form of sensory memory.

A secondary sensory storage medium that includes features but not their locations would be consistent with some work on attention by Treisman and Gelade (1980). Their work was based on earlier findings indicating that attention is needed to search for a target defined by a conjunction of features, such as a red letter "O" among red "X"s and blue "O"s. The role of attention is indicated in that the search time increases with the number of distractors in the display. Treisman and Gelade required that subjects not only determine which of two possible targets was present in each display, but also to locate the target. Targets that were incorrectly localized were identified no better than chance, whereas correctly localized targets were almost always identified correctly. In contrast, targets that could be identified by a single feature, such as a red letter within a field of blue letters, often were identified even when they were not correctly localized. The subjects in this study may rely upon a secondary sensory memory consisting of feature sets with no very accurate locations attached, and an attentional process that allows the perception of specific feature conjunctions in objects at specific locations.

The distinction between the brief-lived, literal visual sensory afterimage and a secondary visual memory (the one consisting of poorly localized features) has been supported also by differences between the stimulus parameter dependencies observed in different kinds of procedure. Eriksen and Collins (1967, 1968) developed a procedure in which two arrays of dots were presented in rapid succession. The two arrays of dots formed a letter trigram (e.g., BEV) when superimposed, but the letters could be perceived only if the first array was still visible (thanks to the afterimage) when the second array was presented. In this sort of procedure, as in the Efron (1970*a*, 1970*b*, 1970*c*) procedure, persistence of an afterimage is inversely related to the duration of the stimulus up to about 160 ms. In contrast, that is not generally the case in partial-report procedures (Di Lollo & Dixon, 1988).

Di Lollo and Dixon (1988) were able to modify the partial-report procedure so that effects of duration were obtained, and they accounted for their results and other results with a mathematical model that included a brief sensory persistence (with a duration that is constant from the stimulus onset) and a second sensory memory (with a longer duration, constant from the stimulus offset). The main difference between their view and the present view is that Di Lollo and Dixon's secondary visual store appeared shorter than the one I have suggested, with rather faster decay than is observed, for example, in the data of Phillips (1974). This could depend on how much detail must be drawn from sensory memory to respond correctly in each task.

This two-process account of sensory memory still leaves unexplained the auditory modality advantage in list recall. One way to explain it without hypothesizing a difference between the durations of visual vs. auditory memory storage is to appeal to the different perceptual encoding capabilities of the two modalities. Visual encoding has a very high spatial resolution, whereas auditory encoding has a lower spatial resolution but is superior in rapid temporal coding. Thus, the direction of the modality effect will depend on the nature of the material to be encoded (Penney, 1975, 1989; Glenberg & Swanson, 1986).

In summary, two phases of sensory storage have been proposed, of similar durations across modalities. The briefer phase is a vivid afterimage of the stimulus. It is not fully clear if the second phase of sensory memory is exactly comparable across modalities, but in each modality it appears to encode some physical features of the stimulus better than others (e.g., pitch better than temporal sequence; visual shape better than location). Later we will question if the second phase of sensory memory is more appropriately viewed as a special case of short-term memory.

Technically, it may not be meaningful to speak of the "duration" of a transient memory store, if the mathematical form of memory decay is one that reaches an asymptotically low level of activation only after an infinitely long period of time (e.g., exponential decay). Instead, what would be needed would be a parameter of decay within a specific decay equation. Within exponential decay, for example, one can speak of the half-life of memory, the point at which the memory reaches half of its original strength. (At three times the half-life, it would reach an eighth of its original strength, and so on.) In these more suitable terms, I am suggesting that the brief afterimage has a half-life of about 50–75 ms, and the secondary sensory memory, a half-life of about 2–4 seconds.

Additional work is needed to ensure that the longer memory in the visual modality actually encodes sensory features. In audition, this conclusion has been supported by some painstaking work. For example, one cannot conclude from the basic suffix effect that sensory features are encoded, but one can draw this conclusion from effects of the acoustic similarity of the list and suffix provided that attention has been ruled out as an explanation of these effects (Greenberg & Engle, 1983). It appears that not much comparable diagnostic work has been done in the visual modality.

2.4 Uses of sensory memory

There are many ways in which sensory memory could be used in information processing, but they boil down to two basic functions, one relatively obvious and one less so. The obvious function is to allow more time for processing. We already have seen how the brief afterimage can extend the duration of processing for stimuli that otherwise would be too brief to be perceived correctly. This in itself could be viewed as tangential to normal processing, although one can find examples of ecologically prevalent brief stimuli that might require the use of this delay function to be perceived (e.g., speech sounds; tones in some musical works; animals visible briefly while scampering among the bushes). For the longer form of sensory memory, the utility of memory persistence is clearer, at least for auditory stimuli. For example, if someone asks a question while one is busy reading, the question often still can be attended to and answered despite a considerable delay (1–2 seconds) in one's switching attention to the speaker. Auditory memory of this sort also might be useful in the processing of attended stimuli; for example, as a means of comparing one's exact pronunciation of words to the pronunciation used by present company. The longer form of visual sensory memory might be used in cases for which the original display disappears. It might be essential in artistic drawing, an activity in which one must switch one's gaze back and forth between the environment to be sketched and the drawing pad, or scan a scene to understand the color arrangement. The utility of visual sensory memory might even be found in the act of transcribing words from one page to another, although in this activity (and to a lesser extent, in drawing also), nonsensory forms of memory undoubtedly are used as well.

Primarily with the brief visual afterimage in mind, and with this passive, information-prolonging function of sensory memory in mind, Haber (1983) suggested that visual sensory storage is not important in daily life (except for unusual occasions such as reading signs in a lightning storm!). The basis of the suggestion is largely the fact that, in daily life, visual stimuli usually do not vanish soon after they are encountered, as do auditory stimuli. Moreover, the extraction of information can be very fast in some circumstances. Rayner, Inhoff, Morrison, Slowiaczek, and Bertera (1981) used a sophisticated eye-movement monitoring device to demonstrate this in the case of reading. Words in the text on a computer screen were replaced with a row of Xs only 50 ms after the subject's eyes landed on them, constituting a brief, effective masking interval; but the text still could be read in this situation.

A better case for the utility of visual sensory memory in daily life can be made, though, for a second, less obvious function of sensory memory. It is the function of sensory integration. On a perceptual basis, sometimes-disjointed fragments of moving visual stimuli must be integrated into a fluid percept. Suppose that two successive sensory events, A and B, must be integrated to form the more meaningful perceptual event A–B. Sensory memory is needed to preserve Event A until Event B is presented. You can demonstrate this phenomenon for yourself by cutting a slit, perhaps 3 mm wide, in an index card. Use the card to cover a picture that is slightly shorter than the slit. By moving the slit rapidly back and forth, the entire object can be perceived behind the slit. The perception is not quite veridical: McCloskey and Watkins (1978) found that subjects tended to report the object behind a moving slit as narrower than it really was.

It is not much of an extrapolation from the moving-slit experiment to a situation in which fragmented, brown images leaping between trees in the forest are integrated to form a deer in the perceptual system of a predator. Of course, for some of the research procedures we already have discussed, subjects also had to integrate two visual images (Eriksen & Collins, 1967, 1968) or two arrays in memory (Phillips, 1974). Even without the presence of trees or other objects partially obscuring the view of the perceiver, it may well be that the visual sensory afterimage still is used to integrate perception across time. Without sensory memory integration, it thus is difficult to understand how fluid motion can be perceived at all. We know this to be true in the perception of motion pictures, but from the point of view of the visual system the situation may essentially be the same for ordinary, fluid motions and transformations of objects. Perhaps a fair model of how the world might appear without visual sensory memory is a case study in which a woman with damage to an area at the border of the occipital and temporal cortical regions experienced a "frozen world" in which changes appeared suddenly, with no fluid motion between them (Zihl, von Cramon, & Mai, 1983).

One situation in which visual sensory storage could provide continuity is in the case of visual eye movements or saccades (Walter Ritter, personal communication, 1992). Gross, Vaughan, and Valenstein (1967), and Adey and Noda (1973), found that the brain's response to visual patterns is suppressed during saccades. Visual sensory memory could serve to tie together the perceptual views from before and after a saccade to avoid the perception of discontinuity in the environment.

Irwin (1991) examined sensory integration across saccades in a modification of the procedure used by Phillips (1974). An array of dots was presented and then was followed by a second array that could differ from the first by at most one dot essentially like Phillips' procedure. However, in some conditions the first array was presented until a saccade was executed, and then the second array was presented. In such conditions, it was found that the task could be performed but that there was no advantage for spatial or retinal correspondence between the arrays, as there was with a short delay and no eye movements. This suggested that the integration across saccades includes only the second phase of visual storage, unlike the case in the absence of saccades.

In the auditory modality, sensory integration may help to allow each phoneme of speech to be perceptually integrated with prior and subsequent phonemes, which are known to affect the categorization of the phoneme in question. For example, the categorization of a consonant depends on the length and quality of surrounding vowels (e.g., see Darwin, 1976). A number of studies suggest that the spectral transitions between phonemes could allow this integration and prevent each phoneme from backwardly masking the prior phoneme (see Cowan, 1984 for a review of the evidence for this).

Cowan (1987) demonstrated a consequence of temporal integration within a single sound. Tones were presented in target-mask pairs and three different intensities of the two tones in a pair were used. All tones had the same frequencies. Subjects were to rate the loudness of both tones separately. The rating of the first (target) tone in the pair was affected in an interesting manner by the SOA between tones. As the SOA increased past 75 ms, the tones were judged more dissimilar from one another but, in addition, the mean judged loudness averaged across the three target intensities increased as SOA increased. One example of this pattern of results, which was obtained in several different experiments, is reproduced in Fig. 2.4. (The graph parameter is the target stimulus intensity.)

The interpretation suggested by Cowan (1987) was that loudness is based on a perceptual integration of each tone, not only for the duration of the tone itself, but across its sensory afterimage as well. The mask presumably terminates access to the afterimage of the target and thereby limits the perceived loudness of the target. This study suggests that the integration of sensory input including sensory afterimages, and not just the immediate sensory data themselves, is a fundamental aspect of perception.

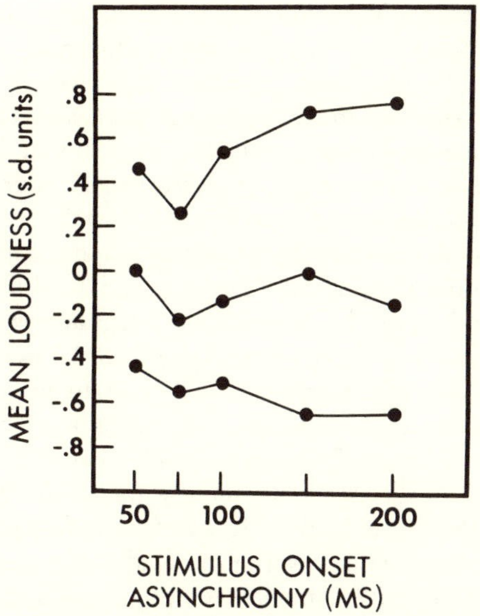

Fig. 2.4 Data on masking of loudness. (From N. Cowan, Auditory sensory storage in relation to the growth of sensation and acoustic information extraction. *Journal of Experimental Psychology: Human Perception and Performance, 13,* p. 209, Fig. 5. Copyright © 1987 by the American Psychological Association. Reprinted by permission.)

A few previous studies appear, at first glance, to be at odds with the findings of Cowan (1987), but they actually agree with them fairly well. Elmasian and Galambos (1975) and Elmasian, Galambos, and Bernheim (1980) examined the effects of two adjacent tones on one another's perceived loudness by having subjects match either an isolated tone or a tone within a rapidly presented tone pair (separated by a 100-ms intertone interval) to a third tone separated from the second by 1.5 seconds. This was done by adjusting the intensity of the third tone. The main outcome of these studies was that a target tone's loudness was altered in the same direction as the nearby contextual tone, no matter whether the contextual tone was presented first or second. (See Loveless, Hari, Hämäläinen, & Tiihonen, 1989 for related results with event-related cortical responses.) These findings do not differentiate the studies, however; Cowan (1987, Fig. 4) found a similar contextual influence. The difference is that Cowan was interested primarily in the effects of the time between the target and mask. In contrast to Elmasian's studies, Cowan did not compare conditions in which a contextual tone was present vs. absent, a comparison that best reveals the contextual effect.

When the contextual effect was minimized in Elmasian's studies by making all tones the same intensity, the result in fact was a decrease in the relative intensity of the first tone (Elmasian & Galambos, 1975, middle column of Table II), or little contextual effect (Elmasian et al., 1980). The results of other studies (Irwin & Zwislocki, 1971, Fig. 2; Peak, 1940) also agree with Cowan (1987) in revealing an increase in the loudness of the first tone in a pair as a function of increases in the interval between tones.

The longer phase of auditory sensory memory might be used in cognitive, as opposed to perceptual, integration. For example, it might be used to retain part of a sentence until it can be semantically integrated with a subsequent phrase. Exemplifying this, Jakimik and Glenberg (1990) examined modality effects on the use of anaphora (phrases that refer to previous ones). For example, a passage about loons mentioned two types of calls, a "long, mournful wail" and an "excited yodeling sound." The subsequent sentence referred to one of the calls either temporally (e.g., "the former call") or semantically (e.g., "the excited call"). It was found that performance was better overall when the sentences were presented in the auditory modality, but the difference was especially large for temporal anaphora when referring to the most recent phrase. This is comparable to the auditory modality superiority in list recall and might be attributed to the better temporal or sequential coding in auditory than in visual sensory memory.

In summary, there are good reasons to believe that both phases of sensory memory are put to good use in vision, as in audition. Doubts about the utility of visual sensory memory (Haber, 1983) have focused on the persistence function but have tended to ignore another possible function, that of the temporal integration of stimuli across time given a moving visual environment.

2.5 Neural representation of sensory memory

Although sensory memory has been only a moderately popular topic recently within cognitive psychology, it has been more popular within the brain sciences. Sensory memory is likely to be more similar across individuals than types of memory that depend more on learned forms of stimulus coding, and it may be an especially suitable topic for physiological research methods that can be used to observe transient processes, such as event-related electrical and magnetic potential recordings.

Some progress has been made examining neural representation with purely behavioral measures. They have been used to ask if the representation is "peripheral," meaning that it exists in neural locations that precede the combination of signals from the left and right sensory organs, or if it is "central," meaning that it is subsequent to the combination of the left and right fields. The most solid progress has been made in the visual modality, because it is possible to present a visual stimulus that appears to be in the same spatial location no matter whether the signal reaches the brain through the left or right eye (using a tachistoscopic apparatus to present stimuli to one eye at a time). Haber and Standing (1969, 1970) presented flashes at a variable inter-flash interval that was adjusted to determine the point at which each flash appeared to fuse with the next, with no perceived gaps between flashes. When the flashes were monoptically presented, the maximal inter-flash interval for this experience was about 200 ms. When flashes were presented to the left and right eyes in alternation in such a way that there was a high degree of perceived spatial overlap between stimuli in the two eyes, the effective inter-flash interval remained the same, which meant that each retina now was being stimulated only once every 400 ms. If the location of the visual sensory afterimage were restricted to peripheral loci, the stimuli should not have fused at this rate. Thus, this study supports the existence of a central locus of visual sensory memory. The earliest such locus probably would be the primary visual cortex, where input from the two eyes is first combined. Neural fibers from the two eyes partially cross earlier, of course, in the optic chiasm; but there appear to be no neural interactions between inputs from the two eyes at that earlier point.

There also is evidence that perception of a target in one eye is susceptible to interference from a following mask in the other eye (Turvey, 1973), and the same is true of the left and right ears (Kallman & Morris, 1984), as explained above. This could be taken to indicate that masking occurs at a central location. On the other hand, in these studies it is logically possible that the sensory store is peripheral and that the mask works by somehow redirecting perceptual processes to itself and away from the sensory trace of the preceding target.

It would be nice if an auditory analogue of Haber and Standing's procedure could be developed to further examine the locus of sensory storage in audition. Unfortunately, that is impossible because any stimulus presented to alternating ears is perceived as having a spatial location that shifts from ear to ear, in strong contrast to the situation in vision. Fortunately, there now is evidence of a central locus from psychophysiological studies in audition.

The first relevant evidence came from studies of event-related electrical potentials of the brain, measured from the scalp. Näätänen (1990) reviewed studies of a negative-going potential in response to a discriminable change in an acoustic feature (e.g., frequency or intensity) in a repeated tone, even when the subject was engaged in a reading task with no response required to the auditory channel. This potential, termed the "mismatch negativity," was obtained only if the inter-tone interval was a few seconds or less (Mäntysalo & Näätänen, 1987). Näätänen (1990) suggested that the mismatch negativity occurs when a sound is automatically compared to the sensory memory of the previous sound and found to differ from it. This comparison presumably could not be carried out if the previous sound's memory had decayed beyond usefulness by the time the next sound arrived.

Additional research suggested that there are at least two potential sources of the negative-going response to a change in ignored auditory stimuli. One of these, termed the "N1 response" (which actually appears to be the composite of several different generators at different brain locations), is a very large, early (peaking at about 80–100 ms) response that occurs for new sounds following a long, silent, period, and for the addition of new stimulus features (e.g., new frequencies or increased intensity), but not for intensity decreases, or feature omissions (Näätänen & Picton, 1987). The N1 response could reflect the recovery of feature detectors that have been inactive for a while. A second, smaller, slightly later component (peaking at about 100–180 ms) is what Näätänen defined as the mismatch negativity response, which also may be a composite of several generators. It occurs for discriminable acoustic changes that entail a decrease as well as an increase in the intensity, and it occurs for the omission of components (Winkler & Näätänen, 1992). Thus, it may reflect the response to any discriminable change from the standard stimuli. The N1 and mismatch negativity responses often overlap temporally, but they have different scalp distributions (Scherg, Vajsar, & Picton, 1989; Näätänen, 1992; Picton, 1992). Magnetoencephalographic recordings, which often can localize electrical generators in the brain more precisely than electrical recordings, indicate that the N1 and MMN (mismatch negativity) responses include generators in slightly different locations within the supratemporal gyrus of the temporal lobes (Hari, Aittoniemi, Järvinen, Katila, & Varpula, 1980; Hari et al., 1984; Sams, Kaukoranta, Hämäläinen, & Näätänen, 1991).

Magnetoencephalographic N1 responses have also been found to decrease gradually across a few poststimulus seconds, with somewhat slower decay for the association cortex than for the primary auditory cortex (Hari, Kaila, Katila, Tuomisto, & Varpula, 1982; Lü, Williamson, & Kaufman, 1992*a*) and with a close relation between the neuromagnetic measure and a behavioral measure of sensory memory across four subjects (Lü, Williamson, & Kaufman, 1992*b*). This could be the locus of auditory sensory memory storage.

On the other hand, there are at least three reasons to be cautious about this conclusion. First, Näätänen (1990, 1992) has summarized arguments that, unlike the mismatch negativity which truly reflects encoded information, N1 is more situation-specific. Its neural refraction may not turn out to be closely parallel to behavioral measures of memory across a variety of tasks. Second, the estimated duration of auditory sensory memory appears somewhat shorter than what has been obtained in some other behavioral estimates (see Cowan, 1984) and in some recent studies using the mismatch negativity (see Näätänen, 1992). Third, and I think most importantly, the correlation between behavioral and N1 responses observed by Lü et al. conceivably might result from a difference in strategy in the four subjects.

Woldorff and Hillyard (1991) showed that the refractoriness of the N1 response in event-related potential (ERP) recordings is much larger for attended than for unattended stimuli. In the study of Lü et al. (1992*b*), subjects who paid more close attention to the stimuli may have produced both better behavioral discrimination at longer interstimulus intervals and a longer-lasting period of refractory N1 responding. The correlation between N1 and behavior still would be interesting, but it might not be the same as what is commonly referred to as sensory memory. To assure that it is sensory memory, it might be necessary to use ignored stimuli for the behavioral task, similar to the methods of Eriksen and Johnson (1964), and Cowan et al. (1990).

Sams, Hari, Rif, and Knuutila (1993) found that a magnetoencephalographic mismatch field (presumably the equivalent of the mismatch negativity) in the supratemporal auditory cortex occurred only if the stimulus tones were separated by no more than about 10 seconds. The correspondence of the mismatch negativity to behavioral indices of sensory memory seems closer than does the correspondence of N1 to these behavioral indices (cf. Näätänen, 1992). For example, the behavioral literature has suggested that stop consonants generally are acoustically too complex to be differentially represented in sensory memory (Crowder, 1971; Cowan et al., 1990). Yet, in an event-related potential study, Picton (1992) reported that a negative potential was obtained when a speech sound sequence changed from /ba/ to /da/, but not from /da/ to /ba/. The response that was obtained appears to have been an N1 refractory response to the change rather than the mismatch negativity. Spectral analyses of the sounds suggested that /da/ includes most of the frequencies present in /ba/ as well as additional higher frequencies, and the N1 can respond to the addition of new frequencies but not to the omission of frequencies.

Nevertheless, there still might also be a contribution of the N1 to sensory memory. It might, for example, account for asymmetries or "time-order errors" that sometimes are obtained in two-stimulus comparison tasks, in which the order of two different stimuli are found to make a difference (Hellström, 1985). One reason that this could occur is that the N1 response would be larger whenever a second sound adds, rather than omits or diminishes, features present in the first one.

So far, the evidence on brain potentials in response to shifts in tones has not clearly established that the memory is "sensory" according to the strict criteria I have mentioned. The mismatch negativity does appear to be modality-specific, but still it remains theoretically possible that this response depends upon a categorical memory. Winkler, Reinikainen, and Näätänen (1993) did link the mismatch negativity to one of the traditional sensory memory procedures. Specifically, they demonstrated that the magnitude of the mismatch negativity response to a change in a tone within a repeated, rapidly presented pair is affected by the SOA between members of a pair in a way that closely resembles the forward and backward masking functions obtained with behavioral measures (Massaro, 1973). This research still does not rule out the possibility that the mismatch negativity results from a categorical code that forms on the basis of sensory memory, although this seems somewhat unlikely given that the tones were to be ignored during their presentation.

A study of Winkler et al. (1990) further suggests that a sensory memory underlies the mismatch negativity. They used nine standard tones differing only in intensity, randomized together in a series in which each tone was presented with equal probability. In a particular trial block, the difference between consecutive standards in the set was fixed at 1.6, 0.8, 0.4, or 0.2 dB, or 0 dB in a control condition. The deviant differed from the standard in frequency, and its intensity was set either equal to the central standard or below the lowest standard. It was found that, with increasing variation in the standard intensities, the mismatch negativity to the deviant decreased and the mismatch negativity to the standards (relative to the central standard) increased. This suggests that the mismatch negativity is based on a memory that is sensitive to rather small variations in the stimulus. Certainly, subjects are unlikely to have preestablished categories for such small variations in sound.

Cowan, Winkler, Teder, and Näätänen (1993) demonstrated that the memory representation of a stimulus as the standard is not one that develops simply with a single presentation of the standard, but rather one that develops across several presentations, can become inactive across a silent period, and then can become reactivated with a single additional presentation. The evidence for this conclusion came from an experiment in which the stimuli were sequences of nine tones in a row, with 11- to 15-second, silent intervals between sequences. In most sequences, one of the nine tones was a deviant tone with a frequency 1/6 higher than the other, standard tones. The deviant could appear first, second, fourth, sixth, or eighth in a series. In the "roving standard" condition, the standard tone changed between sequences, but in the "constant standard" condition, the standard frequency remains the same throughout the session.

In the roving-standard condition, a mismatch negativity occurred for deviants in the fourth position or later. Thus, an adequate representation of the standard (i.e., its status as a standard to be compared with the deviant) presumably could develop after only two or three presentations of the standard. In the constant-standard condition, however, there also was a mismatch negativity when the deviant was second in the sequence, though still not when it was first. In this case, there must have been a representation of the standard that was carried over from the previous sequences, which had the same standard tone frequency. However, for a mismatch negativity to occur, it appears to have been necessary for the subject to hear one presentation of the standard tone following the silent interval, presumably in order to reactivate the memory of the standard tone. Thus, if the mismatch negativity is based on sensory memory, this sensory memory must include the result of stimulus repetition, and it must sometimes be in a dormant or inactive state until it is reactivated with a reminder presentation. This type of finding would be consistent with the suggestion by Cowan (1988) that sensory memory may have properties that are fundamentally no different from other types of short-term memory (see also commentary by Port, 1991).

In summary, the recent physiological research is finding neural counterparts to sensory memory. This is likely to renew the interest in sensory memory among behavioral researchers in the fields of cognitive psychology and information processing. Many important questions remain unanswered, and it is even possible that the slightly waning interest in sensory memory in recent years has been a result of a sense of confusion rather than increasing understanding. It still is unclear which procedures best index sensory memory, how it can be distinguished from other types of memory, and whether this distinction makes an important difference. The mutual assistance between behavioral and physiological fields may be able to sort this out in the not-too-distant future.

2.6 Challenges to the concept of sensory memory

We already have considered the point that the usefulness of visual sensory memory has been questioned (Haber, 1983). Having reviewed evidence for sensory memory and its usefulness in various modalities, it still must be pointed out that the very existence of a transient auditory sensory memory has been questioned. The basis of this questioning is in recent studies of the nature of the auditory modality advantage, and of the suffix effect that decreases this advantage through auditory interference. An advantage of lipread over printed materials has been obtained, and suffix effects have been obtained when the list, the suffix, or both were lipread rather than spoken aloud (for reviews, see Crowder, 1983; Cowan, 1984). Modality and suffix effects also have been obtained with a "through-list distractor technique" in which a distracting task lasting 12 or more seconds is interposed between adjacent items, and between the last item and the memory test (e.g., Gardiner & Gregg, 1979; Glenberg, 1984). These findings appear to indicate that the basis of the auditory memory advantage has to do with a coding difference in the two modalities. Specifically, speech materials (whether presented acoustically or through lip movements) are encoded in a form more readily available for sequential recall than printed materials. This set of findings appears to remove the need to assume that there is a transient form of sensory memory storage involved in the modality and suffix effects. One might even suggest that the burden of proof has shifted, so that it must be demonstrated that it is impossible to account for all of the sensory memory results without assuming the involvement of a transient sensory store.

What this alternative point of view overlooks, however, is that there appear to be subtle differences between the ordinary suffix effects and those obtained without the usual presentation conditions. Turner et al. (1987) found that the lipread suffix effect occurs for materials varying in consonants only, which is not the case for the ordinary suffix effect (Crowder, 1971). Glenberg (1984) found a suffix effect within the through-list distractor technique only if the suffix differed from trial to trial, in contrast to the ordinary suffix effect in which a single suffix can be used over and over. These findings suggest that caution in interpretation is in order. One interpretation is that speech coding offers some mnemonic advantages in addition to the use of a transient auditory sensory memory (e.g., phonetic and articulatory coding), and that these additional advantages result in effects that are similar, but not always identical, to effects based on auditory sensory memory. This issue will be taken up again in a later chapter, when the basis for belief in a separate short-term memory store is examined.

3. Memory activation and attentional focusing

The previous chapter offered the opinion that sensory memory is unique in that it is an internal representation of the physical properties of external events. Short-term memory taken as a whole, including both sensory and nonsensory aspects, is unique in a different way, in that it represents the subject's present mind. Certain memories and ideas are readily accessible by virtue of their appearance in one's recent past and their presence in the focus of one's awareness.

However, theoretical difficulties arise at the fringes of this common experience. How should we classify ideas that are readily accessible but are not in one's current awareness? Are they part of short-term memory, or not? Does awareness make a difference in memory tests? Questions such as these will be addressed in this chapter. The general point is that many previous investigators often have used the term "short-term memory" ambiguously, with reference either to the set of all memory elements in a temporarily heightened state of activation (e.g., Hebb, 1949) or to all memory elements currently in the focus of attention (e.g., James, 1890). After this review, the next chapter will take another, more critical look at the short-term memory concept by treating seriously the possibility that one could account for all memory performance without the concept of separate, transient memory stores (though ultimately this approach will be rejected).

3.1 A brief history of short-term memory concepts

Historically, within the field of experimental psychology, the concept of short-term memory has varied. Some have suggested that there is a capacity limit; others, that there is a time limit; and still others, that there is no special short-term memory function. These historical positions were precursors of the still-controversial role of short-term memory within the modern fields of cognitive psychology and information processing.

3.1.1 Capacity limits of short-term memory

The concept of a content-limited short-term memory can be traced back to William James and his approach based largely on phenomenology and subjective experience. In his text (James, 1890) he pointed out the contrast between the small amount of information that can be kept consciously in mind at any one time versus the vast amount of knowledge that we store in our brains. This was the distinction between a limited, fleeting "primary memory" and a vast, stable "secondary memory."

3.1.2 Time limits of short-term memory

Hebb (1949), within his vision of a plausible physiological coding of memory, developed a different concept of short-term memory than James, and for totally different reasons. He suggested that new information is encoded as a specific pattern of neural firing or "cell assembly," which persists only temporarily but is transformed into a chemical pattern and then consolidated into a pattern of synaptic growth that permanently saves aspects of the original learning. The new synaptic growth would strengthen the neural pathways involved in the original pattern of neural firing, allowing that pattern to be reconstituted at a later date, resulting in "remembering."

Could the cell assembly be a neural coding of James's primary memory? Only if an active neural cell assembly is limited to the information of which the subject is conscious. That is not likely because the types of short-term memory limit appear to differ in the two conceptions. James's conception implies a limit in the total content of short-term memory at any one moment (i.e., a capacity limit), whereas Hebb's conception appears to suggest a limit in the temporal persistence of short-term memory (i.e., a time limit).

The notion of time-dependent forgetting has had a turbulent history. Thorndike (1914) had proposed a "law of disuse" stating that memories decrease in strength over time if they are not used (i.e., retrieved). McGeoch (1932) argued against the generality of this law, noting that disuse is neither a necessary nor a sufficient condition for the decrease in observed memory strength. He cited cases in which memory persisted after disuse (e.g., spontaneous recovery of conditioned responses following a period of extinction; reminiscence) and cases in which memory decreased during use (e.g., negative adaptation).

3.1.3 Monistic memory theories

Researchers in the behaviorist and verbal learning traditions (e.g., Underwood, 1957; Postman, 1961; Melton, 1963) hoped and generally expected that a single set of learning rules would apply regardless of how much time was interposed between a stimulus and the test of the memory for that stimulus. For example, Underwood (1957) was ready to dispense with the concept of memory decay entirely, and he formulated a unified view of the memory system. He suggested that most apparent forgetting depended upon proactive interference (both from previous trials and from the subject's pre-experimental life), which grew as time distanced the subject from any particular learning episode. The remaining portion of forgetting was attributed not to decay, but to retroactive interference from stimuli, events, and thoughts interpolated between study and test. There was no provision in the theory for very recent memories to be treated differently than older memories; the difference was viewed as a quantitative one having to do with the amount of time available for proactive interference to emerge rather than a qualitative one having to do with separate short- and long-term memory stores.

3.2 Short-term memory limits according to cognitive psychology

Both capacity limits and time limits of short-term memory have been discussed intensively within modern cognitive psychology. After a brief description of the logical role of short-term memory in information processing, evidence from cognitive psychology will be examined below for both capacity limits and time limits. Ways in which capacity and time limits are combined in processing also will be explored. Additionally, there are important roles of knowledge and covert processing that will be discussed. All of these factors contribute to the practical use of short-term memory, and in the last subsection its functions in a variety of cognitive tasks will be considered.

3.2.1 Short-term memory and information processing

The rebirth of short-term memory, viewed both as a time limit (Conrad, 1957; Brown, 1958; Peterson & Peterson, 1959) and as a capacity limit (Miller, 1956) coincided with the beginning of modern cognitive psychology (e.g., Broadbent, 1958). The capacity and time limits were important to different cognitive investigators.

There was renewed interest in primary and secondary memory by many of the investigators who initiated the "information processing approach" to learning and behavior. They found that computers must operate with a large data bank (the disk, tape, or drum memory), but also with a more limited set of data that is made available for immediate manipulation (the "read-and-access memory," or RAM). Having these two types of memory seemed to be a rather powerful method of allowing both the retrieval of a vast storehouse of information, which can be accomplished only at a limited speed, and also the more rapid retrieval and use of the relatively small amount of information designated most relevant to the problem at hand. The computer analogy in making a model of human thought processes is evident in the first information processing diagram, which was tucked away as a footnote in the text of Broadbent (1958).

Broadbent (1958) discussed evidence that human beings had a limited-capacity memory. The evidence was basically that subjects could fully attend to only one channel or stream of information at a time. It was natural to search for a reason for that fundamental limit in human information processing. One good reason was that there appeared to be a stark contrast between the complex array of stimuli with which a human sometimes is bombarded (e.g., multiple voices coming through headphones to an airline pilot winding his way through a cloud formation and observing potential landing sights) and the limited amount that could be held in the focus of one's attention at a time.

Broadbent proposed that there was an "attentional filter" severely restricting the amount that gets into the subject's awareness at any one moment. Theoretically, it would be possible for the restricted stream of information passing through the filter to accumulate directly into an unlimited memory store, but this would not be very satisfying teleologically. Why would the attentional processing limit exist? Implicitly, considerations similar to those of James (1890) and Miller (1956) would have suggested that this processing limit existed at least partly in order to make the most efficient use of a limited short-term storage capacity or attentional focus.

The work of Sternberg (1966) helped researchers to envision how a short-term memory store would actually be used. Subjects received a target list to be remembered and then a probe item that was to be classified, as quickly as possible, as present or absent from the target list. They could do that with a high level of accuracy; at least, provided that the list length fell clearly within limits comparable to the 7 ± 2 items noted by Miller (1956). Within such limits, subjects' reaction time appeared to increase about 40 ms for every item on the list. Thus, an item within a set held in short-term memory can be accessed within several hundred milliseconds (e.g., $40 \times 7 = 280$ ms). This is generally much faster than the time it takes to retrieve an item that is not from a predesignated target set.

Subsequent investigators have applied Sternberg's procedure in other ways that support the short-term/long-term memory distinction. For example, Van Dusen, Britton, and Glynn (1992) had subjects process a number with an arithmetic operation that included 1, 3, or 5 steps. In a "short-term store" condition, the subject could mentally prepare for the arithmetic operation just before the target number was presented. This was impossible in a "long-term store" condition because the subject read letters and, on an unpredictable half of the trials, received a cue to recall those letters instead of receiving a target number to process. There was a reaction time advantage of carrying out an arithmetic operation in the short-term rather than the long-term memory situation, and the magnitude of this advantage increased as a function of the number of operational steps. This was taken as evidence that, in the long-term memory situation, the plan had to be re-loaded into a short-term store (i.e., put in an active state) step by step when the number was presented, before the arithmetic operations could be carried out.

3.2.2 Capacity limits of short-term memory

Miller (1956) took a functional approach in observing that, in various domains, human primary memory was limited to a "magical number seven plus or minus two" meaningful items or "chunks." The approach was functional in that a specific mechanism underlying the memory limit, such as a decaying representation or dedicated memory locations, was not proposed. Miller did not discuss theories of forgetting, such as those of McGeoch (1932) or Underwood (1957). Nevertheless, it appears as if those monistic theories of memory have at least no obvious way to account for an immediate memory limit that remains about the same across a wide range of circumstances.

3.2.3 Time limits of short-term memory

Conrad (1957) noted, in a brief report, that subjects' immediate recall was impaired when they were required to recall items at a slow rate of 2.0 seconds per item as compared with a faster rate of 0.66 seconds per item or, better yet, at a self-determined rate. Brown (1958) and Peterson and Peterson (1959) observed severe memory loss of just a few items (e.g., in the Peterson and Peterson study, consonant trigrams) across an interval of up to 18 seconds filled with a distracting task (e.g., counting backward by threes) to prevent rehearsal. This rapid forgetting of just a few items followed by dissimilar interfering material was not expected according to monistic memory theories that placed a great deal of emphasis on specific memory interference, such as that of Underwood (1957). The interpretation that these results required a separate short-term store was soon challenged (Keppel & Underwood, 1962; Melton, 1963), a point that will be taken up in the next chapter. However, these studies did serve to reopen the issue.

Brown (1958) remarked that interference between trials might well have a role in memory, but that it might be only a symptom of short-term forgetting rather than a cause as Underwood believed. According to Brown's proposal, the interference between trials would reflect competing responses that could be made in the test situation, but it would be the transient, short-term memory trace that sometimes allows the subject to distinguish which of those possible responses is appropriate for the current trial.

Baddeley et al. (1975) brought to a head a debate that could have occurred between James (1890) and Hebb (1949), but of course never did; that is, the debate between the notion of short-term memory as a capacity-limited vs. time-limited faculty. Baddeley et al. tested for memory of sets of words of various length (e.g., by varying the number of syllables per word) and also tested the rate at which subjects could quickly repeat words of each type. They found a linear relation between speech rate and immediate memory.

Subjects could recall as many items as they could repeat in about 2 seconds.

Many other researchers have confirmed this finding, in studies obtaining variation in the rate of speech through individual differences, developmental differences, language differences, and differences in materials within a language (Baddeley et al., 1975; Standing, Bond, Smith, & Isely, 1980; Nicolson, 1981; Case, Kurland, & Goldberg, 1982; Hulme, Thomson, Muir, & Lawrence, 1984; Zhang & Simon, 1985; Naveh-Benjamin & Ayres, 1986; Schweickert & Boruff, 1986; Hulme & Tordoff, 1989). One typical, recent example, based on data from Cowan, Keller, et al. (1994), is shown in Fig.3.1.

Such findings led Baddeley et al. (1975) to a theory of verbal short-term memory focusing on a time limit, the "articulatory loop theory" that since has been revised and elaborated upon (e.g., Baddeley, 1986). Baddeley's theory states that verbal information to be recalled is held in a phonological form that is subject to decay within the first 2 seconds. By covertly rehearsing items in a list, subjects are capable of renewing those items in the phonological short-term store. However, an item must be retrieved successfully in order for it to be rehearsed. Therefore, rehearsal is limited to the amount that can be articulated within about 2 seconds, the presumed period of phonological memory decay. The faster the items can be rehearsed, the more items can be rehearsed in a repeating loop before they decay. The assumption that the measured maximal overt articulation rate mirrors the maximal covert rehearsal rate was verified by Landauer (1962).

Recent findings of Cowan et al. (1992) make the time-based nature of memory in short-term word list recall clearer. They noted that, according to the articulatory loop theory, items should decay in phonological memory while other items are being pronounced in the recall phase of a trial. They

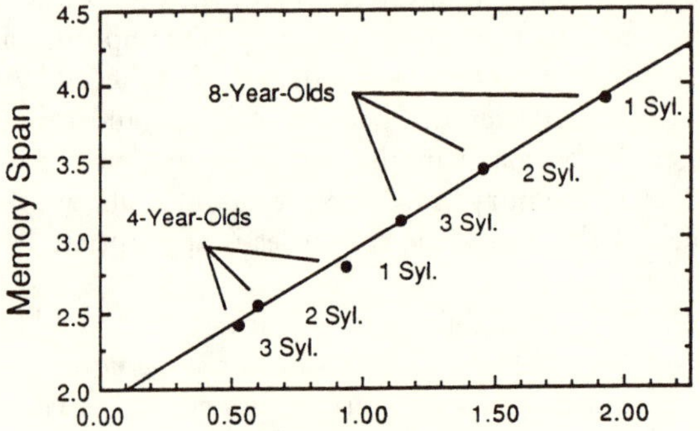

Fig. 3.1 Data on the relation between the maximal speech rate and memory span. (After Cowan, Keller, et al., 1994.)

reasoned that the length of items pronounced first should make the most difference to recall, because those items delay the recall of other items on the list; items pronounced last in recall do not delay anything else. As we will see, this conjecture was strongly supported by the results of experiments in which the length of items in the first and second halves of the list to be recalled were independently varied. (More precisely, each list contained five items and the lengths of the first two and last two items were varied independently. The middle item's length varied randomly and the results were collapsed across different lengths of that item.)

Sets of longer and shorter words were constructed by Cowan et al. on the basis of the time it took to say each word; the number of phonemes and syllables per word was equated across word lengths, in a manner modeled after Baddeley et al. (1975) but with some confounding factors in the stimuli removed. The most critical experiment of Cowan et al. included forward and backward recall conditions. Subjects received a cue after the list, indicating whether the list was to be recalled in the forward or the backward order. The significant factors that were obtained in forward and backward recall are reproduced in Fig. 3.2.

In ordinary, forward serial recall, most of the word length effect depended on the length of words in the first half of the list, and second-half word length was not significant. When backward recall was required, however, it was the length of words in the second half of the list that mattered, and first-half word length was not significant. (In the top half of the figure, the means are collapsed across trials with short and long second-half lengths and, similarly, in the bottom half of the figure, the means are collapsed across first-half lengths.) Thus, in either recall order, it was the lengths of just those words that were to be recalled first that made a difference.

How do these findings affect the status of Baddeley's (1986) working memory theory? The research of Henry (1991) suggests that the limit in recall is partly in the duration of spoken output, as Cowan et al. (1992) demonstrated, and partly in the efficiency of covert, rehearsal-type processes, as Baddeley and his colleagues originally supposed. She conducted a short-term memory experiment with 5- and 7-year-old children in which a pointing response was used instead of spoken recall. The pointing response removed the effect of word length entirely for 5-year-olds, although the effect remained for 7-year-olds. Rehearsal seems the most plausible basis for the remaining effect in 7-year-olds.

When interpreting short-term memory studies, the response mode must be carefully taken into account. Caplan, Rochon, and Waters (1992) reported that, when sets of shorter and longer words were equated for the number of phonemes and syllables (as in Baddeley, et al., 1975 and Cowan et al., 1992), the word length effect disappeared entirely. The authors concluded that it was the phonological structure of a word that determined the magnitude of the word length effect, and not the time it takes to articulate the words *per*

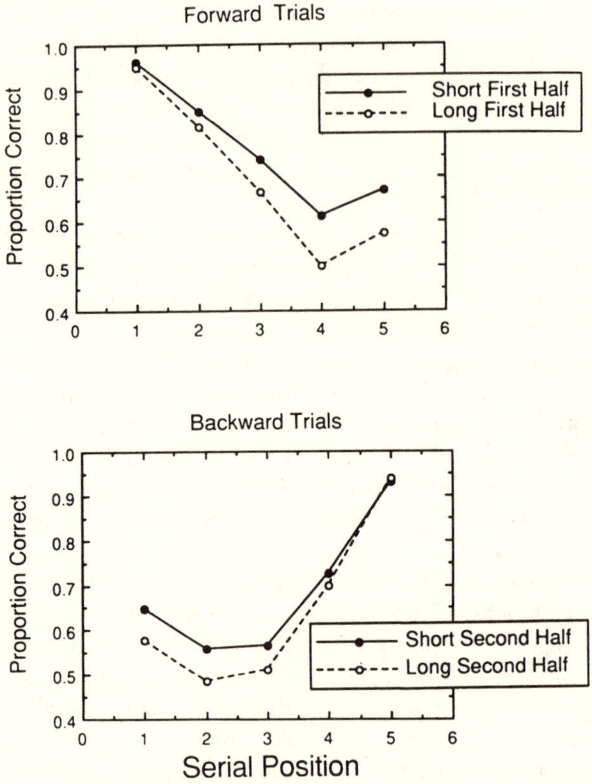

Fig. 3.2 Data on half-list word length effects. From N. Cowan et al., 1992, The role of verbal output time in the effects of word length on immediate memory. *Journal of Memory & Language, 31,* p. 11, Fig. 4. Reprinted by permission of Academic Press.)

se. However, these authors used a response in which subjects pointed to the correct words, which would have eliminated the factor of output time. Thus, although these results may indicate that phonological structure is the factor of most importance in covert rehearsal, I would predict that a word length effect still would have emerged if a spoken response were used.

In many test situations, longer test delays are filled with more interfering stimuli. Such situations cannot be used to demonstrate the existence or nonexistence of pure memory decay (Broadbent, 1971). Consider, for example, the study of Waugh and Norman (1965), who varied the rate of presentation of digits and examined performance on a serial probed recall task as a function of the number of intervening items (which could come from either the stimulus or the response). The subject was to respond to each probe by pronouncing the item that followed it in the list. It was found that performance was a function of the number of intervening items, with only a small effect of the presentation rate that could be attributed to memory decay. However, this may not be a fair test of the potential contribution of decay. Decay should have the greatest effect when there are few intervening items, because intervening items presumably destroy the memory that otherwise would decay.

3.2.4 Combination of capacity and time limits

It should be emphasized that the time-based contributions to short-term memory are not the only contributions, even in the verbal domain. Exemplifying capacity limits, Glanzer and Razel (1974) found that subjects could remember a roughly equivalent number of meaningful units no matter whether the units were single words or idioms such as "a stitch in time saves nine." However, that research involved free recall of a set of items that changed from trial to trial. It appears that the time-limited nature of recall applies only to the serial recall of items selected from a small set, with the same items used over and over among trials so that it is mainly the serial order information that is difficult to remember. Prior evidence supports this suggestion in several ways. Word length effects in serial recall are not eliminated by rehearsal-blacking if the words are drawn from a large set (La Pointe & Engle, 1990), and effects of phonological similarity can be traced to impairment in recall primarily of the serial order information (Wickelgren, 1965). Even in the serial recall of lists composed from a small vocabulary, the time-limited factors of recall are not the only limits that must be considered. A few items of material that are not readily verbalizable, such as free-radical characters in Chinese script, still appear to be held in memory in some nonverbal form (Zhang & Simon, 1985), such as a visuospatial or abstract form (e.g., Baddeley, 1986; Cowan, 1988).

3.2.5 The role of long-term knowledge in short-term memory tasks

If short-term memory results from the activation of long-term memory elements, the quality or organization of what is activated should be important for short-term memory performance. Confirming this, McCauley, Kellas, Dugas, and DeVellis (1976) demonstrated an effect of knowledge on short-term memory. They had fifth- and sixth-grade children study the lists to be used in a search task modeled after Sternberg's (1966) procedure. On each trial, a short list of digits was presented and then a probe digit was presented. The subject was to indicate as quickly as possible, with a button press, whether the probe digit was a member of the list. In one condition, subjects studied each target list to be used in the probe task in their own manner, with items presented one at a time, self-paced. In another condition, however, subjects studied each list with instructions to rehearse each list cumulatively. After each list item was presented in this condition, the entire list up to that point was rehearsed twice. This resulted in much longer study times than the other procedure. In addition, when the studied list was used in the probe task, the subjects who studied the list in their own way turned out to use a slower memory search rate (57 ms per item) than subjects who were instructed to rehearse cumulatively (39 ms per item). Thus, strengthening the links between items in memory with serial, cumulative rehearsai may assist the memory search process.

A finding of Kristofferson (1972) demonstrates that this effect on memory search speed is likely to be a knowledge effect rather than a general practice effect. She examined effects of extensive practice in a Sternberg-type memory search task in which the relevant set continually changed throughout the study. With practice, subjects became faster in the task, but the reaction time slope as a function of memory-set size did not change at all.

With verbalizable materials from a small set used in serial recall, there still appears to be a contribution of lexical knowledge that is not time-related. Hulme, Maughan, and Brown (1991) examined word length effects for sets of English and nonsense words and found the same linear relation between maximal speech rate and memory span for both sets of items, but at a much higher intercept (better recall) for words than for nonwords.

These studies taken together begin to provide clues about the specific role of knowledge in short-term memory. Specifically, episodic knowledge of the links between items in a list affected a processing rate, namely the rate of memory search (McCauley et al., 1976); whereas lexical knowledge of the items in a list was found to affect overall performance in memory span and search tasks, but not in a rate-related manner (Kristofferson, 1972; Hulme et al., 1991).

3.2.6 The role of covert processes in short-term memory tasks

It is likely that covert processes that are used to search for items represented in short-term memory, and to reactivate them, must be understood better before the contributions of time limits can be fully understood. However, there has been considerable recent progress in this regard.

Even though articulatory speed correlates with recall, it cannot be assumed that the correlation implies direct causation. Illustrating this, Smyth and Scholey (1992) found that an adult subject's articulatory rate was a good predictor of that subject's span in a spatial task that was shown not to depend on articulation *per se*. In contrast, measures of movement speed did not predict spatial span. The explanation was that articulatory rate may not itself play a causal role in spatial span, but may be correlated with some more general cognitive speed factor that was causal but was not directly measured.

Some of our recent research (Cowan, 1992; Cowan, Keller, et al., 1994) has focused on the possible role of the speed or efficiency of covert processes that may occur during the verbal response period in memory span tasks. A simple interpretation of the findings of Cowan et al. (1992) on output effects would suggest that memory decays steadily during the response period and that, as a consequence, spoken recall must be completed before the memory has decayed. Given that subjects can recall the amount that they can pronounce in about 2 seconds (e.g., Baddeley et al., 1975), this interpretation would imply that the useful lifetime of the memory trace is about 2 seconds and therefore that the verbal response cannot last much longer than this. Indeed, this hypothesis can be found in the literature (Broadbent, 1958; Brown, 1958; Schweickert & Boruff, 1986; Stigler, Lee, & Stevenson, 1986; Cowan et al., 1992). However, even if the store does decay in 2 seconds, an alternative possibility is that subjects engage in covert processing during the response period that refreshes items and therefore prolongs the duration for which responding on the basis of this temporary store is possible.

To distinguish between these possibilities, Cowan (1992) measured the timing of spoken recall in a memory span task administered to 4-year-old children. (Adults could have been used but young children were convenient because of clearer inter-word pauses.) Pause durations were found to depend on the number of items in the list, and on the subject's short-term memory ability, whereas the duration of word pronunciations was not altered by these factors. Subjects at various levels of memory ability appeared to have equivalent pause durations within their recall of span-length lists (i.e., the longest lists they could recall perfectly), but the pause durations were found to be shorter within the recall of subspan lists. This finding is reproduced in Fig. 3.3 for subjects with the most commonly observed spans on acoustically similar (span = 3) and dissimilar (span = 3 & 4) word sets, tested on various

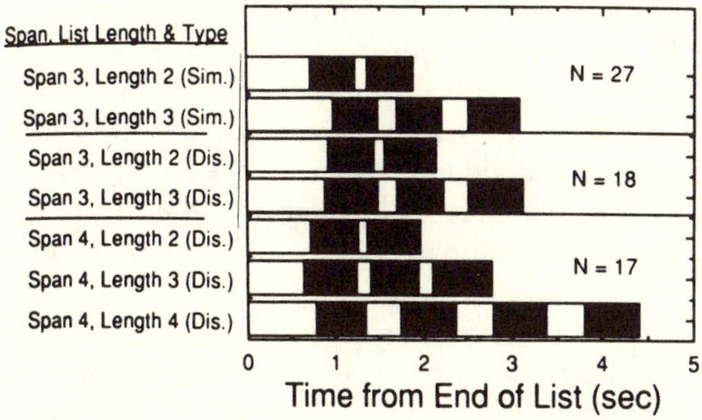

Fig. 3.3 The timing of spoken recall. (From N. Cowan, 1992, Verbal memory span and the timing of spoken recall. *Journal of Memory & Language, 31,* p. 677, Fig. 5. Reprinted by permission of Academic Press.)

span-length and subspan lists. White segments represent mean silent pause times and black segments represent mean speaking times for each serial position.

As shown in the figure, within a subject, pause times were affected by list length whereas speech pronunciation times were not. On average, the greater the number of items on the list, the longer each interword pause lasted. Additionally, subjects with a higher ability level produced shorter pauses during the repetition of lists of a particular length. The data are as one would expect if the subjects used time-consuming, capacity-limited resources somehow to process covertly all items on a list (or, at least, to process a constant proportion of those items), with this covert processing across the entire list being re-initiated every time another item was to be repeated aloud. The covert process might be a memory search necessary in order for the subject to determine which item to say next. The pause times then would depend on both the number of list items and the subject's speed in covertly processing those items. The pauses between responses in spoken recall appear to be too small for substantial covert rehearsal to occur, given that covert rehearsal proceeds at a rate comparable to overt pronunciation (Landauer, 1962). The pauses could be taken up instead with a more rapid memory search process.

Research using procedures in which a rapid response must be made on the basis of a set of items held in immediate memory suggests that memory search is not likely to involve much articulatory rehearsal. Thus, it does not depend upon the length of words to be searched (Clifton & Tash, 1973; Chase, 1977; Sternberg et al., 1978, 1980) as does immediate recall (Baddeley et al., 1975; Baddeley, 1986). Nevertheless, this nonverbal memory search may play a role in immediate recall. In an analysis of results across memory span and memory search rate studies using a variety of stimulus materials, Cavanagh (1972) found that the search rates for different types of verbal stimuli were linearly related to the memory spans for those stimuli.

Brown and Kirsner (1980) found that individual differences in search rate were not useful in predicting memory span differences among normal adults, and Puckett and Kausler (1984) similarly found a relationship between memory span and memory search rate primarily across materials within individuals, not across individuals. However, the reason may be that among these normal college students, as Puckett and Kausler (p. 75) suggested, "search may be a participating, though not a limiting, process in span performance under certain conditions."

Thus, if more intersubject variance in search rate and memory span could be obtained, a relationship between the two might be more apparent. For example, it is possible that increases in search rate that occur with development in childhood are important in predicting developmental improvements in memory span. This has not yet been tested directly in normal children. However, Sininger, Klatzky, and Kirchner (1989) obtained much slower search speeds in language-disordered children than in normal children. Kail (1992) examined a variety of memory span tasks, articulatory rate tasks, and more general processing speed tasks in normal 9-year-olds and adults and found multiple relations between them. There was a relation between articulatory speed and memory span, but there also was a strong relation between general processing speed and both articulatory speed and memory span directly.

Cowan, Keller, et al. (1994) recently have confirmed the importance of both memory decay and covert processing speed during the verbal response period in spoken recall. They measured the timing of spoken recall in a memory span task, as Cowan (1992) did, but with lists of three different word lengths and subjects of two age groups (4- and 8-year-olds). The findings replicated those of Cowan (1992) and, in addition, the effects of age and word length on spoken output timing differed dramatically. Word length affected the time it took to say each word in the response, but it did not affect the interword pauses. In contrast, age affected the interword pauses obtained for lists of a given length, but did not affect the duration of the words in the responses. Age most dramatically affected the duration of the silent preparatory period between the end of the list and the beginning of the response. For measurements taken from responses to span-length lists, the preparatory period averaged across conditions was 1.75 seconds for 4-year-olds vs. 1.16 seconds for 8-year-olds; significantly shorter in the older group even though the span-length lists involved were considerably longer (3.49) than they were for the younger group (2.59).

Thus, it appears that age affects covert processing speed whereas word length affects overt articulation rate, although both have an impact on recall. Word length would affect the amount of time that elapses, and therefore the amount of memory loss that takes place, while the subject pronounces a word, whereas age may affect the rate of covert processing and therefore the subject's efficiency in searching for items in memory, and perhaps reactivating them, between words in the response.

The nature of the covert processing taking place between items in recall is still somewhat of a mystery but, as mentioned above, there are reasons to believe that it may include rapid memory search. For one thing, the speech timing results obtained by Cowan (1992) and by Cowan, Keller, et al. (1994) basically resemble those that Sternberg et al. (1980) obtained when subjects were to pronounce short lists of items as quickly as possible. For example, they too found that the intervals between words in the list were not affected by word length or serial position of the item in the list, but were affected by list length. Their results were attributed to a process in which the subject had to search rapidly through the list to determine which item to pronounce next.

It remains to be seen how much of the variance in recall can be attributed to output times *per se*. Using a nonverbal responses, Dosher and Ma (1992) found that response output time accounted for more of the variance in recall than did articulatory rate. That finding also is consistent with Cowan (1992) and Cowan, Keller, et al. (1994): the length of the response was strongly correlated with memory span.

Given the role of covert processes such as memory search in memory span, however, the precise role of decay in memory span is going to be difficult to determine. Although the results support the notion of a time-limited process in immediate memory, they do not necessarily support the conclusion that it is a 2-second limit. Given the general correlation among the speeds of various mental processes (Hale, 1990; Kail, 1992), the finding that subjects can recall as much as they can pronounce in about 2 seconds may be merely incidental. The important temporal variable may be something else, such as the number of memory items the subject can search through in about 500 ms; or it may be a combination of speeds that is important, for each of the various processes that assist recall.

3.2.7 Short-term memory limits in other cognitive tasks

At least if one considers a broader range of materials to be remembered, the articulatory loop mechanism must be considered incomplete. Not all items can be verbalized. Baddeley (1986) portrayed the articulatory loop as part of a more diversified memory system that was based on a faculty directly linked to attention, the "central executive," that is served by various subsidiary mechanisms. The two such mechanisms mentioned were the articulatory loop and the "visuospatial scratch pad" for nonverbal, visually related materials. Other mechanisms, such as motor systems, also can serve as subsidiary mechanisms (Reisberg, Rappaport, & O'Shaughnessy, 1984).

Within Baddeley's (1986) theory of the memory system, it is not entirely clear where all of memory storage actually resides. It is clear that the subsidiary systems include a passive storage component; for example, the articulatory loop includes both a phonological buffer and an articulation component that serves to reactivate items in that buffer. What is less clear is whether the central executive also includes its own memory capacity. Certainly it contains memory of the procedures that are used to manage the subsidiary systems, but does it also include the ability to remember stimuli in some form, without using any subsidiary systems at all?

The answer would have to be "yes," according to the working memory model of Just and Carpenter (1992). Their theoretical model is supposed to be an elaboration of what goes on in the central executive, the component that Baddeley viewed as relatively intractable, during comprehension tasks. The model can be seen as a bit confusing at first because it incorporates terms with different meanings than in Baddeley's model. The omission of subsidiary systems in working memory is justified on the basis that it contributes relatively little to comprehension. This is based in the neuropsychological finding that subjects with unusually poor short-term memory spans typically have adequate comprehension except when the sentence is especially complex, or when it imposes a rote memory load that cannot be reduced through rapid semantic and syntactic coding. The main evidence of this is that patients with short-term memory impairments show only mild impairments in language comprehension, as is indicated, for example, by the research reported by various chapters in the volume edited by Vallar and Shallice (1990) and reviewed by Martin (1993).

Just and Carpenter say that the amount of information storage and the speed of processing during sentence comprehension both depend upon the amount of available memory "activation." However, the type of activation to which they refer really includes only information that is in the subject's focus of attention. Subjects who have more attentional capacity, or who use it more efficiently, are said to have more available activation. To measure this, Daneman and Carpenter (1980) developed a span measure in which subjects had to comprehend series of sentences and also retain the last word from each sentence. Just and Carpenter note that this measure does not correlate well with the typical memory span measure, and that only their reading span measure predicts reading comprehension skills.

The data presented by Just and Carpenter (1992) support the suggestion that there are two limits in Baddeley's broader concept of working memory. One is the limit in short-term memory span, which correlates well with the speed of articulation. The other is the limit in the simultaneous storage and processing of information, which presumably relies little upon the covert mechanisms (such as Baddeley's articulatory loop) that appear to depend on some sort of processing speed. Supporting this dissociation between processing span and processing speed, Just and Carpenter found that subjects who were high vs. low in reading span did not differ in reading speed, although they did differ in the ability to keep in mind simultaneously more than one potential interpretation of a sentence structure.

Cantor and Engle (1993) also have assumed that there is a limit in the amount that can be activated at one time. They examined the performance of subjects with relatively high vs. low working memory span on tasks that yield fan effects. In these tasks (Anderson, 1974), sentences to be recalled differ in how many other sentences share arguments with them. For example, suppose that one has encountered the four sentences, "The fireman was in the street," "The banker was in the park," "The banker was in the pool," and "The librarian was in the pool" among a number of other sentences, the task being a speeded response confirming or denying that a particular probe sentence was among the list. Among the examples, the reaction time would be slowest for the sentence, "The banker was in the pool," because both "banker" and "pool" appear in two sentences each. The fastest would be the first sentence, because both of its arguments are unique. This difference between sentence types is known as the fan effect. The theory that has been advanced to account for fan effects (Anderson, 1983; Anderson & Pirolli, 1984) states that activation spreads rapidly among related examples but is diluted to an extent related to the number of relevant examples to which activation must spread. Cantor and Engle (1993) found that the magnitude of fan effects was larger in subjects with a lower working memory span, suggesting that, for some reason, those subjects had less available activation to be spread among items.

Engle (personal communication, 1992) pointed out to me that the assumption of rapid spread of activation is strongly supported by studies (Wickens, Moody, & Dow, 1981; Wickens, Moody, & Vidulich, 1985) using Sternberg's probe reaction time technique, but with a backward-counting task sometimes interpolated between the set of items to be searched and the test probe item. This interpolated task presumably interferes with short-term memory and therefore forces subjects to retrieve the search set from long-term memory (that is, to reactivate it) before searching the set for the probe item. The results indicate that the reaction time slope as a function of the search-set size is not altered by the interpolated task, although it does increase the Y-intercept of the function. This is easily explained if all items in the set are reactivated in parallel.

The idea that activation spreads rapidly is supported also by the finding of Neely (1977) in which he separated the contributions of activation and expectancies to semantic priming, basically by sometimes leading subjects to expect a target from a semantic category that was different from the category of the priming stimulus. Neely was able to obtain trials in which the target was semantically related to the prime and expected; related but unexpected; unrelated but expected; and both unrelated and unexpected. The effect of relatedness, presumably reflecting semantic activation, was largest at the shortest target-prime asynchrony that was used in the experiment (250 ms), suggesting that activation related to the prime reaches its peak by or before that time.

Where Cantor and Engle differ from Just and Carpenter (1992) is that Cantor and Engle to not appear to assume that individual differences in the limit in the amount of memory activation depend upon differences in central executive functioning. It remains to be seen what the involvement of the central executive is, as opposed to the alternative possibility of a difference in the amount of automatic activation of memory that can occur.

To summarize the main ideas that have been offered in accounts of working memory, two distinct limits have been suggested. Short-term, serial list recall appears to depend largely upon the speed of processes that may serve to refresh the decaying activation of phonological units in memory. In contrast, comprehension and problem-solving may depend more upon a limit in how much information can be activated at one time.

Though the short-term memory mechanisms that subserve list recall are needed in the service of language comprehension only under especially demanding circumstances (e.g., Martin, 1993), these verbal short-term memory mechanisms are critical in learning new vocabulary. Baddeley, Papagno, and Vallar (1988) found that a patient with a severe short-term memory deficit could not learn new words at all, and Gathercole and Baddeley (1989, 1990) have found that short-term phonological memory in children is a good predictor of their later vocabulary acquisition. These results appear consistent, theoretically speaking, with Hebb's (1949) cell assembly idea. A cell assembly supposedly begins as a transient pattern of neural activation, but it leads to a permanent preservation of the activation pattern through new synaptic growth.

3.3 Cowan's (1988) conception of short-term memory

3.3.1 Basic structure

Cowan's (1988) conception of the memory system was similar to that of Baddeley, with an attempt to be clearer regarding the relation between memory and attention (and the central executive). Within it, there is only one storage medium, which contains information about various past stimuli in terms of their features and feature combinations. For verbal stimuli, these can include acoustic, phonological, orthographic, and lexical/semantic features. However, there are two types of special status that an item and its features can have within memory. First, a subset of items and features in long-term memory can be in an activated state at any one time. This might correspond to active cell assemblies in Hebb's (1949) conception. The items so represented could act as primes for the identification of related items. For example, presentation of the word "doctor" can speed the subsequent recognition of the related word "nurse," as shown in numerous studies of semantic priming. Second, a subset of the activated items and features in memory can be in the focus of attention at any one time. This would correspond to James's (1890) conception of primary memory.

In terms of the working memory theory of Baddeley (1986), the activated elements in memory would be equivalent to the passive stores within the various subsidiary systems, considered collectively. The information within the focus of attention would reflect a storage ability of the central executive itself. Given the hierarchical representation of these concepts in Cowan (1988), however, the ease of attending to an item can be said to depend on how much it is already activated.

It must be acknowledged that there still are important questions about how to measure activation. The traditional measure is priming (i.e., facilitation of responding to one stimulus by the prior presentation of a related stimulus); it is assumed that features of memory related to both the prime and the target were activated by the priming stimulus. However, this may not be totally satisfactory because long-term priming effects also have been observed (e.g, see Squire, 1987). Another possibility, suggested by Cowan (1988), is that the reaction time for the retrieval of activated items should be shorter than the reaction time for the retrieval of inactive items. Waugh (1970) reported data to that effect but, again, there probably also are effects of the status of an item on long-term memory on retrieval times. Given the uncertainty in something as theoretically important as measuring memory activation, the recent physiological studies examining activation and decay of sensory memory, discussed in Chapter 2, are extremely important and should be extended if possible to nonsensory features.

3.3.2 The role of unconscious activation

It presumably is not possible for an inactivated element to be in the focus of attention, but it is possible for an activated element to be outside of the focus of attention. The reason for this assumption is that there can be priming (activation) of information without the use of attention. There has been considerable controversy over whether this actually does occur for semantic information. Holender (1986) reviewed a great deal of possible evidence for automatic semantic activation in the cases of items presented in an unattended channel in selective listening (e.g., Dawson & Schell, 1982), semantic primes presented so quickly that they are subliminal (e.g., Balota, 1983; Marcel, 1983), and items presented in parafovial vision (e.g., Inhoff & Rayner, 1980; Balota, Pollatsek, & Rayner, 1985). Holender concluded that there is no airtight evidence for automatic semantic activation without accompanying conscious identification of the stimulus.

Subsequent evidence by Merikle and Reingold (1990) has been considered stronger. They presented brief masked words, nonwords, or blank fields on each trial. Subjects were to indicate whether or not an item was presented, and then were to choose which of two items was presented if in fact anything was. The nature of the recognition task varied between experiments. In each experiment, on those trials in which a word was presented but subjects indicated that nothing was presented, the level of recognition nevertheless was slightly above chance (about 55%, or 5% above chance) even when a measure of recognition sensitivity (*A*') was used. No such effect was obtained for nonword stimuli, suggesting that subliminal perception occurs only for previously learned units. Unfortunately, though, this effect is dangerously small and the response pattern possibly could be influenced by subtle response demand characteristics. For example, in the fourth experiment in the series, which was considered most critical, the assignment of response keys to responses was not counterbalanced. Among the detection task keys, the "no stimulus" response was always to the left of "stimulus," and among the recognition keys, the "word" response was always above "nonword." Response–response compatibility could have produced a slight, spurious correlation between "no stimulus" detection responses and "word" identification responses.

Perhaps the problem with this research area is that, for any normal stimulus, there is only a small range of normal stimulation that is adequate to affect the nervous system without being registered in awareness. The situation might be different if an abnormal stimulus, such as electrical stimulation of the brain, were used. Recently, Libet et al. (1991) carried out a series of experiments addressing this issue, in patients who have electrodes implanted in the scalp to allow stimulation of the ventrobasal thalamus as a means of alleviating chronic pain. Using relatively mild electrical impulses, it was found that a pulse train of up to about 500 ms is needed in order for the subject to be aware of the stimulation. Using electrical impulse trains of various lengths, both above and below this duration, subjects were asked both to indicate which of two temporal intervals marked with lights contained the electrical impulse, and to indicate how aware they were that an impulse was presented at all. The awareness response was indicated on a 3-point scale (certain yes, uncertain, certain no). Even when subjects were certain that they were not aware of electrical stimulation, they were correct in identifying the interval that contained it about 66% of the time (where chance = 50%), providing perhaps the strongest evidence to date for subliminal perception.

It seems clear that there is an automatic analysis of at least some of the physical features of the environment, at least in the case of sounds. A change in the physical properties of an unattended auditory channel captures one's attention from the attended stimuli (Cherry, 1953), and stimuli that deviate from a repeated standard tone in an unattended channel evoke a mismatch response that can be observed in averaged event-related brain potentials (Näätänen, 1990). According to the model of Cowan (1988), the feature representation of the pre-change, standard sound or sounds must have been present in an activated portion of the memory system outside of the current focus of attention.

3.3.3 The role of multiple-feature activation

Under Cowan's (1988) conception of short-term memory, the second phase of sensory memory, lasting 10–20 seconds, actually is just one of several types of activated feature in memory. This idea follows the lineage of Massaro's (1975*a*) idea that sensory memory is a form of short-term memory, although Massaro attributed physical and semantic features to separate stages of memory, which he termed synthesized visual and auditory memory" and "generated abstract memory," respectively.

As mentioned in Chapter 1, the dynamics of feature activation and decay could be general across feature types. For example, each type of activated feature would be degraded by other stimuli containing similar features.

However, this similarity among features should not be allowed to obscure certain potential differences among features. First, features differ in the type of information that they encode best, corresponding to differences in the sensory analyses leading to these features. Visual features may best encode spatial information, and acoustic and speech-related features may best encode serial and temporal information (e.g., Penney, 1989; Glenberg & Jona, 1991). Second, as mentioned in Chapter 2, it still is unclear whether sensory codes can be activated with imagery processes, or whether there is a type of sensory feature that can be activated only through stimulation. To the extent that imagery processes can activate sensory features, Broadbent's (1958) notion of a return of information from a capacity-limited process to a preattentive buffer store would be justified after all.

Additional evidence that Cowan (1988) overlooked helps to solidify and clarify the view of multiple-feature activation as the basis of passive memory storage. Deutsch (1975) presented evidence that strengthens the view that sensory memory across some seconds is a matter of memory activation. Two tones, that were to be compared to one another in pitch, were separated by six interpolated tones, one of which bore a systematic relation to the first tone to be compared. When it was 2/3 tone away from the first tone in pitch, interference was maximal. Deutsch suggested a lateral inhibition mechanism for tones held in memory. Regardless of the mechanism, systematic, pitch-dependent interactions between tones in memory indicate that it is reasonable and perhaps necessary to think of even nonverbal memory as consisting of activated features rather than a simple, literal representation of the stimulus.

At the other end of the processing spectrum, the recall of a list from long-term memory may require that a hierarchical semantic structure is first activated. Tulving and Patkau (1962) examined "adopted chunks" in a free recall task. Adopted chunks were the groupings of items in subjects' memory, and they were estimated (most likely slightly underestimated) by the number of groups of items that were produced in their original sequential order. Lists differed in word frequency (two levels) and in their degree of statistical approximation to English (five levels), and adopted chunks were examined only for the first trial of each of the 10 conditions. It was found that, although the number of words recalled varied widely across conditions (ranging from 6 to 15 words), the mean number of adopted chunks remained about the same (ranging from 4.60 to 6.04) and bore little or no relation to performance, whereas the size of the adopted chunks closely covaried with performance.

3.3.4 Impact of the model

A repercussion of the Cowan (1988) conception of short-term memory is that it omits part of the stage-like quality of memory that was present in the early information processing models of Broadbent (1958) and Atkinson and Shiffrin (1968). Those models included a sensory memory of unlimited capacity, followed by an attentional filter that permitted only a small proportion of the sensory information to reach a limited-capacity short-term store. This early conception did not do well at explaining "leaks" in the filter that allowed some semantic analysis of items that apparently were unattended at the time when they were presented (e.g., Treisman, 1964*a*, 1964*b*, 1964*c*). In the new conception, part of the analysis of stimuli is carried on automatically. This presumably includes resolution of a great deal of the physical information (producing what I have called the second phase of sensory memory) and perhaps some of the semantic information.

Many researcher are likely to have held a similar view of memory, with attended information seen as a subset of the activated elements in memory, before the review presented by Cowan (1988). However, the view logically was blocked by some of the assumptions of the early models. It was assumed that sensory memory was unlimited in capacity whereas short-term memory was severely limited. Cowan (1988) pointed out that the unlimited capacity of sensory memory had been demonstrated only in the case of the first phase of sensory memory lasting several hundred milliseconds. This distinction (and other such distinctions, for example, the duration of memory persistence) is not well-founded when one is comparing the second, longer phase of sensory memory to short-term memory. Thus, as far as we know presently, physical or semantic information both might occur as activated elements of one's memory, and can be inside or outside of one's focus of attention. The only distinction between them is that it clearly is much easier to focus attention on a physically defined stream of information than it is to focus attention on a semantically defined stream of information (see Johnston & Heinz, 1978). This appears to be a result of the more extensive automatic processing of physical features (Cowan, 1988).

For short-term memory, the end result of the Cowan (1988) view is that both James (1890) and Hebb (1949) are seen to have been correct. As James believed, there is a capacity limit in short-term memory, viewed as a limit in the number of items that can be held in one's attention at the same time. There also is a time limit in the duration for which an item can be kept active in memory, as Hebb would have predicted. Both can be true because the attended information is not synonymous with the activated information, but is only a subset of it.

3.3.5 Short-term memory limits in particular tasks

If there are at least two limits to short-term memory (a time limit to activation and a capacity limit to attended information), how are they reflected in short-term memory tasks? This is a critical but difficult question. Cowan (1988) suggested that there is evidence for both limits in separate procedures. When adult subjects are allowed to rehearse items, they are able to recall about seven of them. According to the theoretical considerations of Baddeley (1986), this would reflect the time limit of activation. However, it does not seem plausible or consistent with the limited-capacity notion of Broadbent (1958) to believe that people could attend to seven items at a time. Accordingly, the prediction is that under circumstances in which the exploitation of strategies that make use of all of activated memory are minimized, memory span should be much closer to the limit of attended information. Consistent with this prediction, results of studies in which the estimated contribution of long-term memory has been mathematically subtracted out (Waugh & Norman, 1965; Watkins, 1974) and from a "running memory span" method in which subjects are quizzed at an unpredictable point within a long list (Pollack, Johnson, & Knaff, 1959; Crowder, 1969) both suggest an attended-item span of no more than about three items.

3.3.6 An analogy

Broadbent (1971, p. 376) suggested an interesting real-life analogy that works fairly well (with some modification) in describing short-term memory limits. Consider an office that includes an in-basket (temporary store), a filing cabinet (long-term store), and a desktop (workspace). I will add additional components: an executive who works at the desk and various lowly assistants (processing modules?) who file and retrieve information, but are not allowed to sit at the desk. Our in-basket is tricky in that items that are not taken out soon enough (within several hundred milliseconds) are dumped directly into a bottomless pit below the office. The assistants are able to keep this type of mishap to a minimum by taking new articles out of the in-basket, doing a cursory search of the files to see if any old information obviously helps in interpreting the new, and placing each new item, with copies of relevant old items attached to it (i.e., partly encoded items), onto the desktop. This represents the process of automatic activation. If the item is of obvious importance (novelty or significance), it is marked with a red flag.

The desktop can become cluttered, but the executive sitting at the desk generally is able to process only one item at a time. He does this as he wishes, but with special attention to flagged items. He often directs an assistant to retrieve copies of additional articles from the files (because the need for these articles is not obvious to them) that are to be attached to the processed items. Then a new file (a fully interpreted memory code) is made for each newly processed item and it, accompanied by relevant material, is filed away for future reference. When an item has remained on the desk too long without the executive turning attention to it (which is unlikely to happen with flagged items), an assistant makes a file for it and returns it in its impoverished, poorly analyzed state to the files, where it is unlikely to be found again.

One unknown in this analogy is whether there is any limit to the amount of clutter that the desk can tolerate or that the executive will allow. Fisher, Duffy, Young, and Pollatsek (1988) presumably would maintain that there is, but see Massaro and Cowan (1993) for cautions.

3.3.7 Relation between short-term memory and working memory

According to the present view, and that of Cowan (1988), the "working memory" of Baddeley (1986) is a valid concept but one with multiple components. It presumably involves information in the activated portions of long-term memory, in the service of the focus of attention as applied by the central executive to the solution of a specific problem.

In contrast to this view, at least two studies (Klapp, Marshburn, & Lester, 1983; Brainerd & Kingma, 1985) purport to demonstrate that short-term memory and working memory are unrelated (Ronald Kellogg, personal communication, November, 1983). Klapp et al. showed that grouping and acoustic similarity effects occurred for an ordered, immediate recall task, but not for a task in which the subject had to find the digit that was missing in an 8-digit sequence. This might have occurred, however, not because grouping and acoustic similarity effects are specific to short-term memory as opposed to working memory, but rather because these effects are specific to ordered recall, whether of a short-term or a long-term nature. Klapp et al. also showed that there was little interference between processing tasks (e.g., reasoning) and storage tasks (e.g., ordered recall). However, that can be explained easily if items were maintained in storage primarily with an articulatory process that was relatively automatic, whereas processing had to be accomplished with central executive processes.

Brainerd and Kingma (1985) found that children's performance on reasoning tasks was independent of their short-term memory for the background facts that were presumably needed in order to solve those tasks. However, it is not clear that subjects had to keep in mind all of the background information in order to get the problems correct. For example, in a typical task problem within Experiment 1, subjects were asked to say whether there were more gorillas or more animals in a previously seen display. However, this type of question can be answered without the subject having encoded exactly how many gorillas there were. A similar criticism may apply to the other tasks. In each trial within Experiment 2, for example, subjects were to take a certain number of one type of animal and a certain number of another type of animal (e.g., seven turtles and three birds) and put them in a container. Then they were to shake the container and answer a probability question (e.g., "If I close my eyes tight and take one picture out of here [the container], do you think I will get a turtle or a bird?"). However, the subject does not have to remember the exact number of each animal to answer this question correctly; only the approximate relative amounts are needed. Thus, the information probed in the short-term memory tasks may have been more detailed than what was needed to solve the reasoning problems.

In summary, though working memory is a more complex concept than short-term memory defined as the sum of activated memory elements, there is no reason to doubt that working memory is based on that activated information along with central executive processes.

3.4 Some unresolved issues in the Cowan (1988) approach

A working theoretical framework is useful partly because it can help one to focus upon areas in which additional research is most sorely needed. In the time since my 1988 article, some interesting questions about the exact nature of short-term memory have come up that were not dealt with adequately in the article. A discussion of some of these will help to illustrate how the theoretical framework could continue to evolve and advance.

3.4.1 How many short-term memory limits?

Although Cowan (1988) proposed a simple structure for memory and attention, it deliberately left open some of the specific descriptions of the components in the structure about which more research is needed. For example, it did not determine the number of factors limiting short-term memory in a broad sense. There theoretically could be four types of limit on short-term memory: either time limits or capacity limits of activated memory and of the focus of attention. The conventional limits in immediate serial recall were said to result from the temporal limits of memory activation. What has not been decisively resolved is whether there are independent capacity limits in activation, the focus of attention, or both.

Engle, Cantor, and Carullo (1992) have summarized evidence from their own laboratory on individual differences in working memory relevant to this point. Engle and his colleagues use terminology more in keeping with Baddeley (1986) than with Just and Carpenter (1992), in that "working memory" was said by Engle et al. to include the entire set of information in an activated state. Within their working memory, Engle et al. also defined a "short-term memory" as "that information that is maintained at a surface level of coding and is within the grasp of immediate consciousness" (p. 990). Thus, they endorsed a hierarchical scheme that appears to be basically similar to Cowan (1988). However, Engle et al. (1992) maintained further that working memory (activated items) and short-term memory (items available to consciousness) appear to make independent contributions to performance on other tasks such as verbal comprehension. La Pointe and

Engle (1990) found that an ordinary word span task correlated with Verbal Scholastic Aptitude Test (VSAT) scores, provided that a different set of words was used in each trial. Articulatory suppression eliminated this correlation, but it did not eliminate the correlation between the VSAT and more complex span measures in which subjects had to carry out processing while remembering the products of that processing, in a manner analogous to the reading memory span of Daneman and Carpenter (1980). Cantor, Engle, and Hamilton (1991) found that these simple vs. complex span measures loaded onto different factors in a factor analysis of VSAT scores and accounted for separate portions of the variance in those scores. Geary and Widaman (1992) reached a similar conclusion in an analysis of skills related to mathematical abilities. Thus, evidence from the psychometric approach suggests that there actually may be at least three different limits on short-term memory broadly defined: a time limit in activation, and capacity limits in both activation and attention.

3.4.2 How is serial order coding accomplished?

Cowan (1988) did not consider in detail the manner in which subjects recall lists in a memory span situation. Serial order information is a critical part of that type of recall situation. If the information that the subject is about to recall is represented as an activated subset of the long-term memory network, then how is serial order information preserved? A naive hypothesis would be that this information is represented by the degree of activation. More recently presented items could be more active in the store, and the subject's performance method would be to discern the item with the least amount of activation remaining (hence, the earliest presented item in the list) and repeat it first. However, this hypothesis would not take into account the assumption (Baddeley, 1986) that subjects reactivate items through rehearsal. This reactivation would imply that the most recently rehearsed, and not necessarily the most recently presented, items would have the most activation.

The information that is in an activated state must include new information as well as the activated set of previously learned information. Links between items and/or between each item and its serial position context must be generated and preserved as additional activated information. The new links comprise an episodic record that will become part of long-term memory, although the distinctiveness of some aspects of this episodic record (such as its specific phonological and lexical content) will decrease as a function of interference from other, similar episodic information in long-term memory; thus the finding that subjects recall only the gist of discourse except for the last phrase or so (e.g., Sachs, 1967).

Electrophysiological evidence may help to clarify the role of attention in serial order coding. In particular, there may be a severe limit to how much serial, episodic information can be encoded automatically. Ritter et al. (1992) examined the mismatch negativity and attention-related (N2b) responses to changes in the pattern of tones that occurred while subjects either attended to them or ignored them and read a book. In some tone sequences, series of repetitions of an identical tone were interrupted by an occasional deviant tone. In other sequences, an alternating pair of tones or a random sequence of tones was presented, and the deviant event was the occasional immediate repetition of a particular tone. The attentional component responded to deviants in all of these situations. However, the mismatch negativity, which presumably indicates automatic detection of a change by the brain, occurred only in the conditions in which the deviants were tone changes, not when they were tone repetitions. This suggests that automatic processes may not keep track of the temporal pattern of tones. The pattern of episodic links between items might have to be established in the attentional focus. This also is in keeping with what will be said in the chapter on the role of attention in long-term memory.

In the last few years, a great deal of effort has gone into producing detailed theoretical models that can predict correctly the serial order information in memory (e.g., Pike, 1986; Gronlund & Ratcliff, 1989; Lewandowsky & Murdock, 1989; Nairne, 1990; Burgess & Hitch, 1992; Brown & Hulme, 1993). Suffice it to say that, at this point, there are many candidates and there is little consensus as to what type of mechanism is most parsimonious. This issue will be discussed further in the next chapter in order to determine which of these proposed systems are compatible with Cowan (1988); some are and some are not.

3.4.3 How modular is short-term memory storage?

Cowan's (1988) model discusses the activated portion of memory as if it consists of a matrix of features corresponding to the items represented, much as Nairne (1990) does (except that Nairne believed that these features were subject to interference only, and not to decay). In contrast, a more modular view is possible. Shallice (1988, Chapter 3) proposed that there are separate visual and phonological short-term storage modules, on the basis of subjects with a selective impairment in phonological short-term memory and generally no long-term memory impairment. The memory was thought to be specific to phonological information for several reasons. Although there was no deficit in speech perception in many of the patients, their digit span was poorer with auditory than with visual presentation, just the opposite of the pattern found in normal subjects; and there was little deficit in short-term memory for nonverbal sounds.

There are at least two parts to this hypothesis of modularity. One is that short- and long-term memory devices are separate, and another is that phonological, acoustic, and visual types of short-term memory devices are separate. First, the separation in function from long-term memory, suggested originally by Shallice and Warrington (1970), is inconsistent with the recent finding in one of these patients that, although word–word associations can be learned normally, word–nonword associations (essentially, new vocabulary learning) cannot be accomplished at all (Baddeley et al., 1988). Thus, phonological short-term memory is quite important for a limited, related area of long-term learning. These results seem more consistent with the hypothesis that short-term memory is an activated subset of elements in long-term memory, along with newly activated links between these elements that is to serve as the episodic record.

Second, the modularity of short-term memory itself that Shallice proposed can be interpreted in several ways. One is that there are several independent mechanisms solely designed for their short-term memory functions. Again this seems incompatible with the interdependence of short-term phonological memory and long-term phonological learning.

An alternative interpretation of modularity in short-term memory is that all of memory consists of different cortical areas specialized in different types of memory feature, with each type strongly connected to the modality of input (with phonological memory near the temporal lobe areas where phonological input is processed in the first place; acoustic memory in nearby or even overlapping areas, and perhaps partly in comparable areas of the nondominant hemisphere; and visual memory in quite different, occipital, temporal, and parietal areas). Then short-term memory would include elements from all of these areas that are temporarily active. According to this account, damage to one area, such as the damage leading to a phonological short-term memory deficit, could leave most of long-term memory intact but not all of it. The only way to get a short-term memory deficit with absolutely no long-term storage deficit would appear to be to damage strategic processing used specifically for short-term retention, in particular covert verbal rehearsal processes. This proposal is speculative but clearly lends itself to further empirical investigation.

3.4.4 How is neuromotor memory coding accomplished?

Another aspect of mental specialization is the possible separation of processes used to retain input vs. planned output. Broadbent (1984) suggested that the human information processing system includes a distinct neuromotor memory store, as well as sensory and abstract (e.g., phonological; semantic) stores. Cowan (1988) proposed that all of these types of transient memory code potentially may be subject to the same dynamic rules. For example, they could have the same rates of decay of activation over time, and each type of code presumably would be particularly susceptible to stimuli giving rise to a similar type of code. It would be assumed that a single stimulus often gives rise to more than one type of code.

The sensory and abstract codes have formed the basis of much of cognitive psychology. The sensory code can be observed whenever the subject uses information that is tied to a particular modality or to stimuli with a particular physical description, and an abstract code can be observed whenever the subject is able to translate information from one modality or stimulus type to another (e.g., pictures to words). However, the possibility of a distinct neuromotor memory code is more elusive and requires careful reconsideration.

There are two possible versions of a neuromotor code: memory for activities that have already been performed, and memory for activities that have yet to be performed. Memory for activities that have already been performed is fairly well demonstrated. For example, modality and suffix effects have been obtained when the list items, the suffix, or both, are mouthed instead of spoken aloud (e.g., Spoehr & Corin, 1978; Nairne & Walters, 1983; for a larger review, see Cowan, 1984, p. 348). Also, Cheng (1974) demonstrated that silently mouthed syllables can be recalled better when they include distinct vowels, independent of whether the heard information includes distinct vowels or not. However, spoken or mouthed speech leaves a sensory trace resulting from the proprioceptive feedback from the muscles (Schmidt, 1988). Therefore, this type of information is no different in principle from sensory storage and can be viewed as a type of sensory storage.

There have been motor memory studies that mirror the studies of short-term memory for other types of codes (reviewed by Schmidt, 1988, pp. 504–508). For example, Adams and Dijkstra (1966) had blindfolded subjects move to a stop that defined a target position, return to the starting location, stay there for a variable retention interval, and then move to the stop location with the stop removed. Errors in movement extent increased as a function of the retention interval. The errors grew in magnitude for about 80 seconds, substantially longer than for three consonants in the Peterson and Peterson (1959) procedure; but seemingly comparable to what would be obtained for the forgetting of a single consonant (Murdock, 1961) if the retention interval were extended for that long. Again, though, it could be argued that the memory in the Adams and Dijkstra procedure was held in a sensory form based on sensory feedback from the previous movement.

The other potential type of neuromotor memory is a representation of motor movements that one is planning to make. One way to represent such planned movement would be by imagining the sensory feedback that one will receive when the movement is carried out. However, that type of memory representation would be no different in principle from an abstract memory code, such as one would generate if a tone were imagined.

What is needed to demonstrate a distinct neuromotor code is a closer link between the memory representation and a subsequent action. For example, one might focus on motor errors that people make. When one accidentally switches two speech sounds, the reason may be that the plan for speaking a subsequent word in the sentence became too activated too soon and was not inhibited. (For an interesting theory of speech errors along these lines see Dell, 1986). However, it still is possible that the plans could be held in an abstract form that is not yet uniquely neuromotor in nature. By that account, only one motor movement is generated at a time from the larger, abstract plan, so that no premotor store is needed.

One stringent criterion for premotor coding is that it inevitably produces a movement and cannot be aborted once the premotor code has been formed. That would not be expected of an abstract memory representation. Rosenbaum (1991), in his review of evidence for a "motor output buffer" (pp. 110–112), appears to hold that view. However, the studies he discusses make clear that, when subjects are engaged in a motor activity and have been instructed to abort the activity when a certain cue appears, they typically persist in their activity only for a very short time (for example, about one keystroke in typing or one syllable in speech). This might reflect the time needed to encode the stop signal, not the contents of an output buffer. In summary, then, we might do without any assumption of a distinctly neuromotor memory code unless future evidence provides a better case for such a code. Abstract plans may be translated into future actions one at a time without a need for transient storage.

3.4.5 What is the proper definition of memory decay?

Like Baddeley (1986), the theoretical framework of Cowan (1988) depends upon the notion of memory decay over time as one factor in short-term forgetting. However, what exactly is memory decay? Assuming that interference also is possible, it is not clear how to tell the difference between interference and decay. Massaro (1970*a*) found that the rate of decay of memory for the first tone in a two-tone, delayed comparison task varied as a function of the acoustic similarity of the tones to be compared to sounds that filled the intertone interval of up to 4 seconds. The fastest memory loss was observed when the interval was filled with another tone, slower memory loss was observed when it was filled with white noise, and almost no memory loss was observed when it was silent. Thus, according to Massaro, there is no decay but rather the influence of the similarity of interference and duration of exposure to it.

For sensory memory, there are data that appear to contradict that view. Cowan, Lichty, and Grove (1990) found a substantial loss of memory for unattended speech presented while the subject was silently reading, across a silent poststimulus delay of up to 10 seconds. Balota and Duchek (1986) used a stimulus suffix procedure in which the suffix was presented after a 20-second delay filled with a silent distractor task. A delayed-suffix effect was obtained, but it did not vary as a function of the acoustic similarity between the list and suffix as it did at a 0-second suffix delay. Apparently, an acoustically specific code decayed within 20 seconds. There are no comparable data specific to phonetic memory, and it is not clear if internally generated phonetic activation should be counted as interference or not.

Even in the case of sensory memory, perhaps neural noise is enough to degrade the memory trace. If so, it appears that there is no such thing as the total absence of interference. It seems to me that, in this case, decay still is a useful concept, although it must be redefined as memory loss in the presence of interference no greater than the minimum amount produced by the subject's own nervous system.

If there is pure memory decay, it can be expected that decay and output interference ordinarily operate conjointly. I will re-examine some classic, elegant studies by Jane Mackworth to illustrate what the ramifications of this conjoint influence might be. In the most critical study, Mackworth (1963) presented spatial arrays of items for a variable duration and measured the duration of the spoken response that resulted as subjects attempted to read as many items as possible out of the array. Subjects did not have to wait for the end of the array to begin speaking and could continue after the array was removed.

When subjects were permitted to read out items as quickly as they could, their correct responses lasted an average of a little less than 2 seconds beyond the end of the array. Increases in the exposure duration of the array (e.g., in Experiment 4, from 0.05 seconds to 2 seconds) dramatically increased the total number of items correctly reported (from about 4 to about 11), but still the duration of report after the end of the array remained about the same (ranging from 1.4 to 1.8 seconds). However, the number of digits reported after the display also remained about the same across display durations (ranging from 3.7 to 4.1 items).

A final experiment of Mackworth (1963) essentially attempted to distinguish between decay and interference hypotheses. The arrays in different conditions within that experiment were formed from digits, colors, letters, or digits on a colored background which also was to be reported. The number of items in the array varied and were adjusted to subjects' ability level with each type of material, and exposure durations of 0.1, 1.0, and 2.0 seconds were used (although the longer two durations were used with only some of the array types). The conclusion was that, although the pronunciation rate depended on the type of item, the duration of response after the array remained about the same.

However, a careful re-examination of data in that last, critical experiment does not support that conclusion. Fig.3.4 summarizes the evidence reported for each combination of stimulus type and array size. (The 1- and 2-second display durations were used only with the three conditions shown as solid shapes). The top panel of the figure shows that the number of items correctly recalled varied widely across conditions. The middle panel shows that the

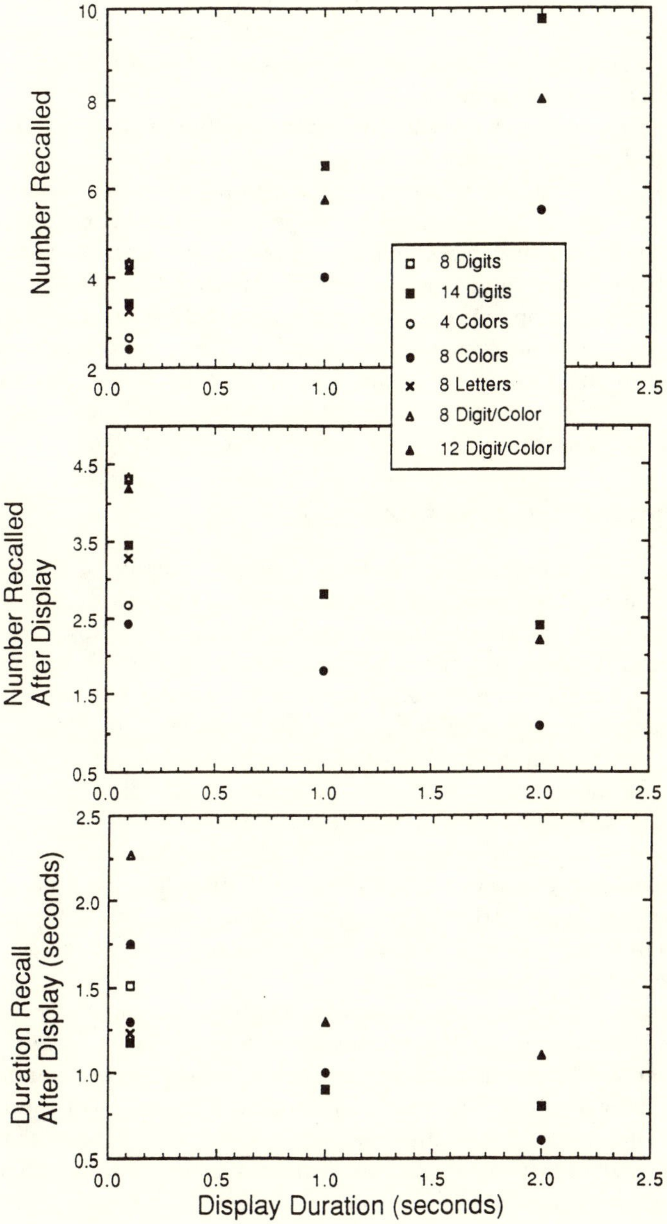

Fig. 3.4 Data on effects of display duration on number of items recalled. (After Mackworth, 1963.)

number of items recalled after the display ended also varied in a consistent pattern. Finally, the bottom panel shows that the duration of report after the end of the array was not nearly constant across conditions, as Mackworth intimated, but varied consistently in a manner similar to the number of items reported after the array ended.

It is true that, within any particular display duration, materials that were better recalled were so recalled without the recall period lasting longer than in other conditions. It also is possible (although by no means certain) that this figure reflects the upper bounds of the persistence of the memory store necessary for recall. However, even if this experiment can be taken to suggest an upper bound of memory persistence of just over 2 seconds, in most conditions subjects stopped recalling considerably before this upper bound even though many items remained to be recalled. Thus, performance in this task thus may be limited by some combination of decay and output interference. Similar observations apply to another study in which the duration of auditory memory was estimated (Mackworth, 1964).

3.4.6 Are process boundaries fuzzy?

Cowan's (1988) theoretical framework distinguished between items in vs. out of the focus of attention, and between items in vs. out of the activated portion of memory. Either of these boundaries could be fuzzy without doing harm to the basic notions of the framework. However, several added assumptions do seem necessary for activation and attention to be meaningful concepts despite fuzzy boundaries. The first is that activation of any particular information in memory decays within some seconds if not refreshed through central executive processes involving the focus of attention. The second is that the amount that can be activated beyond some baseline level is very small relative to the entire amount stored in memory, which presumably stays at the baseline level most of the time. These assumptions are needed to rule out the possibility of a smoothly graded continuum in which various items are at various levels of activation all of the time and encompass all of memory.

Still, the task of operationally defining short-term memory remains a difficult one. For one thing, the advantages of activation may be mimicked by the contextual relevance of certain items in long-term memory. A discussion about a zoo may make it easier to perceive animal words minutes or even hours after the discussion, but that does not mean that the information stayed "activated" all of that time; not in the sense in which I am using the word activation. Still, in borderline instances it might be difficult to tell empirically what is activated and what is not. Also, the concept of graded activation complicates some potential methods of testing for activation. For example, although Cowan (1988) suggested that one could use a reaction time measure to distinguish between items in vs. out of the focus of attention, that would not be very meaningful unless there were a relatively sharp discontinuity in reaction time between items in and out of the focus.

A related question is whether the difference between memory in vs. out of the focus of attention is a qualitative or a quantitative one. It could be that when features or items in memory are activated to a certain degree, they automatically enter the focus of attention. Alternatively, it could be that items in the focus of attention possess some neural status that cannot be encoded along the same level-of-activation dimension. A logical argument in favor of the latter, more complex possibility is that, in cases of sleepwalking (Kelly, 1985) and sometimes in epileptic seizures (Martin, 1985), a person can carry out ensembles of actions seemingly without any awareness. The same may be true in various other pathological and unusual states of awareness, at least as judged by the patient's later inability to recall activities during the unusual state (Hilgard, 1986). Thus, the action schemes apparently can be activated enough to be expressed in overt behaviors, and yet can be cut off from the focus of attention.

3.5 Neurophysiology of short-term memory

From the prior sections of this chapter, it should be clear that behavioral researchers have their hands full in trying to determine the nature of short-term memory. Until recently, they could reasonably act as if this investigation could proceed without detailed knowledge of the neural structures underlying the behaviors. In the last few years, however, neural science has advanced to the point where it no longer can be ignored. This makes many behavioral researchers, including myself, uncomfortable inasmuch as it will be difficult for any one researcher truly to master and keep abreast of both literatures. Moreover, such interests must run deep as well as broad, because cursory literature reviews perpetuate errors in interpreting the results and send those errors into the secondary literature. Perhaps the behavioral researchers will be willing to engage in this broadening of their field of enquiry (e.g., perhaps tripling the number of journals that they view as relevant) as more neurophysiologists in turn realize how critical behavioral studies are for their interests.

One way we can tell that a behavioral field needs neurophysiological input is when a behavioral researcher frames a research hypothesis in neural terms. One well-known example of this is the neural metaphor used in connectionist modeling of behavior (McClelland et al. 1986). An example more immediately pertinent, however, is the proceduralist view of memory, which Crowder (1993) stated as an alternative to the multistore view. The proceduralist view is that memory is an aftereffect of the prior stimulus processing and, as such, is stored in the same locations within the nervous system that are involved in the initial processing.

From recent research involving electrical recording and brain lesions in animals (reviewed by Goldman-Rakic, 1992), we can say that the proceduralist view is only partly right and fails in an important way. It does appear that the memory of recent events is stored with the involvement of association cortex in disparate parts of the brain that appear relevant in processing particular types of material. In the visual and spatial memory tasks discussed by Goldman-Rakic, the parietal lobes are mentioned in this regard, whereas abnormal auditory short-term memory has been obtained with temporal lobe lesions (Colombo, D'Amato, Rodman, & Gross, 1990). However, as Goldman-Rakic makes clear, a critical area for working memory is the prefrontal cortex. Single-cell studies indicate that certain prefrontal cells respond, not when the subject is processing the stimulus, but when that stimulus is being retained in memory in order for the subject to complete a response following an imposed delay. Moreover, lesions of the prefrontal cortex impair this working memory without impairing the processing of the same stimuli in a nondelay situation. These prefrontal areas also are implicated in object permanence tasks like those that Piaget (1954) used to show behavioral immaturity of memory in infants. Goldman-Rakic proposed that the prefrontal cortex does not contain the memory representations, but is instrumental in keeping those representations active through cross-cortical stimulation during working memory tasks. In terms of the model of Cowan (1988), the prefrontal area must be included as part (or all) of the neural substrate of the central executive and/or the focus of attention, whereas the diffuse areas of the association cortex in other parts of the brain must be included as part (or all) of the neural substrate of memory elements that can be placed in a temporarily heightened state of activation.

Schacter (1989) suggested a further distinction on the basis of human neuropsychological evidence. Whereas patients with frontal lesions tend to have well-known difficulties in planning and executing series of activities, patients with lesions in certain parts of the parietal lobe do not necessarily have this problem, but do display various abnormalities and lapses of awareness. On the basis of evidence that Schacter summarized, one might hypothesize that the central executive is at least partly localized in the frontal lobe whereas the focus of attention, though directed partly by frontal lobe structures, is itself represented in parietal lobe structures instead. Both Goldman–Rakic and Schacter emphasized the especially abundant neural pathways connecting the frontal and parietal lobes. What do we make of the neurological evidence? It is not conclusive, but it is enough to cause interest. The evidence will be discussed in more detail in the final chapter of this book.

4. Actual versus "virtual" short-term memory phenomena

The discussion so far has sketched out converging sources of evidence on the nature of sensory and short-term storage. However, it is possible that converging sources can be deceptive. While some investigators go on assuming that sensory and short-term stores exist, and go on working on refinements in characterizing them, a few have begun to reopen the question of whether the concept of multiple stores is necessary at all or whether, instead, one set of theoretical principles can explain all memory phenomena in the same way. The latter, as mentioned above, will be termed a "monistic memory" view. This view presents a challenge to the interpretations of both the sensory storage and the short-term memory phenomena discussed in the previous two chapters.

The basis for questioning the need for a functionally distinct short-term memory is that it turns out to be possible to mimic many of the results of conventionally accepted short-term memory procedures using types of long-term memory tests, and vice versa. An alternative, monistic account of memory states that it is not the absolute amount of poststimulus time that is important in predicting forgetting, but only the amount of time relative to the timing of the stimuli that have been presented.

The present view is that both theoretical orientations have some merit. Although many short- and long-term memory phenomena can be made to mimic one another, there are subtle but important differences between them, so that a distinct short-term memory function is still needed. On the other hand, some of the phenomena that have been explained with the short-term memory construct may not actually reflect short-term memory.

The situation is somewhat analogous to the concept of "virtual memory" in computer terminology. Part of the hard disk of a microcomputer can be made to function in the same way as active, read-and-access memory (RAM), and this deceptive, apparently distinct memory storage device is termed virtual memory. In a similar way, the principles of retrieval from long-term memory are such that they sometimes mimic the functioning of short-term memory, forming what could be termed a virtual short-term memory. While the demonstration of a virtual short-term memory is of course important, it does not necessarily rule out the possibility that an actual short-term memory also exists. The important empirical task becomes one of distinguishing between them.

The results of Nairne (1992) will serve to illustrate the motivation to reconsider a monistic, or unitary, view of memory. Nairne investigated the fate of serial order information for lists after test delays ranging from 30 seconds to 24 hours. The finding was that serial order information diminished gradually across that period. It did so in a way that previously (Lee & Estes, 1981) had been attributed to short-term recall. Specifically, items were often exchanged with other items nearby in a list, as if the variability in serial order coding gradually had increased. Lee and Estes had attributed this pattern to perturbations that presumably occurred when the subject rehearsed the list. Obviously, though, perturbations in rehearsal are not likely to be involved after 24 hours.

This period of the loss of serial order information would not be surprising according to the account of memory described here, however. New serial order information would be represented as new activated information, which would become a part of long-term memory. Changes in context between study and test would account for the gradually diminishing ability of subjects to recall the serial order information. This account predicts that the original study context might be reinstated in some way that would renew the subject's serial order recall.

4.1 A challenge to multiple-store accounts

4.1.1 Through-list distractor procedure

Nairne's finding of a long-term recall pattern matching what is usually found in short-term recall is not a unique case. Bjork and Whitten (1974) found a recency effect in long-term recall, in a procedure that I will refer to as the "through-list distractor" technique. In their procedure, pairs of words were used. A distracting task 12 seconds long was interposed between each item pair, with a 20-second version of the distracting task (arithmetic) added between the final pair and the recall task. The items were presented in pairs to encourage subjects to focus on each pair separately rather than rehearsing the list across all items. It is impossible to maintain that subjects could preserve the list-final items in short-term memory across the final period of distraction, but a long-term recency effect still was obtained. Tzeng (1973) reported similar long-term recency effects in a study in which the items were individual words rather than word pairs. Moreover, unlike Bjork and Whitten (1974), the long-term recency effect remained even in final free recall. It appears that serial position must have affected something other than short-term memory, such as the relative distinctiveness of various words in the list.

Gardiner and Gregg (1979) and Glenberg (1984) carried this argument further by showing that the typical auditory modality superiority is obtained with this "through-list distractor" technique developed by Bjork and Whitten. Glenberg and Swanson (1986) proposed that the acuity of serial position coding is better in the auditory modality, accounting for the greater distinctiveness of list-final items.

Watkins, Le Compte, Elliott, and Fish (1992) recently succeeded in demonstrating that the short-term memory for exact temporal intervals in lists with irregular timing is in fact superior in the auditory modality. However, this modality effect was obtained only when the list consisted of repetitions of a single stimulus and when articulation was suppressed. This, and the research reviewed by Watkins et al., suggests that the auditory modality advantage in list recall may be an advantage in sequential order coding, though not in temporal location coding as Glenberg's theory states.

Other studies have shown that additional features of recall typically attributed to the dual-store system can be replicated with the through-list distractor technique. Gregg and Gardiner (1984) found phonological similarity effects that resembled those typically obtained in ordinary immediate recall, and Greene (1986) found a pattern of word frequency and list length affects (on the prefinal serial positions only) that were the same as in ordinary immediate recall. These findings suggest that, if there is a separate short-term memory, it at least cannot be demonstrated simply by the characteristics commonly associated with it.

One study using the through-list distractor technique (Koppenaal & Glanzer, 1990) has directly questioned the monistic interpretation of long-term recency effects. In their first experiment, Koppenaal and Glanzer used two different distractor tasks: word reading and arithmetic. Some subjects performed the same task during every distractor interval, but others performed one task between items to be recalled and the other task in the interval between the final item and the recall test. In the subjects who received a constant distractor task the long-term recency effect was obtained, but in the subjects for whom the distractor task changed just before the test, no recency effect was observed. The authors' interpretation was that subjects learn to rehearse some of the to-be-remembered words during the distractor task, which produces a recency effect because the most recent words are still being rehearsed when the list ends. A change in distractors was said to disrupt this covert rehearsal, eliminating the recency effect. Thus, the result was taken as evidence against the monistic, distinctiveness account of the long-term recency effect.

However, this interpretation of the data did not prove to be correct. Thapar and Greene (1993) re-examined the issue in several ways, the most striking of which was to require a different distractor task after each item in the list. This condition produced a strong recency effect, even though there was no recency effect when a distracting task was placed only between the last item and the recall period. Thus, the recency effect cannot be accounted for by a short-term memory mechanism and truly must be accounted for instead by a longer-term encoding factor such as the temporal distinctiveness of list items.

It remains possible, of course, that when short-term memory is present it causes a recency enhancement above the level that results from such distinctiveness factors. It has been found, in fact, that the recency effect is larger in immediate recall than in an otherwise identical through-list distractor recall procedure (Cowan, Wood, & Borne, 1994).

4.1.2 The monistic view

Crowder (1989*a*, 1993) has questioned the existence of separate short- and long-term stores and maintains that the procedures that previously had been taken to index short-term storage (counting, incidentally, sensory memory as one variety of short-term storage) could be accounted for entirely according to the properties of a single memory store. Part of the reason is the finding of long-term recency and modality effects, but there are other reasons. For one, the Peterson–Brown results (rapid forgetting of a very short list during performance of a distractor task as shown by J. Brown, 1958; Peterson & Peterson, 1959) have to be interpreted in light of the finding (Keppel & Underwood, 1962) that very little forgetting occurs during the first few trials. This result is illustrated in Fig. 4.1.

The monistic memory account states that forgetting is due to proactive memory interference across trials. The detrimental effect of test delays on performance then is interpreted as a result of the changing test context. When the test is immediate, the last list is relatively distinctive in memory and therefore relatively impervious to interference from previous trials. At longer test delays, this special distinctiveness of the final list is lost, and items in that list cannot be discriminated as easily from items in previous lists.

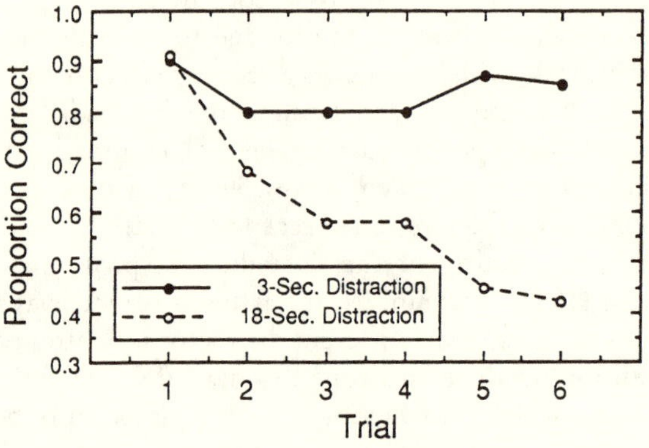

Fig. 4.1 Data on proactive interface. (After Keppel and Underwood, 1962.)

This distinctiveness interpretation could be considered to be strengthened by the finding that a high proportion of the errors in recall are not random, but consist of intrusions from previous lists (Drewnowski & Murdock, 1980; Lee & Estes, 1981). The distinctiveness principle also would apply to the recall of items in a longer list, and to accompanying phenomena such as the suffix and modality effects.

Crowder (1989*a*) discussed still further reasons why he doubts the reality of the short-term memory (STM)/long-term memory (LTM) distinction. To establish the logic for his concerns, he drew a distinction between "coding dissociations" and "process dissociations." A coding dissociation is a case in which two different memory codes (e.g., phonetic vs. semantic coding) exist and lead to different memory retention characteristics. A process dissociation is a case in which, regardless of the type of coding, two different memory processes are said to apply. The STM/LTM distinction is one that supposedly reflects a process dissociation, but Crowder warns that this conclusion is a mistaken one in which the process is confounded with the type of coding. Specifically, the concern is that what has been taken as evidence for an STM/LTM distinction actually reflects only a phonetic/semantic coding distinction. Phonetic coding lends itself well to the task of memory rehearsal, whereas semantic coding may be better suited for long-term memory retrieval.

The remaining behavioral realm in which there appears to be evidence for a type of short-term memory is the set of evidence in favor of an "articulatory loop" (Baddeley, 1986). Crowder notes that this memory presumably relies upon a coding trick, namely the covert repetition of items to be recalled. The typical handful of items in STM (e.g., the 7 ± 2 items of Miller, 1956) can be retained only with such a trick, as evidence on the effects of articulatory suppression (Baddeley et al., 1975; Cowan, Cartwright, Winterowd, & Sherk, 1987) demonstrates. One way to reduce the effects of covert rehearsal severely, even without articulatory suppression, is to present a very long list of items and to stop at an arbitrary point to require backward recall. It is impossible to cumulatively rehearse so many items, and with this "running memory span" procedure (Pollack, Johnson, & Knaff, 1959; Crowder, 1969), typically only two or three items can be recalled. Although not mentioned by Crowder, similar small estimates of the items in short-term storage at any one time are provided by techniques in which the estimated contribution of long-term storage to short-term recall is subtracted out (for a review see Watkins, 1974). Crowder (1989*a*) suggested that these two or three items reflect the set currently in consciousness and doubted that this set could be meaningfully interpreted as a short-term store of practical, mnemonic value.

Another idea questioned by Crowder (1989*a*) was the sacrosanct notion of memory consolidation. Crowder's review of the animal research literature suggested that there is little valid evidence for it. Previous research indicated that electroconvulsive shocks, or the blockage of protein synthesis immediately following a learning episode, prevented any demonstration of long-term memory of the episode, even though the animal's short-term performance had been adequate. However, subsequent research has suggested that these were examples of state-dependent learning and that shock or protein blockage at the time of recall revealed that memory consolidation had taken place after all.

4.1.3 Neurological and neurochemical evidence

Finally, Crowder noted that cases of neurological dissociation between types of memory have been used to distinguish between short- and long-term stores. In the most celebrated case, a patient denoted as H.M., who had a bilateral hippocampectomy as a cure for severe temporal lobe epilepsy, displayed essentially normal short-term processing but little or no explicit long-term memory of events following the operation. For example, he might learn to solve a puzzle, and later would show savings when attempting to relearn the puzzle; but he nevertheless would not recall having worked on the puzzle before, nor would he recall the people whom he had met since the operation. The conventional account of this finding is that short-term memory and long-term procedural memory are intact, but that the information is not coded in a way that allows it to be stored for long-term declarative retrieval.

Crowder's (1989*a*) analysis of such cases of amnesia was brief but consistent with his other views. He noted that the amnesia can be considered as a type of coding deficit in which the relation of the episode to its temporal context is not coded. Thus, this was viewed as another example of a coding dissociation rather than process dissociation.

Crowder might also have said something similar about the rare cases in which an individual's performance on short-term memory tasks is severely impaired even though performance on long-term memory tasks is normal (Shallice & Warrington, 1970). Is it a special type of store or a type of coding that is impaired? Baddeley et al. (1988) found that this type of deficit leads to the inability essentially to learn new vocabulary. Therefore, it could be argued that a specific type of phonetic coding is impaired, not short-term storage *per se*. Of course, the only type of model in which a deficit of STM should not lead to any deficit of LTM is one in which short- and long-term stores are arranged in parallel (Shallice & Warrington, 1970). Nevertheless, it appears as if the neurological deficits of memory are not going to include cases that provide a clear, clean demonstration of the dissociability of short- and long-term memory after all, as many would have hoped.

Recent findings on the neurochemistry of learning and memory have been cited as evidence for the separability of short- and long-term memory, but it is likely that even this evidence can also be called into question. For example, consider research that Fanselow (1993) reviewed on two types of neural receptors, termed NMDA and non-NMDA on the basis that only one type binds the chemical NMDA (*N*-methyl-D-aspartate). The types of receptor react differently to the neurotransmitters that they accept. The non-NMDA receptors consistently react by opening a neural channel, causing an excitatory change in the neuron. However, the NMDA receptors cause channel-opening only when the cell is depolarized. Moreover, this type of channel-opening causes chemical changes in the cell that last a long time. The result is that NMDA receptors permit long-term potentiation (increases in reactivity) in the neuron, and this occurs only if the NMDA receptor is activated at the same time that a strong neural stimulus has been received. This, in fact, was proposed as the mechanism of conditioning (and, by implication, possibly other types of long-term learning). At least in the case of fear conditioning, the NMDA receptors involved are found in the hippocampus and amygdala (Fanselow, 1993), areas known to be involved in long-term learning (e.g., see Squire, 1987).

Whereas NMDA receptors appear to mediate at least some types of long-term learning, non-NMDA receptors may mediate short-term memory. However, as suggested above, the interpretation of the relevant findings may be complex. For example, Kim, Fanselow, DeCola, and Landeira-Fernandez (1992) administered an NMDA antagonist to rats who were subjected to shock associated with a particular testing apparatus. The fear reaction (freezing of motion) occurred but lasted only 3 minutes in NMDA-blocked animals, whereas the fear reaction lasted at least 6 minutes in the saline-injected control animals. The authors concluded that a short-term memory process was independent of NMDA, whereas a longer-term memory process was NMDA-dependent. Although this is plausible, the data do not appear to favor that interpretation strongly because the NMDA-blocked animals never reached the same level of maximal freezing behavior that the control animals did. (In both groups, that behavior did not peak until the second minute of testing.) The peak level could be intrinsically related to the persistence of the behavior across extinction trials. The data only show, therefore, that the entire learning process was impeded by the NMDA antagonist.

Perhaps equivalent levels of behavior would be observed if the animals could be tested on a behavior that peaks more rapidly, and thus more clearly within the period of short-term memory activation (which could be as short as 10 seconds, if rats resemble humans in this regard; see Cowan et al., 1990; Sams et al., 1993). Thus, it may be that the recent, exciting neurochemical leads have not yet been linked to clearly identifiable short- and long-term memory faculties.

In summary, it appears from discussion above that the concepts of memory distinctiveness and contextually dependent recall, along with modality differences in temporal vs. spatial coding, may be able to predict the basic recency, modality, and distractor effects in recall, as well as neurological and neurophysiological evidence, without the need for a theoretical distinction between short- and long-term storage. Crowder's interpretation of the data was along these lines. It was based on the monistic concept of "proceduralism," in which it was assumed that memory is a residue of the processing that took place when the stimulus was first encountered and is stored in the same places in the brain that mediate these encoding processes. However, arguments and evidence against this view will be presented below.

4.2 Arguments against the monistic view

Crowder suggested that, given the evidence reviewed above, it is now up to the agonist of multiple stores to provide a logical defense of those stores. It is my attempted defense that follows, as I still believe that a monistic memory store cannot account for all of the detailed evidence that exists and must be considered. Let us reconsider Crowder's points one at a time.

4.2.1 Through-list distractor procedure reconsidered

The first and perhaps most central point involves the long-term recency, modality, and suffix effects obtained with through-list distractor techniques (Bjork & Whitten, 1974; Gardiner & Gregg, 1979; Glenberg, 1984). They could be taken as evidence against the two-store distinction, but only if they display the same properties as the ordinary effects obtained in immediate recall. To understand why this might not be the case, one must realize that multiple codes can be involved in any particular memory phenomenon that is observed. Different memory codes might produce analogous influences on the pattern of recall. This in itself does not rule out a monistic explanation, given that multiple types of coding are expected within that view. However, a monistic explanation should not include the possibility that some codes decay quickly whereas other codes last longer. Whenever minor differences are observed between generally analogous short- and long-term memory phenomena, one must consider if the differences result from the use of a different combination of memory codes in shorter- vs. longer-term recall, and if that different combination in turn is the result of drastically different rates of decay for different memory codes.

A rarely cited paper by Richardson (1979), in which an ordinary immediate recall procedure was used, makes clear the preliminary point that recency, modality, and suffix effects are based on multiple codes. Richardson demonstrated different effects for lists of letters, which presumably have only an impoverished lexical code, than for lists of words, which have a richer lexical code. In one experiment, when sets of letter stimuli were used, an auditory modality superiority for recall of the most recent items was obtained but was eliminated when the items in a list were made phonetically similar, which is in keeping with the previous findings of Watkins, Watkins, and Crowder (1974). However, when sets of word stimuli were used instead of letter stimuli, a respectable modality effect remained even when the words were phonetically similar. This suggests that the modality effect for the words did not depend on vowel distinctness as did the modality effect for letters. Additional experiments demonstrated that for letters, but not for spoken words, (a) the suffix effect was eliminated by phonetic similarity between the items to be recalled, and (b) the suffix effect was diminished by the acoustic similarity between the voices in which the list and suffix were presented. These results appear to indicate that some code that is unaffected by acoustic similarity was available for words, but not for letters. Richardson suggested that it is a lexical code that was richer for the word stimuli. The findings also are reminiscent of the observation by Turner et al. (1987) that the suffix effect for lipread speech stimuli is unaffected by phonological similarity among items in the list, unlike the suffix effect for heard speech stimuli.

Close comparison of the ordinary vs. the through-list distractor procedures for immediate recall suggests that a different mixture of codes is used in the two procedures. Ordinarily, the suffix effect (i.e., retroactive interference specific to auditory suffixes placed after auditory lists) can be obtained using the same suffix on all trials (e.g., Morton et al. 1971). In contrast, in the through-list distractor procedure, Glenberg (1984) found no suffix effect when the suffix stimulus remained the same from trial to trial, as shown in the top panels of Fig. 4.2. A suffix effect was obtained only when the suffix changed from trial to trial, as shown in the bottom panels of the figure. This may suggest that the suffix effect in the distractor technique occurred because of interference with lexical or long-term phonological processing, in a way that is not important in ordinary immediate recall procedures.

Neath and Crowder (1990) approached the distinctiveness theory in a way that is different from most other studies. Instead of simply replicating the traditional immediate recall results with a through-list distractor technique, they presented lists with irregular timing in order to test further predictions of the distinctiveness theory. Some lists began with relatively long interstimulus intervals that grew shorter across serial positions, some lists began with short intervals that grew longer across positions, and some lists had constant intervals. The best example of the latter is the final item in a list with increasing interstimulus intervals. A "ratio rule" predicted that the recallability of a particular item is related to the ratio of the interval between that item, and the previous item and the interval between that item and the response period. Items presented close together and far from test are relatively disadvantaged; items presented far apart and close to test are the most advantaged.

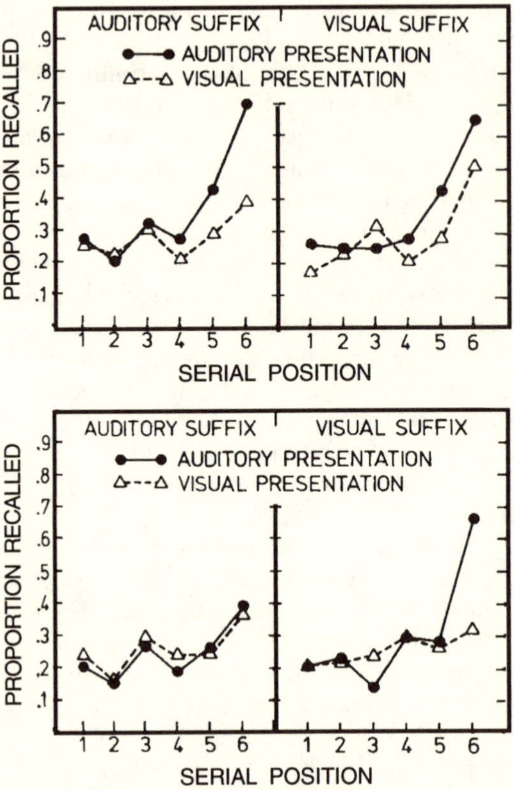

Fig. 4.2 Data on long-term suffix effects. (From A. Glenberg, A retrieval account of the long-term modality effect. *Journal of Experimental Psychology: Learning, Memory, & Cognition, 10,* p. 25, Fig. 5 (top panels) & p. 27, Fig. 6 (bottom panels). Copyright © 1984 by the American Psychological Association. Adapted by permission.)

The results of two experiments with an immediate recall procedure and bimodal presentation (items visually presented but read aloud by the subject) generally matched the predictions of the distinctiveness theory. Specifically, lists with increasing interstimulus intervals across items (and therefore increasing inter-presentation/retention ratios) showed larger recency effects than lists with a constant interval, which in turn showed larger recency effects than lists with a decreasing interval. Given a constant interstimulus interval, the magnitude of the recency effect was related directly to the duration of the interval. However, in these experiments, each interstimulus interval was filled with digits that the subject was also to read aloud, so this procedure is not strictly comparable to ordinary immediate recall. A dual-store theory would make predictions similar to the ratio rule, because the longer interstimulus intervals also included the most acoustic and phonetic interference.

In a third experiment, a through-list distractor technique was used, the intervals between items were filled with a silent arithmetic task (with each interval lasting up to 32 seconds), and the modality of the list items was manipulated. In this situation, the distinctiveness account fits well enough for the visual lists but proved irrelevant to the findings with auditory lists. For those lists, there was simply a very pronounced recency effect regardless of the presentation schedule.

It is possible that these results could be accounted for in a monistic memory system, with separate distinctiveness and acoustic cues. However, this would complicate the account, so that the monistic explanation still would be a two-process explanation. It also remains possible that the acoustic cues used when the list presentation is auditory are from auditory sensory memory. The time periods through which auditory sensory memory would have to be carried in this procedure are within the range of the persistence of auditory sensory memory discussed in the sensory memory chapter of this book (e.g., Watkins & Todres, 1980 ; Watkins & Watkins, 1980; Cowan, 1984; Cowan et al., 1990).

Studies of the output order and serial position functions in ordinary recall (Dalezman, 1976) and through-list distractor procedures (Whitten, 1978) also differentiate between the two. Dalezman (1976) carried out immediate and delayed free recall procedures in which the order of output was semi-controlled. In three different conditions, subjects were to recall items from the beginning, middle, or end of the list before recalling other items. There also was a free recall condition. One basic finding was an advantage for items recalled first, but there was an especially large advantage for the most recent items when they were recalled first. This enhanced recency effect matches what one would expect from a transient memory store that held the most recently presented items. Moreover, free recall most closely matched recall in this recency-first condition, suggesting that subjects ordinarily do make use of short-term memory in this type of procedure. In a delayed recall condition, there still were output-order effects, but without the special recency benefit obtained in immediate recall. Specifically, the serial position function in delayed free recall most closely matched the primacy-first output condition, not the recency-first condition.

Whitten (1978) carried out the same manipulation of output order as Dalezman (1976), with a through-list distractor procedure. In contrast to the clear pattern of results that Dalezman obtained, no significant effects of output order were obtained here. It is as if long-term serial position effects in this study resulted from a pattern of memory about the trial that was in a form impervious to output interference, different from the one Dalezman (1976) observed.

In summary, although it may be possible to account for the basic results of the through-list distractor technique without invoking any type of short-term memory storage, a close inspection of the results suggests that there are details that are difficult to understand with a monistic account. There are subtle but important differences between the patterns of results that have been obtained in immediate recall vs. through-list distractor recall procedures.

It is worth noting that a distributed trial procedure was tried considerably before the through-list distractor studies of Tzeng (1973) and Bjork and Whitten (1974). Setting the scene for this procedure, Baddeley (1966, Experiment 1) had different groups of subjects learn lists of 10 words that were acoustically similar, semantically similar, or neither. The answer choices were provided on a response card, so the test was one of order and not item information. In four identical, successive trials of this immediate recall task, there was a phonological similarity effect but no semantic similarity effect. Then subjects engaged in a different (digit recall) task for 20 minutes as a distractor. Finally, subjects were asked to write down as much of the word list as they could, in the appropriate order. In this delayed recall test, there was no effect of similarity of either type. These results are reproduced in Fig. 4.3 (top panels).

In Experiments 2 and 3, Baddeley (1966) interposed the 20-minute task either between each list and the response, between each response and the next presentation of the list, or neither. In each case, there also was a final distraction period and then a retest on the words, as in Experiment 1. The through-list task manipulation did not alter the effects of acoustic similarity, but it did alter the effects of semantic similarity. A digit task between each list and the response to the list dramatically impaired performance for semantically similar lists relative to control lists on the later trials and the retest. These results are shown in the bottom panels of Fig. 4.3.

Apparently, turning the task into one of long-term retention made subjects more reliant on semantic features, whereas in immediate recall they were more reliant on acoustic features. (This may be because of the difference in memory maintenance strategies subjects can use in short- vs. long-situations, as Cowan, 1988 suggested). Placing a distracting task between trials had, if anything, a facilitatory effect on later trials, perhaps because it permitted more distributed practice. It is clear from this study that it would be an oversimplification to state that one simple set of rules (e.g., related to the discriminability of items) describes performance across short- and long-term memory procedures.

An experiment by Cowan, Wood, and Borne (1994) provides what may be the strongest evidence to date that there is a short-term store of the sort assumed within the articulatory loop. One condition was a replication of the study in which the length of words in the first and second halves of a printed list to be recalled were varied separately (Cowan et al., 1992). In this

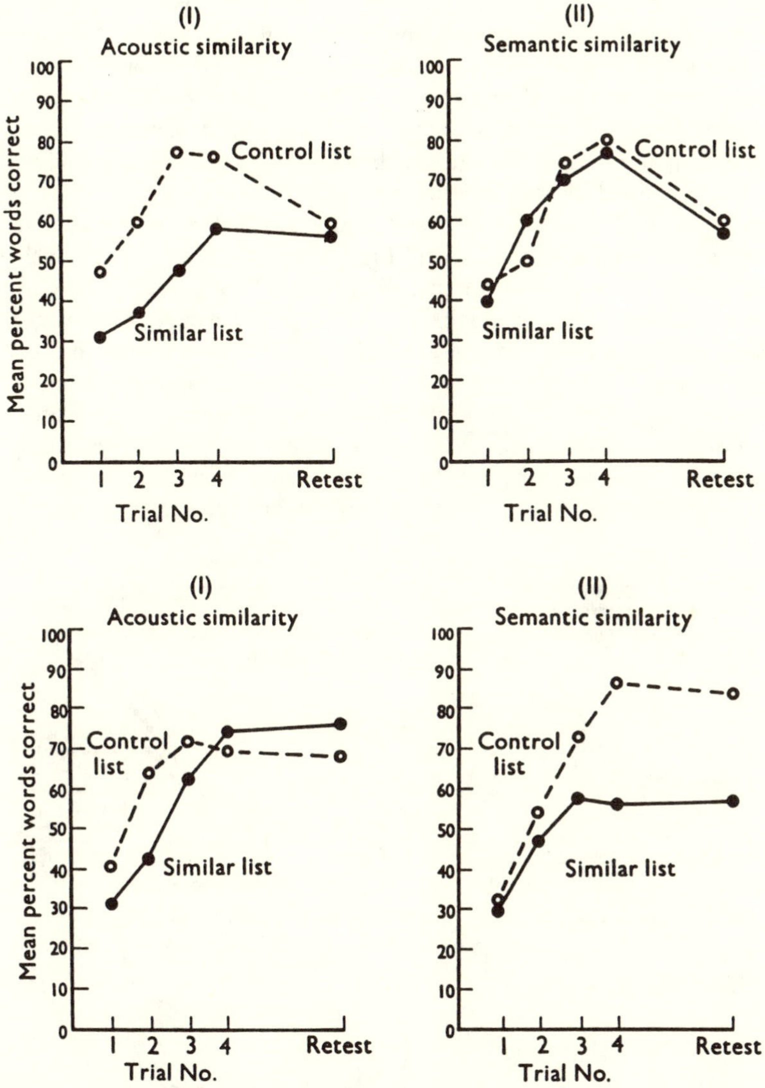

Fig. 4.3 Data on effects of similarity in an early distributed-list procedure. (From A. Baddeley, 1966, The influence of acoustic and semantic similarity on long-term memory for word sequences. *Quarterly Journal of Experimental Psychology, 18,* p. 304, Fig. 1 (top panels) & p. 307, Fig. 3 (bottom panels). Adapted by permission of *Quarterly Journal of Experimental Psychology.)*

particular replication, one- vs. three-syllable words were used. Subjects were to pronounce each item aloud as it appeared on a computer screen. In a second condition, however, the same lists were to be recalled but a through-list distractor procedure was used. Specifically, subjects were to pronounce aloud not only the words to be recalled, but also digits that appeared on the computer screen at a rapid rate of 2 per second, for intervals of 15 seconds before the first word and after each word in the list. Because of the time-consuming nature of the through-list distractor procedure, only backward recall was examined in this experiment.

The results of the immediate presentation procedure were very similar to the ones shown in the bottom half of Fig.3.2. Specifically, lists with a short second half were recalled better than lists with a long second half. Unlike previous studies of the through-list distractor procedure, however, the results of that procedure here were not like the results of immediate recall. In fact, there was no advantage of short words over long words at all.

Recency effects did occur in both procedures and cannot be attributed to short-term storage mechanisms. However, the finding that word length effects were specific to immediate recall is consistent with Baddeley's (1986) theory in which such effects depend upon a short-lived form of memory.

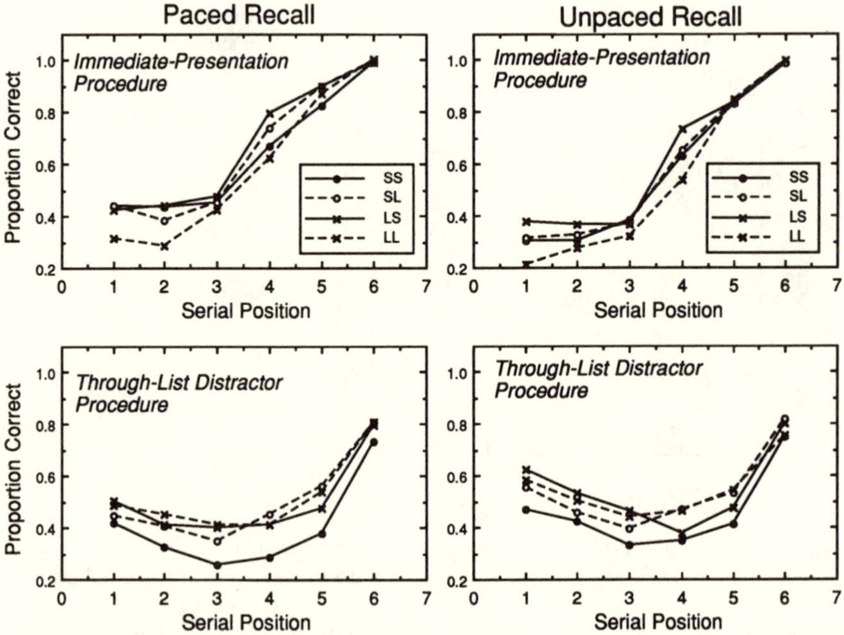

Fig. 4.4 A detailed view of the data set on which Cowan, Wood and Borne (1994) based their report. Notice that the paced and unpaced recall groups yielded almost identical patterns of means. SL = short first half-list & long second half-list; etc.

This difference between short- and long-term memory procedures thus is an answer to Broadbent's (1971) call for greater emphasis to be placed on searching for differences between short- and long-term memory procedures, rather than similarities.

It must be admitted that the critical effects were rather small, so that one still can argue that the role of short-term storage mechanisms in processing may not be overwhelmingly large. It is likely that the influence of distinctiveness cues was larger; thus there were large recency effects in the through-list distractor condition, as well as the immediate recall condition. However, the evidence for short-term memory was very clean. There were two groups of 48 subjects and, though not shown in the published article because of space limitations, the graphs of the results for those two groups were remarkably similar. These are shown in Fig. 4.4.

The difference between the procedures used for the two groups of 48 subjects was in the response protocol. Half of the subjects were to recall at a carefully controlled pace of 2 seconds per word, whereas the other subjects were to recall at any pace they wished. The absence of an effect of response pacing is inconsistent with the simple view that short-term memory decays monotonically during the recall period. It is more consistent with the theory of Cowan (1992) and of Cowan, Keller, et al. (1994), that short-term memory decays primarily while subjects are recalling a word and that little decay occurs during the silent pauses between words. The number of words to be recalled was the same regardless of the recall pacing, which can explain the absence of an effect of recall pacing.

4.2.2 Peterson & Peterson procedure reconsidered

Crowder's (1989*a*) next point of contention was the Peterson and Peterson (1959) procedure. However, the proactive interference that builds up in that procedure is at least compatible with a dual store explanation (e.g., see Cowan, 1988). The explanation would be that subjects can respond on the basis of either short- or long-term memory. When the test delay is long, the short-term representation fades and only long-term memory still may be available. After the first few trials, however, the proactive interference from previous trials renders the long-term representation of the current trial unusable, so that the trials after the first few become relatively pure indexes of short-term memory in the absence of useful contributions from long-term memory.

One would not know from current literature that the issue of proactive interference actually was considered by Peterson and Peterson (1959). It was not considered for the first few trials separately, but for successive blocks of 12 trials of a particular range of delays in Experiment 1. The results of this analysis are shown in Fig. 4.5. Over the entire experiment, it is true that the amount of decay increased steadily across trial blocks, but not because of

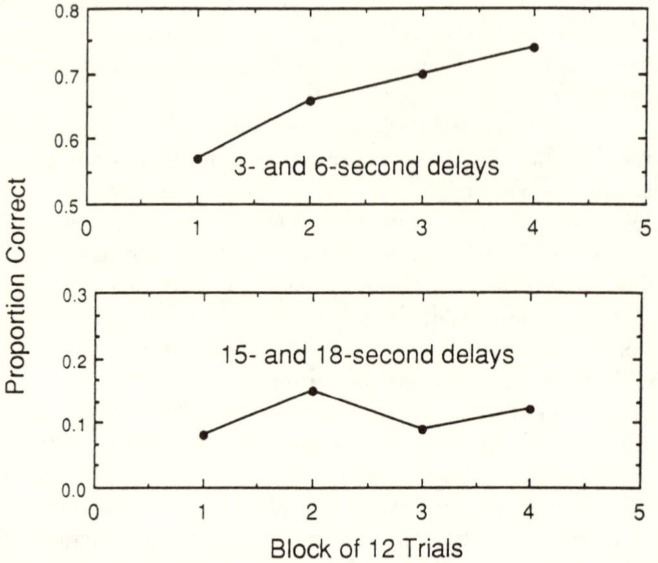

Fig. 4.5 Data on practice effects in delayed recall. (After Peterson and Peterson, 1959, Experiment 1.)

increasing proactive inhibition at the longer delays. Instead, the significant change was an increase in performance for the shorter delays, with no significant change in performance for the longer delays. It appears that subjects become better at using short-term memory with practice. In contrast, a pure interference theory with no separate short-term memory component would predict a steady decline in performance at the longer delays as interference builds.

Broadbent (1971) addressed the issue of proactive interference and other general memory principles in the Peterson and Peterson procedure, and in other short-term memory procedures, as follows (pp. 342–343):

> There remain to be considered two points urged by interference theory: the existence of effects on short-term memory from previous long-term experiences, and the continuity which seems to exist between memory at long and short periods of time. The first of these must be admitted straight away, and is perfectly consistent with a view of short-term memory as due to recirculation into and out of a decaying buffer storage ... In general one must beware of concluding that the appearance in short-term memory of an effect known from longer-term studies is evidence for identity of the two situations ... Only the success or failure of attempts to show *differences* between the two situations is of interest in distinguishing the theories.

He suggested that short- and long-term procedures involve similar mechanisms, but that the relative emphasis on a recirculation of information in and out of a buffer store will be greater in short-term procedures, with a gradual continuity rather than a sharp break between different types of procedure. Broadbent (1971) provided further analysis of various procedures of the day in this still-raging debate between monistic and dualistic views of memory.

Baddeley (1986) reviewed other studies supporting the contention that, although interference does play a role in the Peterson and Peterson procedure, it isn't everything. Conrad (1967) found that errors in this task were phonological confusions at short delays, but not at long delays. This is what would be expected if there were a transient phonological memory representation that lost some of its accuracy (at short delays) and then decayed entirely (at longer delays). Baddeley and Scott (1971) tested a very large number of subjects with a single trial each and observed forgetting as test delays increased across several seconds, although the estimated decay was less than what one would think on the basis of the work of Peterson and Peterson (1959). Thus, though it may seem unparsimonious to some to propose both a long-term interference process and a transient memory store, the data viewed in detail do appear to require this sort of two-process analysis.

There is another, related criticism that has been leveled at the Peterson and Peterson (1959) procedure. Muter (1980) questioned how much of the memory in that task depended upon subjects rapidly and intentionally encoding the items for later recall. To examine this, a computerized version of the task was used, and it included a few critical trial in which subjects had no advanced warning that they would be asked to recall the consonant trigram after the intervening task. That circumstance was achieved as follows. After each consonant trigram was presented, subjects encountered either a cue to perform a distracting task (for example, in Experiment 1, a three-digit number from which the subject was to count backward) or a 2-second blank interval followed by a cue to recall the consonant trigram ("Letters?"). On the very infrequent critical trials, however, either the Letters cue was presented immediately or the distracting task cue was presented first and then, 2, 4, or 8 seconds later, the Letters cue was unexpectedly presented. The result was that performance fell from almost 100% of the consonant trigrams correct with a 0-second delay to almost none correct (about 40% of the individual letters correct) after only a 2-second distractor-filled delay on critical trials. This was in striking contrast to the near perfect memory performance on trials with a 2-second blank delay, in which the Letters cue was expected. The implication appeared to be that, with the long-term memory encoding contribution removed in the critical trials, there was little memory left beyond what the subject was thinking about at the moment. This research would call into question the proposition (e.g., Cowan, 1988) that there is a subset of memory that is in an activated state even though it falls outside of the current focus of one's attention.

In answer to this criticism, Cunningham, Healy, Till, Fendrich, and Dimitry (1993) noted that the comparison of the 0-second delay with the next, 2-second delay and subsequent delays was not a fair one because subjects were not misled at the 0-second delay. The trials counted as 0-second-delay, "critical" trials could not be distinguished, from the subject's point of view, from the trials with a 2-second blank delay. Thus, recall at the 0-second delay was expected, unlike the critical trials at longer delays. It was between the 0- and 2-second delays where the sharp dropoff in performance occurred, and this cannot be taken as a valid decay function. Between 2 and 8 seconds, the number of trigrams correct was at floor level; but if one examines the number of consonants correct, one sees a decay function between these delays that is similar in form to that obtained in previous studies, although at a lower overall level of performance (Muter, 1980, Fig. 3). Of course, the low performance after only 2 seconds of distraction is in itself a striking result. However, one has to bear in mind that the distractor items may not only block rehearsal, but may also displace the consonants in short-term memory. Thus, the contribution of activated memory across 10 or so seconds is quite vulnerable to interference, but it does appear to exist.

4.2.3 Articulatory loop reconsidered

Crowder's next point had to do with the articulatory loop. Although it does postulate a strategic "trick" as he says, namely the use of covert rehearsal, it was designed to account for a time-dependent property of immediate serial recall; that the amount that can be remembered is linearly related to the rate at which the subject can pronounce the materials. The explanation of this finding relied critically on the existence of a phonological memory that decays over the course of a few seconds. It is not clear how one would explain this correlation in a monistic memory system. The finding of Cowan, Wood, & Borne (1994) that the word length effect did not emerge in a through-list distractor procedure also would be difficult to interpret with a monistic view.

A related point Crowder made is that the few items typically recalled in a running memory span procedure (Pollack et al., 1959; Crowder, 1969) may be of no psychological relevance. However, recall that Cowan (1988) suggested that short-term memory is composed of both an activated subset of memory and a focus of attention on just part of the activated memory. It is quite logical that running memory span would be based primarily on the information in the focus of attention, whereas larger estimates of memory span depend on methods (i.e., tricks) that permit more of the activated memory to be used in the task.

In many situations, the contents of the focus of attention might well be of more behavioral significance than the traditional memory span. It may not always be feasible to carry out strategies such as covert rehearsal in order to keep items in memory in the midst of a larger task. For example, being a good conversationalist may require a listener to draw the correct pragmatic inferences, which might in turn require that several pieces of information are kept in mind while attention continues to be devoted to the speaker, rather than to rehearsal of the critical information. If this line of conjecture is correct, then various skills in problem-solving, comprehension, and so on should show a non-negligible correlation with running memory span.

4.2.4 Hebb's approach reconsidered

Next, we revisit Hebb's notion of consolidation and the domain of neurophysiological research. Although there may be no evidence for the process of memory consolidation *per se*, there also is no evidence against it. Even Crowder (1993) remarked that some such process must exist, although he questioned its behavioral relevance. However, recent findings in neurophysiology reveal that a stimulus produces a localized burst of neural activity in the primary sensory cortex, which outlives the stimulus by several seconds and then fades away (Lü et al., 1992*a*, 1992*b*; Näätänen, 1992; Sams et al., 1993). At least some of this neural activity appears to be behaviorally relevant. Subjects display a mismatch negativity to stimulus contrasts that they can behaviorally discriminate, but not to contrasts that they cannot discriminate (Näätänen, 1991). The relevance of this neural activity to memory *per se* is circumstantial, but it does seem to be the case that the behavioral decline in memory over time (Eriksen & Johnson, 1964; Pisoni, 1973; Cowan et al., 1990; Sams et al., 1993) covers about the same time course as the decay of the neurophysiological activity (Lü et al., 1992*b*; Sams et al., 1993). It is hard to see how this neural activity could reflect just the distinctiveness of the upcoming item relative to the list.

In the area of amnesic deficits, the interpretation of human evidence is complicated by the lack of experimental control over the deficits. However, a study in rats conducted by Meck, Church, Wenk, and Olton (1987) provides an interesting model of human amnesia. Animals were placed in a delayed response procedure in which they had to press a bar 40 seconds after the beginning of a warning signal in order to receive a food reward. If the warning stimulus is temporarily turned off and then back on (e.g., for 10 seconds), normal rats will delay their bar presses by the duration for which the warning was turned off. Thus, the animals appear to keep a memory record of the warning stimulus that is carried over across the blank interval. The same was true for rats with frontal lobe ablations, suggesting that this ability does not place excessive demands on attention (unlike some other manipulations that Olton, 1989 discussed). However, in another group of rats, the neural tracts to and from the hippocampal regions were cut (similar to the critical lesions in amnesic patients). These rats reset their internal clock after the gap. This suggests that they failed to recall the information that occurred before the gap. Again, it is difficult to see how to interpret this kind of finding in terms of the lack of contextual coding of information in the hippocampal animals, as Crowder's theory would have it.

4.2.5 Detailed models of short-term memory phenomena

A final research area that might be examined for evidence of the monistic vs. dualistic nature of memory is on detailed mathematical and computer-based simulations. It is only recently that researchers have attempted to model the phenomena that I have taken to reflect temporary memory decay, the most important of which is the word length effect (see Baddeley, 1986). The question is whether researchers have found it necessary to posit a temporary memory to model this effect, or not.

In one type of model, each item is represented in memory by a matrix of features (e.g., see Pike, 1986). Nairne (1990) presented a feature-based model of immediate memory that posited no decay of memory on the basis of time alone; all memory loss was caused instead by interference. A primary memory vector of each stimulus, susceptible to degradation through interference from items with similar features, was compared to a non-degraded secondary memory representation. With too much degradation, the primary memory representation no longer matches the secondary memory representation and cannot be used in recall. This model accounted well for modality and phonological similarity effects. However, it appeared to flounder when it came to word length effects. To account for those effects, it was suggested that the representation of item positions is perturbed with the passage of time as suggested in the model of Estes (1972) and Lee and Estes (1981). However, in retrospect it is doubtful that the perturbation process occurs on the basis of temporal decay, given Nairne's (1992) finding that the loss of positional certainty continues in the long term. This is important, but it leaves the Nairne (1990) model without a viable mechanism to account for word length effects—unless a decaying source of memory is independently added to the model.

A major attempt to model serial order learning (Lewandowsky & Murdock, 1989) involved the convolution of item representations together into a common memory trace. This was successful in modeling serial order learning (although, see Pike, 1986) without the use of the concept of temporary memory activation. However, it did not address word length effects.

Another recent type of approach uses connectionist models. Brown and Hulme (1993) suggested one such model to account for short-term memory phenomena. To account for serial order learning, their approach incorporated concepts from Lewandowsky and Murdock. However, they did endorse the concept of memory activation. As they put it (pp. 122–123):

... short-term memory capacity is an essential part of any recurrent net, because any new input to a net must be accompanied by some context-giving representation of the recent outputs of the net. The network usually represents (in its 'state' or 'context' units) some function of the recent history of the network outputs. It should therefore be theoretically possible to reconstruct from the state units the previous outputs of the network.

Finally, the most explicit attempt to deal with the word length effect and other short-term memory phenomena in a simulation model (Burgess & Hitch, 1992) is another network model that explicitly incorporates the notion of activation that decays with time.

4.3 Where do we search for short-term memory?

If anything is clear from this discussion, it is that a definite priority for research in short-term memory has been established. The most important research can forget about the niceties of particular theories and focus on experiments that might shed further light on whether short- and long-term memory storage is carried out by two separate types of neural mechanism or not.

Perhaps the most difficult aspect of this research goal is that short- and long-term memory could function separately but still could produce similar phenomena. From the point of view of Hebb (1949) or Cowan (1988), that is what one would expect if short-term memory representations consisted of electrochemical patterns of activity, that later were transformed into long-term memories consisting of neural growth resulting from those electrochemical patterns and permitting the pattern to be reinvoked at a later date. For example, the long-term recency effect could be produced at the time of retrieval as the list structure is transferred from long-term storage to short-term storage. The information about the absolute durations in the list may be inconsequential at that time, so that the structure transferred to short-term storage now looks like an ordinary list from the point of view of the conscious processing system.

There may be a problem in using various types of explicit recall to index a time-limited short-term memory, because there always will be a confounding between time and context. (A relevant discussion of this point is provided by Neill, Valdes, Terry, and Gorfein, 1992). As time passes, what is the important change, the decay of information or the change in the temporal context? One way to distinguish between these mechanisms might be to use measures that typically are found to be context-free.

Priming is a process that usually is preserved even in amnesiacs who do not appear able to make use of contextual cues to recall (Schacter, 1987; Squire, 1987). If one observes the decline of priming over time, that should reflect a decay of the relevant information rather than a change of context.

Anderson (1983, p. 104) reviewed research on the decay of semantic priming and concluded that the estimates of the half-life of activation range from 400 ms to 4 seconds. Assuming that useful information exists somewhat beyond the half-life, these estimates are within the range of the typical assumptions about the duration of short-term memory. Within the model of Cowan (1988), this would reflect the rate of loss of activation when the activated information no longer is in the focus of attention.

Given that the focus of attention is not the issue here, perhaps we would only like to count as relevant the portion of the priming effect that is due to automatic memory activation. Neely (1977) has demonstrated one way in which that process can be separated from the priming based on conscious expectations. In a prototypical priming experiment, the subject might come to expect a target to be related to a preceding prime. However, Neely presented some conditions in which a semantically unrelated prime was expected (e.g., "expect a bird to be followed by a type of furniture"). The subject's expectations were met on 80% of the trials. The finding was that semantic relatedness played a large role in priming at short intervals between the prime and target, whereas conscious expectations appeared to play more of a role at longer intervals. The apparent dissipation of automatic semantic activation was in the same range as the one that Anderson suggested.

Until recently, one also might have considered negative priming (Allport, Tipper, & Chmiel, 1985) to reflect a variety of automatic memory activation. The basic situation is a dual-stimulus situation in which each trial includes both a relevant and a related but irrelevant stimulus, as in the well-known Stroop (1935) task in which subjects must quickly name the color of ink used to write conflicting color words (e.g., name the ink color "red" when the red ink forms the printed word "blue"). However, to demonstrate negative priming, an irrelevant stimulus from trial n–1 is made identical to the relevant stimulus in Trial n. For example, in the Stroop situation the word "red" in blue ink could be followed by the word "green" in red ink. On average, the mean reaction time in this red-relevant trial is slowed by the fact that it was immediately preceded by an irrelevant presentation of the word that now has become the correct response. The original interpretation of this finding was that there is an active attentional inhibition process that reduces the activation of the elements below their baseline level. Thus, the irrelevance of certain items could in itself constitute a type of information in activated memory. Neill and Valdes (1992) showed that negative priming declines for several seconds as the interval between the irrelevant and relevant presentations of the repeated information increases.

The results of a subsequent study by Neill et al. (1992) argue against this interpretation, however. They found that negative priming depends not only on the interval between the irrelevant and relevant information (that is, the interval between Trials n–1 and n), but also on the previous interval between trials (that is, between Trials n–2 and n–1). When the interval between trials is held fixed within a series, little decay of negative priming is observed. This result was interpreted by Neill et al. according to a new theory of negative priming based on the distinctiveness of the negative priming trial (*n*–1). The more temporally distinct this trial is from the preceding one, the more likely it is that the inhibiting information will be retrieved at the time of test.

Perhaps the logic of priming and short-term memory will turn out to be similar to the logic of unattended stimuli and short-term memory. Neill et al. (1992, p. 998) pointed out that several studies indicate that negative priming is eliminated when the prior prime is followed by a pattern mask and thereby made unavailable for conscious report, and that positive associative priming effects are obtained instead. By removing the prime from the focus of attention, the pattern mask may weaken or eliminate the contextual, episodic information about the prime, although neural activation remains. Thus, automatic activation and unattended speech may turn out to be two ways to examine short-term memory free of the contextual distinctiveness cues that allow some of the other "short-term memory procedures" to be mimicked by features of long-term memory.

4.4 Refrain: what is short-term memory?

In case one wanted to talk of short-term memory as a structure that is separate from long-term memory, Cowan (1988) explained why that seems improbable. Basically, incoming information must make contact with the long-term knowledge store in order for it to be categorically coded. Moreover, it seems clear that at least some of this coding (at the very least, some of the physical coding) occurs automatically, without the involvement of attention. The coded information at some point must count as activated information outside of the focus of attention. The behavioral and physiological data suggest that there probably is a time limit on this automatically held information.

Short-term memory then would be viewed as a hierarchical set of processes occurring within memory. A large amount of information can be activated and automatically held, but with a time limit in the range of seconds. A small subset of this activated information falls within the current focus of the subject's attention. Short-term memory often has been described as the focus of attention (James, 1890) or the sum of the activated information (Hebb, 1949), but it is better viewed as both of these together (Cowan, 1988; also see Baddeley, 1986) and not to assume that they are synonymous.

It might be said that the view of short-term memory as activated and attended subsets of memory is midway between the view that short- and long-term memory stores are completely separate (e.g., Shallice & Warrington, 1970) and the truly monistic view in which there is only one type of memory with one set of rules. More work will be needed to distinguish between these views. Notice, though, that parsimony may no longer be on the side of the monistic memory view, given that many different concepts would have to be invoked within such a view to explain the full range of phenomena described in this chapter. The burden of proof appears to have shifted back to the monistic camp.

Part II

Selective Attention Phenomena

5. Attentional filtering and orienting

> That the stopping of an unfelt stimulus may itself be felt is a well-known fact: the sleeper in church who wakes when the sermon ends; the miller who does the same when his wheel stands still, are stock examples. Now (since every impression falling on the nervous system must propagate itself somewhither), Müller suggests that impressions which come to us when the thought-centres are preoccupied with other matters may thereby be blocked or inhibited from invading these centres, and may then overflow into lower paths of discharge.
>
> William James (1890)
> in *Psychology*, p. 457

Cognitive researchers have long marveled at humans' ability to fix attention rather easily on one stream or "channel" of stimuli out of a larger spatiotemporal array, provided that the channel is distinguished from all other concurrent stimuli by physical characteristics such as the spatial location, voice quality, or color of the information in that channel (Broadbent, 1958). This ability is purchased with the also remarkable inability to learn very much about the unattended stimuli, except for some of the material that occupied the last few seconds before a recall cue (e.g., Norman, 1969; Glucksberg & Cowen, 1970). On the other hand, Cherry (1953) found that subjects did notice a change of the speaker's voice in an unattended speech channel, although they usually did not notice changes in the language spoken or in the topic of discussion within that unattended channel.

The problem of attentional filtering will be examined in detail in this chapter. It will be proposed, in accord with Cowan (1988), that the concept of the habituation of orienting helps in addressing many of the problematic aspects of attentional filtering. Nevertheless, there are unresolved issues about the mechanisms of attention and habituation that also will be discussed.

5.1 The problem of attentional filtering

This specific pattern of human abilities and limitations inspired Broadbent's (1958) suggestion that most stimuli are filtered out by the attentional system before they can reach short-term memory, which was conceived as a limited-capacity storage system. All stimuli presumably are registered in sensory storage and receive a primitive feature analysis at that stage, but only a limited amount can pass through the filter and therefore receive a more complete, physical and semantic analysis and be included in the focus of the subject's attentive processing.

Much of the modern research on selective attention has been a reaction to Broadbent's hypothesis. A great deal of research has suggested that some semantic features can be extracted from stimuli without any allocation of attention to these stimuli. Some researchers (Deutsch & Deutsch, 1963; Duncan, 1980) made the counter-proposition that all stimuli are completely analyzed and that observed limits in processing occur because the subject is unable to respond to all stimuli at once. This has been termed a "late-filter theory" (because the attentional limitation was said to occur late in the progression of processing from stimulus to response) as a contrast to Broadbent's theory, which has been dubbed an "early filter theory." Other researchers (Treisman, 1964*a*, 1964*b*, 1964*c*; Norman, 1968) took an intermediate stance. Treisman proposed that the stimuli in unattended channels do reach the processing system, but only in an attenuated form. Differences between the thresholds of different items in long-term memory determine whether or not a particular attenuated input causes semantic activation strong enough to influence the subject's responses. For example, one's name would have a particularly low threshold of activation, so that hearing one's name in an unattended auditory channel often should attract the subject's attention, as Moray (1959) reported. Norman (1968, p. 528) similarly suggested that "nonattended inputs remain only partially interpreted." For example, he thought that language might be decoded to the morpheme or word level, but not integrated across these units into more meaningful messages.

Given that the allocation of attention is very difficult to measure, Holender (1986) was able to cast a reasonable doubt on the conclusion that there is some semantic analysis of unattended stimuli, and to assert in his extensive review that adequate data still do not exist, even after decades of research on the question. Cowan (1988) also reviewed the literature and noted shortcomings in the methods of many early experiments, including those of Moray (1959) and Treisman (1964*a*); but, on the whole, the evidence did seem to favor some intermediate-level filter, in general agreement with Norman and with Treisman.

The problem addressed by Holender (1986) actually was slightly different from the problem of the level of the selective attentional filter. Holender's question was whether semantic activation can occur without concomitant awareness of the material. Assuming that the answer is "no," as Holender suggested, there still is the question of whether attention must precede semantic activation or whether semantic activation can come first, provoking an attention shift. There is some evidence suggesting that the latter may occur (e.g., Treisman, Squire, & Green, 1974; Yates & Thul, 1979; Wood & Cowan, in press). Nevertheless, this issue is difficult for the same reason that

Holender's issue is difficult: there is no foolproof, complete measure of the allocation of attention.

What is agreed upon in all of the models of selective attention is that some information is extracted from each incoming stimulus. In the late- or intermediate-filter models, the extracted information includes the activation, or tagging as relevant, of at least some of the semantic features of long-term memory that describe the incoming stimuli. According to the early-filter model, it is restricted to physical features of the stimuli. However, these still might be considered part of long-term memory. Although there are some seemingly innate feature detectors for some physical features (e.g., Hubel & Wiesel, 1963), feature detectors appear to be tuned by early experience (e.g., Werker & Tees, 1984).

Cowan (1988) maintained that, if we wish to propose that incoming stimuli automatically make contact with and activate features in long-term memory (no matter whether the semantic features are activated along with physical ones or not), then Broadbent's (1958) linear representation of processing is not ideal. In Broadbent's model, information appears to make contact with long-term memory only through the mechanism of short-term memory, which itself was conceived as a limited-capacity processor. There was no provision for the automatic activation of memory elements without the involvement of attention. That aspect of processing is better represented by a scheme in which the incoming stimuli automatically make contact with long-term memory and activate some elements, as in the views of Treisman (1964*a*), Norman (1968), and Cowan (1988). One can hold such a view while leaving open the question of just how much of the semantic memory system can be activated through this automatic process.

Next, one is faced with the question of where to put attention back into the system. In doing so, Treisman (1964*b*) considered that automatically activated information can attract attention. Cowan (1988) incorporated this point into a model in which three entities were represented hierarchically. Currently activated memory elements were represented as a subset of long-term memory, and the focus of attention was represented in turn as a subset of the currently activated memory elements.

Cowan's model was left deliberately vague on the question of what quality is necessary for an element to be included in the focus of attention. It may be that elements activated beyond a certain level automatically enter the focus of attention (which assumes that there is some way to quantify the level of activation, say through the amount of priming resulting from that activation), but it also is possible that there is some qualitative difference between attended and unattended memory elements that cannot be reduced to a quantitative measure of the amount of activation. For example, according to Schacter's (1989) suggestion, attention and awareness might result from a process in which signals from disparate parts of the brain are conveyed to certain areas in the parietal lobes. Damage to those areas results in deficits in awareness without any obvious deficits in automatic, unaware processing of the information.

5.2 Habituation of orienting as a selective filter

Cowan (1988) tied together two research literatures. The literature on selective attention introduced by Cherry (1953), Broadbent (1958), Moray (1959), and Treisman (1964*a*, 1964*b*) deals with the factors determining the direction of attention (among other issues). That is partly under the subject's control, but it is partly beyond control (for example, when there is a particularly salient stimulus that breaks through a monotonous background). The second literature, on the orienting of attention (Sokolov, 1963), deals with the physiological and behavioral mechanisms that accompany shifts of attention, whether or not they happen to be under the subject's control.

Although many stimulus conditions may cause orienting, they appear to reduce to two situations: stimulus novelty, and stimulus significance for the organism. The orienting response is most easily observed when elicited by a novel stimulus imposed on a monotonous background, such as a tone breaking into a silent background, or perhaps a sudden shift in the color of the room lighting. However, more subtle novelty in the pattern of stimulation also can evoke an orienting response, and it presumably can be evoked by stimulus significance (Öhman, 1979; Gati & Ben-Shakhar, 1990) as defined either by the task (for example, a stimulus that yielded a shock last time it was presented) or by the subject's pre-experimental dispositions (for example, the subject's own name).

The orienting response includes several indicants: behavioral quieting; often, adjustment of head and eye position, and ear position in some animals, so as to be maximally sensitive to further stimulation from the same source; activity in the parasympathetic nervous system, including a momentary slowing of heart rate and a momentary reduction in skin conductance; and evidence of high-priority processing of the eliciting stimulus. Repetitions of the eliciting stimulus result in a reduction or "habituation" of the orienting response.

Sokolov's (1963) theory behind the orienting response is that it allows a neural model of the stimulation to be formed. (That is to say, some spatiotemporal pattern of nerve cell firing is established that occurs uniquely and nonrandomly as a response to the particular stimulus features that are present, thus representing those features in memory.) Each incoming stimulus is compared with the neural model and elicits an orienting response only if (1) the neural model is not yet developed enough to describe the stimulus, or (2) the stimulus has changed in a way that makes it discrepant from the neural model.

It seems worth noting at this point that the relation of attention to the formation of a neural model is not yet well worked out. Sokolov's model appears to imply that the neural model of a stimulus ceases to develop further at the same time that attention to the stimulus ceases, and that no refinement of the neural model can take place in the absence of attention. On the other hand, Näätänen's (1990, 1992) theory of information processing underlying the mismatch negativity component of brain potentials includes the assumption that a sensory analysis of the stimulus (resulting in a kind of neural model) proceeds in the absence of attention. Näätänen's conclusion has, however, been disputed by other researchers (Woldorff et al., 1991; Trejo, Ryan-Jones, & Kramer, 1992) who have shown an effect of attention on the magnitude of the mismatch negativity and even may believe that the mismatch negativity would not occur if there were absolutely no attention devoted to the channel that the subject is supposed to ignore.

Regardless of whether the neural model continues to develop in the absence of attention, the exciting relevance of the orienting response and its habituation is that these processes can serve, along with the subject's voluntary attentive processes, as a plausible mechanism for both Broadbent's attentional filter and Treisman's leakage of unattended information through that filter. Orienting presumably works in combination with effortful, attentive processing to define the overall distribution of attention (Kahneman, 1973; Posner, 1980). As Cowan (1988) proposed, all incoming stimulation makes contact with long-term memory and activates some of the relevant features, although it is not yet certain if this includes semantic features (Holender, 1986). Newly activated features presumably tend to attract attention; that is, to cause orienting. However, with repetition of a stimulus or simple stimulus pattern, there is habituation of this orienting response so that attention no longer is automatically recruited. When this happens, the subject is free to select among the activated elements using voluntary attentional processes, without strong competition from external distractors. Of course, a compelling speaker may use the orienting response repeatedly to direct attention toward, rather than away from, the source to which the listeners presumably are voluntarily trying to attend as well. With a monotonous speaker, on the other hand, one must struggle harder to maintain attention even if the semantic content of the speech is quite interesting.

With habituation of orienting as an attentional filter, it appears that no other automatic attentional filter is necessary. This habituation-based account of attentional filtering can address some basic aspects of attention that otherwise have remained puzzling. One is that subjects appear consistently to notice gross changes in an unattended stimulus channel. According to Broadbent's (1958) early-filter theory it is not very clear why they should be able to do that. It is true that some sensory analysis must precede the attentional filter or be incorporated into it, in order for the filter to know what stimuli fit a specific selection criterion. However, that would not explain how subjects would notice a change that was irrelevant to the selection criterion. For example, assume that the subject's task is to attend to some demanding visual stimuli and ignore auditory stimuli. A change in the voice of the unattended auditory stimuli does not make the sounds any more relevant to the selection criteria, and therefore should continue to be rejected. Yet, such changes are easily noticed.

A late-filter theory also can explain why physical changes are noticed, because such changes make contact with long-term memory. However, according to the late-filter view it is not clear why semantic changes are not also easily noticed, assuming that the incoming information makes contact with semantic as well as physical features in memory.

The explanation according to the habituation theory is that the subject's neural model of the unattended stimuli can be compared with new stimuli only on the basis of automatically analyzed features of the new stimuli, which are primarily physical in nature. Therefore, a change in the physical features is much more likely to create a detectable discrepancy from the neural model, leading to dishabituation of the orienting response, than is a change in semantic characteristics that is not accompanied by blatant physical changes.

The theoretical view described here and by Cowan (1988) also can account for effortful, as well as effortless, forms of attention. Johnston and Heinz (1978) found that subjects could attend selectively on the basis of semantic features, although with more effort and less efficiency than is found with attention to physical features. In a well-developed set of experiments, a binaurally-presented tape recording included two concurrent speeches that differed in the speaker's voice only, in topic only, or in both voice and topic. Subjects were to shadow (repeat) one channel and to perform a subsidiary task, pressing a key as quickly as possible whenever a visual signal was presented. The visual reaction time served as a measure of attentional allocation. The finding was that the reaction times were shorter when a physical cue was present than when it was absent, with little added benefit of semantic separation between the channels.

According to the habituation model, voluntary selective attention always requires an effortful selection process. However, this process can be assisted by the neural model of all of the stimuli. Because there are multiple channels, it is not possible for all of the neural comparison processes to include all of the semantic properties of the stimuli. For selective attention on a purely semantic basis, the potentially relevant information must be effortfully coded in order for the correct items to be identified. In the case of selective attention based on physical features, however, the necessary codes are already activated in memory and the voluntary task is limited to further processing of the stimuli with the desired features. It should be noted that event-related brain potentials also have revealed a distinction between components that can be observed for discriminations made on a physical basis (N2) vs. a semantic basis (N400) (Kutas & Hillyard, 1980; Deacon, Breton, Ritter, & Vaughan, 1991).

Johnston and Heinz (1978, Experiment 2) further supported the notion that physical selection is relatively effortless. They compared a condition in which there was one channel to be ignored (two channels total) with a condition in which there were two channels to be ignored (three channels total). In the latter condition, the to-be-attended channel was presented in a female voice and the to-be-ignored channels, in two different male voices. Almost identical probe reaction times resulted in the two- and three-channel situations. This would not be expected if it took an independent effort to filter out each channel, but it is expected according to a habituation theory in which the maintenance of a neural model is automatic and effort is needed only to focus attention voluntarily on one channel, despite its habituation along with the other channel or channels. This topic will be taken up again later on, in a discussion of a prior, more extensive study of the effects of multiple irrelevant channels on attention (Treisman, 1964*a*).

Although the orienting response has been associated here with an involuntary shift of attention, in theory there also could be an orienting response accompanying the voluntary control of attention. However, it often would not show up in autonomic indices of attention because it would no longer be time-locked to every stimulus. A slow, tonic component of attention spanning a number of stimulus presentations can be hard to measure. What is easier to measure is the attentional response to a stimulus that has been given significance within the experimental setup. For example, a subject who is supposed to count the high tones but ignore the low tones could show an orienting response selectively to high tones, even if they were rather frequent in the stimulus stream. If the tones are presented too quickly for heart rate or skin conductance measures to be observed, a related response still can be observed in the form of attentional components of event-related, electrical brain potentials recorded from the scalp (Näätänen, 1992). Thus, the focus of attention at any time would depend upon the competition between voluntary and involuntary forces acting upon a common attentional orienting system.

5.3 Evidence linking orienting and selective attention

The evidence relating the orienting response to attentional selectivity will be presented in several subsections. The first three subsections strive to establish the relation between orienting and selective attention. Specifically, it will be argued that (1) habituation of orienting to a stimulus limits the effect that this stimulus subsequently can have as a distractor in a selective listening task, (2) introducing a new element into the unattended stream of stimuli attracts attention, and (3) habituation of orienting is accompanied by a neural model of the stimulus that can be of use in selective attention.

The next three sections strive to establish the conditions under which orienting and its habituation and dishabituation can occur. They examine (4) the codes that are included in vs. excluded from the neural model used in the habituation of orienting, (5) the characteristics of novelty and significance that appear critical for dishabituation of orienting, and (6) the involvement of the active attentional focus in orienting. Last, (7) some possible objections to the hypothesis of habituation of orienting as an attentional filter will be addressed. Many (although not all) of these areas were addressed by Cowan (1988), but there has been important progress since that time. Below, I will briefly explain the older evidence but focus on the newer evidence in each area.

5.3.1 Effects of habituation to unattended stimuli

Mackworth (1969) suggested that habituation of the orienting response serves as a selection device. She noted that the neural model built up to a stimulus "acts as a selective filter, inhibiting reaction to a stimulus which closely matches it." Waters, McDonald, and Koresko (1977) may have been the first to test this concept. They used a primary task in which subjects were to solve a set of arithmetic problems presented aurally in a male voice. In some conditions, subjects simultaneously heard two-digit numbers and arithmetic symbols that were presented in a female voice as a distractor. Subjects who had been exposed to this distracting tape ahead of time oriented to it less during the arithmetic task (according to a skin conductance measure), and performed better on the first few arithmetic problems, than did subjects who had been exposed to a tone or no tape ahead of time.

The behavioral results for the first 3 trials are illustrated in Fig. 5.1. Performance was best in a control group of subjects who received the voice

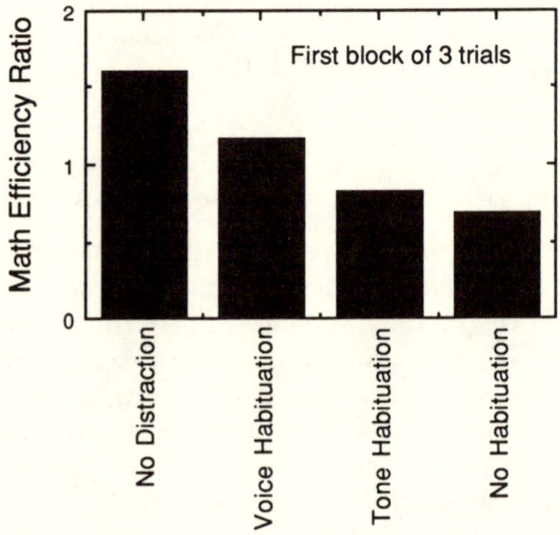

Fig. 5.1 Data on habituation of distractors. (After Waters et al., 1977.)

or tone tape as a habituating stimulus, but then did not receive any distracting sounds during the math problems. Among three groups who received voice distraction during the math problems, performance was best following habituation to the same voice tape, poorer following habituation instead to a tone, and poorer still following no habituation at all. The significant voice/tone distinction is the critical one. Apparently habituation is relatively rapid, inasmuch as the difference disappeared by the second block of 3 trials.

Comparable behavioral results were obtained by Lorch, Anderson, and Well (1984) and by Lorch and Horn (1986) with pre-exposure to picture stimuli that would serve as distractors in a speeded classification task. Thus, the finding of benefits of habituating pre-exposures is similar across the auditory and visual modalities.

Morris and Jones (1990) showed that habituation of orienting to a distracting channel of stimulation can play a role also in a short-term memory task. Previously, Salamé and Baddeley (1982) had demonstrated that recall of a list of visually presented verbal items is impaired by the concurrent presentation of irrelevant speech sounds. Morris and Jones repeated this type of manipulation, using Italian prose as the irrelevant speech. However, before the memory task in the presence of the irrelevant speech, subjects listened to 20 minutes of one of four habituating tapes: Italian prose, English prose, humming (all three in the same voice as the irrelevant speech would be), or pink (band-limited) noise. A clear irrelevant speech effect was obtained only in the pink noise condition, which appears to suggest that prior exposure to merely the basic voice characteristics of the irrelevant speech was enough to prevent an irrelevant speech effect.

The results of Morris and Jones actually present what might be viewed as a theoretical puzzle for the working memory theory of Baddeley (1986). Within that account, the irrelevant speech interference effect is said to occur because the irrelevant speech is automatically entered into phonological storage, a process that has nothing to do with attentional recruitment by the irrelevant speech. Baddeley supported this automatic-entry hypothesis by two observations. First, irrelevant speech cannot be ignored and was found to be more damaging when it was phonologically similar to the attended, visual items (Salamé & Baddeley, 1982). Second, the detrimental effect of phonological similarity among items to be recalled can be eliminated through articulatory suppression if the items to be remembered are presented visually, but not if they are presented auditorily; presumably, the formation of short-term phonological storage can be blocked only for visual lists (Peterson & Johnson, 1971; Cowan et al., 1987). What is the correct explanation of the irrelevant speech effect, automatic short-term memory contamination or the recruitment of attention away from the visually presented stimuli to be recalled?

Jones, Madden, and Miles (1992) and Jones and Macken (1993) have obtained findings that improved the understanding of the irrelevant speech effect, though they could be accounted for either by a type of corruption of phonological short-term memory (in terms of Cowan, 1988, corruption of activated memory) or by attentional recruitment (in terms of Cowan, 1988, corruption of the focus of attention). Specifically, interference with memory for visually presented verbal items was caused not only by irrelevant speech, but also by irrelevant tones provided that there were multiple sound onsets rather than a steady tone; and little if any irrelevant speech effect resulted from a steady-state vowel. Jones and his colleagues account for these effects with an "object-oriented episodic record" model in which the irrelevant sounds enter the record that is used for the memory task every time there is a change in the physical state of the sounds. However, a change in the physical state is also the likely precondition for the orienting of attention (e.g., Sokolov, 1963; Cowan, 1988). In fact, some researchers have suggested that the entry of a new object into the memory record is precisely what captures attention. Thus, in summarizing his work on the conditions leading to the visual capture of attention, Yantis (1993, p. 161) stated that "new object files are created by abrupt visual onsets or any perceptual event that segregates an element from its background." This suggests that, in the irrelevant speech effect, it is going to be difficult to separate the roles of automatic short-term memory contamination and attentional recruitment away from the stimuli to be recalled.

It is not even clear any more if there is any role of automatic memory contamination at all. Jones and Macken (in press) have called into question the effect of phonological similarity between the relevant printed and irrelevant spoken materials. They note that Salamé and Baddeley (1982) used monosyllabic words for their printed materials and phonologically similar irrelevant speech, but disyllabic words for their phonologically dissimilar irrelevant speech. The disyllabic speech could have interfered less only because the rate of word presentation was slower. Jones and Macken used all monosyllabic words and still manipulated two kinds of phonological similarity. They manipulated the phonological similarity of items within the relevant printed channel and within the irrelevant spoken channel, and they also manipulated the similarity between the relevant and irrelevant channels. The finding was that between-channel similarity made very little difference, whereas the effect of within-channel similarity made a much larger difference. The authors appeal to the object-oriented episodic record model as their favored interpretation, but attentional recruitment to changing irrelevant stimuli could account for them also.

Separate roles of contamination of a short-term memory representation, on one hand, and recruitment of attention away from the relevant stimuli, on the other, is beginning to become clearer in work on another type of irrelevant speech, the "cross-modal Stroop effect" of Cowan and Barron

(1987). They replicated the well-known color-word interference effect but also found an additional detrimental effect of conflicting spoken color words. The set of color names presented in the irrelevant auditory channel was the same as the set used as color responses, but the irrelevant color words were presented in an order and timing that was unrelated to the visual stimuli or to the correct responses. This effect is more restricted than the irrelevant speech effect of Salamé and Baddeley (1982), in that no cross-modal effect was obtained across trials with words that were unrelated to color words. Other demonstrations of auditory–visual, cross-modal interference effects also exist in previous literature (Morton, 1969; Greenwald, 1972; Lewis, 1972; Navon, 1977).

Cowan and Barron (1987) suggested that the cross-modal Stroop-like effect may reflect interference within a pre-speech memory buffer, given that a similar previous study using a button-press response produced no effect (Thackray & Jones, 1971). Dyer (1973, p. 107) reported a similar failure but the response mode was not specified. Another critical factor may be that, in the tapes of Cowan and Barron, the visually presented colors and spoken color words did not always conflict. At any time, there was a 1/5 chance that the items in the two modalities would match, perhaps increasing the difficulty of ignoring the spoken color words at other times. This is an unresolved methodological issue at present.

Subsequent work with a procedure modeled after Cowan and Barron has suggested, however, that there may be a temporary attentional distraction effect regardless of the identity of the irrelevant speech sounds, superimposed on a longer-lasting, automatic memory contamination effect for irrelevant color words. Cowan (1989) presented a replication of the cross-modal effect in which responses were especially slow at first because the color words that the subjects were instructed to use were relatively rare ones: *lime, crimson, sepia, beige, turquoise,* and *lavender.* There were two color audiotapes, one containing *lime, crimson, and sepia* and the other containing *beige, turquoise,* and *lavender.* There also were tapes of matched non-color adjectives: one containing *dire, smothered,* and *changeable*, and the other containing *strict, lesser,* and *dastardly.* On each trial, 16 colors were to be named. The experiment was organized into 4 blocks of 10 trials, with color-tape blocks alternating with control-tape blocks.

For all trial blocks, the speed of performance increased across trials within a block as subjects got used to the irrelevant channel. (The range was from about 800 ms per word at the beginning of the experiment to about 600 ms per word at the end.) However, this improvement across trials in a block was obtained equally for the color-word and noncolor-word tapes. The magnitude of the difference in performance with the two types of tapes, which is what was meant by the cross-modal Stroop effect, was about 20 ms per word across trials.

Miles and Jones (1989) stated that they failed to replicate the results of Cowan (1989), but they did not provide enough methodological detail to determine why the attempt may have failed. We have replicated the effect in two additional experiments (Cowan et al., 1994) that also clarify the origins of irrelevant speech effects in a cross-modal Stroop procedure.

The procedure was similar to the one described above, except that the subjects also heard 30 seconds of an audiotape before each cross-modal Stroop trial. Each audiotape presented before the Stroop trial shared some or all of the features of the items on the following distractor tape. During this pre-exposure period, subjects had to attend closely to the audiotape, tallying the number of presentations of each word. Sometimes the pre-exposure audiotape was identical to the tape to be used as a distractor. In other trial blocks, the tapes were produced in the same voice, but contained different subsets of the words. For example, some subjects heard randomized presentations of *lime, crimson,* and *sepia* in the pre-exposure period followed by *beige, turquoise,* and *lavender* as distractors during color naming. For other subjects, the words always were the same during pre-exposure and color-naming test phases of a trial, but they sometimes were presented in different voices during those phases.

Regardless of the nature of the pre-exposure period, color-naming performance was better in the presence of non-color than color words. This cross-modal interference effect persisted across the experiment and was superimposed on a practice effect in both conditions. No effect of pre-exposures was significant across the experiment. However, there were some significant effects of pre-exposure in Block 1 of each subject's data. When the pre-exposure was composed of the same words as the distractor tape, but in a different voice, this was worse for performance than when the pre-exposure and test tapes were identical, by 150 ms in the first trial. This effect occurred for subjects who received either color or noncolor audiotapes in this first trial block. When the pre-exposure was made in the same voice as the distractor but was composed of different words, this was helpful to performance in the first trial block, relative to the case of identical pre-exposure and test tapes, by 110 ms on the average. Again, this occurred for subjects who received either color or noncolor audiotapes in this first trial block. In summary, pre-exposure to the voice of the distractor tape temporarily facilitated performance, whereas pre-exposure to the words in the distractor tape temporarily impeded performance.

In another experiment, both the voice and words either changed or remained the same between pre-exposure and test tapes. To obtain more power in examining a transient effect, 96 subjects were included and the different conditions were examined between subjects. Only the noncolor tapes were used in this experiment in order to focus on the distraction effect. The overall finding was that no change was better than change, by 139 ms in Trial 1, but with the difference decreasing quickly across the first few trials.

In other words, the effect of physical habituation predominated over the effect of semantic priming. An ongoing experiment with a more complete design is under way to determine if voice and semantic attributes might interact.

These data are consistent with the notion that physical features of stimuli are used to form a neural model that allows habituation of orienting to the distractor tape. Presumably, pre-exposure to the voice of the distractor tape contributes to the neural model that permits habituation of orienting and thereby improves selective attention. The finding that the semantic features cannot be used in the same way makes sense given the fact that the irrelevant tape was to be ignored during color-naming. According to the model of Sokolov (1963), the habituation and dishabituation occurs through a process in which the neural model of previous stimuli is compared to new stimuli, with a mismatch producing orienting. The neural model of the attended pre-exposure tape may well contain semantic features, but it might be impossible for subjects to extract the semantic features of the spoken words presented but ignored during color-naming, so that a comparison of the semantic features in the two tapes does not take place. On the other hand, the semantic features activated by the pre-exposure tape would be more easily re-activated by subsequent stimuli, which would result in more recruitment of attention to the irrelevant tape in the same-word pre-exposure conditions.

In summary, the irrelevant speech effects in what Cowan and Barron (1987) termed the cross-modal Stroop procedure appear to include two attentional effects that do not last long (orienting to novel physical features and to primed semantic features of the irrelevant tape), and a more specific color-word interference that lasts throughout the experiment and probably can be attributed to the contamination of the pre-speech memory buffer.

5.3.2 Effects of orienting to changes in unattended stimuli

Another prediction of the habituation hypothesis is that changes in the unattended channel in a selective attention task attract attention, provided that these changes occur in features of the stimuli that can be analyzed without attention. The fact that at least some automatic analysis occurs is evident from the original finding (Cherry, 1953) that subjects generally notice changes in the voice of an unattended channel in selective listening.

In the study of Lorch et al. (1984) using picture stimuli, detailed predictions involving dishabituation to unattended stimuli were tested. Specifically, not only was the primary task disrupted after the distractors were changed to novel ones but also, after subjects had habituated to these stimuli, a switch back to the original distracting stimuli led to renewed distraction or dishabituation.

Although habituation is predicted for novel stimulus features in an unattended channel, habituation would not necessarily be predicted for any stimulus features that can be automatically perceived and are of special significance to the subject. Nielson and Sarason (1981) found that shadowing was disrupted by the presentation of a sexually explicit word in an unattended auditory channel. Comparable findings were obtained by Von Wright, Anderson, and Stenman (1975), who paired auditory items with shock and subsequently presented them as distractors in selective listening. There was continued physiological response to the conditioned items, and shadowing performance tended to worsen with their repeated presentation. The experiment was run originally to test the concept of subliminal perception, but the results actually suggest that, at the very least, the perception became less subliminal as time went on.

It is possible to arrive at the habituation theory through an analysis of event-related potential (ERP) data as well as behavioral data. In fact, Woods (1990) has made such a proposal on the basis of a selective listening experiment in which ERPs were recorded. Both channels contained standard stimuli and slightly different target stimuli, and subjects were to keep track of target stimuli in one channel only. Occasionally, though, a very different novel sound was unexpectedly introduced in one channel. This elicited a response that included the mismatch negativity, N2, and $P3_a$ components, equivalently, no matter whether the novel sound was presented in the attended or unattended channel. In contrast, the latter two components did not occur for either standard or target stimuli of the unattended channel. Woods explained this result in terms of an "attentional parasol" that inhibits attention to stimuli fitting the familiar description, but not to novel stimuli differing from that description. This appears to be a close physiological counterpart to the habituation theory.

In the studies we have discussed so far, distraction by novel stimuli has been cast as a sort of nuisance that interferes with primary task performance, appearing to leave in question the ecological value of this mechanism. However, that is primarily a result of the procedures used, which were designed to show evidence of attention shifts and not to demonstrate the function of these attention shifts. The value of attention shifts would be that novel stimuli are more likely than familiar stimuli to be important. They therefore require further, attentive evaluation to determine their actual importance.

Johnston et al. (1990) carried out a series of experiments that demonstrate well this potential function of orienting. Subjects saw series of rapidly presented arrays of four words at a time. Some such arrays were followed by a question-mark probe, to which the subject was to pronounce aloud the word that had appeared last at the probed location. Some of the words were presented repeatedly in a number of arrays, but sometimes a word appeared for the first time, along with three of the familiar words. Other times, all of the words were familiar or all were novel. Although familiar words were identified more accurately than novel words when they were organized into separate arrays, novel words were identified more accurately than familiar words within mixed arrays. This effect was termed "novel popout" to indicate that the novel item presumably emerged from the mixed array by some preattentive mechanism, much as a row composed of the letter X would appear to pop out from a background composed of the letter O. The novel stimuli appear to have captured attention and to have obtained a more complete perceptual analysis than the familiar stimuli within the same array. In subsequent experiments, other explanations were ruled out. For example, there was no comparable popout of a familiar word when embedded in an array of three novel words (Experiment 3). Taken together, the results suggest that familiar words are perceived rather automatically and that attention is attracted to an isolated stimulus for which the automatic perceptual process is not proceeding smoothly or, in the terms of the habituation theory, for which the stimulus does not match the internal neural model.

This is not to say that all changes have an equal impact on the neural model. There is some evidence that stimulus onsets and offsets have more of an impact than other types of feature changes. Yantis and Jonides (1984) and Yantis and Johnson (1990) presented a target letter on each trial followed by a placeholding array composed of copies of the figure "8" in a square digital font. This figure can be changed into a variety of letters by taking away some of the seven lines making up the digit (e.g., F, L, E). Following the placeholding array, an array of letters appeared. Some (or all) of them appeared where copies of the figure "8" had been, whereas one or more other letters sometimes appeared at new locations. The latter were considered "abrupt onset" stimuli because they were new objects in the array rather than changed objects. The target, if it appeared in the letter array, could be either an onset- or a no-onset letter. In both studies, it was found that targets were detected more quickly when they occurred at new onset locations.

Yantis and Jonides (1984) concluded that the special status applied only to onsets and not to offsets, because all of the letter stimuli in their arrays other than the abrupt-onset stimulus were formed through line offsets (from the figure 8 to the letter) that occurred at the same time as the abrupt onsets, and yet did not eliminate the onset effect. However, Miller (1989) pointed out that the number of lines involved in each stimulus offset was not as large as the number involved in each onset. He repeated the Yantis and Jonides experiment, but with additional lines added as Xs inside the top and bottom portions of the figure 8 in order to accentuate the stimulus offsets. Under these conditions, much of the effect of onset stimuli was eliminated by the concurrent offsets.

Jonides and Yantis (1988) and Yantis and Hillstrom (1992) recently found that this effect of onsets does not generalize to other abrupt changes in the stimuli. In a procedure basically similar to Yantis and Johnson, they replaced each of the placeholders in the array with a letter, but presented one of these letters in a new color that had not appeared in the placeholding array. No attention-attracting effect of the color change was observed. (This finding did not depend on a perceptual limitation given that, when the changed color consistently cued the target, a large benefit of this extra cue was observed.) It still is possible that an attention-capturing effect of the color change exists in principle, but was overwhelmed by an attention-capturing effect of the abrupt offsets of lines in each of the stimuli as they changed from placeholding "8s" to letters, which would tend to distribute attention across all of the stimuli. Nevertheless, it can be said that abrupt color changes have failed in conditions similar to those in which abrupt onsets have succeeded.

The special status of abrupt onsets and offsets is indicated by physiological data, as well, in this case primarily through work in the auditory modality. For example, Näätänen (1992) has reviewed evidence that stimulus onsets and offsets elicit a strong response in the auditory event-related potential at about 80 to 100 ms, termed the "N1 response." (The N1 response habituates across presentations, however, at fast enough stimulus rates.) This N1 response is weaker in the case of changes in stimulus features and absent when the change consists of the removal of a feature or the decrease in intensity. In contrast, the mismatch negativity component is slightly later in time and occurs for any discriminable change in the auditory stimulus, but not for new stimulus onsets in the absence of a previous standard stimulus. Näätänen (1992, Chapter 4) suggested that both N1 and mismatch negativity responses tend to attract attention, but the generally larger magnitude of the N1 response would make it the potentially stronger influence on attention, which could account for the behavioral results of Yantis and Hillstrom (1992) on the special status of onsets.

Cowan (1988) proposed that the focus of attention is determined jointly by automatic attentional recruitment and voluntary "central executive processes." There presumably can be a tension between these two influences. The results of Yantis and Jonides (1990) indicate where the boundary between these combined influences lies. They found that a precue permitting focused attention on the location at which the target was to appear was capable of totally overcoming attentional capture by an abrupt onset at a different location in the array.

This behavioral research is consistent with a further distinction that has been drawn in the psychophysiological literature, between a neural "call for attention" and an answer to that call or actual reallocation of attentional resources (Siddle, 1991; Näätänen, 1992; Öhman, 1992). The N1 and mismatch negativity responses in ERPs presumably would reflect a call for attention, whereas later measures of attention in ERPs and autonomic measures of the orienting response would reflect an attentional reallocation. For example, in the case of an abrupt onset that occurs while attention is closely focused elsewhere (Yantis & Jonides, 1990), there presumably would be an N1 response, but not an orienting response or some of the later attentional components of the ERP.

Some of the studies that support the notion that orienting is an answer to the call for attention, rather than the call itself, include reaction time to a probe stimulus as a direct measure of attentional allocation. When attention is allocated to a primary task, the reaction time to a secondary probe task increases (Posner, 1978; Posner & Klein, 1973). In one psychophysiological study, Siddle and Spinks (1992) presented subjects in an experimental group with 24 auditory stimuli followed by one vibratory stimulus, or vice versa, whereas control subjects received 25 presentations in one modality. A secondary task involved reaction time to a visual probe stimulus. Reaction time increased markedly at the point of the modality change in the experimental group; in fact, it was larger than for even the first stimulus in the prechange series. A skin conductance response measure of orienting showed a similar pattern across trials. These results were taken by Siddle (1991) to suggest that the full-strength orienting response results when there is a stable, well-developed neural model from which a changed stimulus can be found to differ.

The detection of change at an automatic level of neural processing apparently is not enough to elicit orienting dependably. Lyytinen, Blomberg, and Näätänen (1992) showed that the relatively automatic, mismatch negativity response to a discriminable change in an irrelevant auditory channel often is not accompanied by autonomic indices of orienting (e.g., heart rate deceleration and skin conductance responses).

A seeming contradiction to the assumption that autonomic indices register attention shifts appears in the findings of Dawson, Filion, and Schell (1989). Their subjects were to count the number of deviant (longer-than-usual) tones in a series presented in one ear, but they were to ignore the tones in the other ear regardless of their qualities. Concurrently, subjects were also to press a button in reaction to a light that could occur at various intervals during the tone task. In the early trials, there was an apparent contradiction between the reaction time to the light and the orienting response to the tones. Tones in the irrelevant channel slowed reaction times more than tones in the relevant channel when the visual reaction time stimulus was presented 150 ms after a tone. However, skin conductance responses to tones were larger when these tones were presented in the relevant channel.

The simplest explanation of this contradiction may be that attention can switch rapidly, whereas skin conductance is a gross, temporally imprecise measure. There may be a brief attentional shift to stimulus onsets in the irrelevant ear followed by a longer period of attention to the relevant ear, with the latter dominating the skin conductance responses. This interpretation was supported by further research (Filion, Dawson, Schell, & Hazlett, 1991) showing that the dissociation disappears when the relevant and irrelevant channels occur in different modalities. The attention-switching may be more likely to occur when the relevant and irrelevant channels are more similar and therefore relatively difficult to tell apart automatically. Of course, other studies show that subjects can attend to one ear in selective listening relatively automatically (e.g., Johnston & Heinz, 1978), but perhaps not in a situation such as the one Dawson et al. used, in which the stimuli in the two channels are not presented simultaneously. That situation makes attention shifts on the basis of abrupt onsets more likely to occur. For further verification of the conclusions of Filion et al., though, it would be informative to use this procedure while measuring earlier attention-driven processes that show up in ERP recordings (Näätänen, 1992). No dissociation between these components and reaction time should result if the present analysis of the results of Dawson et al. is correct.

Results described by Öhman (1992) using a very different procedure suggest that the difference between a call for attention and the actual allocation of attention may be a continuous one. He conditioned subjects to a happy vs. an angry face, presenting mild electric shocks after one (which served as the CS+) but not the other (the CS–). On test trials, subjects saw each face either in isolation, or followed closely by a neutral face as a mask, while skin conductance data were collected. In the no-mask conditions, it did not matter whether the stimulus associated with shock was the happy face or the angry face. In either case, a hefty skin conductance response resulted. In the masked trials, though, the response disappeared when the CS+ was the happy face. It remained but was diminished when the CS+ was the angry face. This result was obtained even though subjects were able to recognize the happy face at slightly shorter masking intervals than was the case for the angry face. These results may suggest that a small amount of measurable orienting occurs with minimal, perhaps fleeting, allocations of attention that can be elicited at least by certain ecologically important stimuli (such as the angry face). However, autonomically measurable orienting that is more sustained and larger in magnitude appears to occur only following a more complete perceptual analysis of the stimulus.

5.3.3 Formation of a neural model

From the research that we have discussed so far, we can conclude that the repeated exposure to particular stimuli results in a decrease in the recruitment of attention to those stimuli, which can be either helpful or detrimental depending on the task that the subject is trying to perform. The theoretical mechanism proposed to underlie these findings is the construction and refinement of a neural model of the repeated stimulation. However, up to this point the neural model construct has not been demonstrated. In fact, it might be viewed as odd in that something positive (refinement of a neural model) has been proposed to account for something negative (declining attentional recruitment to the stimulus channel). What is needed, in principle, is a way to observe the positive aspects of a neural model apart from its effect on attentional recruitment.

Kraut and colleagues have conducted relevant research in several articles. Kraut and Smothergill (1978) proposed that the neural model built up through repeated exposures to a stimulus would enhance encoding of the stimulus, as well as decreasing the amount of attentional recruitment or "alerting" to the stimulus. In the experimental situation they designed, the two factors work in opposition. Subjects received familiarization exposures to one of two colored circles that were to serve as choice reaction time cues. The familiarization consisted of thirty 2-second presentations of either a red or a blue circle. Then, in the reaction time task, the subject was to press one of two response buttons depending on which circle was presented. The reaction time depended on the type of cue, but the direction of the difference depended on the duration of the period between the familiarization exposures and the reaction time test. When the reaction time test was presented without delay, there was an advantage for the novel circle of about 10 to 20 ms (estimated from figures). However, when a delay of 15 or 30 minutes was imposed between familiarization and reaction time test, the advantage was for the familiar stimulus. This advantage increased between 15 and 30 minutes, from about 15 to about 30 ms. The theoretical account was that the habituation of attention to the familiar cue wore off over the period of the delay, whereas the superior encoding of the familiar cue did not wear off. In the no-delay condition, the difference in alerting presumably was of predominant importance, but with the diminution of the alerting difference following a delay, the superior encoding of the familiar circle could be seen to be important also.

A study by Kraut (1976) with 6-year-old subjects went a little further in separating alerting and encoding effects of familiarization. The task was similar to that of Kraut and Smothergill, except that a warning signal was followed by a cue to respond. The warning and the cue stimuli could be either familiar or novel. When the warning stimulus was novel, a familiar response cue elicited the fastest performance. However, when a novel warning stimulus was not used, the novel response cue worked best. This suggests that it is best to have a novel stimulus to alert the subject, but a well-encoded familiar one as the signal to which the choice response must be made, provided that a different stimulus had provided optimal alerting. Kraut, Smothergill, and Farkas (1981) extended these conclusions to adult subjects and to word stimuli, though they found that "alertness decrement appears to be relatively stronger for colors than words, but encoding facilitation seems stronger for words than colors" (p. 1310).

5.3.4 Codes included in vs. excluded from the neural model that leads to habituation of attentional orienting

The fact that the encoding and alerting functions of a neural model can have countervailing effects (Kraut, 1976; Kraut & Smothergill, 1978) makes it a bit more difficult to apply the theory conscientiously to particular situations, because it can permit prediction in either direction. This therefore is an area where additional, careful thought is needed. For example, consider an experiment (Johnston, 1978) in which subjects became familiar with some spoken passages that were to be used as distractors in a selective listening task (with either one familiarizing presentation of each passage, in a moderate-familiarity condition; or 15 presentations, in a high-familiarity condition). A concurrent, visual reaction time task (pressing a button whenever a special light source increased in intensity) served as a measure of the attentional cost of selectivity. When there were physical cues that distinguished between the relevant and irrelevant channels in selective listening, the familiarity of the distractor did not matter, although there was a cost of filtering in comparison to a condition in which there was no irrelevant channel. However, when there were only semantic cues to distinguish between the relevant and irrelevant channels, there was an effect of familiarity: the probe reaction times tended to be slower with higher levels of familiarity of the speech on the irrelevant channel. This result of Johnston (1978) appears to contradict the finding of Waters et al. (1977) that familiarity with the distractor should reduce the amount of distraction, at least at the beginning of the selective attention task.

One account of Johnston's result is that the neural model that is formed for an attended stimulus, that later is to serve as a distractor, can contain features that cannot be used to assist in filtering out the distractor. Specifically, although the neural model formed through attentive pre-exposure to the distractors would contain semantic as well as physical features, this neural model might be useful as a filter only in the physically distinct distractor condition. The reason is that filtering would work only if the incoming distractor stimuli could be adequately analyzed automatically. If the automatic analysis did not include semantic features, then only the physical features could be automatically compared to the neural model. Given that the subject therefore would have to attend to physically similar, semantically distinct distractors in order to establish their irrelevance to the task, the familiarity of their semantic features could cause them to be activated more, thus making them more distracting.

A more complete investigation of the nature of the neural model used in habituation will have to examine separately the status of each of the identifiable codes that was mentioned during the chapters on short-term memory. For example, in the above discussion of the unpublished research of Cowan et al. (in prep.), it was stated that pre-exposure to the physical features of the distracting tape assisted in attentional habituation, whereas pre-exposure to the words of the distracting tape did not, and in fact caused some priming of words in the distracting tape. In more precise terms, though, a match between words includes both semantic and phonological matches. We do not yet know what the separate effects on attention of pre-exposure to semantic and phonological features are.

Reisberg, Baron, and Kemler (1980) conducted a visual Stroop-like task that provides information on the role of phonetic codes in Stroop performance. Their subjects were quickly to count sets of numerical words or symbols (conflict situation) or non-numerical words or symbols (control situation). For example, subjects might have to report how many symbols are present in the display "3 3 3 3," the correct answer being "four." At a certain point, the distractors were changed in order to determine the extent to which training would generalize to different distractors.

Transfer of training to the changed distractors appeared to depend on lexical identity. For example, when the distractors had been the digits "1, 3," there was better transfer of training if the distractors were changed to the words "one, three" (same lexical identities) than if they were changed to other numerical words ("two, four"). Another experiment indicated that "to, for" as distractors were nearly as damaging as "two, four," suggesting that the phonological representation played an important role. However, there was no control condition in which a word that was not homophonic with a number word was used as the distractor. All of the words caused much more interference than the symbols used in the original training, and it is not clear if the effects obtained in this study reflect effects of pre-exposure *per se*, or effects of practice ignoring particular distractors.

5.3.5 The roles of novelty and significance in the neural model

In addition to the question of the nature of the neural model that is formed, one can question the nature of the comparator process that evaluates incoming stimuli in comparison to that neural model. Gati and Ben-Shakhar (1990) noted that Sokolov (1963) "and his followers made no attempt to specify the nature of the matching mechanism" and proceeded to address this question in an important way. They proposed that the subject not only has a neural representation of the standard stimuli, but also a neural representation of task-relevant stimuli. The amount of orienting was said to depend upon both the novelty and the significance of incoming stimuli, but the determination of novelty and significance both were said to depend on a feature matching process. The greater the degree of match between a current stimulus and the representation of the standard, the less the perceived novelty of the stimulus; but the greater the degree of match between the stimulus and the representation of task-relevant stimuli, the higher the perceived significance. A mathematical model based on these ideas provided a good fit with experiments in which various features of cartoon faces were varied.

The task used by Gati and Ben-Shakhar was one designed to produce lively autonomic responses. The subject was to pretend to be a murderer and to appear innocent when shown the face of the victim. First, the victim's face was memorized, and then a series of faces was shown. Within this context it was possible to manipulate independently both the level of novelty of a face (the match with recently shown faces) and the level of significance (the match with the victim). Both factors contributed to the magnitude of orienting as measured by skin conductance responses.

Having affirmed the importance of this study, it is should be pointed out that, although both novelty and significance contribute to orienting, it has not been determined if both factors play a role in attentional filtering. In the study by Gati and Ben-Shakhar, like most studies, the subject was able to devote full attention to each stimulus. If the task were to attend to one channel while ignoring another, the neural model of the unattended channel might not be as complete, and it might not be compared to the neural model of prior or relevant stimuli as completely as is an attended channel. From the point of view of understanding selectivity, the question now is, what part of the neural model can be formed and used automatically in the comparison process?

5.3.6 Role of the active attentional focus in orienting

Assuming that the orienting of attention depends upon a comparison of the neural model to the incoming stimulus, it makes sense that the depth of the comparison, and therefore the likelihood of orienting to a stimulus change, should depend on how much attention was available to analyze the channel to be compared to the neural model. Hulstijn (1979) obtained results consistent with this suggestion using electrodermal indices of orienting to changes in auditory stimuli. Orienting to physical traits was obtained whether or not the subject attended to these physical traits, whereas orienting to changes in semantic features was obtained only when subjects were assigned a task in which they paid attention to the semantic features, rapidly pressing a button if an item came from one particular category.

Another role of attention in selective filtering might be to form a set of expectations that could be included in the model of task-relevant stimuli. Sokolov (1963) suggested that each stimulus actually is compared with an expected stimulus. This might be true, but attention might influence the expectations in some circumstances. For example, suppose that the unattended channel in selective listening contains a series of tones that form a known melody. It might be predicted that a deviation from the melody, that does not violate general qualities of Western music, might trigger orienting only if the subject were allowed to listen attentively to the melody.

In addition to the observation that attention affects orienting, it is undoubtedly true also that orienting and its habituation affect selective attention. In fact, I have proposed that the effect of habituation to irrelevant stimuli, making it easier to selectively attend to other stimuli, is the primary function of habituation. However, there also is a cost of habituation to relevant stimuli. A simple example is the relative difficulty of attending to a monotonous speaker even if the words that are being spoken are very interesting. An experiment demonstrating the cost of habituation was carried out by Posner, Cohen, Choate, Hockey, and Maylor (1984). As in earlier studies by Posner and others, a visual reaction time probe was preceded by a directional cue on each trial. However, rather than the cue always changing from trial to trial as in previous studies, in this study the cue sometimes remained valid for an entire short block of trials. It was found that the repeated cue provided much less benefit than a cue that changed from trial to trial, suggesting that subjects habituated to the repeated cue and could not be alerted by it as easily as by a novel cue. The directional cue in this study may be serving two functions: that of a bearer of directional information, and that of an alerting stimulus as in the study by Kraut (1976) discussed above.

5.3.7 Habituation of orienting vs. suppression of attention

Finally, it should be noted that the habituation of orienting is not the only way in which activated elements of memory are kept out of the focus of attention. Another way is through the active suppression of information. A key example of this active suppression is the "negative priming" effect observed by Neill (1977), Allport et al. (1985), and others. The procedure is one in which a distracting stimulus property in one trial becomes a relevant property in the next trial. For example, Neill (1977) presented a series of color-word stimuli with contingencies such as the word *red* in blue ink followed by *green* in red ink, where the task was to ignore the word and name the color. When a vocal response was used, the irrelevant word from Trial n–1 (in our example, the word "red") slowed the naming of the color on Trial n (the ink color red) more than when no such contingency between trials was present.

When a manual response was used, there was facilitation rather than inhibition from the prior irrelevant word. However, Tipper, MacQueen, & Brehaut (1988) obtained different results in a similar study of negative priming involving letter stimuli. Each display contained two adjacent letters with a bar near to one of them indicating that the subject should respond to that letter. Displays were paired, with the first display in a pair serving as a prime and the second display, as a probe. Some subjects were to respond to each prime display verbally and others with a key press. The same was true of the probe displays, and all four combinations of prime and probe response modalities were used, in different groups of subjects.

No difference between groups in the magnitude of negative priming were observed. This suggests that, in negative priming across trials, it is not the particular motor response that is inhibited. (A similar conclusion was reached by Neill, Lissner, & Beck, 1990.) On the other hand, it is not the specifics of the perceptual code that are inhibited, either. Tipper and Driver (1988) obtained negative priming even when the irrelevant item in Trial $n-1$ was a picture and the relevant item in Trial n was the corresponding word, or vice versa. Thus, it appears to be some kind of more abstract semantic and/or lexical representation of the irrelevant prime item that is inhibited, not just the features of the relevant stimulus percept or motor response.

One developmental study allows us to operationalize the difference between habituation and active inhibition. Tipper, Bourque, Anderson, and Brehaut (1989) used separate manipulations in a Stroop-like task to examine these two phenomena. To elicit habituation, they included a condition in which the irrelevant word stayed the same from trial to trial (e.g., the word *brown* presented in successively different colors of ink). To elicit active inhibition, they used a negative priming procedure as outlined above. Habituation was observed as readily in second-grade children as in adults, but that was not the case for active inhibition.

A remarkable series of 10 experiments conducted in an earlier era (Greenwald, 1972) may make these points even clearer. Subjects were to read digits while hearing as distractors various types of series of spoken items that could include repetitive or changing digits, or tapping sounds as a control. Both habituation (referred to as perceptual filtering) and negative priming (referred to as response suppression) could be separately observed in various ways. Exemplifying habituation, there was less interference when the distracting series was repetitive than when the distracting digit kept changing. Exemplifying negative priming, responses were slower when the current visual item was the same digit as the previously presented series of distractors. Driver and Baylis (1993) replicated the cross-modal negative priming and interference effects with a slightly modified design.

5.3.8 Potential objections to habituation as an attentional filter

Broadbent (1958) and Treisman (1964*b*) brought up the possibility that habituation of the orienting response is the same mechanism that permits subjects to ignore repeated patterns of stimulation. However, Treisman was concerned that orienting often occurs even when the stimuli change only in their semantic characteristics, unlike selective filtering, which proceeds much more efficiently on the basis of physical rather than semantic properties. She therefore suggested that "a different system may control habituation from that which controls selective attention with competing and highly informative inputs."

This suggestion appears to overlook one point about orienting to semantic changes: it typically has been obtained with attended stimuli (e.g., Siddle & Spinks, 1979). When the target stimuli are unattended, evidence for orienting to semantic features is less impressive, the same as with behavioral evidence (see Holender, 1986). It seems likely that the types of changes that will elicit an orienting response depend upon the sophistication of the analysis of the current stimulus, which is to be compared to the neural model. This, in turn, should depend on the amount of attention devoted to the current stimulus. The habituation that automatically filters out unchanged patterns of stimulation would be based on a less sophisticated analysis of the stimuli to be compared to the neural model (because those stimuli are unattended), no matter how detailed the neural model itself was.

Another possible objection to the habituation hypothesis of selective filtering is that it is not clear how to account for the results of Treisman (1964*a*) in experiments with multiple irrelevant channels. She conducted an interesting selective listening experiment with a number of conditions in which there could be either one or two irrelevant channels. The relevant channel, to be shadowed, was presented either to one ear or to both ears (i.e., binaurally), and the irrelevant messages always differed from the relevant message in voice, spatial location, or both. Also, when two irrelevant channels were present they sometimes, but not always, differed from one another in voice or spatial location.

When the relevant channel was presented to one ear, it was found that there was little detrimental effect of a single irrelevant channel presented contralaterally, even though it was presented in the same voice as the relevant channel (94% correct performance, vs. 96% when there was no irrelevant message). A same-voice irrelevant channel presented at a central location (i.e., binaurally) did result in somewhat lower performance (88% correct), but performance was lower still when both the contralateral and central same-voice irrelevant channels were presented (79% correct). Similarly, when the relevant channel was central, performance with a same-voice irrelevant channel presented to the right ear (95% correct) was much better than when separate irrelevant channels in that same voice were presented to the left and right ears (66% correct).

If the orienting response to multiple channels can become habituated simultaneously, as suggested by Cowan (1988), then shadowing should theoretically not depend on the number of irrelevant channels in this way; Treisman's results thus appear to contradict this part of the habituation hypothesis. However, her results lend themselves to other interpretations. When different stimuli are presented in the same voice at three locations, subjects' ability to encode the relevant input perceptually, let alone attend to it, may be impaired.

The importance of adequate perceptual encoding is illustrated by the fact, mentioned above, that a single, centrally-located irrelevant message, in the same voice as the relevant message, presented to one ear resulted in a performance level (88% correct) that was substantially lower than when the irrelevant message was contralateral to the relevant message (94% correct). A central location entails binaural stimulation, which means that the irrelevant message stimulates the ear of the relevant message and may cause peripheral masking.

The importance of adequate perceptual encoding is illustrated also in another way, by excellent performance in conditions in which the relevant channel was presented to one ear, and both of the same-voice, irrelevant channels were presented at a single location, either centrally (94% correct) or contralateral to the relevant channel (97% correct). In these conditions, it seems likely that the perceptual encoding of the irrelevant items was made difficult because they masked each other, which could have greatly reduced their distraction effect.

Treisman also included conditions in which the relevant channel was presented in one ear, one irrelevant channel was presented in the same female voice as the relevant channel, and the other irrelevant channel was presented in a male voice. Perceptual encoding should have been easy for one of the irrelevant channels (the male voice). No matter whether the two irrelevant voices were presented to the central and contralateral locations (83% correct) or both to the central location (84% correct), performance was not much worse than when a single same-voice irrelevant channel was presented at a central location (88% correct). This suggests that, except for the added difficulty of perceptual encoding, an additional irrelevant channel does not much increase the difficulty of selective attention. There are some additional leads suggesting that this is probably true (e.g., Cherry & Bowles, 1960; Moray, Bates, & Barnett, 1965; Johnston & Heinz, 1978), though it has not yet been proven in complete generality. It is, of course, interesting how much work remains to be done on key topics first investigated so long ago and then largely abandoned by the field when other topics seemed more urgent or attractive.

5.4 Some unresolved issues related to the habituation hypothesis

The research that we have discussed can be taken in two opposite ways. It does confirm that there is a critical mass of behavioral and psychophysiological research that supports the utility of the concept of habituation of the orienting response and its link to selective attention; but it also makes clear that there are numerous unknowns that remain to be investigated within this account of attentional filtering. Below, just two of these areas of ignorance will be considered as illustrations. The first of these is that the exact preconditions of habituation remain unclear. The second is that there are many phenomena that could reflect habituation of orienting but might instead reflect something else.

5.4.1 Preconditions for habituation

The preconditions for habituation of orienting are not entirely clear. Näätänen (1990) noted that Cowan's (1988) approach is inaccurate in that habituation can occur even if there is stimulus variation. For example, habituation of orienting may occur if the stimulus is a series of tones with some variation in physical properties. What I actually believe, but perhaps did not make clear in Cowan (1988), is that the basis of a neural model presumably is not a single stimulus but the perceived pattern of stimulation. If the stimulus stream is simple enough so that some type of repeating pattern can be observed, with no consequential new elements or variations, then habituation of orienting presumably will result.

Of course, this formulation in itself leaves a lot undetermined. How much complexity can the stimulus pattern include and still permit habituation of orienting? Presumably, that depends on the richness of the neural model that has been formed. I would expect that a neural model might include information like "a series of tones that ascends in pitch for several tones in a row, and then starts over at the lowest pitch," or "five colors that repeat in random order." For example, the subject might learn to ignore the repeating series of five tones ascending in pitch, in a matter of minutes or even seconds. However, if that pattern were then violated so that the series began to descend, renewed attentional orienting to the tones would be expected.

In turn, the detail of the neural model could depend on how much voluntary attention the subject already had devoted to the stimulus stream. The more attention, the more complete the neural model that could be formed. However, the aspects of the neural model that can be used in selective attention should not be confused with the subject's potentially more complete model or intellectual understanding of the stimulus series. For example, a subject may have learned through counting that every seventy-third tone in a series has a deviant pitch. Nevertheless, if the subject began to ignore the tone series, orienting to the deviant tone probably would occur because the tones cannot be counted automatically in order to be compared to the knowledge in memory.

It is a matter for future research to determine how complex the neural model can be, how long it takes to develop such a complex model, and how much of it can be used in an automatic comparator process. Also, it may not be necessary to develop the neural model all in one session. For example, in an experiment in which sirens are used as distractors, a subject who is more familiar with sirens (and perhaps one who lives in a larger city and hears sirens more regularly) might learn to ignore the sirens more quickly in the test situation. The hypothesis that habituation of orienting is a mechanism of attentional filtering provides a framework leading to clearly specified directions of research, both on the necessary and sufficient conditions for habituation of orienting, and on the relation of orienting to the voluntary direction of attention.

5.4.2 Candidate phenomena of unclear status

If something looks like a duck and walks like a duck, then . . . it still might not quack like a duck, and therefore it might be some other kind of bird. When one is excited by a theory, it is all too easy to perceive a wide variety of phenomena in terms of that theory when it actually does not apply. This may be the case for habituation theory, which an overzealous theorist might try to apply to various cases in which stimulus repetition leads to some sort of diminished responding to the channel containing the repetition. Although some sort of neural model may well be involved in those cases, the adequate demonstration of the relevance of habituation theory to the phenomenon would also have to establish at least that attention to the stimulus channel declines. In an effort to avoid such excess zeal, it is worth considering several phenomena that are interesting candidates for the habituation theory, but for which the evidence one way or the other still is lacking.

Watkins and Sechler (1989) obtained results with a version of the list-final suffix procedure in auditory list recall (see the chapter on sensory memory) that would have to be judged surprising from the modal point of view of memory stores. Instead of presenting the suffix item only after the list, they presented the suffix repeatedly at a regular 1-second interval, between list items as well as after the list. This procedure cut the magnitude of the suffix effect approximately in half. The part of the suffix effect that was not eliminated still could reflect sensory memory. However, it already had been demonstrated that there also is an effect of attention in the suffix effect, at least at prefinal serial positions (Greenberg & Engle, 1983). A suffix that is acoustically similar to the items in the list may be especially difficult to filter out and may curb processing of the list by switching attention to the suffix. Attentional habituation to the suffix item could limit the attentional effect of the suffix.

On the other hand, attentional habituation might make it more difficult for the subject to attend to the list itself, which should hurt recall. Also, in some of their experiments, Watkins and Sechler (1989) found an effect of habituation to the suffix item on recall of the item in the final serial position, in contrast to the attentional effects that were observed by Greenberg and Engle (1983) at prefinal positions only. It is possible to articulate other theories, such as one based on the promotion of figure/ground separation between the list and suffix, that need not appeal to the concept of attentional filtering. In fact, the research of Frankish (1989) showed that perceptual grouping is especially important for auditory stimuli. When lists were separated into subgroups of three successive items, the result was separate bowed serial position functions for stimuli in the auditory, but not the visual, modality.

Two phenomena involving the higher-level processing of attended stimuli are of special interest in pointing out just how little we actually know about the domain and exact mechanisms of the habituation theory. In principle, both of them might be explained by the habituation theory but, inconveniently, they appear inconsistent with one another.

The first of these is the phenomenon known as "semantic satiation" (Smith, 1984; Smith & Klein, 1990). Smith (1984) carried out a simple task in which subjects had to judge whether or not a particular word was a member of a particular category. However, before each trial, the subject was to repeat a category name either 3 or 30 times. The category name sometimes matched the category of the item to be tested. For example, the subject might repeat the word "fruit" and then have to determine if a pear is a fruit, or if a car is a vehicle. It was found that repeating a category name 30 times slowed judgments referring to that category (but not other categories) in comparison to trials with only 3 repetitions. However, in another task, the subject repeated the category name 3 or 30 times and then was to make a lexical decision about the following test item (i.e., to determine if it is a word or not). No effect of the number of repetitions was obtained in this task. Therefore, the satiation effect is specific to tasks that draw upon semantic, as opposed to lexical, representations. One possible interpretation of this effect is that a neural model of the repeated word's semantic features is built up over 30 repetitions and that subsequent words sharing these semantic features cannot attract attention as much as they otherwise would.

The second phenomenon is termed "repetition blindness" (Kanwisher, 1987; Kanwisher & Potter, 1990). A sentence is presented with the words in rapid succession. Within these sentences, a word may be repeated, as in "When she spilled the ink there was ink all over." The basic finding is that subjects recalling this type of sentence tend not to notice the second occurrence of a word, even at the expense of the meaning of the sentence. In the above example, many subjects fail to detect the second presentation of the word *ink*, and they repeat the sentence without it. Kanwisher and Potter found that this phenomenon is based on orthographic units rather than phonetic or semantic units. Thus, if the critical words were homographs as determined by sentence context (e.g., she *rose* from her seat to accept the *rose*), the repetition blindness effect was obtained, but when the words were synonyms (e.g., *sofa* and *couch*) or homophones (e.g., *ate* and *eight*), no effect was obtained.

It is possible that the activation of the neural model of a word by the first presentation prevents an attentional response to the second presentation, and that this lack of an attentional response is responsible for the subject's failure to realize that the word was presented twice. However, the nature of the underlying representation or neural model clearly requires further study.

That representation appears to involve semantic features to the exclusion of lexical ones in semantic satiation, and just the opposite in repetition blindness. Together, though, they help to illustrate useful areas for future research related to the habituation of orienting. We should make sure that any failures are considered along with the successes, as a successful theory must have clear boundary conditions.

6. Attention and long-term memory

Clearly, two of the most central topics in cognitive psychology are long-term memory, or what one learns, and attention, or which of the incoming stimuli are selected for special processing. The extent of the psychological research literatures on these topics would be difficult for the layman to believe. The main objective of this book is to understand the essential mechanisms of the processing system and how they interact. So as not to be seriously distracted from that aim, I will not give an extensive, well-rounded review of research on either long-term memory or attention. However, this chapter will focus specifically on the relationships between long-term memory and attention.

The general gist of the chapter is that, although some simple associative learning goes on automatically, learning involving specific episodic contexts for events is attention-dependent. This was the conclusion of Cowan (1988) also. However, some of the learning mechanisms that were left unspecified by Cowan (1988) will be considered in more detail here.

In James's (1892/1961) briefer course in psychology, the first two chapters are entitled "Habit," and "The stream of consciousness." Although this sequence of topics may seem arbitrary at first sight, it leads to a clear theme. The mind is partly like a machine or, in modern terms, like a well-programmed computer; but unlike a machine, it also is the direct cause of all that we feel and experience. The relation between the topics is a fascinating one. What had been the focus of one's attention and awareness is recorded in memory and becomes less a matter of attention as it becomes more completely ingrained in memory.

Is the only road to "habit," or in broader terms long-term memory storage, through awareness and attention? In the past 20 years or so, an empirical claim that has spawned vast amounts of research is that the answer is "no," that learning and memory storage of some types can take place without the involvement of awareness of, or attention to, the relevant stimuli. A related claim is that information stored in memory, no matter how it was learned, can affect performance on a particular task without the subject being aware that this memory is being used. Before discussing these claims, it is necessary to examine the status of some distinctions that have been drawn between different types of long-term memory.

6.1 Dissociations between direct and indirect memory measures

Direct memory measures (e.g., recall; recognition) are those in which the subject is asked to report information explicitly about a previous event. In contrast, indirect measures (e.g., completing a fragment of a word; identifying a physically degraded word or picture) are those in which the effects of exposure to an event on subsequent tests are examined, no matter whether or not the subject consciously knows that the memory exists or that it is influencing responses (Richardson-Klavehn & Bjork, 1988). One of the oldest indirect memory measures is the free association task that Freud used to examine the unconscious mind, but modern tasks have been simplified in order to reveal more elementary operations in memory.

Strikingly different results have been obtained using direct vs. indirect measures of memory. The difference was at first closely tied to the dissociation between short- and long-term memory. The early research on H.M., the patient whose hippocampal areas were removed to treat severe epilepsy, suggested that he no longer could learn anything new, although short-term memory was preserved as was memory for events that took place before the operation. For example, he showed no evidence of remembering having met a new person, and his knowledge of current events remained forever frozen at the time at which the hippocampectomies were performed (Scoville & Milner, 1957). However, subsequently it was discovered that H.M. showed savings when presented with the same puzzle on multiple occasions, even though H.M. denied that he ever had encountered the puzzle before. This occurred both for a motor-oriented task in which a star was to be traced while the subject viewed his hand in a mirror (Blakemore, 1977) and for a more complex cognitive puzzle, the "tower of Hanoi" task in which a tower of disks is to be moved from one peg to another without placing larger disks on smaller ones (Cohen & Corkin, 1981). It has since been learned that a similar type of dissociation between direct and indirect memory measures is obtained, to varying degrees, in most amnesic patients with damage to the hippocampal areas, including many stroke victims and patients with Korsakoff's syndrome (e.g., see Squire, 1987; Shallice, 1988). The general pattern is that, following a cerebral accident leading to amnesia, indirect measures of memory reveal learning even though direct memory measures show more impairment.

Initially, one might have wanted to draw a distinction between verbal and nonverbal forms of memory. However, Warrington and Weiskrantz (1970) studied four amnesic patients and found that priming was preserved when the word that had appeared as a prime was encountered again in word fragment completion and identification tasks, even though recognition of the same materials as having come from the prior set was severely impaired. Verbal priming in other tasks in amnesic patients also has been observed (see Shimamura, 1986 for a review).

A common account of these results is that there are at least two different memory systems, and that amnesia involves an impairment of one of these memory systems. The systems have been given many different names. Squire (1987, pp. 168–169), for example, listed these various distinctions, which include, among others, the distinction between "episodic, semantic, and procedural" memory (Tulving, 1985); "explicit vs. implicit" memory (Schacter, 1987); and "knowing that vs. knowing how" (Ryle, 1949). Squire defended the advantages of his own distinction between "declarative and procedural" types of memory. Procedural memory would be knowledge of how to do something, without the subject or patient necessarily knowing that memory was being used. Declarative memory, on the other hand, would be the kind of knowledge that allows the subject or patient to state, or declare, that a particular stimulus event was encountered.

Considerable research has been devoted also to finding parallels of the research on amnesiacs in normal individuals. The typical situation is that stimuli are either presented or tested under two different conditions, with both direct and indirect tests being given. The manipulation typically has a large effect on the direct measure and only a small effect on the indirect measure. In the best cases, there is a dissociation between performance on the direct and indirect measures (Tulving, 1985). For example, in a typical study of this type, Graf, Mandler, and Haden (1982) found that the type of orienting task (i.e., the depth of processing) that the subject had to carry out when words were first encountered affected explicit recall of the words, but did not alter the amount of priming seen when the same words were used in a word stem completion task.

One fine point that is not captured in Squire's division of all memory into procedural and declarative memory is that the result of a new experience in an amnesiac may result in new declarative knowledge, although not knowledge directly about the target episode. In a classic example of this, a doctor shook hands with an amnesic patient with a pin concealed in his hand, giving the patient a mild pinprick. When the doctor held out his hand at a later date, the patient refused to take it, saying that "doctors frequently conceal pins in their hands." This type of indirect knowledge is not limited to amnesiacs. In a personal example, I once was discussing the Mardi Gras in Rio de Janeiro with my brother when he commented that the closest he ever came to the Mardi Gras was his visit to me in Ann Arbor (in 1972). I questioned him repeatedly about the basis of his comment, and all that he could come up with were rather remote, far-fetched connections, such as that Ann Arbor at night had a party-like atmosphere with lots of lights. (Ordinarily he would censor a remark that was so "off-the-wall," but he was quite tired at the time.) My brother did not recall that, when he visited me in Ann Arbor, we went to a movie called *Black Orpheus*, which is all about the Mardi Gras in Rio. These types of phenomena suggest that the procedural/declarative division of memory may not be the best one.

Roediger, Weldon, and Challis (1989) questioned the validity of studies that are based on findings of dissociations in normal individuals. They point out that a dissociation need not result from the involvement of two separate memory systems, such as "declarative and procedural" (Squire, 1987) or "explicit and implicit" (Schacter, 1987) memory systems. In their own experiments, they were able to obtain dissociations between different types of implicit memory test, and between different types of explicit memory test, by varying the modality and nature of the learned materials.

Roediger et al. remarked on a processing distinction among the typical direct and indirect memory tasks in the literature. The direct tasks tended to require "conceptually-driven processing," whereas the indirect tasks tended to require "data-driven processing." As an example of this distinction, they described a study by Jacoby (1983). Subjects received stimuli with one of three orienting tasks. In a data-driven "read" condition, subjects simply had to read the target word, such as the second item in the pair, "xxx-COLD". In a conceptually-driven "generate" condition, the subject had to fill in the target word mentally, as in the pair "hot-xxx" where the subject had been instructed to generate opposites and should generate "COLD." Last, in an intermediate condition, either or both types of process could be used, as in the pair "hot-COLD." In a second phase of the experiment, subjects received both a recognition test for the target words and a perceptual identification task for them. In the latter task, the targets and other words were tachistoscopically presented one at a time and had to be identified, without explicit reference having been made to the first part of the experiment. The finding was that the "read" orienting task led to the best performance in the perceptual identification test, whereas the "generate" orienting task led to the best performance in the recognition test. The intermediate orienting condition produced results that were in fact intermediate. In short, memory performance was best when the types of processes carried out during the initial encoding closely matched the types of processes needed at the time of test, very much in keeping with Tulving's (1983) principle of transfer-appropriate processing.

Roediger et al. were able to account for the dissociations that they obtained entirely according to the data-driven vs. conceptually-driven processing distinction. This distinction does not imply two separate types of storage device in the brain, but simply two or more types of encoding process, both involved in any one task to varying degrees.

This controversy may seem somewhat reminiscent of a discussion in the section on short-term memory. (Similarly, see Crowder, 1989*a* on the various dissociations in memory.) In the short-term memory literature, one question has been whether there are separate short- and long-term stores, or simply separate processes (such as maintenance rehearsal vs. elaboration) in an essentially unitary memory system. My answer was that this is a false choice and that there is an intermediate solution; that fundamentally there is one memory system, but with processes (activation, attention) that define a short-term memory storage set within that memory system. Thus short-term memory is functionally distinct from, but embedded in, long-term memory.

My basic answer to the question of the existence of separate types of memory store is similar. There may be fundamentally only one type of memory storage medium, but with different types of memory storage process. In particular, I will appeal to a distinction between those memory processes that occur automatically, and those that occur only with a substantial investment of attention both at the time of encoding and at the time of retrieval. Data-driven processing and the formation of procedural knowledge often can go on to some extent with little or no commitment of attention, although they may be susceptible to attentional effects; whereas conceptually-driven processing and the formation of declarative knowledge typically require considerable attention in order to occur at all. In amnesic patients, attention itself is normal, but there may be a disconnection between these attentive processes and the consolidation of memory that normally occurs as a result of those attentional processes (Schacter, 1989).

6.2 The importance of attention for long-term memory

Hasher and Zacks (1979) drew an important distinction between effortful and automatic processes. Some processes, such as recall and recognition, presumably require effort, whereas other processes, such as frequency estimation, presumably do not (Zacks, Hasher, & Sanft, 1982). Given that effort is assumed to require attentional capacity, the effortful processes presumably indicate an effect of attention on long-term memory. However, even the supposedly automatic processes in these studies have been elicited with the subject basically attending to the stimuli, although without the intent of memorization when stimuli are presented. Moreover, these still are direct memory measures. Therefore, these studies do not answer the more stringent question of whether some (perhaps indirect) measure of memory would reveal learning of truly unattended stimuli. However, some studies possibly relevant to this question will be reviewed below.

6.2.1 Attentional manipulations in memory tasks

Several early studies indicate that divided attention limits performance with a direct measure of memory more than it limits performance with an indirect measure. In one particularly striking study, Grand & Segal (1966) presented various words in different ink colors and then required that subjects name the ink colors, in one condition, or cross all vowels, in another. Notice that color-naming permits that the word be ignored entirely, whereas vowel-crossing involves more direct attention to low-level aspects of the word. Color-naming resulted in a stronger priming effect from the unattended words, even though vowel-crossing resulted in more words being consciously recalled. Koriat & Feuerstein (1976) found little effect of incidental vs. intentional learning conditions for priming effects, although incidental learning conditions resulted in far less conscious recognition or recall than intentional learning.

These early studies left several of the details about memory and attention unaddressed. Does the complete absence of attention eliminate all evidence of declarative memory? Is procedural memory always hurt by diminished attention to the stimuli? Is it eliminated by the total absence of attention? Finally, is direct vs. indirect testing the distinction of greatest relevance where attention is concerned, or is it something else such as the data-driven vs. conceptually-driven processing distinction? More recent evidence provides clues to the answers to these questions, although they remain unresolved.

Eich (1984) conducted a study that appeared to indicate that unattended information affected an indirect measure of memory without any evidence of direct recognition. Subjects in one experiment heard a dichotic tape that included an essay presented to one ear, to be shadowed, and a series of word pairs presented to the other ear, to be ignored. The series of word pairs included some that specified the less frequent of two homophones, such as the second word in "taxi-FARE". ("Fare" is less frequent in English than "fair"). After the selective listening task, subjects received both a recognition task and a spelling task that included the critical words. It was found that subjects were slightly but significantly more likely to select the spelling of homophones consistent with the irrelevant channel in selective listening (.35) than in the case of control words that had not been presented in the tape (.22), even though subjects were not able to identify words that had occurred in the dichotic tape any better than chance. On the other hand, in a second experiment in which the list was attended, there was good recognition and a much larger effect of the critical words on subsequent spelling.

The control of attention in Eich's study can be questioned. Words in the irrelevant channel were presented at a 1-second rate with 2-second intervals between pairs, and this is slow enough that some attention may have been drawn to the irrelevant words (cf. Cowan et al., 1990). This is especially true because the rate of shadowing of attended prose was relatively slow. Some of the irrelevant stimuli may have been attended to momentarily and then forgotten. Nevertheless, the study does show that memory encoding may be indicated by an indirect measure and still not show up in a direct measure. Moreover, it appears to be memory that includes the episodically introduced link between adjacent words in the irrelevant channel.

A study by Balota (1983), using a very different method, appears to be at odds with the conclusion of Eich (1984). Words were presented and followed by a mask at an interval that made them either supraliminal or subliminal in a detection task. (For the present purposes, it is not necessary to be concerned about whether the allegedly subliminal threshold was truly subliminal or not; for that issue, see Holender, 1986). The masked words served as primes for subsequent target items in a lexical decision task.

Semantic priming was obtained at both masking intervals. Subsequently, subjects received a recognition task that included prime-target pairs. Among these were homophone targets that were distinguished by the word that had been the prime (e.g., "grape jam" as opposed to "traffic jam"). Whereas preserving the context that had been present in priming was very helpful for the supraliminal priming condition, this context made no difference in the subliminal priming condition. This result suggests that subliminally presented words can activate memory representations without being useful in forming an episodic memory trace.

One important difference between the Eich (1984) and Balota (1983) studies is that the test of episodic memory was indirect in Eich's study but direct in Balota's study. Thus, these studies taken together are consistent with the belief that rudimentary episodic memory traces can form with little or no awareness of the stimuli, although episodic memories formed in this way are not necessarily available to conscious recollection. On the other hand, inadequate control of attention in the study of Eich (1984) might account for the difference between studies. This issue will be addressed in further detail below.

Kidd and Greenwald (1988) carried out an extension of the "Hebb effect." In Hebb's original studies (e.g., Hebb, 1961), subjects improved over time in the recollection of a repeated sequence of verbal items, even when they expressed no awareness of a repeating sequence. Kidd and Greenwald copied this design within a selective listening task, but placed the repeating sequence either in an attended voice or in a concurrently presented, unattended voice. Unattended repeating sequences later were presented in the attended voice for testing purposes. Although attended sequences were learned implicitly, as in Hebb's studies, absolutely no implicit learning of unattended sequences was observed. This finding appears at odds with the study of Eich (1984). The critical difference may be that Eich had subjects shadow a prose passage (at a slow rate of 85 words/minute), whereas Kidd and Greenwald had subjects shadow words that were presented at times synchronized to the unattended channel. It should be much more difficult to attend to items on both channels under these circumstances.

Parkin and Russo (1990) administered a task in which, on each trial, a picture of a common object was shown first in an incomplete form and gradually became more complete until the subject could identify it. Half of the subjects also carried out a tone detection task concurrently. In a second session 24 hours later, half of the subjects in each condition received a surprise recall test for the names of the items presented previously. Then all subjects proceeded to redo the picture identification task, with the indirect measure of memory being savings from the first session. There were substantial savings, from a score of about 5.3 initially to about 2.7 in the second presentation. Divided attention greatly impaired recall, but it had no noticeable effect on savings in the picture identification task. These data show that substantial memory coding can occur with only a moderate amount of attention to the stimuli. The absence of an effect of attention on savings suggests that some memory processes are indeed fairly automatic.

Hawley and Johnston (1991) carried out a perceptual recognition task that was similar to the indirect measure that Parkin and Russo used. There first was a study phase in which subjects read words that were presented briefly (33 or 83 ms) and followed by a pattern mask. Then, in each trial of a subsequent test phase, a word was presented, at first obscured by an array of dots. The dots were gradually removed over the course of 6 seconds until the subject could attempt to identify the word. In one experiment, attention during the study phase was manipulated. Subjects attended to the words during this phase fully, only partly (with attention devoted also to digits flanking the words), or not at all (with attention devoted solely to the digits).

In contrast to the findings of Parkin and Russo, however, Hawley and Johnston found that attention had a large effect on the perceptual identification measure. It is not clear why the results of these two studies disagree. One possibility is that the physical match between study and test was much closer in the Parkin and Russo study, in which the measure was simply savings during retest, than it was in the Hawley and Johnston study. Perhaps automatic processes provide only a very narrow, difficult-to-generalize memory trace, whereas more attention is needed to extrapolate from one task to another. A second possibility is that the attentional manipulation in the Hawley and Johnston procedure was a more powerful one. More research reconciling these findings would clearly be useful.

Smith and Oscar-Berman (1990) carried out an experiment that is procedurally a hybrid between Parkin and Russo (1990) and Hawley and Johnston (1991). The task was one of speeded lexical decision. Similar to Parkin and Russo's picture identification task, the indirect memory measure was the amount of savings when a stimulus was presented for a second time. On the other hand, similar to Hawley and Johnston's task, the attentional measure involved attending to vs. ignoring characters flanking each word or nonword stimulus. The findings, also, can be considered intermediate. For word stimuli, the finding was more in line with Parkin and Russo. Specifically, the savings were just as large under divided attention circumstances as during full attention to the words. On the other hand, for nonword stimuli, the result was more like that of Hawley and Johnston. The amount of savings was severely reduced by divided attention. In a second experiment, it was shown that amnesia had an effect similar to the effect of divided attention.

One interpretation of the Smith and Oscar-Berman results is that attention is needed to form a coherent memory representation of nonsense-word items. In an earlier chapter, we saw that a subject who had an abnormally small short-term memory span apparently could not learn new vocabulary words at all (Baddeley et al., 1988). Perhaps a divided attention condition is much like a short-term memory limitation. The links between phonemic units in an unfamiliar item appear not to be formed when attention is limited, whereas the activation of familiar units appears to occur more readily under these circumstances.

One thing that is needed is careful analysis of the similarities and differences between all of these tasks and of all of the means of manipulating attention. For example, learning links between phonemic units in a nonword may require the same processes as learning links between word units in multiword sequences. If they do, the inability of subjects to benefit from repetition priming in the case of unattended nonwords (Hawley & Johnston, 1991) is at odds with the ability of subjects to benefit from exposure to unattended word pairs (Eich, 1984). However, as mentioned above, the control of attention by Eich (1984) is questionable.

It is difficult to definitively control attention, but easier to at least observe if the subject can report awareness of the relation between stimuli in different phases of an experiment. Bowers and Schacter (1990) carried out several priming studies in which a word-presentation phase was followed by an indirect memory task, in which the subject was to complete word fragments. In the first phase, the subject was to judge semantic or physical properties of each word. In the subsequent, word fragment completion task, the fragments could be completed in multiple ways and often could be completed as words that has been presented earlier. So far, this experimental design is typical, but there was an unusual aspect of this study. After the fragment completion task, subjects were questioned as to their awareness that some words presented in the first phase later appeared in the fragment completion task as well.

In Bowers and Schacter's first experiment, words from Phase 1 were presented individually. It was found that subjects who did vs. did not report being aware of the repetition of stimuli in the two experimental phases gave these words as responses to word fragments equally often. In subsequent experiments, words were presented in arbitrary pairs, and the second word in a pair could be presented as a fragment in the next phase of the experiment either in the same or in a different episodic context (e.g., "rain-tennis" in the first phase and either "rain-ten__" or "jacket-ten__" in the second phase). Unlike the outcome for simple repetition priming observed in the first experiment, the beneficial effect of preserving the same episodic context was dependent on awareness. In fact, subjects who reported being unaware of the repetition of words in the two phases of the experiment showed no evidence of episodic priming.

6.2.2 Attention, memory, and amnesia

Bowers and Schacter (1990) also pointed out the relation between this study and the amnesia literature. Whereas the priming of individual words occurs in all types of amnesia (e.g., Graf, Squire, & Mandler, 1984; Squire, Shimamura, & Graf, 1985), priming based on newly exposed, arbitrary sequences does not usually occur in cases of severe amnesia (Cermak, Talbot, Chandler, & Wolbarst, 1985; Schacter & Graf, 1986; Shimamura & Squire, 1989), although it does in more mild cases of amnesia (Schacter & Graf, 1986) and in normal subjects (e.g., McKoon & Ratcliff, 1979). This makes sense if severe amnesia in the absence of other deficits involves effects on memory that are similar to effects of divided attention, as was suggested, for example, by Cowan (1988) and Smith and Oscar-Berman (1990). This dissociation between types of priming would not be found in all severe amnesias; not in those involving damage to diffuse cortical association areas in which long-term information is stored, such as Alzheimer's disease (Butters & Miliotis, 1985), and probably not consistently in Korsakoff's syndrome, in which various parts of the thalamus and other diencephalic structures are affected (Joynt and Shoulson, 1985), but in those involving severe damage specifically to the frontal or hippocampal areas (e.g., see Squire, 1987).

The suggestion that attention is important for memory is supported neuroanatomically, by the finding that amnesia can result from frontal as well as hippocampal damage (Shallice, 1988, pp. 374–379; Schacter, 1989). Both of these authors proposed that frontal lobe amnesias reflect the involvement of attention and supervisory control in memory storage and/or retrieval. The frontal lobes are closely connected to the hippocampal areas, and it has been suggested that they work together. (Some of the evidence for this statement will be examined in the last chapter of this book.)

Posner (1984) suggested that "the amnesic can bring information to attention but has a problem in storing the products of that attentive act." He further suggested that there could be a neurobiological "write" signal that occurs when an event is recorded in memory with the involvement of the hippocampus. It is likely to be the frontal lobe that sends such a write signal to the hippocampal areas in the first place.

The special connection between the frontal and hippocampal areas was also noted earlier, in the discussion of working memory (Goldman-Rakic, 1992). This should not be surprising if, as I suggested earlier, the type of working memory that those studies examined actually involved the focus of attention. The connection would be that items in the focus of attention are important for both working memory and long-term storage of declarative information.

Relating organic amnesias to the attentional system even though attention itself is unimpaired in these patients would also help to explain non-organic sources of amnesia that occur as part of dissociative syndromes such as fugue states (Hilgard, 1986, 1992; Kihlstrom, 1992), which involve no known specific brain damage and appear to have their origin instead in environmental traumas. Consider, for example, the case of multiple personality disorders. Nissen, Ross, Willingham, Mackenzie, and Schacter (1988) carried out a study in a subject with several personalities, each of which claimed to be unaware of the others. In various direct and indirect tests, information was presented in one personality and tested in another personality. It was found that indirect tests of memory sometimes revealed transfer of the information from one personality to another, whereas direct tests of memory did not.

It can be speculated that there are both similarities and differences in the link between attention and loss of conscious memories in amnesias of an organic vs. psychological origin. In both cases there would be some way in which attention and awareness would act to integrate new knowledge into a coherent, conscious set of knowledge schema. In organic amnesias, the attention still occurs but presumably no longer serves its normal function in integrating schemas. In non-organic, psychologically derived amnesias and memory dissociations, there are separate schema sets for each personality and attention is limited to the schema set of the currently active personality. The following theoretical framework helps to strengthen these speculations a bit.

6.2.3 Attention and taxonomies of memory

Schacter (1989) reviewed a wide range of neuropsychological syndromes in which a process is left intact, but in which conscious awareness of the process is eliminated. In his words (p. 360), "Just as amnesic patients show implicit memory for information that they do not consciously remember, these patients show implicit knowledge of stimuli that, depending on the exact nature of their impairment, they either cannot perceive, identify, recognize, or understand consciously." Examples included prosopagnosia, or difficulty recognizing familiar faces, in which implicit familiarity appears to be spared; blindsight, or the ability to make above chance judgments concerning the attributes of stimuli that the patients claim not to see at all; alexia, in which patients unable to read printed words still can make above-chance lexical decisions; and various types of agnosia and aphasia in which the consciously impaired process still influences implicit tests. Furthermore, in each of these cases, the impairment is domain-specific and there is no evidence of a general impairment in conscious awareness.

In accounting for these diverse cases, Schacter proposed (p. 363) that "specific processing and memory modules are *selectively disconnected* from the conscious system, thereby resulting in a domain-specific deficit of conscious experience." In the terminology of Cowan (1988), which seems very compatible with Schacter's account, particular types of percepts or memory traces that are normally formed only after the relevant information enters the focus of attention are deficient in patients with these various deficits, although the focus of attention itself still may operate normally in such patients.

In passing it should be noted that Fendrich, Wessinger, and Gazzaniga (1992) questioned the phenomenon of blindsight resulting from occipital cortical damage, on the basis that their blindsight patient showed spared visual function only in a small region of the visual field for which the cortical representation itself was spared. Although this calls into question the routine interpretation of blindsight, it still was the case that vision in this spared area occurred without the patient's awareness; and blindsight also occurs in hemispherectomized patients (e.g., Ptito, Lepore, Ptito, & Lassonde, 1991). Therefore, it still may be that Schacter's general hypothesis applies to blindsight.

6.2.4 Contrasting theories of memory and amnesia

It is not yet fully clear what implications Schacter's proposal has for other theories of memory and amnesia. According to Tulving's (1985) proposal, episodic memory involves self-awareness, which seems consistent with the finding of Balota (1983) and others that an episodic memory trace is not formed in the absence of awareness of the stimuli. However, it is not clear if there is non-episodic information that also can be learned only with the same involvement of attention. If so, and if it is impaired in amnesia, that would favor Schacter's theory over Tulving's.

According to Squire's (1987) theory, the basic types of memory are declarative and procedural memory, with only the latter typically intact in amnesia. Priming is said to be a type of procedural memory, explaining why it usually is unimpaired. However, the observation that the priming of episodic information usually is impaired in amnesiacs compared to normal subjects (Bowers & Schacter, 1990) appears to favor Schacter's theory over Squire's.

6.2.5 Control of the type of processing

Most of the studies mentioned in this section have focused on the effects of attention on direct and indirect measures of memory. There still do not appear to be studies taking the cue from Jacoby (1983) and Roediger et al. (1989), investigating the effects of attention on data-driven vs. conceptually-driven processing. It seems likely that such effects would be obtained. More importantly, there are not studies in which the effects of attention on direct vs. indirect measures are examined with the nature of the processing (data- vs. conceptually-driven) held constant. It is not at all certain if those effects would be obtained.

Merikle and Reingold (1991) noted that the direct and indirect tasks should be matched in all characteristics except instructions for the comparison to be valid. In such a comparison, they found that the indirect measure exceeded the direct measure for two blocks of trials, with the direction of the difference reversed in the third block of trials. More specifically, performance on the direct measure increased across trials and performance on the indirect measure decreased. The likely reason for the decrease is that the indirect task was one in which the noise background presented along with a previously encountered word was judged quieter than the same level of noise background presented with an unencountered word (Jacoby, Allan, Collins, & Larwill, 1988). There may be a discounting mechanism whereby a recognized word is less likely to have the perceptual effect, which would lead to a decrease in the indirect measure as a result of the increase across blocks in the direct measure. At any rate, the empirical dissociation between the direct and indirect measures provides strong support for the basic concept that there can be memory without awareness.

6.3 Dissociation of automatic and attention-related factors

Jacoby and his colleagues have carried out a set of experiments on the effects of attention on memory that has quickly become important in the field, primarily because it does not focus on direct and indirect tests *per se* but, rather, on how to examine the fundamental processes of memory that may underlie performance in these tests. They proposed that performance is based on a combination of two processes: familiarity, which presumably takes place automatically; and recollection, which presumably involves strategic processes and requires attention.

Jacoby, Woloshyn, and Kelly (1989) based their study on the observation that, when one encounters a name, the tendency to consider it "famous" should be based on both familiarity of the name and the belief that this familiarity did not arise solely from some earlier encounter with the name in the test situation itself. Their subjects read a series of names in what was considered a study phase, and then were tested on a longer series of names, only some of which had been included in the study phase. They were to give both fame judgments and recognition judgments for each of these names. Either the study phase (in Experiments 1 & 2) or the test phase (in Experiment 3) was sometimes conducted under divided attention conditions. In the two most critical experiments (2 & 3), subjects knew that none of the names encountered in the study phase were famous. Familiarity of a name thus could be discounted if the subject recollected that the name had appeared in the study phase. The most important result was that divided attention at either study or test made subjects more likely to call a name that had appeared during the study phase "famous," and less likely to call a name that had not so appeared "famous." In other words, it made them more likely to rely on familiarity rather than recollection.

Jacoby and Whitehouse (1989) used a procedure that did not rely upon a divided attention task. First, there was a study phase in which subjects read a large number of words. Then, in a subsequent test phase, subjects were to indicate if each test word had appeared in the study list or not. However, each test word was preceded by a context word surrounded by visual masks. Sometimes, the context word matched the test word. In the "aware" condition, the duration of exposure to the masked context word was long (200 or 600 ms in different experiments) and the subject was informed that the context and test words might match. This would allow them to discount the feeling of familiarity likely to be produced by the context word. In the "unaware" condition, the duration of exposure to the masked context word was much shorter (50 or 16 ms in different experiments) and the subject was not informed about the context word. The most important result was that the match between context and test words increased the number of false alarms (i.e., the incorrect belief that the test word had appeared in the study list) in the unaware condition, but not in the aware condition. Awareness presumably allowed the recollection process to be used to discount familiarity when it resulted from the context word.

Jacoby (1991) conducted a study to demonstrate that familiarity and recollection can be dissociated and quantified. This idea was realized most completely in his third experiment. In a first study phase within that experiment, subjects solved anagrams, and also read words, in separate trial blocks. In a second study phase, subjects heard words. Then two different types of memory test, referred to as "inclusion" and "exclusion" recognition tests, were administered to different subgroups of subjects. In the inclusion test, an item was to be labeled "old" if it had occurred anywhere in the experiment, whereas in the exclusive test, an item was to be labeled "old" only if it had been heard in Phase 2 of the experiment. Subjects should be able to make the inclusive judgments on the basis of some combination of familiarity and recollection. On the other hand, the exclusive judgments pit these sources against one another. An item that is familiar may be "old," but it nevertheless is to be considered "new" if one recollects that the item was seen or generated rather than heard.

In explaining the mathematical model, I will rely on terms that do not appear in Jacoby (1991), but do appear in some later reports (Joordens & Merikle, 1993; Debner & Jacoby, 1994). Familiarity is assumed to be independent of the subject's conscious awareness, and the proportion of items represented in this unconscious form of memory is labeled U. In contrast, the proportion of items that can be consciously recollected is labeled C. According to Jacoby's model, these forms of memory are said to operate independently. In the inclusion condition, the probability of calling an item "old,"which will be termed I, was the joint probability of it being either unconsciously familiar or, if not familiar, consciously recollected:

$$I = U + (1 - U)C \tag{6.1}$$

In this and in subsequent formulas, the parameter values were assumed to differ between the "Anagram" and "Read" stimuli, but I will omit those subscripts for stimulus condition as a matter of simplicity.

The probability of calling an item "old" in the exclusion condition, E, was said to be the probability that it was familiar, but still not determined through recollection processes to be from the first phase of the experiment:

$$E = U(1 - C) \tag{6.2}$$

On the basis of these equations and simple algebra, Jacoby could calculate C and U from the data in each condition of the experiment:

$$C = I - E \tag{6.3}$$

$$U = E/(1 - C) \tag{6.4}$$

Verification of the theory was obtained from a comparison of the theoretical parameter U (based on Experiment 3) with the result of the divided attention condition of Experiment 2. In that experiment, an exclusion memory task was conducted, but half of the subjects engaged in a secondary task, monitoring a tape for runs of three odd numbers, while taking the recognition test. The results for the full attention group in this experiment were similar to those in the third experiment. However, for the divided attention group, the recognition scores for items that had appeared in Phase 1 were almost exactly what one would predict if recognition were accomplished entirely on the basis of familiarity, with no contribution of the recollection process. It was concluded that divided attention removes almost all recollection but leaves familiarity intact.

Jacoby, Toth, and Yonelinas (1993) described new findings that strengthen the process dissociation framework. In their study, both inclusion and exclusion recall conditions were examined under both full and divided attention. Subjects encountered a set of words in a study phase of the experiment and then, on each test trial, were given the first three letters of a word as a response cue (e.g., the word "motel" followed by the trigram "mot" as a cue). To strengthen the attention manipulation further, subjects were informed in advance that they would be tested on the words presented in the study phase only in the full-attention condition. In the inclusion condition, they were to attempt to recall the corresponding word from the list or, if they were not able to do so, to guess with the first word that came to mind. In the exclusion condition, on the other hand, they were to complete the trigram with some word that was *not* from the list. Producing a studied word in the exclusion condition thus can be taken as an indication that recollection of that word has failed. As shown in Fig. 6.1, this

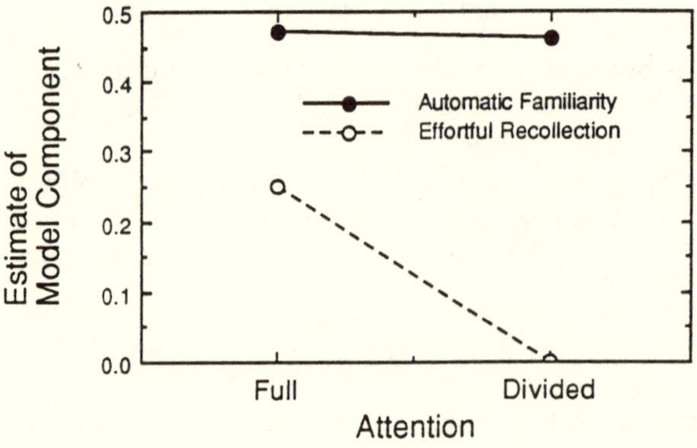

Fig. 6.1 Data on attention effects in memory. (After Jacoby and Kelly, 1992, p. 177, Table 1.)

experiment produced an estimate of automatic familiarity that remained stable across attention conditions, and an estimate of recollection that fell to 0 in the divided attention condition.

6.4 Separate or embedded memory processes?

The concepts of familiarity and recollection proposed by Jacoby and his colleagues are very much in accord with what Cowan (1988) proposed in a review of research on memory and attention processes. There it was suggested that there are some elementary memory storage processes that take place automatically (although some minimal amount of attention may have to be expended in order for the perceptual coding of the stimuli to be adequate in the first place). Memories stored in this way could be automatically activated, leading to a feeling of familiarity, and they would be predominant in indirect tests of memory. Cowan (1988) concluded also that there are other storage processes that occur only with the devotion of more attention, which also can be fully retrieved or activated only with more attentional involvement. These memories would enable conscious recollection and would link together isolated items into a coherent, contextually defined episodic stream.

However, Jacoby's theoretical framework has differed from that of Cowan (1988) in a subtle but potentially important way. Jacoby (1991) discussed familiarity and recollection as if they were independent entities. According to the framework suggested by Cowan (1988), they theoretically should not be entirely independent because it should not be possible to recollect an episode without that episode also appearing familiar. Thus, one would have to distinguish between familiarity based on automatic processes and the additional familiarity produced effortfully, as a byproduct of recollection processes. The converse case is different: it still should be possible to have familiarity without recollection. The attention-related processes thus might be said to be *embedded in* the automatic processes, not independent of them. We will re-examine this conclusion shortly, however.

Joordens and Merikle (1993) brought up a similar issue. They noted that the estimate of unconscious memory (U) changes if one uses a model in which conscious memory (C) is embedded within it. As shown above, Jacoby's estimate was $U = E/(1 - C)$. However, if C is embedded within U rather than independent from it, then C makes no independent contribution to performance in the inclusion condition, and the estimate of unconscious processing must be equal to performance in that condition: $U = I$. This embedded or "redundant" processes model was shown to lead to different estimates of U for the data of Jacoby et al. (1993).

6.4.1 The importance of correcting for guessing

Whether one prefers the independent processes model of Jacoby (1991; Jacoby et al., 1993) or the redundant processes model of Joordens and Merikle (1993), it is important to note that neither of the models appear to have been properly corrected for guessing, and that this guessing correction makes a big difference in the estimate of unconscious processing (Cowan & Stadler, in preparation).

Jacoby et al. (1993) obtained a measure of the base rate of guessing (which I will term G), the proportion of trials in which the stem was completed with a particular target word that had not actually been presented to the subject in the study phase of the experiment. They then suggested a correction for guessing in which the true measure of unconscious memory was said to be the estimate of U minus the baseline guessing rate. That is,

$$\text{“Corrected } U\text{”} = U - G \tag{6.5}$$

The rationale was that the raw parameter U was said to reflect a "sophisticated" guessing process in which both the true familiarity of the item and pure guessing make contributions.

The trouble with this estimate is that it requires the unfounded assumption that there is no overlap between the studied items that are represented in the unconscious memory and the studied items that did not make it into unconscious memory but still were guessed. If one assumes instead, as seems more likely, that guessing is independent of unconscious memory, then there are likely to be some items that are in unconscious memory but would have been guessed in the stem completion task even if they were not in unconscious memory. On the basis of this assumption, Jacoby's model of performance in the inclusion task (Equation 6.1) must be revised. Performance would equal items retrieved from unconscious memory, plus those not in unconscious memory but consciously recollected, plus those not in either source of memory but still guessed:

$$I = U + C(1 - U) = G[1 - U - C(1 - U)] \qquad (6.6)$$

In this formula, unlike Jacoby et al. (1993), the term U refers specifically to unconscious memory and does not include within it the guessing process, G.

The estimate of conscious memory still is $C = I - E$ because, in the exclusion condition, subjects presumably use the same items as in the inclusion condition except for those that are consciously recollected. One can derive an estimate of U by substituting $I - E$ for C in Equation 6.6 and rearranging terms with simple algebra:

$$U = [E - G(1 - I + E)]/\{[1 - I] + [E - G(1 - I + E)]\} \qquad (6.7)$$

This equation is complex, but notice that the denominator exceeds the numerator by exactly $(1 - I)$. As performance in the inclusion task increases, so does the estimate of U, though the strength of the relation depends on E and G.

Joordens and Merikle (1993) did not correct their redundant processes model for guessing, but the correction is easy to make. Assuming that conscious memory is embedded within unconscious memory, and assuming that guessing is independent from memory, the conceptual model would be as shown in Fig. 6.2. Performance in the inclusion condition would equal items in unconscious memory plus items not in unconscious memory but guessed anyway:

$$I = U + G(1 - U) \qquad (6.8)$$

One can derive a new estimate of U simply by rearranging terms:

$$U = (I - G)/(1 - G) \qquad (6.9)$$

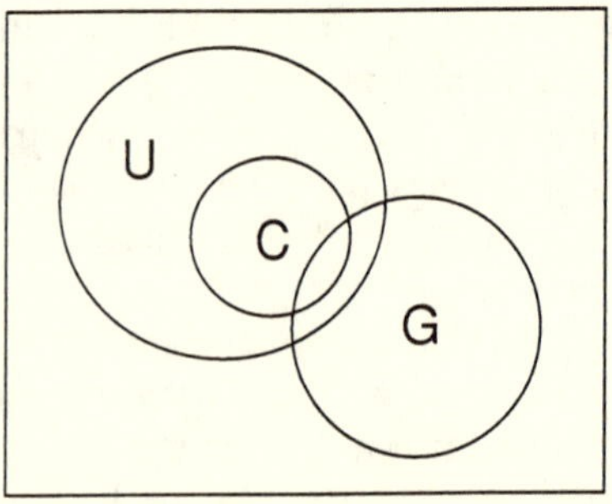

Fig. 6.2 A representation of Joordens and Merikle's (1993) redundant processes model with guessing processes taken into account.

When the baseline guessing rate is fairly high, the correction for guessing can make an enormous difference for the estimate of unconscious memory. Consider Experiment 3 of Jacoby et al. (1993) in which, during the study phase, subjects read some words and received others as anagrams. In the Read condition, the mean proportion of word stems filled with the studied word were .82 in the inclusion condition and .49 in the exclusion condition, and the baseline guessing rate for nonpresented target words was .55. If one uses the Jacoby et al. method of estimating unconscious memory (the uncorrected U minus the baseline guessing rate), an estimate of .18 is obtained. However, using the version of their independent processes model with the present correction for guessing (Equation 6.7), the estimate rises to .40. Joordens and Merikle (1993) did not correct their estimates of unconscious memory for guessing, but when the Jacoby et al. correction (subtracting the baseline rate) is applied to their redundant processes model, the resulting estimate is .27. Finally, using the redundant processes model with the present correction for guessing (Equation 6.9), the estimate increases dramatically, to .60.

For the Anagram condition of the same experiment, the only difference in the means is that subjects used the target word only .25 of the time in the exclusion condition. For this condition, the differences between models in the estimates of unconscious memory were even more extreme (independent processes U minus baseline, .03; independent processes with the present correction, .07; redundant processes U minus baseline, .27; and redundant processes with the present correction, .60). It seems fair to conclude that our understanding of unconscious memory depends almost entirely on the model that is adopted, and that the nature of the correction for guessing plays an especially important role in the models.

This correction for guessing even makes a difference in the viability of the redundant processes model. If one simply uses the Jacoby et al. method of correcting for guessing (subtracting the baseline rate), then the redundant processes estimates of unconscious memory in Jacoby et al., Experiment 3 (.27 in both conditions) is less than the estimates of conscious memory in the same experiment (.33 in the Read condition, .57 in the Anagram condition), which would make the redundant processes model unviable. However, with the present correction for guessing, the estimates of unconscious memory (.60 in both conditions) remain higher than the estimates of conscious memory, and the redundant processes model remains viable.

6.4.2 Partial overlap between conscious and unconscious memory: modeling the general case

Joordens and Merikle (1993) noted that the independent processes model and the redundant processes model are two endpoints of a continuum of models that differ according to how much overlap there is between conscious and unconscious memory processes. It is possible to modify the present approach to obtain equations for the more general model that subsumes both extremes.

The general model is depicted in Fig. 6.3. Conscious memory is split into two portions: conscious memory for items that also were automatically familiar, C_F, and conscious memory for items that were not automatically familiar but were remembered through a deliberate recollection process, C_R. Performance in the inclusion condition reflects all items that were automatically familiar, plus those not familiar but still recollected, plus those not familiar or recollected, but guessed:

$$I = U + C_R + G(1 - U - C_R) \qquad (6.10)$$

The exclusion condition is based on the same information but is reduced by the exclusion of C_R and also C_F:

$$E = U - C_F + G(1 - U - C_R) \qquad (6.11)$$

This leads to the expanded formula for conscious memory:

$$C = I - E = C_R + C_F \qquad (6.12)$$

It also leads to a new formula for unconscious memory:

$$U = (E + C_F - G + GC_R)/(1 - G) \qquad (6.13)$$

How should the new components of this model be interpreted? It is possible that automatic familiarity is a continuously variable quantity and that, when familiarity reaches a certain level of strength, the item enters conscious awareness. That entry of an item into consciousness on the basis of vivid familiarity could occur with probability C_F. On the other hand, items that do not reach conscious awareness in this way still could enter awareness on the basis of a more deliberate, elaborate memory search process, and this could occur with probability C_R. These processes appear to correspond to

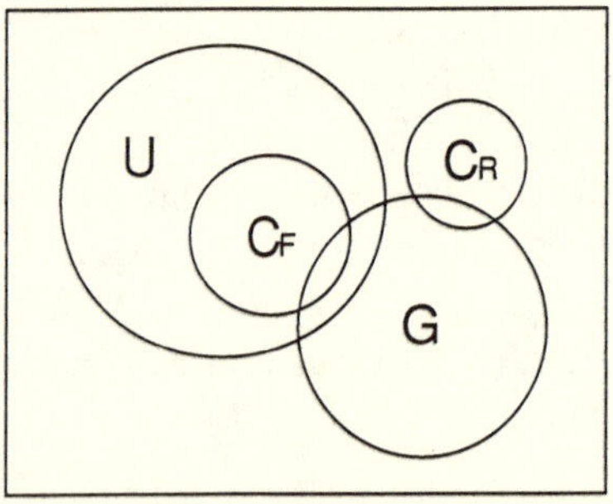

Fig. 6.3 A representation of a more general process dissociation model.

those of memory "familiarity/integration" versus "retrieval/elaboration" as discussed in an article on the recognition process by Mandler (1980). They also appear to correspond to involuntary vs. voluntary influences on the focus of attention (Cowan, 1988).

The general formulas can be reduced to the uncorrected formulas of Jacoby et al. (1993). First, one must set $G = 0$. The independent processes assumption holds when the proportion of U that also is conscious is the same as the proportion of the remainder ($1 - U$) that is conscious; that is, when $C_F / U = C_R / (1 - U)$. Under those conditions, by simple algebra one can show that $C_F = U(C_R + C_F)$ or, in the terminology of the prior models, $C_F = UC$. Making this substitution in Equation 6.11, with $G = 0$, results in the Jacoby et al. equation for E and also leads to their equation for U.

The formulas also can be reduced to the uncorrected formulas for the redundant processes model of Joordens and Merikle (1993), simply by setting $C_R = 0$ (that is, no conscious memory for unfamiliar items) and $G = 0$ (no guessing).

Of course, there is a big problem with the more general approach: we do not yet have a way to obtain separate empirical estimates of C_F and C_R. However, some clues to manipulations that might separate these quantities are found in the experiments reviewed by Mandler (1980). For example, one would expect that either stimulus repetitions or repetitive, maintenance-type rehearsal should increase C_F but not C_R, whereas elaborative rehearsal, in which the subject is instructed to make up some sort of coherent story or theme in which to place the studied items, should increase C_R more than C_F. Recognition generally should place relatively more emphasis on C_F, and recall, more upon C_R.

It may also be possible to separate these components if and when one can assume that the difference in ability between two groups of subjects is a matter of a difference in elaboration processes, not in familiarity. An experiment conducted by Zacks et al. (1982, Experiment 3) illustrates this point. Subjects in higher- and lower-ability groups received a list of words including many repetitions, under instructions either to expect a recall test, to expect a word frequency judgment test, or to expect both. This last condition was considered a divided-attention task, inasmuch as subjects appear to prepare differently for the two tests. In each case, both types of test were actually given.

The frequency judgments revealed no effects of either instructions or ability level. In contrast, the recall measure revealed large effects of both instructions and ability level, suggesting that they influence elaborative recollection processes. There also was an interaction of instructions with ability level. The effect of ability level was largest when recall was expected, whereas it was eliminated when only frequency judgments were expected. When both tests were expected (the divided attention condition), the effect of ability level was not eliminated even though scores were depressed relative to the expect-recall condition. This suggests that divided attention did not totally eliminate elaborative recollection processes. It is possible that the modeling framework given above can be applied to results such as these to produce estimates of C_F and C_R, the two subcomponents of conscious memory.

The divided attention manipulation in the Zacks et al. experiment probably was weaker than the one used by Jacoby et al. (1993), which apparently reduced all recollection ($C_F + C_R$) to 0. However, it is worth noting that, in a wide variety of studies in which dual-task methods have been used, the effect of one task on performance in the other rarely has been completely devastating even when both tasks are fairly complex (e.g., see Gopher & Donchin, 1986; for a review). It may be that divided attention at the time of study has a more severe effect on C_F than on C_R, and that the total elimination of recollection processes by divided attention can be observed primarily in situations in which C_R is negligible to begin with. The elimination of conscious memory in Jacoby et al. (1993, Experiment 1) may have occurred because subjects in the divided attention condition were not told that they would have to remember the printed words presented during the study phase.

Providing one possible argument for the independence of conscious and unconscious memory, Cowan and Stadler (in preparation) found that invariance in the estimate of unconscious memory across full and divided attention conditions (Jacoby et al., 1993; Debner & Jacoby, 1994) could not be produced by any model in which the ratio of C_F to C_R remains fixed acoss experiments. In the independence model, the ratio increases as the estimate of unconscious memory increases.

How is this result to be reconciled with the logic of Cowan (1988)? It should be noted that the items that become familiar only as an indirect consequence of effortful recollection would not show up within the estimate of automatic memory in the independence model. Therefore, it is quite possible to have a structural embedding of conscious memory within unconscious memory, conceptually reminiscent of Joordens and Merikle (1993), while still dividing the familiar items into those automatically familiar and those familiar only via effortful recollection, in conformity with either the independence model or the more general class of models described above. Also, in certain circumstances it might be possible for a subject to deduce that an item must have been presented, without that item becoming familiar as a result.

Finally, the general model described above still adheres to the assumption that the components of the model, C_F, C_R, U, and G, remain the same within the exclusion and inclusion tests. Graf and Komatsu (in press) have found reasons to question these assumptions under some circumstances and have presented a general model in which these equalities were not assumed, though the independence of unconscious and conscious processes was assumed (but without much confidence).

6.5 Specific mechanisms of attention in memory storage and retrieval

It is one thing to demonstrate that attention affects memory and another thing to understand exactly what mechanisms take place and why. As many of the papers most relevant to the issue of the effects of attention on long-term memory have been published only within the last few years, it is doubtful if we are yet in the position to satisfy these more demanding goals. However, one way to begin to generate more specific hypotheses is to look for similarities in function across areas of inquiry. As it turns out, the issue of attention has been investigated much more thoroughly with respect to perception than it has with respect to memory.

6.5.1 Perception and attention in relation to memory

A leading theory of how attention works is that it is used to link together features after those features are automatically perceived. Without getting into details sufficient to sidetrack the discussion of attention and memory, Treisman and Gelade (1980) proposed that single features are perceived differently from feature conjunctions. For example, when subjects search for a blue T embedded in a field of red Ss and red Ts, they can detect the blue T simply by observing the presence of the color blue. This kind of search appears automatic in that it can be completed at a speed that does not depend on the number of non-target items present in the field, which must be processed in parallel. However, when subjects search for a blue T embedded in a field of red Ts and blue Ss, both the color blue and the letter T are present in non-targets, so that one must search for the correct conjunction of these features in a single object. That kind of search appears attention-demanding, in that the time to complete it increases steadily as a function of the number of non-target items.

There has been a controversy concerning whether or not searching for feature conjunctions truly is the critical difference between automatic and attention-demanding perceptual search. Duncan and Humphreys (1989, 1992) demonstrated that search can be made attention-demanding by increasing the difficulty of the target/non-target distinction in ways that do not involve feature conjunctions. Their theory was that similarity between the features of the target and distractors makes search more difficult, whereas similarity among the features of the distractors with one another makes search easier. The evidence on this issue will not be reviewed in detail here, but can be traced by reading Treisman (1992*a*) and the literature cited.

Either theory of attention can be viewed, though, as a variant of Posner and Snyder's (1975*a*, *b*) basic theoretical description of perception. In that view, there is an early, preattentive phase of perception in which features in the environment are automatically activated. There also is a secondary phase of perception that can take place only with the allocation of attention to particular elements in the stimulus field. For the selected objects, the percept can be much more integrated, complete, and semantically rich than for other objects in the perceptual field.

These theories of attention and perception are relevant to long-term memory because subjects cannot be expected to store information that they have not encoded. If materials are learned in a divided attention situation, then the encoding is likely to involve features of objects that have not been totally conjoined to form the correct objects. Moreover, it may well be the case that the idea of attentively conjoining elements applies not only to features within an object, but also to features and objects within a perceived event in the environment. In order to encode an entire target event fully and coherently, one would have to form associative links between successive target objects (e.g., between successive words in a list to be recalled), between each target object and surrounding contextual objects (e.g., between the list and the experimental room, apparatus, and experimenter), and perhaps even between each target object and an abstract, internal context based on the particular features of memory that are currently active or accessible (e.g., the subject's mood state; the ideas made most relevant by the experimental instructions). Any or all of these associative links might be diminished or absent in a divided attention situation.

The application of feature conjunction theory to memory thus would appear to be a rich area for future exploration. For example, the level of recognition of various perceptual features of stimuli within an unattended channel should be high even when the recognition of the stimuli themselves is relatively poor (and the recognition of particular sequential orders of the stimuli, even poorer). Among objects that are not fully attended, feature recombinations should occur in memory, as they do in perception (e.g., Treisman & Schmidt, 1982). Of more interest, though, the allocation of attention needed to conjoin features of an object in perception might not be as great as the allocation needed in order to remember the object that way explicitly. Although these hypotheses about attention have not yet been explored, there already is evidence (Reinitz, Lammers, & Cochran, 1992) that conjunction errors in memory (false recognition of new items composed of familiar features) do occur more frequently than feature errors in memory (false recognition of items with some new and some familiar features).

6.5.2 What occurs in implicit serial learning?

One potential counterexample to the proposal that sequentially linking objects requires attention comes from the work of Nissen and Bullemer (1987). In their task, subjects pressed a series of response keys as they lit up one at a time at four different locations. Unknown to the subjects, there was a repeating pattern embedded in the test. Subjects improved in their performance without any awareness of the pattern. They claim to have shown that this type of learning is eliminated in a dual-task situation, which would mean that implicit serial learning requires attention.

However, Stadler (1992) has shown that there probably was contamination from the particular distracting task that Nissen and Bullemer used. The task involved listening to a tone after each serial response and keeping track of the number of presentations of one kind of tone (e.g., the low one). Stadler suggested that the need to update the count may act as an event that divides the sequence. He was able to interfere with implicit serial learning just as much without a dual task, by inserting a long pause (e.g., 2 seconds) at each point where an update in the count would have been necessary.

Stadler's result suggests that implicit serial learning, with limited attentional allocation to the task, may be possible after all. However, what is being learned in this sort of situation? Curran & Keele (1993) suggested that it is associative chaining between adjacent stimuli, but not the learning of an integrated context as may occur with full attention.

Findings of Willingham, Nissen, and Bullemer (1989) suggested that what is learned in implicit serial learning is not a temporal sequence, but rather a situationally specific set of condition-action links. In their third experiment, they tried a variation in which the color of the signal light, rather than its location as in the Nissen and Bullemer procedure, determined which response key to press. For some subjects, the colored lights appeared in a repeating pattern of locations, though the sequence of colors and thus of response locations was random. This condition was meant to test for perceptual learning. Another group received a repeating series of colors, which resulted in a repeating pattern of correct response locations though the lights were presented in random locations. Implicit learning of the pattern occurred only in the latter group, indicating the involvement of a response-related component. In a subsequent generalization phase, the colors were removed and Nissen's original task was used (so that the stimulus location indicated the response location), and the learning that occurred in the first phase in the response-related learning group did not generalize. Thus, it was not the response pattern *per se* that was learned, but a series of condition/action contingencies.

Another way to explore the role of attention in serial learning is to examine its relation to short-term memory. Using a serial learning task based on Nissen and Bullemer (1987), Frensch and Miner (1994) found that serial learning ability correlated with short-term memory span under certain circumstances. After Cowan (1988), they argued that activation and the focus of attention are separate entities. They proposed that the short-term memory limit reflected the amount of information that could be activated, and that it correlated with serial learning ability only in situations in which the capacity limit of short-term memory was taxed. This occurred when the interstimulus interval was short (leading to many items activated at once) and the task instructions were intentional as opposed to incidental, which presumably permitted activation of memory up to the limit; or a dual task was imposed, reducing the availability of the focus of attention to maintain memory activation; or the population was elderly, limiting the capacity of the subjects' focus of attention to maintain activation. These data appear compatible with the notion that the focus of attention serves to allow the memory storage of organized conjunctions of items, rather than just individual items and their low-level associations.

The studies reviewed so far have considered the role of attention in only very simple types of serial learning. Some other researchers have considered learning in more complex tasks also (e.g., Berry & Broadbent, 1988; Hayes & Broadbent, 1988; Stadler, 1989; Fendrich, Healy, & Bourne, 1991). It would take us too far afield to review these, but they all seem consistent with the notion that simple contingencies may be learned automatically whereas context-specific information may be learned with more attention to the task.

In summary, it may be helpful to view the storage of items in their larger context as analogous to the perception of feature conjunctions. Both of these require attention. Nevertheless, some simple associations apparently can occur without attention. This seems to be a fertile ground for further research.

6.6 Automaticity, attention, and long-term memory

So far, we have investigated ways in which attention alters memory for stimulation. It also is possible to consider the converse case, in which prior stimulation results in a memory representation that modifies the attentional response to the stimulus. One important phenomenon in which this can be observed is that of "automaticity," as described by Shiffrin and Schneider (1977).

It may be helpful to consider automaticity in a somewhat unusual light. In the case of the habituation of orienting, like the case of automaticity, it is said that the involvement of attention in the processing of a particular type of stimulus declines as a memory representation of the stimulus is built up. After discussing automaticity briefly, similarities and differences between automaticity and habituation will be considered, as well as a general processing view of these phenomena.

6.6.1 Description of automaticity in search tasks

The description of automaticity by Shiffrin and Schneider was related to a basic task in which subjects searched through an array of one, two, or four characters to determine if a target item that belonged to a set of one, two, or four memorized items was present in the array. In a "variable mapping" condition, any of the items within the set held in memory on one trial could be used as distracting items on the next trial, and prior distractors could become part of the next memory set. In contrast, in a "consistent mapping" condition, items used as targets were never used as distractors or vice versa; two consistently separate sets of items were maintained. The basic finding was that search times in the variably mapped condition depended heavily on the number of items in both the memory set and the visual array, even after extensive practice in the task. Search times in the consistently mapped condition began in the same way, but with practice the functions become nearly flat across memory size and array size.

The account of the data offered by Shiffrin and Schneider (1977) was based on the notion that there is a limit in the attentional resources needed to search through items in memory or in an array. In a variably mapped search these resources must be divided among items, either by sharing resources concurrently or by examining items one by one.

In a consistently mapped search, it is clear that the processes change with practice. In a practiced subject, adding memory items or array items no longer increases the response time. Shiffrin and Schneider assumed that a parallel search of all items, that is no longer limited by attentional resources, becomes possible because the perception of the particular items in the target set has become "automatized." The evidence suggests that it is the category-specific significance of the stimuli that becomes automatized, and not just the perceptual identification. Specifically, when a consistently mapped search is followed by a session in which the previous targets become the distractors or vice versa, with the status of the entire ensembles of items switched in unison, there is so much interference that responses become slower than if subjects had gained no practice at all in the task (Shiffrin & Schneider, 1977).

6.6.2 General description of automaticity

A more formal description of automaticity is needed if the concept is to be applied across a wider variety of tasks. Shiffrin (1986) summarized the criteria that have been used by various investigators to define automaticity, although each of these criteria is in some way controversial. Drawing loosely from his discussion, automatic processes have been said to require relatively few attentional resources and little effort; to permit other, attention-demanding activities to be accomplished with little interference from concurrent automatic processes; and to require little advanced preparation. It has been said that a great deal of repetition is needed for automaticity to develop and that, once developed, automatic processes run to completion quickly and are difficult to modify or abort. Finally, it has been said that automatic processes can be carried out with little awareness and may leave behind very little of a memory trace that can be accessed in a direct memory task.

6.6.3 Some controversies about automaticity

Perhaps the most controversial aspects of the concept of automaticity have involved memory and its relation to the focus of attention. One issue concerns the processes by which automaticity takes place. Does one kind of search process become faster with practice, or is there a change in the type of process that takes place? A paper by Logan and Stadler (1991) provides rather convincing evidence that, in the case of consistently mapped memory search, there is a switch in the processes used from an active search of the target items in short-term memory to an automatic long-term memory retrieval of information about well-learned targets. The basic procedure of their study followed that of the consistent mapping condition of Shiffrin and Schneider (1977). Specifically, the set of items that subjects were to look for within a visual display changed from trial to trial, but were drawn from the same ensemble; no target item ever was used as a distractor in a later trial, and no distractor later was used as a target. Subjects were to respond "yes" or "no" as to whether a member of the target set was present in the visual display. However, unlike Shiffrin and Schneider (1977), Logan and Stadler included trials in which items that were members of the target ensemble, but were not selected as targets on that particular trial, sometimes were included as distractors in the visual display. Subjects had a strong tendency to make false alarms to those items or to reject them slowly, suggesting that they stopped using the short-term memory of the particular target set defined for each trial individually and responded instead on the basis of membership of visually displayed items in the larger target ensemble.

There is no evidence that this "superset strategy" is used in visual search, however, which is consistent with the observation that memory search and visual search use different processes (Hockley, 1984). Use of an ensemble appears most consistent with the idea that subjects could easily learn to conduct a parallel memory search of items in the memorized ensemble, whereas visual search may become parallel only with more extensive practice.

The notion of memorizing and using the target set ensemble is not one that necessarily translates straightforwardly to a wider variety of tasks in which automaticity has been observed. However, the idea that automaticity results from learning is of wider applicability. Logan (1988*a*) articulated a theory of automaticity based on the learning of instances. The theory states that there often are two ways of accomplishing a task: by applying an algorithm or by retrieval of learned information. A simple example is in a simple arithmetic problem (e.g., 8 + 4 = ?), where one can either perform a calculation or retrieve the answer from memory. If the answer is not stored soundly in memory, the algorithmic method will be faster, but retrieval of the answer directly may become faster and more accurate as the subject's knowledge base improves (Siegler, 1986; Geary & Burlingham-Dubree,

1989). The theory further states that knowledge is stored in the form of individual instances rather than memory strength based on a generalization across instances. Logan (1990) further found that the instance theory also explains results from repetition priming studies; in both repetition priming and automaticity, the increase in the number of instances experienced leads to improvement in the presumed retrieval time according to a predictable power function.

Logan's is not the only theory of automatization based on memory retrieval. Schneider (1985) and Schneider and Detweiler (1988) also proposed such a theory, but their theory states that repetitions increase the strength rather than the number of instances of memory representation. It remains for future research to try to determine which of these theories is correct.

The memory-based theories of automatization receive further support from a study by Strayer and Kramer (1990). They reasoned that, according to the instance theory, the role of a limited capacity "working memory" should diminish as automaticity develops. Before automaticity, the memory set must be compared to the probe item in a time-consuming fashion that presumably requires rehearsal of the memory set items. After automatization, the memory set is retrieved automatically from long-term memory in the same way, whether or not it is being rehearsed in a working memory. To assess these predictions, between the memory list and the probe item they inserted a rehearsal-preventing distraction task (determining if each Digit *N* in a series matched Digit *N*–2), a manipulation modeled after the studies by Wickens et al. (1981, 1985). In a consistently mapped task, it was found that all effects of the distracting task disappeared with practice, as expected.

The redefinition of automaticity in terms of underlying processes frees it from a dependence on the descriptive criteria that have been so controversial (mentioned above). There is no reason in the instance theory why all automatic processes must be beyond the subject's conscious control. Logan (1989) summarized evidence that, although subjects cannot always interrupt automatic perception and memory retrieval, they typically can interrupt the actions to be carried out on the basis of this memory retrieval. The typical procedure to investigate this question involves providing a stop-signal and determining if the process or action was stopped as requested, which can be determined by the presence or absence of priming effects of the process in question on a subsequent trial. Category and rhyme judgments could not be stopped (Logan, 1983, 1985), but retrieval of arithmetic facts could be stopped (Zbrodoff & Logan, 1986).

Another controversy has been whether or not automatically perceived stimuli produce a memory trace that can be used in a direct test of memory. Hasher and Zacks (1979) distinguished between automatic and effortful mnemonic processes, but both supposedly could be examined through direct tests. A key example of an automatic task was frequency judgments, which were found to be independent of the intentional vs. incidental nature of the learning based on task instructions and which did not appear to differ as a function of aging. In contrast, recall did depend heavily on both instructions and age differences. Both are direct tasks, but frequency judgment presumably is automatic and recall presumably is effortful.

Fisk and Schneider (1984) investigated the question of memory for automatic processes in a very different way, in two experiments using a divided-attention version of the search task. On each trial, subjects saw a word flanked by digits, which appeared either in the upper left and lower right corners or vice versa. One task involved detecting digits, and another involved detecting words of a particular category membership. Each word was presented 1, 5, 10, or 20 times in order to permit a test of frequency judgments in addition to a recognition test after the search task.

In one experiment, the emphasis on the word task varied between conditions. In different sessions, each subject was to make a semantic judgment of each word, try to remember it, make a graphemic judgment, simply "look" at it, or ignore it, while carrying out the digit task. There was almost no recognition or frequency memory in the "ignore" or "look" conditions, a bit more in the graphemic judgment condition, and much more in the other conditions. This experiment thus indicates that even frequency judgments are not totally automatic, as Hasher and Zacks proposed; they build up only when the words are attended at the time of presentation.

In Fisk and Schneider's (1984) second experiment a semantic category judgment of each word was required, but the judgment was permitted to become automatic through repetitions. After eight sessions, the new category members were used and new distractors also were used. This time, it was the memory of the new distractors that was at issue. Even though subjects succeeded in detecting almost all of the new targets, they displayed almost no recognition or frequency judgment memory of the new distractors, and could distinguish them from items that had not been presented at all only slightly better than chance.

In order to reconcile the results of Fisk and Schneider (1984) with those of Hasher and Zacks (1979), it is necessary to consider the precise role of attention in each case. In the case of the incidental recall condition within Hasher and Zacks' tasks, subjects were ignorant to the need to recall but they still devoted attention to the stimuli at the time of their presentation. Thus, perception was accomplished with attention but additional, deliberately mnemonic encoding was not carried out. This is apparently sufficient for a frequency judgment task, whereas the automatic perceptual encoding observed by Fisk and Schneider (1984) in their second experiment was not sufficient. A remaining unanswered question is whether or not memory for automatically perceived items would show up on an indirect test. The result obtained by Eich (1984) may suggest that the answer is "yes" but, as indicated above, control over attention in that study is suspect.

6.6.4 A comparison of automaticity with habituation of orienting: two perspectives on memory and attention

This chapter and the last have dealt with two separate cases in which memory affects attention, and they are in some ways analogous. In the case of the habituation of orienting, a repeating pattern in the physical environment leads to a neural model that limits the degree to which additional input matching that pattern recruits attention. In the case of automaticity, repeated exposure to a particular class of stimuli allows additional stimuli of that type to be processed and responded to adequately with a minimal involvement of attention.

On the other hand, there are important differences between habituation of orienting and automaticity. Whereas it is difficult to maintain attention on habituated stimuli, automatized processes sometimes trigger attention. For example, as mentioned above, items that have been used as targets in a consistently mapped search situation, and then become distractors in a subsequent experimental phase, continue to attract attention, now to the detriment of performance (Shiffrin & Schneider, 1977). This aspect of automatization seems quite unlike habituation of orienting; in fact, it seems more like the dishabituation of orienting that occurs when a significant stimulus is presented. Is it possible to describe habituation and automaticity within a common theoretical framework that captures the similarities and differences between them?

The general framework provided by Cowan (1988), amended to incorporate the general view of automaticity as a learning phenomenon, can do so. The essential players are simply long-term memory, activated memory, the focus of attention, and voluntary, central executive processes (Fig. 1.5). First, in habituation, immediate repetitions in the environment have set up a neural model within the activated memory. Provided that there is no discrepancy between the incoming stimuli and that model, and provided that there is no match detected with a "significant" template, the focus of attention will be free to be controlled by voluntary processes and there will be no obligatory recruitment of attention. (One unknown in this scheme is whether the templates for significant stimuli can be held within inactive portions of long-term memory, or whether they must be active to be used.)

Second, in automaticity, repetitions of the stimuli and their relation to the task that are stored in long-term memory permit the correct perception and response to be automatically activated. Until this automaticity is achieved, the focus of attention must be used to assist the activation of the correct units if the task is to be carried out correctly. After it is achieved, the focus of attention is free to be elsewhere, at the whim of voluntary processes. However, when targets that have been learned to the point of automaticity suddenly are used as distractors, significant templates for responses can be activated in what has become an inappropriate circumstance.

Summarizing across phenomena, habituation and automaticity are two types of process that act to free up the focus of attention. Habituation does it following the automatic activation of certain basic stimulus features in memory, by preventing what otherwise would be an obligatory recruitment of attention to the stimuli. Automaticity, on the other hand, does it through the automatic activation of more complex memory units that previously could be activated only with a voluntary devotion of attention.

6.7 A reassessment of attention and memory in Cowan's (1988) model

In retrospect it is possible to re-evaluate how the model proposed by Cowan (1988) fares in light of our discussion of long-term memory and attention. The basic, simple architecture proposed in that paper still has merit. For example, consider the asymmetrical relation that occurs between procedural and declarative memory (or some similar distinction) in amnesia. One finds many cases of what appears to be deficient declarative memory without a deficiency in procedural memory, but not the converse case in which procedural memory is damaged but declarative memory is spared. Anatomically, this makes sense if all of memory shares a common, diffuse representation in various cortical areas of the brain (see also Humphreys et al., 1989 for this idea) whereas declarative memory requires the additional involvement of hippocampal and frontal areas, as the anatomical research suggests.

Of course, it also has been suggested that the declarative/procedural distinction is not quite right and that a better distinction is between memory that takes place with vs. without the involvement of conscious awareness (Schacter, 1989). If this is so, then the anatomical architecture maps onto the cognitive architecture of Cowan (1988) well. Learning in vs. outside of the focus of attention is the important distinction to be drawn in normal individuals.

It is important to acknowledge, however, that the links that would be damaged in the typical amnesia are not specifically represented in Cowan's (1988) model, although they do not conflict with it. Crosson (1992, Chapter 8) brought up an apparent difficulty for Cowan's model that appears to be based on a misunderstanding of that point. He noted that the amnesic subject can recall newly presented information if tested immediately; therefore, the information should have been encoded in an attended manner and should be available for later explicit recall. In a normal individual, with connections between memory and attention intact, that would be the case. A dissociation between implicit and explicit memory in normal subjects can be obtained only by depriving the subject of complete attention to the target stimuli, but it does not follow that the same must be the case for amnesic patients.

A more fundamental problem is how the Cowan (1988) model is to account for new explicit learning at all, in normal subjects. The focus of attention was said to contain activated elements that already existed in long-term memory, so how does this result in the laying down of new memory traces for the new episodes? Presumably, the connection between these elements is new because they never have been activated at the same time before. In other words, the combination of target element and context is new. This new combination then can be encoded in long-term memory with the help of attention, so that new memories are formed from old elements.

This account of explicit memory encoding is the same as the account that was given previously for short-term serial recall. This leads to the prediction of similarity between these two types of events. For example, there should be little short-term serial recall of events that were unattended at the time that they were presented, just as there is presumably very little explicit memory for such events. The findings of Nairne (1992), that forgetting of serial information across 24 hours mirrors what previously has been observed in short-term forgetting, tends to confirm this similarity between short-term serial recall and episodic encoding.

7. The attentional focus and conscious awareness

I swear to you, gentlemen, that to be hyperconscious is a disease, a real positive disease. Ordinary human consciousness would be too much for man's everyday needs . . .

Fyodor Dostoevsky (1864/1960)
in *Notes from Underground*

Perhaps like many other researchers of cognitive and neural functioning, what brought me into research originally was an intense curiosity about the physical mechanisms that could produce consciousness. To exactly what mechanisms should we attribute our status as aware, thinking, reflective organisms? The type of model I have proposed (Cowan, 1988) could, I hope, serve as a general framework for the conscious mind. Within that model, like many others, the focus of attention is assumed to be the same as the contents of conscious awareness. However, there are many tough questions for such an approach that should not be glossed over.

Consciousness, as a phenomenological term, of course cannot be observed in scientific study directly; it can be observed only through introspection and through the interpretation of others' seemingly deliberate verbalizations and behaviors. I will assume that if a subject is consistently able to respond appropriately to a direct question about the presence or absence of a type of stimulus, either verbally or through a manual indicator, then the subject is conscious or aware of the stimulus when it is present, though failure of such an index does not necessarily imply unawareness of the stimulus.

One difficulty in linking conscious awareness to attention is that attention typically is used as a relative term, whereas consciousness typically is used as an absolute term. One cannot totally control the subject's attention, but one can observe attentional effects obtained through instructional differences between conditions. Thus, we speak of graded amounts of attention to a stimulus, in a continuous fashion. The situation is different for consciousness because we usually take the subjects to be conscious of whatever they say they are conscious of. Of course, people usually make a discrete judgment (perhaps based on some criterion level) and rarely state that they are "sort of" or "partly" conscious of a particular stimulus. To be consistent, though, we must be able to speak theoretically of the possibility of graded amounts of conscious awareness of a stimulus.

Having said this, I will continue to refer to items "in" vs. "out of" the focus of attention for the sake of simplicity. This is partly a matter of convenience of discourse, and partly reflects a belief that it is a tolerable simplification because *most* items are clearly in vs. clearly out of the focus of attention, despite the fuzzy boundary.

Not every investigator would agree that the content of consciousness is the same as the focus of attention (e.g., for various kinds of dissent see Allport, 1980; Wickens, 1984; Shallice, 1988). However, if one is to discuss a phenomenological concept like consciousness meaningfully, it seems important to link it to some fairly simple, coherent quantity that can be observed through experimental manipulation. Otherwise, the term becomes scientifically intractable. As we discussed in the last chapter, though, human subjects can carry out many types of information processing, including some verbalization, without expressing awareness of it and without explicitly recalling the automatically executed behaviors. Theoretically linking the concept of awareness of an event to that of attention to the event has the benefit of making it likely that the thoughts we identify as "conscious" will be the same ones that are found to be recalled in a direct memory test (e.g., Fisk & Schneider, 1984; Jacoby, 1991; Jacoby et al., 1993).

It seems clear that a better scientific understanding of consciousness requires the help not only of cognitive and neural scientists, but also of philosophers. Interesting philosophical debates about the nature of consciousness, making use of psychological and neurophysiological data, have been raging lately (e.g., Searle, 1984; Penrose, 1989; Dennett, 1991). Indeed, for any understanding at all, a philosophical attitude must be taken with respect to all sorts of data on the mind and brain. The psychologist's most important tool still may be the armchair (Arnheim, 1971).

Consider, for example, the question of whether or not consciousness requires a human brain or some similar biological organ. Computer programs can carry out many complex processes that appear to resemble, or at least to be competitive with, some aspects of higher-level cognitive thought in humans (Anderson, 1983; McClelland & Rumelhart, 1986; Newell, 1990). Are the programs conscious?

A computer simulation of intelligent behavior usually is fed one stimulus, or at most one type of stimulus, at a time for consideration (with the exception of certain systems specialized for interruptions or time-sharing operations). Contrast this with the view of human information processing that we have been entertaining. Multiple stimuli presumably reach the organism in a barrage. Automatic, parallel processing of basic features of many of those stimuli takes place, and these processed features serve as a resource base for a narrower core of attention-demanding, limited-capacity processing of higher-order features. Some of what humans do consciously, computer programs (e.g., Anderson, 1983) can simulate, but the processes in the computer appear to progress automatically and unconsciously. Some of what we do automatically, computer programs (e.g., McClelland & Rumelhart, 1986) can simulate, again automatically. In short, in computer simulations of human thought there have been interesting simulations of cognitive processing, but a general neglect of the concept of attention and, consequently, little work related to consciousness directly.

What essential purpose would consciousness serve in humans? One possible answer is that it, or a mechanistic correlate of it at least, adds flexibility and adaptability to behavior. It allows various subsets of the automatic, parallel processes to be specially selected as a basis for further, relatively more serial processing. It may allow different facts relevant to a particular choice to be considered together and weighed, much more meaningfully than could be accomplished with automatic processes alone. Thus, it may permit a coordination of broad, parallel processing and flexibility in the choice of the best material for further processing of a limited-capacity nature (cf. Baars, 1987, 1988, 1992).

The goal of this chapter is to consider the strength of the concept of consciousness as a unitary entity that is the same as the focus of attention, and the empirical validity of the unitary attention concept itself. The validity of this conceptual framework has been challenged in several interesting ways: by research in cognitive science, including both behavioral research on the possibility of multiple processing resources and neurological research on the disconnection of mental processing modules from one another; by other research in psychology, on dissociated states of mind in normal brains; and by the arguments of some philosophers, on the absence of any type of central observation point within the human mind. The concept of a unitary attentional focus will be explored in greater detail, and then the objections to this framework will be discussed and countered.

7.1 The concept of a unitary focus of attention

There are several key assumptions made about the nature of a unified attentional focus, and they are of special importance in our understanding of the human mind and will be discussed below. If these assumptions are false, the model of Cowan (1988) is false along with many other models (e.g., Atkinson & Shiffrin, 1968; Schneider & Detweiler, 1987; Baars, 1988).

7.1.1 Limited attentional resource

In these approaches to information processing, although it has been assumed that there may be multiple processing mechanisms that operate in parallel to one another, attention has been viewed as a single limited resource. The limited resource presumably can be concentrated on one channel, idea, or process, or can be divided up to provide some enhancement for two or three processes at a time. Whether focused or divided, though, it is assumed that allocating some attention to one task reduces the amount of attention available for any other task.

The hallmark of attentional resource limitations is a "performance trade-off" between two tasks that are performed concurrently (Norman & Bobrow, 1975). Attentional resource limitations are said to be in effect if better performance on one task (which can be induced by manipulating the relative importance, difficulty, or complexity of that task) can be achieved only at the cost of poorer performance on the other task. As Navon (1985) has pointed out, the notion of a performance trade-off is more than just the assumption that there is such a thing as selective attention. For example, there theoretically could be selective attention only because the subject would rather not encode useless information, and not because selection is needed in order to conserve a limited attentional resource. Thus, evidence will have to be viewed carefully.

7.1.2 Unity of attention and awareness

It is assumed also that awareness is a unified entity (cf. Baars, 1988). One presumably can speak of information in and out of the focus of attention and awareness, but not two separate, conscious awarenesses in a single, neurologically normal human brain. As we will discuss, the same might not apply to a patient with a lesion of the corpus collosum, the neural fiber bundle that normally connects the two cerebral hemispheres.

Attention clearly can be divided among channels, but under the assumption of the unity of conscious awareness, the perceived contents of the attended channels should be somehow integrated or combined. As a simple supporting example, if one is instructed to divide attention between visual and auditory channels, and one perceives the printed word "dog" and the spoken word "cat," there should be no difficulty in determining that the two words are semantically related; stimuli that can be consciously perceived simultaneously can be compared to one another, as awareness serves as a "global workspace" (Baars, 1988).

It is more difficult to verify the unity of conscious awareness than it is to verify the unity of the focus of attention, given that there is no direct measure of awareness. Some would hold that information that can be verbalized is in awareness, but then, it seems possible to speak without awareness, as when one automatically and as it were "thoughtlessly" gives a cursory "uh-huh" response to a question without interrupting one's work and without fully processing or remembering the question. Other, less ordinary examples include sleep-talking, automatic speech in epilepsy, and automatic speech in dissociated states (Hilgard, 1986).

Given the failure of verbalization to be a definitive indicant of conscious awareness, some would just as soon permit multiple response modalities and require that multiple criteria of awareness be met (e.g., Allport, 1988). If the subject coherently describes the stimulus, can report on it through multiple response modalities, and can recall it, awareness of it might safely be assumed.

One general principle to which we will return is that conscious awareness should be general enough to hold across response modalities. For example, if a subject can respond to a certain dim light flash by saying "I detect it," and can respond to a certain soft tone by pressing a button, then the same subject should be capable of saying "I detect it" for the tone and pressing the button to the light.

7.1.3 Distinction between "attention" and "selection"

Neumann (1990) has noted that there are many instances in which one item is selected from a larger field automatically. For example, holding a complex discussion while walking does not ordinarily make one fail to select correctly from the visual field and therefore to bump into a wall. Neumann still would like to call this type of automatic selectivity "attentional selection," in contrast to Neisser (1967), who had called it "preattentive processing." Unlike Neumann, I will reserve the term "attention" to refer to new, unpracticed selections, preserving the close relation between attention and conscious awareness. This will be distinguished from "automatic selection," which does not require awareness or take up attentional capacity.

Selective filtering on the basis of a physical cue (e.g., listening to the message presented in one ear within a dichotic tape recording) is another example of what I am calling automatic selection. According to the theory I have presented above and in Cowan (1988), habituation of orienting permits this type of automatic selection. Johnston and Heinz (1978) showed that selection based on physical cues does not very much increase the reaction time in a secondary task, unlike selection on the basis of a semantic distinction.

Attention, as I am defining it here (as a limited resource) does come into play in tasks that involve automatic selection, of course, in that the ability to automatically filter out irrelevant channels leaves one better able to attend to the *message* that occurs in the selected channel. In other words, voluntary automatic selection does not use much of a limited attentional resource, so it leaves one free to use this resource to better analyze the selected stimuli.

7.1.4 Internal vs. external attentional focus

Neumann went on to pose a more subtle distinction (p. 257):

> As I raise my eyes from the monitor screen that displays this text and look through the window, I see a huge wing of the university building facing me. Now I start shifting my attention [to other objects] . . . What has become of the university wing at this point in time? I am no longer attending to it, and yet it would be incorrect to say that I am not conscious of it.

This description restricts attention to the physical environment, whereas consciousness is allowed to include items in memory as well. In contrast, Cowan (1988) stipulated that both attention and consciousness could be directed either externally or internally. The level of attention and awareness in this example also would appear to be less for the recently attended university wing than for the currently attended object, reinforcing the notion of a fuzzy boundary of awareness and attention that was mentioned above.

Although it would be possible to write an entire book examining these assumptions and elaborating upon the nuances of attention and awareness, others recently have written thorough, excellent treatises on conscious awareness and information processing (e.g., Baars, 1988; Dennett, 1991; Velmans, 1991). Instead, I will concentrate on important challenges to the notion of a unified conscious field that have arisen from work in cognitive science, other areas of psychology, and the more inclusive field of philosophy. These challenges have been discussed by various other investigators but have not been considered thoroughly and in one place.

7.2 The challenge from cognitive science: multiple resources

The notion that there is a limited, central pool of attentional capacity that can be applied to tasks of all types is a standard idea in cognitive psychology that can be traced at least from Broadbent (1958) through Atkinson and Shiffrin (1968), Kahneman (1973), Norman and Bobrow (1975), Shiffrin and Schneider (1977), and up through the present time. However, as Allport (1980) pointed out in an influential, powerfully written article, this concept of a central capacity limitation is difficult to disprove and probably has been grossly over-used. Alternative formulations have been suggested and must be considered seriously. They have been based on cognitive research with both normal subjects and patients with brain lesions leading to dissociations of function.

It would be difficult to deny that there is such a thing as "attention," or selection of some items for further processing at the expense of others, but that is not as strong a claim as the statement that a central pool of capacity must be allocated across tasks. The key indicant of a capacity trade-off was supposed to be the decline in performance in one task with the increase in the difficulty or priority of another, concurrently performed task (Norman & Bobrow, 1975). However, there are other ways in which trade-offs can occur. For example, there might be interference between a reading task and a listening task because they rely upon some of the same linguistic processing modules in the brain. It might be difficult to find two tasks that had absolutely no specific processes in common, in order to observe a task trade-off in pure conditions that could reveal a capacity limitation.

Another difficulty for the capacity theory is that the total capacity available in the system cannot be assumed to be a constant, as it depends on the subject's motivation and arousal (Kahneman, 1973). If a trade-off between tasks is not obtained, one always can hypothesize that the total available capacity was greater than what was used. Conversely, any less-than-perfect performance can be accounted for on the basis of limitations in processing other than those of a central attentional resource, which Norman and Bobrow (1975) termed "data limitations". For these reasons, it is difficult to formulate the central capacity limit hypothesis in a way that is empirically falsifiable.

7.2.1 Allport's objections

On phenomenological grounds, it is difficult to doubt that there is such a thing as conscious awareness and that it can include a limited amount of information at any one time; it is the "primary memory" of James (1890). However, in a more recent article, Allport (1988) has challenged the usefulness of even that basic point in understanding a range of behavioral data. He points out several instances in which a brain-lesioned subject's apparent awareness of a visual object depends on what the response is. For example (p. 164), patients with right parietal lesions generally appear to neglect the left halves of objects. If such a patient is asked to bisect a horizontal line, the bisecting mark therefore is placed too far to the right. However, it has been observed that perception of the same stimulus in these patients seems more normal in a different task, in which the patient is to use the horizontal line as the base of an imaginary square and is to draw the right-hand side of the square. The paradox is that the subject seems relatively unaware of the left-hand side of the horizontal line in one task but not another, though the line itself is similar in the two tasks.

Bisiach (1988) pointed out similar cases. In one task (p. 111), subjects were to press a response key of the same color as the stimulus. Both the stimulus and the appropriate response key could be either on the left or right side, producing four different stimulus–response mappings. One patient with an extensive right frontal lesion could respond to a right-sided stimulus either verbally or with a right-sided button press. However, when the response button was on the left, he often gave no reaction to the same right-sided stimulus, and sometimes declared that no stimulus had occurred. The indication of awareness again was response-dependent.

7.2.2 Response to Allport

These examples indicate that task factors help to determine what information will enter awareness, but they do not seem fundamentally to challenge the unified awareness view. In the first example, it is not likely that there are two separate, aware minds in hemispatial neglect patients, one that ignores the left half of a line and one that does not. Instead, it appears somehow that the stimulus design influences awareness. The vertical line may provide a cue that permits better attention to the horizonal line. In the second example, the subject's observation of his or her own manual response may serve as a precondition for the verbal response because the subject is observing his or her own behavior and wants it to be consistent (cf. Gazzaniga, 1985). A manual response failure with the left-hand, reflecting the neural damage, therefore may be succeeded by denial that a stimulus had occurred.

In the face of these uncertainties, Allport (1988) suggested that the notion of conscious behavior can be applied, but only sometimes. There are different possible criteria of conscious awareness, and the term "conscious" may be used safely only when the subject's behavior appears "fully *integrated* and *coherent*," so that all possible criteria apply (p. 165). This is a reasonable, conservative suggestion, but I still would hold the assumption that conscious awareness continues to exist even when it is difficult to measure.

7.2.3 The multiple resources approach

Navon and Gopher (1979, p. 247) noted that "many experimental findings would embarrass the *strict* model of central capacity interference." These included many circumstances in which performance on one task is affected only minimally, or not at all, by the presence or difficulty level of a second task. It also included situations in which task difficulty and the relative emphasis placed on each task both have an effect, but in which there is no interaction between these factors even though both of them theoretically should affect the same quantity, the amount of processing capacity that is available for the performance of each task. In response, Navon and Gopher kept the notion of resources, but suggested that there is more than just one central resource. This allowed them to propose that two tasks would show performance trade-offs only to the extent that they had the same "demand compositions" or resource requirements.

This suggestion of multiple resources must be viewed as somewhat radical. Kahneman (1973) already had acknowledged that "structural" similarities between tasks could cause dual task interference that was not based on the division of a central attentional resource. Navon and Gopher's proposal goes beyond this, stating that various processing resources can be divided among tasks that need them.

The distinction between a structural similarity and a sharing of resources between tasks could be considered a fuzzy one. In Kahneman's theory, structural factors were distinguished from a central resource in that only the latter was thought to be an attention-related effect; but in the multiple resources view, it would seem untenable to hold that each of many resources is like a specialized attentional pool. The absence of a central, multipurpose attentional resource in the multiple resources view thus appears to be the most important difference between the views as they have been expounded.

Wickens (1980, 1984) has proposed a structure for resources involving three dimensions: stages of processing (e.g., early, encoding stage vs. later, responding stage), codes (e.g., spatial vs. verbal input codes; manual vs. vocal response codes), and modalities (e.g., visual vs. auditory). The similarity between tasks in a three-dimensional space of task characteristics presumably determines the amount of interference between them. Wickens (1984, p. 85) described evidence in support of this view. He found nearly perfect dual task performance between a visual tracking task and a Sternberg-type memory search task with items presented acoustically for a vocal response. When the stimulus or response modalities of the memory search task were visual, more interference was obtained. Other studies have found successful dual task performance on more complex tasks. For example, Allport, Antonis, and Reynolds (1972) found that subjects could learn to sight-read music and engage in auditory shadowing simultaneously.

7.2.4 Response to multiple resources approach

To explain dual task performance with very little task interference within the central capacity view, several options still are open (Broadbent, 1982). First, one may propose that many aspects of one or both tasks have become automatized and no longer require attention. Second, one may propose that subjects are able to learn to use efficient time-sampling and attention-switching strategies to carry out both tasks simultaneously. Sensory memory could be used to allow more flexibility as to precisely when items in each stimulus channel are sampled. To appreciate these points, one particularly influential experiment will be analyzed below in considerable detail.

7.2.5 Detailed analysis of a critical dual task study

Hirst, Spelke, Reaves, Caharack, and Neisser (1980) carried out a study that attempted to refute such criticisms, as is implied by their title, "Dividing attention without alternation or automaticity." The findings were dramatic, and their article is perhaps the most often-cited example of successful dual-task performance (even though the authors discussing this article generally ignore its claim that automaticity and attention-switching have been ruled out). Because of the importance of this study in the literature, and its interpretation, it seems useful to evaluate thoroughly the theoretical claims that were made and, in the process, to illustrate a number of difficult methodological pitfalls that hinder research on the combination of complex tasks.

Subjects learned to read and take dictation simultaneously, following much practice. They apparently learned to read as quickly, and with as much comprehension during dictation, as when the reading task was performed alone. The possibility of alternation of attention between the two tasks was dismissed because subjects took dictation equally well when reading relatively easy story passages and when reading more difficult encyclopedia passages (which should have required a larger percentage of task time if attention were alternated). The possibility of automatization was dismissed because of an assumption that there should be no comprehension or semantic integration for a language task that is performed automatically, whereas various measures were used to demonstrate that comprehension did take place for both tasks. Hirst et al. concluded that "so far as we know now, performance is constrained only by obvious peripheral factors . . . and by an individual's willingness to practice" (p. 114). Below, however, I will reconsider the logic of both of their experiments.

Experiment 1 of Hirst et al. (1980) had two purposes: first, to replicate the finding of Spelke, Hirst, and Neisser (1976) that subjects could learn to perform two complex tasks at the same time; second, to demonstrate that subjects do not accomplish this task by alternating attention from one task to the other. The first goal appears to have been accomplished well. Subjects learned to read and take dictation at the same time, and when they were fully practiced they apparently could read just as quickly, and with as much comprehension, with or without taking dictation concurrently.

The attempt to rule out attention alternation is more questionable. In the relevant manipulation, subjects who had been trained in dual task performance were transferred from supposedly easy story passages to supposedly more difficult encyclopedia passages, and vice versa. It was assumed that, if subjects really did alternate attention between tasks, they would not attain the same level of dual task proficiency for the encyclopedia passages; these passages would require a larger percentage of the task time for equivalent performance than would story passages. It was further assumed that, if alternation of attention took place, a transfer from stories to encyclopedia passages (but not the other way around) would disrupt dual task performance. Contrary to these predictions of the attention alternation hypothesis, no significant differences between performance for the two types of reading passages were observed.

One limitation of this logic is that it assumes that the total pool of attentional capacity is the same for both levels of reading difficulty. A different possibility is that, because the amount of effort varies from moment to moment depending on task demands, only a portion of the maximum total capacity may be available in many circumstances (Kahneman, 1973). One might observe no difference in reading scores for an easier vs. a more difficult reading sample because more effort was exerted (rather than more time allotted) for the more difficult task. This is a testable notion if one believes that there are valid psychophysiological indices of effort (see Beatty, 1982, for a review of research on one apparently successful index, pupillary dilation).

Second, there is a problem with the operational definition of reading task difficulty. Although the encyclopedia passages were shown to be less predictable than the story passages, there was no evidence that subjects actually devoted more time or effort to the encyclopedia passages. Perhaps the comprehension questions that followed the encyclopedia passages could be answered with less thorough understanding than those that followed the story passages. In the data, the mean reading speeds were only slightly different for the two tasks, and the reading comprehension scores during the first testing phase actually were somewhat (perhaps nonsignificantly) higher for subjects who read the encyclopedia passages. (When transferred to the story passages these subjects continued to obtain slightly higher scores, so perhaps sampling error accounts for the group differences.) If subjects did not actually devote more time to the encyclopedia passages and did not have to do so to achieve similar reading scores on the two types of passage, then the absence of an effect of the reading material is not inconsistent with an attention alternation hypothesis.

Finally, dictation performance may well have been affected by the reading task. As Broadbent (1982) pointed out, there was no measure of dictation accuracy in Experiment 1. The rate of dictation was reported as 10.2 words per minute (wpm) in the pretest and a comparable 10.3 wpm in the subsequent three sessions combined, but this information does not necessarily imply that the rate of dictation-taking was constant across task situations. Moreover, subjects worked in a group, so the rate of dictation presumably was the rate required by the slowest subject in the group.

In summary, there are at least three reasons to doubt that the absence of reading difficulty effects rules out a role of attention alternation in Experiment 1. First, the difficulty of the reading material could influence the total effort exerted rather than time devoted to each task. Second, there is insufficient evidence to determine if the intended manipulation of reading difficulty was effective. Third, performance in taking dictation was not monitored in this experiment.

The second experiment of Hirst et al. (1980) was designed to examine the possibility that one of the two tasks in dual task performance became automatic with practice. If it did not, the logical alternative was that attention was devoted to the dictation task with no cost to performance in the reading task. Sets of short sentences and random word strings were dictated during reading, and multiple measures of performance on both tasks were reported. Each task was also conducted alone as a control. The argument against automaticity rested on the assumption that, by any reasonable conception of attention, semantic comprehension and integration should not occur for automatically processed material.

Reading speeds and comprehension measures were collected, as in Experiment 1. Three measures of memory and comprehension of the dictated material were used in addition to copying speed: (1) a measure of the accuracy of copying for sentences vs. random word strings, (2) a measure of cued recall for sentence vs. random strings, and (3) a measure of semantic integration across sets of three sentences. The general finding was that the use of sentential organization for dictated materials occurred without any cost to passage reading speed or comprehension. However, the interpretation of these results is questionable.

Subjects copied and recalled sentences more accurately than random word strings, presumably because they made use of syntactic or semantic redundancies in the dictated sentences. (Dictation performance was much poorer in the dual task situation, but the advantage of sentences over random word strings persisted.) Thus, either sentence constraints can operate automatically or, as Hirst et al. proposed, the dictation task required attention even after extensive practice.

The assumption that comprehension of dictated sentences could not occur automatically is not well justified; opposing views are possible. For example, Fodor (1983, pp. 53 & 92) favored the view that there is an autonomous syntactic parsing device that operates automatically. There also was semantic information in the Hirst et al. sentences that did not appear in the random word strings. The sentences often contained pairs of words that were semantically related (e.g., "*Doctors* recommend *aspirin*"), whereas the random strings generally did not contain related words (e.g., "Money rain scratch"). Correct perception of some words in the sentences might have been reinforced by activation spreading from related words, and this spreading activation generally is assumed to include an automatic component (Posner & Snyder, 1975*a*, 1975*b*; Neely, 1977).

Even if comprehension does require attention, this does not necessarily mean that attention can be divided between two simultaneous tasks, given that the attention alternation hypothesis was not adequately ruled out. There could also be a combination of the two extenuating factors, with some automatic processing and some alternation.

The semantic integration measure of dictation performance was rightly deemed to be the most critical one, because semantic integration is the skill that is least likely to occur automatically. In this measure, modeled after Bransford and Franks (1971), sets of three consecutive dictated sentences formed a coherent passage (e.g., "The rope broke; Spot got free; Father chased him"). Every time that 10 such sentence triads were dictated, a signal was given for subjects to stop reading and take a recognition test in which each probe sentence was to be judged "old" (encountered in dictation) vs. "new." Within this test, three types of probe sentences were presented: (1) those taken directly from the dictated material (e.g., in the above example, "Father chased him"), (2) those with a semantic content that was "implied" by a combination of the dictated sentences (e.g., "Spot's rope broke"), and (3) those termed "unrelated," composed of some of the dictated words in an order that did not express the same ideas as the dictated sentences (e.g., "Spot chased Father").

In the pattern of results that Bransford and Franks (1971) took to reflect semantic integration across sentences, the implied sentences were judged familiar more often than the unrelated sentences even though neither type of sentence had been encountered before. Hirst et al. obtained a pattern of responses that seemed consistent with this conclusion, even in subjects who read while taking dictation (although the effects were attenuated in comparison with control subjects who only took dictation). Dictated sentences were judged most familiar, but implied sentences were still judged more familiar than unrelated sentences.

A fundamental problem with this approach is that semantic integration did not have to occur while the subject was taking dictation, as was implicitly assumed. Instead, the subject could retrieve separate representations of the sentences and integrate them at the time of recognition testing, or perhaps even between segments of dictation. Until this can be ruled out, the argument that attention was used to take dictation is much weaker.

It would not even be necessary for subjects to retrieve all of the dictated sentences in order to generalize to implied sentences. The pattern of results that was obtained might emerge, for example, if subjects remembered only one sentence within each dictated triad. Many of the implied sentences, as well as additional dictated sentences, could seem familiar at the time of the recognition test only because they were semantically compatible with the sentence that actually was remembered. In contrast, the unrelated sentences generally would seem inconsistent with the remembered sentences.

To illustrate, within one triad used by Hirst et al. the third dictated sentence was, "The owners moved." Suppose that a subject retained only that sentence. The dictated sentence that was included in the recognition test, "The stores closed," seems consistent with this remembered sentence, as does the implied probe sentence that was presented, "Stores went bankrupt." However, the unrelated sentence, "The stores moved," seems to contradict the remembered sentence. Hirst et al. (Table 3) presented 10 sentence triads as examples of their stimuli, and the problems discussed here seem relevant to most of these examples. Thus, one cannot dismiss the possibility that subjects remembered only a fraction of the dictated sentences and tagged others as familiar because of the semantic compatibility with the remembered sentences.

A further potential problem is that the sense of familiarity of any one sentence probe might be affected by sentences tested previously. For most recognition probe sets, the dictated and implied sentences were compatible with one another, whereas the unrelated sentence was usually less compatible with them. After a dictated sentence was presented in the recognition test, an implied sentence might be judged familiar, or vice versa, only because of the compatibility between those two sentences.

Finally, the test stimulus materials were confounded with conditions; one cannot rule out the possibility that the dictated sentences were the most plausible on the average, and the unrelated sentences, the least plausible. Consequently, it is possible that similar results would be obtained with these test materials even in subjects who had not received any of these sentences within the dictation phase.

These points do not necessarily apply to the original study of semantic integration by Bransford and Franks (1971). In that study, there was no attempt to argue that semantic integration took place during sentence reception rather than at a later time. Also, Bransford and Franks found that new sentences that contained more of the original propositions than any one of the originally presented (old) sentences were rated more familiar than those old sentences, whereas Hirst et al. did not attempt to replicate this additional evidence of semantic integration.

In summary, in this second experiment of Hirst et al., there is no evidence that subjects engaged in semantic integration of dictated materials while they were taking dictation, and there are insufficient grounds to eliminate the possibility that the use of sentence constraints, when taking dictation, can take place automatically. It is also unclear how much of the dictated material had to be remembered in order to perform the semantic integration task. Across both experiments, although the success of the dual task performance was indeed striking and fascinating, neither automatization nor attention-switching can be ruled out, any more than they can in other studies of successful dual-task coordination.

7.2.6 A more analytic approach to resources: the PRP paradigm

Pashler (1993) has argued persuasively that more progress can be made in understanding the structure of human resources with the use of punctate tasks. When two such tasks are presented in close succession, and speeded response to each one is required, the amount of interference between them and changes in this interference as a function of the stimulus onset asynchrony (SOA) are diagnostic of the source of interference. Pashler noted that this "psychological refractory period" (PRP) paradigm has a long history (e.g., Vince, 1949; Welford, 1952, 1967) although it has been ignored in recent years.

Fig. 7.1, after Pashler (1993), illustrates why PRP tasks may be diagnostic. Based on past research, it has been suggested that there are two types of interference between tasks. First, there is often some interference between perceptual processing of the first stimulus (S1) and the second stimulus (S2). Second, it typically proves to be impossible for the subject to select and initiate two responses at the same time. Therefore, there is a "bottleneck" in

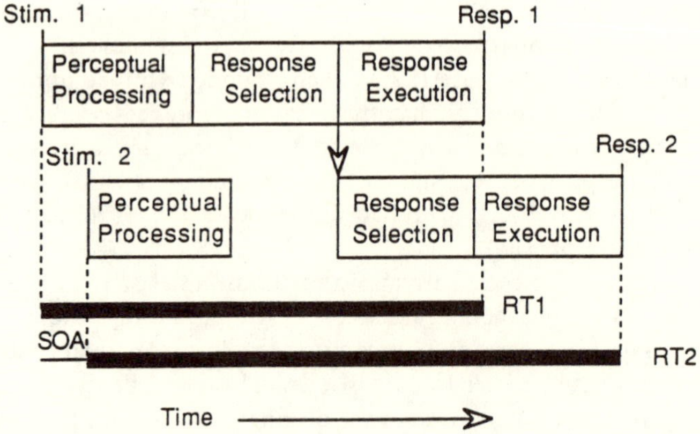

Fig. 7.1 Timing bottlenecks in a dual task. (After Pashler, 1993, Fig. 11.1).

processing at some point after perceptual processing, tentatively marked in the figure as "response selection". Interference in perceptual processing will diminish across SOAs, because at short SOAs there will be more time for perceptually processing the second task; the second response selection process cannot begin anyway until the response selection process for the first task has been completed. It thus has been argued that interference between tasks that holds steady across SOAs results from the response selection bottleneck.

One question that Pashler has asked is why much poorer performance typically has been obtained when the two tasks require the same response modality. Pashler (1990) found this to be the case only when the order of responses to be made was unpredictable. With a predictable response order, there still was interference between tasks at short SOAs, but it no longer was exacerbated by similarity between the response modalities. It was suggested that the difficulty typically lies in interference between task responses in short-term memory. The notion was that with response order unpredictable, both responses have to be held in a similar state of readiness in short-term memory, and that when this is the case with two similar responses, there can be confusion between them. Thus, response modality effects can be explained within a unified system and do not lend support to the multiple resources view.

Another question that Pashler has asked is if various perceptual and cognitive processes rely upon the same resource as whatever causes the response-related bottleneck? It was clear that some types of cognitive processing did rely on the same resource. An example was a task (Carrier & Pashler, 1992) in which the subject received a category and a letter and responded with an exemplar (e.g., a correct response to "VEGETABLE-A" is "asparagus"). When subjects were busy with a choice reaction time response to a tone, they were not able to accomplish any measurable processing on the second task. This was the case even in a situation in which the tone task was repeated for 10 seconds, with a tone coming immediately after each response to the previous tone. Thus, conceptual processing did not occur while the subject was busy making the series of speeded responses to tones. Of course, this finding is consistent with Jacoby's (1991) view that recollection is attention-demanding, unlike the automatic retrieval that leads only to a sense of familiarity.

Pashler (1991) obtained findings regarding perceptual processing that appear to provide more support for a multiple resources view. The first stimulus was a tone requiring a speeded response, and the second stimulus was a display of eight letters along with a probe indicating which letter to report. The probe was a peripheral marker or a central arrow pointing in the direction of one location. The display was followed by a masking array, so that the correct letter had to be selected quickly or it would be too late. Almost no effect of the tone task on the level of accuracy in the letter task was obtained, although the response to the second task was dramatically delayed. Pashler (1993) obtained similar results when the second task was to hold in mind a spatial array of squares (modeled after Phillips & Christie, 1977) to be compared to a second array. All of the results were taken together to indicate that perception and some aspects of short-term memory do not rely upon the same pool of attentional capacity as decision- and response-related processing. It was suggested that the term "attention" be reserved for perceptual selection, whereas the term "bottleneck" be used to describe any decision- and response-related conflicts. This, of course, supports Wickens' (1980, 1984) distinction between resources for earlier vs. later stages of processing.

7.2.7 Response to Pashler

A problem with Pashler's view is that the perceptual processing required by the letter selection and visual short-term memory tasks may be almost totally automatic. Even with a centrally located positional cue in the letter selection task, the perceptual process may quickly become automatized, much like following a one-way sign when driving. This view predicts that there would be little interference between the letter selection process and another perceptual selection process that did not share specific processing structures with visual letter selection, such as a tone discrimination task.

Of course, even in these cases of automatic selection, a speeded response does require attentional capacity and did act as a source of conflict between tasks. More complex perceptual selection also might be expected to require attentional capacity. For this reason, Pashler's research findings provide insufficient grounds on which to conclude that there are multiple pools of processing resources. They do not really disprove Kahneman's (1973) view.

Posner, Sandson, Dhawan, and Shulman (1989) recently obtained results that contradict the conclusion of Pashler (1991, 1993). They used a more demanding first task (shadowing) and found that the shift of visual attention to a second task was, in fact, significantly delayed.

7.2.8 Attention-division vs. attention-sharing

Navon (1984, 1985) has rethought the problem of resources in a penetrating fashion. Aside from offering formal criteria for identifying resources, he made the general point that what is taken for attention-division may only reflect what he terms "attention-sharing." The following analogy illustrated the difference between these concepts (p. 138):

> . . . imagine a room in which one boy is practicing violin while his sister is practicing piano. Presumably, both will not do very well. The cause is an outcome conflict that is due to the limited efficiency of human attentional selectivity. Would it make sense to argue that the siblings are *splitting* the room space? Of course, they could have queued for the usage of the room. But once they decided to use it simultaneously, room space is *shared* by them rather than *divided* by them . . . For example, can the boy use, say, two-thirds of the room space leaving the rest for his sister?

Hirst and Kalmar (1987, Experiment 3) obtained an interesting result that may shed light on the possibility of "attention sharing". Subjects heard a dichotic tape in which series of nouns were presented. On some trials, series of body part names were presented to one ear and series of animal names were presented to the other ear. On other trials, the category of items presented to the left and right ears was the same (both body parts or both animals). In the most interesting condition, subjects listened for a particular target item within each series and pressed a key once for each target heard. When targets occurred on both channels simultaneously, subjects detected both targets about 60% of the time with mixed categories, as opposed to only about 40% of the time when the same category occurred on both channels. In a selective attention condition, on the other hand, in which subjects listened to only one of the channels, it was found that the combination of semantic categories did not make a difference. This condition was intended to rule out a potential contribution of "structural interference" of a type that Kahneman (1973) might have warned against, due to having the same category in the unattended background channel.

What, then, is the nature of the interference? Hirst and Kalmar noted that it was unlikely that there are separate pools of attention-type resources for every semantic category, so a different explanation of the result was sought. They ended up endorsing a type of structural interference, but one in which the term "structure" referred to "any aspect of the cognitive system that defines the *state* of the system," which would "be both numerous and flexible" and would include "data structures, long-term memories, and semantic memories."

With some freedom of speculation, more specific proposals along these lines might be suggested. For example, some studies suggest that there is a "center-surround" organization of semantic memory retrieval, such that the process of retrieving one item inhibits retrieval of other items, with more inhibition of items that are similar in some way (Walley & Weiden, 1973; Jones, 1989; Carr & Dagenbach, 1990; Dagenbach, Carr, & Barnhardt, 1990). Assuming that there is one central pool of attentional capacity, there thus may be structural limits in the extent or ease with which it can focus upon similar items simultaneously, an "attention sharing" problem.

Other investigators also have been thinking along similar lines. Polson and Friedman (1988) argued that manipulating task difficulty in a dual task situation is likely to elicit differences in nonresource, structural factors of the tasks involved (e.g., the physical complexity of visual displays), and that the pure observation of resource factors instead requires the manipulation of task priority within a dual task situation. With this type of manipulation, they note that they have been unable to observe some of the resource factors that Wickens (1980, 1984) proposed. However, they have found what they believe to be separate pools of resources for the left and right hemispheres. This possibility will be addressed below.

7.2.9 Resources and hemispheric functioning

One of the best-known and important areas within neuropsychology entails the study of patients who received an operation, in order to diminish the effects of severe epilepsy, in which the corpus collosum connecting the left and right hemispheres of the brain was cut (Gazzaniga, Bogen, & Sperry, 1965; Gazzaniga, 1985). Most of those patients respond as if the information presented to the left hemisphere (through the right visual field) cannot be collated with the information that is presented to the right hemisphere (through the left visual field). This can be said because the left hemisphere maintains primary control over speech and the right hand, whereas the right hemisphere maintains primary control over the left hand. For example, the split-brain individual denies knowledge of stimuli presented to the right hemisphere, but the left hand indicates good knowledge of it.

In a split-brain individual, it seems clear that two conscious minds exist. Without that assumption, one would have to assume that the right hemisphere is able to follow instructions and report on stimuli coherently without being conscious. One cannot even use the verbal modality as a criterion separating conscious from unconscious behavior: when a purely verbal response is required, some split-brain patients have displayed verbal responses to conflicting left- and right-sided printed stimuli that alternate between hemispheres. First the left hemisphere verbally reports what it has seen; then the right hemisphere temporarily controls the speech apparatus, verbally reporting what it has seen; and then the left hemisphere amends its report, making up a response that appears to amalgamate the material from the two hemispheres, as if it is attempting to make sense of everything that has been said. In one example (Gazzaniga, 1985, p. 90), the left hemisphere received a series of words comprising the sentence, "Ann, come into town today" while the right hemisphere concurrently saw "Mary may visit the ship." The initial response and ensuing dialogue between the subject (S) and the experimenter (E) went as follows:

S: Ann, come into town today.
E: Anything else?
S: On a ship.
E: Who?
S: Ma.
E: What else?
S: To visit.
E: What else?
S: To see Mary Ann.
E: Now repeat the whole story.
S: Ma ought to come into town today to visit Mary Ann on the boat.

Notice that, although this type of response indicates that consciousness is surgically divisible, it does not necessarily imply that consciousness is ever divided in normal individuals.

Gazzaniga's (1988) recent work further indicates that normal cognitive functioning is not cleanly divisible into left and right hemispheres even in split-brain patients. Specifically, for some subjects, there were tasks that could be carried out easily pre-operatively, but could not be carried out well by either the left or the right hemisphere after the corpus collosum had been split (e.g., a "block design" task in which red and white colored blocks are to be arranged to match a picture). Gazzaniga suggested that there is a general action-control structure, typically in the left hemisphere, that uses a combination of information from both hemispheres in the normal individual.

According to Gazzaniga's theory, the left side of the brain ordinarily would play a special role in consciousness. It makes inferences about the incoming information and combines it into a coherent account of what happened and why. In the case of split-brain patients, and presumably in normal individuals at times, the left side of the brain must carry out self-interpretations without having access to sufficient information to do this correctly. For example, in one instance a split-brain patient was presented with the word "bottle" to the left hemisphere and the word "pink" to the right. The patient selected a pink bottle from among bottles of various colors. When asked why, the patient simply said, "pink is a nice color." In other instances, something presented to a split-brain patient's right hemisphere caused laughter and the left hemisphere came up with spurious explanations of what was funny. In contrast to these examples of excessive inference, the right hemisphere in split-brain patients generally has seemed incapable of making inferences at all.

A comparison of different types of neural disorders by Weiskrantz (1988, p. 192) makes clear that the type of self-inference displayed by split-brain patients depends upon the integrity of a specific neural apparatus and is not simply a general adaptive response that occurs across many varieties of brain damage. Whereas the speaking left hemisphere in split-brain patients believe that it is privy to information that it actually does not possess, "blindsight" patients, who have damage to the visual cortex but can localize objects accurately in the damaged part of the visual field if forced to guess, nevertheless insist that they see nothing. More like the split-brain syndrome, patients with Anton's syndrome are partly blind but deny that there is any loss of ability.

Given the divisibility of consciousness observed in split-brain patients, it seems reasonable to ask about a related but more behaviorally oriented concept in normal individuals, namely the allocation of resources. Are there separate pools of attentional resources for each hemisphere of the brain? Polson and Friedman (1988) argued that there are, primarily on the basis of two previous experiments that yielded comparable results (Friedman, Polson, Dafoe, & Gaskill, 1982, Experiment 2; Herdman & Friedman, 1985, Experiment 1). In both experiments, a memory load task was used in which the stimuli were visually presented sets of two to four bisyllabic (CVCVC) nonwords that subjects were to read aloud, retain, and then recall verbally. This presumably was a left-hemisphere-dominated task. A second task involved same–different matches of visually presented names (Friedman et al., 1982) or tone memory (Herdman & Friedman, 1985). In the first case, names were presented to either the left or right visual field, to channel stimuli to one hemisphere. In the second case, two different tones were presented to the two ears but the subject was to attend to just one ear, again so that the attended stimulus would be lateralized.

Tasks were presented singly or jointly, with the second task presented during the retention interval of the verbal memory task. Subjects were instructed to emphasize the verbal memory load task or the lateralized task. To ensure this, there was a set rate of payment for correct answers on the tasks when performed singly, and this amount was split between the two tasks in unequal proportions in the dual task situations. Only subjects who appeared to have strong left-hemisphere dominance (the prototypical case) were used.

Regardless of the hemisphere of presentation of the name-matching or tone memory task, decrements in both tasks were obtained relative to single-task performance. However, the amount of interference between tasks was greater when one of the tasks was lateralized to the left, as opposed to the right, hemisphere. More importantly, with left-hemisphere lateralization of the lateralized task, the amount of task interference depended on the task emphasis, whereas there was no effect of task emphasis with right-hemisphere lateralization of that task. Given the assumed left-hemisphere specialization for the verbal memory load task used in this study, the results appear to indicate that there was a performance trade-off only when both tasks were performed by the same (left) hemisphere. Polson and Friedman (1988) also cited other studies with somewhat similar findings.

However, it still seems possible in these experiments that the "resource" shared in this study was some specific left-hemisphere process rather than attention. For example, it could be that generation of the covert response labels "same" or "different" uses some of the same verbal processes as the verbal memory task.

A series of studies conducted on split-brain patients indicates that, in fact, surgically separating the hemispheres so that they cannot share specific information still does not create two independent attentional resource pools (Holtzman, Volpe, & Gazzaniga, 1984; Gazzaniga, 1985). A study by Holtzman and Gazzaniga (1982) illustrates this clearly. The task involved the tachistoscopic presentation of independent but simultaneous sequences of three shapes to the two visual fields, as illustrated in Fig. 7.2. One field's sequence of shapes (column A) was followed by a probe shape, and the subject was to indicate as quickly as possible whether or not that shape had been presented as part of the sequence (i.e., it was a Sternberg-type task). As shown in the figure, the unprobed hemisphere could receive either the same three shapes seen by the probed hemisphere (column B1) or three repetitions

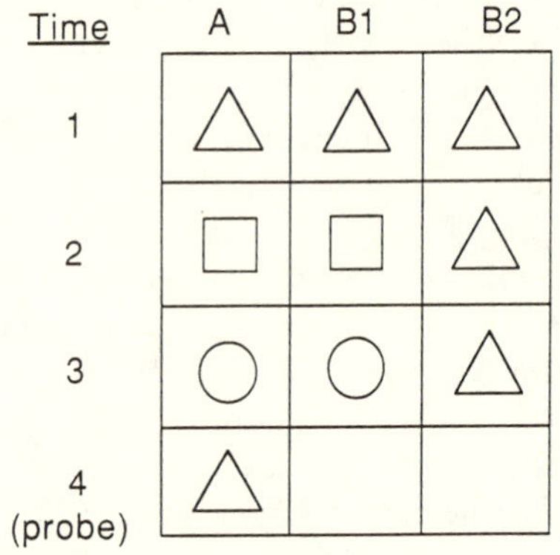

Fig. 7.2 Illustration of the experimental procedure of Holtzman and Gazzaniga (1982).

of one shape (column B2). For normal subjects, the mean response time to the probe naturally was less when the unprobed field contained the same items as the probed field. However, for the split-brain subject, the redundancy of the two fields was not helpful, because the subject could not collate the information in the two fields anyway; they were processed by opposite hemispheres. (This interpretation was confirmed in a followup experiment in which there was a cost of having totally different shapes in the two fields for normal subjects, but not for the split-brain subject.) Moreover, the split-brain subject's reaction times were actually *longer* for the parallel condition (B1) than for the condition with three repetitions of one shape in the unprobed field (B2).

It should demand less of resources to process the same item three times than to process three different items. Accordingly, the obvious interpretation of the above findings appears to be that the probed hemisphere in the split-brain subject performed better when the unprobed hemisphere placed a smaller demand on resources. Neurophysiologically, it may be that energizing structures in the brainstem, such as the reticular activating system, somehow distribute a limited amount of available activation to the hemispheres in a manner that takes into account their current activity levels. Alternatively, the hemispheres may inhibit one another's activity through remaining connections between them, such as the anterior commissure. In either case, the finding suggests that there is a truly central attentional resource that is not divided even when consciousness itself is severed.

Other studies of split-brain patients reviewed by Holtzman et al. (1984) appear to confirm this interpretation. For example, in one experiment, reaction times were recorded to visual stimuli that sometimes were preceded by a warning cue indicating which hemisphere would receive the test stimulus. On some trials, a left-hemisphere cue could indicate that a right-hemisphere test stimulus was to follow, or vice versa. It was found that the cue reduced reaction times to whichever hemisphere was indicated. On other trials, simultaneous cues were presented to both hemispheres, and these cues were found to be of no value. If there were separate attentional resources for the two hemispheres, it should be possible to energize both of them concurrently.

A recent study by Luck, Hillyard, Mangun, and Gazzaniga (1994) presents different results. Split-brain and control subjects carried out a task in which they were to search an array of figures, each of which consisted of a red and a blue square adjoined to form a vertically oriented rectangle. Within most of the rectangles, the blue square was on top, but the subjects were to search for a target item in which the red square was on top. This is a situation that requires a processing-capacity-limited search, so that the search time is a linear function of the number of rectangles in the array. Sometimes the array was presented entirely to one visual field (unilateral presentation), whereas other times the same number of items was divided equally between the two visual fields (bilateral presentation). It was found that, for the control subjects, the search time increased at the same rate as a function of the set size no matter whether a bilateral or unilateral array was used. In contrast, the split-brain patients were able to search the array at twice the speed when the array was presented bilaterally. Apparently, in those patients the two hemispheres are able to search concurrently, each through its own distinct array.

How are the findings to be reconciled? Luck et al. suggested that the relevant distinction is that the studies indicating a central attentional resource in split-brain patients dealt with a response bottleneck, whereas the study by Luck et al. dealt with a perceptual input limitation that apparently existed separately in the two detached hemispheres. That may be, but there is another possibility. The two hemispheres searched different arrays, but they still could have been guided through the arrays in tandem. In other words, though the content of the left- and right-hemisphere searches differed, the left and right foci of attention might have shifted through their respective visual fields in parallel. This might be tested by presenting identical n-item arrays to the left and right hemispheres. If the separate-resource interpretation is correct, then there should be a reduction in reaction time in comparison to a condition in which the n-item array is presented to one hemisphere only (because this situation presumably would capitalize on the fastest scan time in either hemisphere). There should be little or no difference between these conditions if both hemispheres are driven by the same attention controller.

The status of attention in split-brain patients is uncertain. One point to consider is that some specific information, and not just attentional control, apparently can be transferred between the hemispheres in these patients, though the speech side of the brain remains unaware of the information obtained from the nonspeech side (see Gazzaniga, Holtzman, and Smylie, 1987; Lambert, 1993). More research is needed to sort out the nature of attentional control, as opposed to information transfer, in these patients.

7.2.10 Resources and automaticity

According to the approach of Shiffrin and Schneider (1977), more practiced processes come to use less attentional capacity and thus become more automatic. As we have discussed in the previous chapter, Logan's view of automaticity is instead that subjects become more able to retrieve the required information rapidly from memory, and thus are less likely to derive the information in an algorithmic fashion. If Logan's hypothesis is correct, what impact does this view have on the possible existence of a central attentional capacity limit?

Although Logan's work sometimes is cited by investigators as a reason not to believe in the construct of attention, it need not have that effect. Logan (1988*b*) pointed out that a "resource theory" and his "memory theory" could be compatible. Specifically, he observed (p. 588) that "the strengths and weaknesses of resource and memory theories seem complementary: resource theory is strong on explaining novice performance and weak on learning, whereas automaticity-as-memory is the opposite." That is, the domains of applicability of the resource and memory theories appear to differ.

7.2.11 Resources and intelligence

The debate about whether or not a central attentional resource exists can be seen as a rather close parallel to the older, and conceptually related, debate about whether or not a "g factor" in intelligence exists. Spearman (1904, 1927) proposed that an individual's performance on an intellectual task can be explained on the basis of two individual difference factors: a general one, common to all tasks (g), and a task-specific one (s). This view seems analogous to Kahneman's (1973) approach to attention, which included a general central resource and task-dependent "satellite structures" that are used by the resource. Subsequently, in intelligence research, Thurstone and Thurstone (1941) proposed a system with no g or s factors, but seven primary mental abilities. This seems analogous to the position that Friedman, Polson, and Dafoe (1989) have taken, tentatively identifying at least three resources. Finally, Guilford (1967) proposed that intelligence factors are organized according to three dimensions: operation, content, and product. This dimensional scheme of course seems analogous to Wickens' (1984) dimensional treatment of processing resources according to processing stages, codes, and modalities.

Actually, the parallels between research on intelligence and resources may be more than just coincidental. If there is a g factor, a good candidate for it is the efficiency and flexibility of executive functioning (Norman & Shallice, 1985), which amounts to control of voluntary processing and attentional resources and presumably includes control of the focus of attention (Cowan, 1988), which serves as the active agency within a working memory system (Baddeley, 1986). It has been proposed that a main component of reasoning ability is, in fact, working memory capacity (Kyllonen & Christal, 1990). Executive functioning appears to be an important component of intellectual development in childhood (see Welsh, Pennington, & Groisser, 1991) and of the decline in intellectual abilities with age in elderly adults (e.g., Hasher, Stolzfus, Zacks, & Rypma, 1991).

Perhaps contemporary answers to the question of the structure of intelligence can be applied to the newer, less-researched question of the structure of resources. In addition to a host of specific factors, Carroll's (1988) review of individual differences in cognitive functioning finds some evidence for a general "fluid intelligence" or ability-to-learn factor. One of the strongest empirical studies was that of Gustafsson (1984), who administered a battery of tests to approximately 1000 sixth-grade subjects. The LISREL statistical technique yielded evidence for a hierarchical structure of intelligence. "First order" or primary factors were similar to those suggested by Thurstone and Thurstone (1941). These factors appeared to be organized into "second-order" factors that included fluid intelligence, crystallized intelligence (the sum of what has already been learned), and visualization ability. However, the fluid intelligence factor turned out to be exactly the same as a single third-order factor, namely the g factor. This research on intelligence thus seems to provide convergent support for the notion of a central, limited-capacity attentional resource.

Finally, the child development literature also seems consistent with the emphasis on general attentional resources in learning. Specifically, the infant performance measures that are the clearest known predictors of later intelligence are recognition memory and the speed with which an infant's orienting of attention to a repeated stimulus habituates (see McCall & Carriger, 1993).

7.2.12 Unified vs. multiple attentional resources: a summary

The findings on split-brain subjects reviewed by Holzman et al. (1984) appear to rule out a version of the multiple resources approach in which there is no central attentional capacity. Moreover, none of the other results provide clear evidence of *attentional* resources other than the central one. The situation seems to be as Kahneman (1973) suggested, that dual task trade-offs are caused both by a central capacity limit and by a host of specific structural similarities among tasks and the processes they require. The research on the factors of intelligence is convergent with this view as well.

On the other hand, the split-brain results also pose an important challenge to the central attentional capacity approach as it typically has been conceived. In this approach, it is assumed that conscious awareness is to be identified with the focus of attention. Split-brain patients apparently have two independent foci of attention (in the left and right hemispheres) but still some sort of central pool of processing capacity. If so, this demonstrates that processing capacity and conscious awareness are, in principle, separable. However, a separation of left-brain and right-brain conscious awarenesses in normal, adult individuals never has been demonstrated. In the normal case, a totally unified attention-and-awareness entity still could exist.

7.3 The challenge from psychology at large: dissociated states and awareness

The one weak link in the chain of inferences leading to the idea of a unified awareness is that the concept clearly breaks down in the case of neural damage. With sectioning of the corpus collosum, one apparently finds two conscious minds, although they apparently share a common pool of attentional resources (analogous to how Siamese twins share nutritive resources?). If truly similar phenomena could be obtained in neurologically normal individuals, it would disprove the concept of a unified attentional focus.

All of the evidence relevant to this possibility has not been considered in one place and, in fact, various groups bearing conceptually related but very different kinds of evidence have had little to do with one another. For example, Hilgard (1986, 1992) has summarized evidence on a variety of "dissociated states" in which the subject appears to be conscious and functioning cognitively but is, at the same time, unaware of a large amount of self-knowledge that ordinarily would be part of conscious experience.

Evidence of this sort is rarely discussed by the authors who examine single- vs. multiple-resource accounts of attentional capacity limitations. Perhaps this is not surprising, because the two groups display very different attitudes toward psychological theory. The resource theorists generally hesitate to discuss "consciousness" very much, owing perhaps to the difficulty in operationally defining it. In contrast, the dissociation theorists sometimes freely state that subjects were conscious (or unconscious) of a particular activity; one sees this, for example, in studies of hypnosis. However, there are important studies with well-controlled and clever manipulations in both fields. Below, I will overlook the difference in attitudes in an attempt to find what is most useful in the dissociation literature.

7.3.1 Dissociated states

Dissociated states considered by Hilgard (1986) include fugue states, in which someone temporarily forgets his or her personal identity; multiple personality disorders, in which the patient has one personal identity at one moment and a different personal identity at another moment, with each alternative personality having not only its own name, but also its own separate episodic record of events that occurred when it was "out" (Nissen et al., 1988); and, most relevant to the present concerns, dissociations induced through hypnosis. It is not contrary to the concept of a unified attentional focus if some information that ordinarily would be accessible to conscious awareness is made inaccessible, as in these states; but it would be damaging to the concept if two parts of the mind could be induced to have separate conscious experiences at the same time.

Hilgard (1986) carefully and thoughtfully evaluated evidence from dissociated states in neurologically normal individuals. However, one of the more speculative statements in the book can be used to illustrate why and how care must be taken. Hilgard suggests (p. 185) that the typical case of daydreaming may be a dissociated state in which we are dividing attention between, and simultaneously aware of, both an external episode and an internal fantasy. This interpretation could be wrong for at least two reasons. First, it is possible that all of one's attentional resource actually may be devoted to the fantasy, so that the residual overt actions of the daydreamer may be accomplished automatically. They may be available for later direct recall only if the person in question intermittently snaps out of the daydream, switching attention back and forth.

Second, whenever a subject truly does divide attention between overt events and covert images, creating in effect two areas of the focus of attention in the model of Cowan (1988), those areas should affect one another by sharing information. Theoretically they could do this because concepts activated by each focal area would break into the other focal area uncontrollably, due to their mutual pertinence (Norman, 1968). However, this does not seem like a reasonable account of daydreaming, which seems relaxing whereas divided attention usually seems stressful to the subject (e.g., Cowan et al., 1990).

Fig. 7.3 depicts adaptations of the general model of the focus of attention of Cowan (1988) to three different situations that can occur. In the first (top panel), a divided attention situation is depicted. A limited capacity resource must be split between two focal areas that share information. In the example shown, a cashier is attending to operation of the cash register but also to a customer complaining that the fruit is too expensive. There can be a flow of relevant information between the focal areas, perhaps linking them into one unified focus: in the example, the pertinence (Norman, 1968) of the word "fruit" to the cashier's duties is noticed by the cashier and causes a reorganization of activities.

In the second situation, simultaneous attended and automatized activities are depicted. Specifically, the cashier is more experienced and is able to operate the register automatically. However, there still can be a flow of information between activities. The automatic activation of the concept "fruit" during cashier's duties secondarily activates the concept "tropical," and both concepts together feed the current focus of attention, a fantasy about a vacation on a tropical island.

Finally, the last adaptation depicts the abnormal case in split-brain patients. Although a limited capacity resource still must be split between two foci of attention, one in the left hemisphere and one in the right, there can be no sharing of specific information between the hemispheres.

In fugue states and multiple personality disorders, the case may be like the middle panel because there is no evidence that more than one conscious state

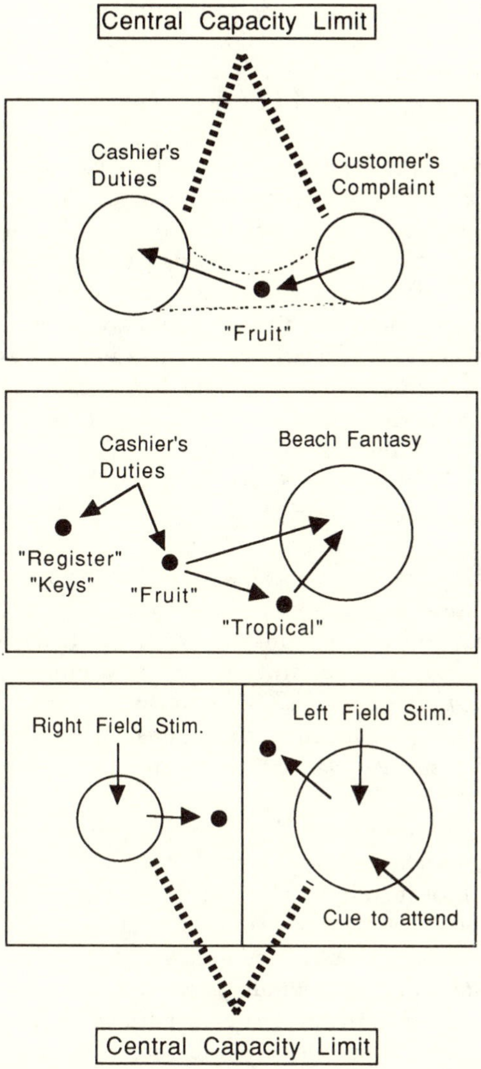

Fig. 7.3 Three hypothetical instances of attentional allocation and its effects.

is present at a time. For example, in multiple personality disorders, no one has given one personality a problem to work on and then found that this mental work continues while the personality is in a latent state, taking processing capacity away from whatever other personality becomes active.

On the other hand, within hypnosis there is a phenomenon known as the "hidden observer." It is based originally on the ability to obtain "automatic writing" from a hypnotized subject (Binet, 1889–1890; James, 1890). A hypnotized subject could be made to believe that he felt no pain and had a very insensitive two-point threshold. However, "automatic writing" obtained from one arm attached to a "planchette," a small board supported by casters and a pencil, indicated that the stimuli were sensed and caused pain.

In more modern times, Hilgard (1986, p. 186) has recounted a seminal episode in which an unnamed classroom "instructor" had told a hypnotized subject that he would not hear anything that occurred during hypnosis (i.e., "hypnotic deafness.") Having achieved that state to his satisfaction, a student asked if "some part" of the subject might be aware of sounds. The instructor agreed to try something new. He told the hypnotized subject that "there may be intellectual processes . . . of which we are unaware, such as those that find expression in night dreams. Although you are hypnotically deaf, perhaps there is some part of you that is hearing my voice and processing the information. If there is, I should like the index finger of your right hand to rise as a sign that this is the case." To everyone's surprise, the finger did rise. The subject then said, "Please restore my hearing so you can tell me what you did. I felt my finger rise in a way that was not a spontaneous twitch, so you must have done something to make it rise, and I want to know what you did."

In a subsequent session, it proved possible to speak to the same part of the subject's mind that had raised a finger, with the instructions (p. 187) that "When I place my hand on your arm like this (he demonstrated) I can be in touch with that part of you that listened to me before and made your finger rise . . . " With the hand on, the subject recounted all that had occurred; with the hand off, the subject claimed to know nothing about what had happened.

In subsequent experiments, Hilgard investigated the hidden observer phenomenon more systematically. Groups of subjects in these experiments have been selected for high hypnotizability; most potential subjects do not qualify. Even among those who are selected, only some display the hidden observer phenomenon. Hypnotized subjects in one set of experiments were subjected to a pain-inducing stimulus (e.g., submersion of a hand in cold water) under "hypnotic analgesia." The pain reports were very low, but it was possible to get a very different response if subjects were asked to rate the pain with a hand hidden from view. The hand often reported that the stimulus did hurt, as much as was observed in nonhypnotized subjects.

Hilgard (1986, p. 188) cautioned that "'the hidden observer' is merely a convenient label for the information source tapped through experiments with automatic writing and automatic talking" and does not imply that there is "a second personality with a life of its own." It seems likely that interpretation of the hidden observer phenomenon will depend largely on the interpretation of hypnosis itself.

Sarbin (1992) brought up the possibility that subjects in whom the hidden observer phenomenon can be obtained excel in adopting the theory of mind that is implicit in the experiment, and in producing behavior that would be consistent with that implicit theory. In his words (p. 56), is a statement of unawareness by the hypnotized subject "the result of an effort at disattending in order to make good the occupancy of the status of good hypnosis subject?"

This type of account appears to be in conflict with some of the detailed observations of hypnosis, however. One type of evidence (Hilgard, 1986, p. 143) has to do with the continued compliance with instructions over time. Hilgard reasoned that this compliance should be limited by the subject's unwillingness to continue in the face of the self-observation of irrational behavior. In one study, the suggestion for posthypnotic behavior was to say "February" whenever the number "3" was encountered in any form. Compliance dropped off severely after the number was encountered for the third time. Hilgard attributed this to subjects becoming aware of the bizarre responses they were making. In contrast, compliance with a less obtrusive suggestion (automatically writing the opposite of each spoken answer) actually increased across repeated opportunities.

This evidence reported by Hilgard seems somewhat preliminary. However, in passing, it is worth noting that the inhibiting influence of awareness on behavior has been suggested in other contexts. Baars (1988) suggested that the striving for internal consistency is an important function of awareness. Nisbett and Wilson (1977) pointed out that some behavioral phenomena are essentially irrational and might not occur if the subject was aware of them (p. 247):

> For example, if people were aware of the effects of the presence of other people on their tendency to offer help to a person in distress, they would surely strive to counteract that influence, and would therefore not show the typical effect ... If people knew that their judgments were subject to influence from other judgments made about an object or from judgments just previously made about other objects, or from the order in which the object was examined, then they would correct for such influences and these effects would not exist.

A second form of evidence against Sarbin's view of hypnosis as social role-playing involves the processing limitations observed under hypnosis. For example, Stevenson (1976) had subjects carry out counting and addition tasks by writing the answers with a hand hidden under a box. Highly hypnotizable subjects were hypnotized and then were to commence with the writing when the posthypnotic cue "begin" was given. In the "conscious" condition they were supposed to remain aware of the writing, but in the "unconscious" condition they were instructed to be unaware of it. A second group of subjects, of low hypnotizability, were instructed to simulate hypnosis. They were told that they would be dismissed from the experiment if the experimenter (who was blind to the subject's status) was able to discover the simulation. The result was that counting and addition task performance in hypnotized subjects was degraded severely when the subject was to be unaware of the writing. In contrast, the instruction to act aware or unaware made no difference for simulators. Given that subjects were told to do their best on all tasks, the hypnotized subjects should not have let their performance slip in the "unconscious" condition if they were acting in order to comply fully with the task demands.

Knox, Crutchfield, and Hilgard (1975) carried out additional experiments with hypnotized subjects, confirming that there is a processing cost of following the instruction to keep an activity unconscious. They had subjects engage in two tasks (naming colors, and pressing keys in a repeating pattern of three left, three right), with instructions to be conscious of both tasks or, in a different condition, to be unaware of the key-pressing task. The usual dual task interference on both tasks was obtained. In addition, there was a cost of being unaware of one task, which showed up as an 11% increase in the number of key-pressing errors with the key-pressing task to be held unconscious.

Do the costs of blocking awareness and of performing dual tasks occur for similar reasons? The authors replied that they did because a fairly high, significant correlation ($r = .69$) was obtained between subjects' key-pressing error scores for the unaware, single-task condition and for the aware, dual-task condition. (This correlation of raw scores is meaningful because it is the same as the correlation between two kinds of key-pressing error difference scores, *conscious single task–unconscious single task* and *conscious single task–conscious dual task*.) Using the individual-subject data that were reported in the article, one can find assurance that this finding is not due to individual differences in key-pressing error levels, because the correlation between each of the difference scores and conscious single-task scores was near zero.

To summarize, although there are certain posthypnotic suggestions that are thwarted when the subject becomes aware of the irrational behavior (e.g., responding "February" to the number "3"), the need to hold a task unconscious adds a processing load that is not duplicated in subjects simulating hypnosis.

Although the pattern of findings in hypnosis goes against the suggestion that hypnotized subjects simply are doing a good job at role-playing, and suggests that they really do believe they are unaware of certain information, it also argues against the independence of the processes occurring with the "overt" and "hidden" observers. There is a single processing capacity limitation that apparently cannot be increased through hypnotic instructions, just as it cannot be increased through a split-brain operation.

The best interpretation of the hidden observer phenomenon still remains unresolved, however. There are at least two possibilities, the first being simply that the information obtained through the hidden hand takes up little attention and is not in awareness enough for the subject to remember it when later probed, similar to the finding that items perceived automatically are not remembered (e.g., Fisk & Schneider, 1984). One difficulty with this view is that it would appear inconsistent with the findings of the prior studies discussed by Hilgard (1986), in which a hypnotized subject was instructed to be amnesic, the forgotten material was brought out and retrieved verbally in the guise of a "hidden observer," and the subject subsequently displayed amnesia again, when the hidden observer was not being specifically addressed (see above). This appears to suggest a second possibility, that two aspects of the mind both can become conscious according to verbal report and responsivity criteria. However, in that case, one still does not speak to the amnesic individual and the hidden observer at the same time. Thus, only one part of the mind was in awareness at a time.

The amnesia instructions may elicit different schemata or idea structures for the amnesic part of the individual and the hidden observer. This difference may be large enough that the two schemata serve as separate, noninterchangeable recall contexts. If this is the manner in which the hidden observer works, however, then information obtained through the hidden observer should be available to the amnesic part of the individual in an indirect memory test. That specific prediction apparently has not been examined, but it has been found in a number of studies that information presented during hypnotic amnesia affects performance on indirect memory tests (see Kihlstrom, 1987 for a review).

A different account of the hidden-observer phenomenon is that, at least in the case of the hidden observer displayed in the form of a hand under a box, there really are two consciousnesses at the same time. Hilgard (1986) argues for that view, which would be closely analogous to the situation in split-brain patients.

From the point of view of phenomenology, the question is whether or not two separate, noncommunicating parts of the mind can be in a state of awareness or consciousness at the same time. This question seems scientifically almost intractable, at least at the present time. However, it has counterpart in behavioral terms. In these terms, the question becomes whether or not two parts of the mind can share a limited-capacity, central attentional resource without also sharing specific information. The answer in the case of split-brain patients appears to be "yes." The answer in the case of psychological dissociations obtained through hypnosis in neurologically normal individuals is unknown because we do not know how much of the hidden observer's report is automatic.

In any case, other types of mental dissociation may be related to hypnosis. Bowers (1991) pointed out that most patients with multiple personality disorders prove to be easily hypnotizable, although most hypnotizable subjects are mentally quite normal. It may be that the preconditions necessary for multiple personality disorders to emerge include both a psychological disturbance or trauma and high suggestibility.

Another parallel might be drawn to dissociations that occur within dreams. For example, Borges (1984, p. 35) recounted a dream in which a man insisted on keeping his hand inside his coat for an unknown reason. When the man finally drew his hand from the coat, it turned out to be a bird's claw, to a horrible effect. Somewhere in the mind, the surprise apparently had been set up, keeping another part of the mind in suspense temporarily. Even if this account is correct, however, the part of the mind that set up the suspense could have been operating outside of attention and awareness no matter how it is defined.

To summarize, dissociated states need not necessarily reflect multiple independent awarenesses in the individual, although the jury is still out. To maintain the unified-awareness view, however, it must be allowed that unconscious processing can accomplish some rather sophisticated things, such as weaving part of a plot or responding to an external stimulus. The review by Kihlstrom (1987) attests that this may be the case.

7.4 The challenge from philosophy of mind: multiple perceptual drafts

In the words of Miller (1987), noted by Velmans (1991), "consciousness is a word worn smooth by a million tongues." Nevertheless, it has been largely a multitude of philosophers who deserve credit for keeping the interest in conscious awareness alive through thick and thin times in psychology. The following discussion will be limited primarily to one recent book that has provoked an exceptional amount of interest, *Consciousness Explained* (Dennett, 1991). It is long, complex, and thoughtful, and argues against the unitary view.

7.4.1 Is there a Cartesian theater?

Dennett characterizes the traditional view of consciousness as the view of the "Cartesian theater." Descartes held the view that the information from various sense organs could not reach consciousness until they were combined to project a unitary view of the environment. He thought this occurred in the pineal gland, located in the center of the brain and very near where the input from the two eyes meets. According to Descartes, for example, a visually observed object would project images onto the retinas of the left and right eyes, but this information would become conscious only after reaching the pineal gland. Although Descartes long ago was shown to be clearly wrong about the specific neural projections, a modern version of this view flourishes. It states that there is a place where information from various sources in the brain all comes together and is projected to consciousness (the Cartesian theater) somewhere in the brain.

Dennett's view is that there is no such central place; no theater and no homunculus inside the head to watch it. Instead, the information that comes into the system presumably exists in the form of "multiple drafts" that are not necessarily consistent with one another, and then a coherent story is formed from them. Two applications of this idea will make it clearer.

7.4.2 Phi phenomenon example

As one good example of a phenomenon resulting in conflicting multiple drafts, Dennett (1991; also Dennett & Kinsbourne, 1992) cited a variation of the apparent motion or "phi" phenomenon. In this phenomenon, described originally by the early Gestalt psychologists, two lights that are flashed in rapid succession, at an interlight interval falling within a certain range, appear as a single light moving between the two poles defined by the actual positions of the lights. The specific variation of the phi phenomenon that was of most interest to Dennett was one in which the two lights were of different color (e.g., a red light followed by a displaced green light). This apparently resulted in the perception of a moving light that changes color in the middle of its perceived trajectory (Kolers & Von Grünau, 1976). The lights that produced this motion were each 150 ms long, separated by a 50-ms blank interval.

Dennett (1991, p. 115) highlighted the paradox of this effect as follows:

> Suppose the first spot is red and the second, displaced, spot is green. Unless there is "precognition" in the brain (an extravagant hypothesis we will postpone indefinitely), the illusory content, *red-switching-to-green-in-midcourse*, cannot be created until *after* some identification of the second, green spot occurs in the brain. But if the second spot is already "in conscious experience," wouldn't it be too late to interpose the illusory content between the conscious experience of the red spot and the conscious experience of the green spot? How does the brain accomplish this sleight of hand?

Dennett saw this paradox as evidence for a multiple drafts theory of perception. According to this theory, the percept of a stationary, first light is discarded when it no longer fits into the overall scheme of the perceived event. The percept of a moving object presumably is constructed after the second light appears and then is put in its proper place within the perceived event, so that the sequence of the *perceived* times of occurrences of events in this example is not monotonically related to the sequence of times at which the events were first registered or constructed in the brain. Time is viewed as a feature that is signalled by some neural configuration, in a manner analogous to any other kind of physical feature of the environment.

7.4.3 Gap-filling examples

One way that the phi phenomenon had been described in the past (e.g., Goodman, 1978) is as a situation in which the mind "fills in" the sequence of events as it is perceived. Dennett (1991, p. 127) objected that "What Goodman overlooks is the possibility that the brain doesn't actually have to go to the trouble of 'filling in' anything with 'construction'—for no one is looking" (i.e., there is no Cartesian theater). He continues, "As the Multiple Drafts model makes explicit, once a discrimination has been made once, it does not have to be made again; the brain just adjusts to the conclusion that is drawn, making the new interpretation to the information available for the modulation of subsequent behavior."

Dennett (1991) applied this same principle to achieve a reinterpretation of other common phenomena that typically are understood through gap-filling, such as the fact that the visual blind spot rarely is noticed. He suggested that, because there is no Cartesian theater, there need be no filling in for its sake. Instead, the absence of information in the blind spot simply is ignored. One compelling example (p. 345) was the case in which an observer stares at a field of plaid. No discontinuity in the field is noticed, but Dennett finds it implausible that the observer could fill in the blind spot with a plaid pattern.

7.4.4 Parallel and serial processing with multiple drafts

Somehow, multiple drafts of an event are combined into a coherent story that the subject believes to be the truth. How does this occur? Dennett proposed that the brain is a massively parallel processing device, but that there is a layer of organization that is intermediate between this parallel processing architecture and our serial stream of consciousness. The intermediate layer is what he calls the "virtual machine" of the mind.

The virtual machine is a simulation of one kind of machine by another; in the case of the brain, simulation of a serial processing device by the parallel brain. Just as a digital computer, traditionally a serial processing machine, can be made to simulate a machine with parallel processing capabilities (e.g., simultaneous operation of two or more programs in different windows), the basically parallel-operating brain can be made to simulate a serial processing machine. This simulation is important because it forces a resolution of disparate, sometimes conflicting pieces of information to create a coherent view, and thus a more often coherent and decisive course of action for the individual. Information is accepted, distorted, or rejected as needed to fit the prevailing conscious view. The virtual machine that produces this serial sequence of ideas is, Dennett proposes, the individual's conscious mind.

Notice that Dennett's virtual machine seems similar in its actions to the "inference engine" suggested by Baars, 1988 and assigned specifically to the left hemisphere by Gazzaniga, 1985. Notice also that the model of a virtual serial machine within a parallel architecture resembles the parallel/serial processing model of Schneider and Detweiler (1987).

7.4.5 A general critique of the multiple drafts view

I am receptive to the clever notion of a parallel architecture that produces information one is not directly conscious of, and a serial virtual machine that produces information that one is conscious of. However, there appear to be at least three shortcomings in Dennett's approach.

First, Dennett did not adequately discuss the factors that determine which information enters consciousness. He appeared to suggest basically that the fate of any particular piece of information is determined by how it fits in with the subject's current conscious view. There was little mention, however, of a selective attention process that would give some information special status within the virtual machine.

When attention is considered, it seems likely that Dennett's virtual machine would include only the attended information and would exclude unattended information. As we have seen in the previous chapters, there is a wealth of information that is processed unconsciously, in parallel, and remains generally unavailable to conscious perception. All processed information presumably becomes activated in some way, but only the attended subset of the information reaches consciousness and becomes part of the personal history or explicit memory of the subject (e.g., Schacter, 1989).

The second criticism, which is related to the first, is that the evidence for the absence of a Cartesian theater was weak; Dennett's arguments merely suggested that a Cartesian theater would not be logically necessary for consciousness. There may well be multiple drafts of information processed inattentively, but there still may be a Cartesian theater, in particular, one related to awareness and attention. If so, it would exist in the sense that some information undergoes special, separate, enhanced processing, not in the sense that there is some agent inside the head experiencing the theater. Thus, it would be a "theater" in the sense of a subordinate meaning offered by *The American Heritage Dictionary* (Morris, 1976): "a place that is the setting for dramatic events." Only some of the unconscious information would be expected to reach this theater and thereby to be available for deliberate action and explicit recall. The concept of multiple drafts and their coherent resolution thus is not inconsistent with this Cartesian theater concept.

Third, given that the present view disagrees with Dennett (1991) in the analysis of both attention and perception, it is not surprising that there is a disagreement about the nature of working memory as well. Dennett's conception of working memory is as a global workspace, similar to that in

Anderson's (1983) theory of information processing. That kind of workspace would consist of the collection of all information that is currently in a heightened state of activation; in Hebb's (1949) terms, the currently active cell assemblies. For example, Dennett writes (1991, pp. 270–271):

> The consensus in cognitive science ... is that *over there* we have the long-term memory ... and *over here* we have the workspace or working memory, where thinking happens, in effect. And yet there are no two places in the brain to house these separate facilities. The only place in the brain that is a plausible home for either of these separate functions is the whole cortex—not two places side by side but one large place ... That means, then, that the workspace has to avail itself of the very same neural tracts and networks that apparently play a major role in long-term memory.'

That view of working memory does not distinguish between attended and unattended activated information. It may be complete for most intelligent computer programs, but only because selective attention generally has not been installed in such programs. Serial programs require no attention because they are fed one stream of stimuli at a time. However, attention should be an important topic for programs that simulate parallel sets of activated information. Laird, Rosenbloom, and Newell (1986) thus mentioned that "the issue for the standard computer is how to be interrupted, whereas the issue [for computer models of cognition] ... is how to keep focused."

In summary, the psychological concept of an attentional spotlight may be the basis of a Cartesian theater. It has been suggested that attended information receives its special status through the involvement of particular areas within the brain acting in a rather modular fashion (see Posner & Rothbart, 1991). Therefore, we should turn to neuroscience in more detail to assess the possibility that there may be a Cartesian theater, and will do so in the next chapter.

Dennett would say that a reintroduction of any kind of Cartesian theater renews the problem of how multiple drafts become resolved into a coherent picture to be shown to the Cartesian theater. However, it seems that Dennett may be underestimating the sophistication of unconscious, automatic processing (Kihlstrom, 1987). Let us examine such processes for two specific examples that were mentioned above, the phi phenomenon and the blind spot.

7.4.6 Critique of Dennett's interpretation of the phi phenomenon

For the phi phenomenon, Dennett offers us only two choices: a metaphysical reinterpretation of time, which he of course rejects, or a multiple drafts model in which inconsistent drafts of perceptual events are excluded from the final interpretation. A third possibility, though, is that the context-specific nature of processing often prevents inconsistent drafts from occurring in the first place.

Consider first the notion that an initial draft is formed of the first light as a stationary object, which is then discarded from the final draft. Actually, there is no evidence that this information is discarded. My informal observation of the phi phenomenon suggests that the first light appears stationary for a split second before it appears to begin to move; it does not look like a shooting star, which appears to move from the moment it is first seen. Thus, there actually is no contradiction here. It is quite possible that the perception of immobility proceeds briefly (i.e., until shortly after the second light is presented) and then is succeeded by an impression of movement, but an initial "draft" need not be discarded.

Now consider the progression of movement. According to the multiple drafts view, the perception of movement cannot be constructed until after the second light is perceived, but when it is constructed, impressions of two stationary lights would be discarded. However, there is no reason to assume that a stationary impression of the second light is, in fact, formed so rapidly. The presentation of the second light, in the context of the first one having just been presented, could result in the perception of movement first, and the perception of a stationary second light only subsequently.

Finally, the color-phi phenomenon may not be as perceptually striking as Dennett believed, which would mean that there is less to be explained. Subjects in the relevant experiment (Kolers & Von Grünau, 1976) were assigned the task of selecting a color that matched the color of the illusory moving object at various points along its movement trajectory. However, the indication of an abrupt change in color, from that of the first light to that the second, could have been made on the basis of a reasonable response to the task demands. Subjects were not given the option of saying that the moving object was colorless, but when I reconstructed the stimuli in my laboratory, I in fact experienced the illusory moving object as colorless except at the endpoints of its trajectory.

Boring (1957, p. 146) recounted a simple experimental paradigm that is similar in its impact to the phi phenomenon, but illustrates a limitation in the multiple drafts approach. A pointer swept over a scale and a bell rang at a certain time during the pointer's movement. In subjects' perceptions there sometimes was a negative displacement of the bell, so that it might appear to coincide with "4" on the pointer's scale though it actually had not been rung until the pointer reached "5." William James (1890) noted that Von Tchisch had suggested that this was a miracle in that you could hear the bell before it sounded, but James ridiculed that interpretation. Later work indicated that it was an example of the phenomenon of "prior entry:" because one is listening for a bell, it sometimes enters awareness with a shorter delay than does the pointer.

Dennett's multiple drafts account would not find this phenomenon problematic, but the result would seem arbitrary. Why should the representation of the arrival time of the pointer be modified to seem sooner than it actually was? This result can be understood best by appealing to the notion of selective attention, which may affect the relative times at which different stimuli enter awareness. The multiple drafts interpretation is based on an amalgamation in which all information is taken into account to produce a rational or coherent outcome in conscious awareness. This, of course, is different from the present view, which is that an attentional device only permits some of the sensory data to participate in conscious awareness and its rationalization function.

7.4.7 Critique of Dennett's interpretation of the blind spot

Dennett exaggerated the neural-computational difficulty of examples such as "filling in" the blind spot with plaid. Plaid is constructed of a collection of straight lines and colored fields. All it would take to "fill in" plaid would be for each line or field broken by the blind spot to be completed or filled in separately.

Crick and Koch (1992) summarized evidence that the brain does fill in. Some of this evidence came from neurophysiological sources. Perhaps the most logically compelling evidence, however, comes from perceptual research summarized by Ramachandran (1992). Absence of information from the blind spot need not be ignored, as is proposed in the multiple drafts approach; it can attract attention. In one example, the visual field contained a multitude of white disks, each with a black dot inside it. When the blind spot falls in the middle of one of the white disks, its black dot is invisible and the white disk that it centers upon appears perceptually to pop out from the others. No doubt there is some truth to the blind spot generally being ignored, but that alone cannot account for the popout that was observed; filling in apparently does take place.

7.4.8 General comment on Dennett's thesis

Dennett proposes that there are multiple drafts that get resolved on the basis of coherence by a "virtual machine" in the brain, as an alternative to the view that there is a Cartesian theater in which some information must be reprocessed. However, the concept of multiple drafts and of a Cartesian theater are theoretically independent. There might be multiple perceptual drafts, typically on an unconscious level, along with a reprocessing that occurs for attended information only.

Investigators who have emphasized the existence of multiple contradictory perceptions have tended to take Dennett's stance against a Cartesian theater. For example, Bisiach (1992) offered the example of a patient with neural damage that makes her simultaneously realize, and yet doubt, that her left hand belongs to her. One can think of examples of logically contradictory perceptions even in normal people. For example, place one hand about 3 inches from your face, directly in front of one eye, and stare at something across the room. The percept is of a hand that is transparent, with the distant object appearing to be seen with both eyes. This percept does not match our knowledge of reality.

In contrast, investigators who have emphasized examples of the inability to access multiple perceptual drafts simultaneously have tended to argue against Dennett's stance. For example, Crick and Koch (1992) noted that, in some binocular rivalry situations, one view is partly or completely suppressed by the other.

In actuality, Dennett's view still seems loose enough to handle either type of phenomenon. Either multiple drafts can be observed, or the virtual machine eliminates all but one. Similarly, in an opposing view in which there is privileged processing of attended information (a kind of Cartesian theater), it is acknowledged that multiple perceptual drafts often exist, but in some circumstances only one of them can be attended. The argument for or against the existence of a Cartesian theater thus is not illuminated by these examples of multiple drafts.

7.5 Response to challenges to a unified view of attention and awareness: a summary

Various phenomena in cognitive psychology and neuropsychology, dissociative phenomena, and philosophical inquiries into perceptual phenomena, all have been used to question the concept of a unified focus of attention and awareness, and have raised the possibility of multiple co-existing agencies to take its place.

My response in some of these situations is that much of the processing that is attributed to awareness goes on automatically. For example, in situations in which a subject is able to carry out two tasks concurrently at a proficiency approaching either task when performed alone (Hirst et al., 1980), there is no evidence that both tasks are in the focus of awareness and attention simultaneously. There is evidence that, at least sometimes, they are not, or at least that both are not recalled as one would expect of attended stimuli (Fisk & Schneider, 1984). In dissociated states, also, there may be multiple cognitive structures or schemata that remain informationally isolated from one another, but there is no good evidence that both of them use a limited attentional resource at the same time.

Separate domain-specific patterns of task interference do not imply domain-specific attentional resources. Instead, they may reflect domain-specific processing mechanisms leading to "structural" sources of task interference, as suggested by Kahneman (1973). Similarly, just as task interference does not always imply an attentional limitation, stimulus selection does not always imply that attention has been used. Some selection can occur on an automatic basis. Also, considerable perceptual preprocessing is done automatically, so that many potential perceptual conflicts are resolved before the point in processing accessed by the focus of attention.

The postulation of a unitary attentional spotlight in normal subjects does not imply that a single neural center mediates this spotlight. In split-brain patients, it does seem likely that the left and right hemispheres are informationally isolated though they share a central attentional resource limitation. However, information is shared more broadly throughout the spotlight of attention in neurally intact subjects, because of the rich interconnectedness of the attentional system. Dissociated and isolated cognitive subsystems may co-exist, but they typically do so outside of this focus of attention. The unitary view of attention and awareness thus appears to remain as the most parsimonious view.

The discussion turns now to the relation between neural and cognitive models of attention, awareness, and memory, in which the unitary phenomena will be dissected, if at all possible.

8. Concluding observations, with steps toward neuroscience

Creating a new theory is not like destroying an old barn and erecting a skyscraper in its place. It is rather like climbing a mountain, gaining new and wider views, discovering unexpected connections between our starting point and its rich environment. But the point from which we started out still exists and can be seen, although it appears smaller and forms a tiny part of our broad view gained by the mastery of the obstacles on our adventurous way up.

Albert Einstein
as quoted by Asimov and Shulman (1988)

We're all amateurs; we don't live long enough to be anything else.

Charlie Chaplin
in the film *Limelight*

This book began with a simple and, I believe, intuitively plausible framework for human information processing, the model suggested by Cowan (1988). Some critics might tend not to fault the model as far is it goes, but they might argue that it does not go far enough. They might well argue that the simple concepts of the model, such as temporary memory activation and selective attention, are fine, but that the components of memory and attention should be subdivided, either according to neurological and neurophysiological evidence (e.g, Shallice, 1988; Posner & Rothbart, 1991), or according to behavioral evidence (e.g., Wickens, 1984; Baddeley, 1986). This may be, but I have adopted a level of analysis at which subdivisions are avoided until they are shown to be fundamental. I believe that this level of analysis should remain useful as long as the basic constructs of short-term memory and selective attention, and the relationship between them, still require further research.

Instead of worrying about subdivisions of the basic, intuitively obvious concepts, I have found that these concepts are not intuitive and obvious to all. In fact, most of the book is concerned with carefully weighing the support for the basic concepts. Chapters 2 through 4 dealt with the concept of short-term memory broadly defined. Chapter 2 reviewed the evidence in favor of sensory memory concepts, and Chapter 3 reviewed other evidence in favor of short-lived memory activation. Chapter 4 examined evidence that has led some researchers to question the separate existence of short-term memory mechanisms. The conclusion of these chapters was that there is a short-term memory, although it is not solely or even primarily responsible for many of the key phenomena originally attributed to short-term memory.

Chapters 5 through 7 dealt with the concept of selective attention. Chapter 5 reviewed new evidence in favor of the proposition that the construct initially termed an "attentional filter," which has remained somewhat mysterious in cognitive psychology, operates through the more specific mechanism of habituation of the orienting response. Chapter 6 reviewed evidence that one of the most important (perhaps *the* most important) distinctions for long-term memory is the distinction between memory stored and retrieved automatically vs. memory stored and retrieved with the benefit of the attentional system. This may not be a controversial conclusion, but it is a point that has been emphasized in the research literature only recently. Finally, Chapter 7 re-examined the concept of attention as a unitary construct in behavioral science, and awareness as its phenomenological counterpart. Many types of evidence against this unitary nature of attention and awareness and in favor of subdividing it, were examined but in the end the validity of the unitary construct was upheld.

Rather than further explaining the rationale for this basic approach, which would essentially be a reiteration of Cowan (1988) and Chapter 1 of this book, the following discussion will do several things. The first part is a summary of some of the ways in which memory and attention appear to be closely interrelated. This may be of use because it consists of observations that could be drawn from the text, so far, only by cutting across chapters. Second, possible directions for future change in the theoretical framework will be considered briefly. The purpose of this is mainly to explain the direction that the next section takes, which is to attempt to map the constructs from Cowan (1988) onto known structures and processes of the brain. Third, the fruits of that effort are to be discussed. Thus, the book ends by launching in a new direction.

8.1 Relationships between memory and attention

This book has reviewed ramifications of two aspects of the human mind: temporary memory and selective attention. The emphasis has been on the close, inseparable, reciprocal relationship between memory and attention. Let us briefly review that relationship, and pose some unanswered questions, before going on to ask how the most useful models for further inquiry might be formed.

8.1.1 Effects of attention on memory

The most meaningful division of memory appears to be a division into memory that is dependent upon vs. independent of attention and awareness of the stimuli, both at the time of encoding and once more at the time of recall. Memory would appear to be based upon a progression of fundamental processes: encoding, activation, decay or inactivation, retention, reactivation, and context-dependent retrieval; but attention can affect all of these processes. Without attention to the stimuli, there still is encoding of at least many of the sensory features of a stimulus. Those sensory features are temporarily in a privileged or activated state that can be seen both behaviorally (e.g., Broadbent, 1958; Cowan et al., 1990) and neurally (e.g., Mäntysalo & Näätänen, 1987; Sams et al., 1991; Lü et al., 1992*a*,*b*). This activated state soon is lost. Although it is uncertain, it appears that some trace nevertheless is left on the nervous system and that if the trace is reactivated by another, "reminder" stimulus, it can affect performance in the future (Eich, 1984; Cowan et al., 1993).

What the automatic processes alone cannot accomplish is (1) a more complete encoding of the stimuli, (2) longer-lasting activation, and (3) a more deliberate, conscious retrieval process. Let us examine these in turn.

First, better encoding of the physical features, somewhat better encoding of structural categorical features such as phonemes, and incomparably better encoding of semantic features appears to take place for attended stimuli (e.g., Cherry, 1953; Broadbent, 1958; Moray, 1959; Treisman, 1964; Cowan et al., 1990). When multiple, similar stimuli are present, it also appears to take attention to bind features together to form objects in the correct combinations (Treisman & Gelade, 1980; Treisman, 1992*a*).

Second, information that otherwise would decay out of activation can be prolonged with rehearsal and attention (e.g., Vallar & Baddeley, 1982; Baddeley, 1986; Cowan et al., 1990). Rehearsal may go on semi-automatically, but it appears to take some attention to initiate and regulate the rehearsal process (Guttentag, 1984; Cowan et al., 1987).

Third, more deliberate recall is possible when attention is present at the time of encoding and retrieval. Thus, the effects of amnesia can be mimicked by imposing a divided attention task (Hasher & Zacks, 1979; Smith & Oscar-Berman, 1990). Attention at the time of encoding may help the memory to be stored in a way in which, similar to the attentional binding of features in perception (Treisman, 1992*a*), events are bound correctly to the context in which they occurred. It has been proposed that amnesiacs, who typically have normal attentional processes, nevertheless have a disconnection between these attentional processes (or conscious awareness) and the store of contextually specific memories (Schacter, 1989). Thus, both divided attention and amnesia greatly impair performance on direct memory tests but leave memory as measured by indirect tests relatively unimpaired. In the terms of Jacoby et al. (1993), automatic familiarity processes are intact but conscious recollection is impaired.

It is not yet clear how independent these effects of attention on memory are from one another. To some extent, they must be separable. Some effects of attention on long-term memory could result indirectly from the poorer encoding of unattended stimuli or from poorer methods of rehearsal. However, these cannot account for all of the effects of attention, given that distraction during the retrieval phase alone can have effects comparable in magnitude to distraction at the time of encoding (Jacoby et al., 1989).

Short-term memory can be viewed as a hierarchical structure consisting of all of the activated portion of memory, on one hand, and the portion of this activated memory that is in the focus of attention, on the other hand. Cowan (1988, 1993) assumed on the basis of available evidence that the limit on the focus of attention is a capacity limit, whereas the amount of memory that can be activated concurrently is unlimited, although a time limit applies. In contrast, Cantor and Engle (1993) recently have assumed that there is a limit in the amount of activation that can exist, as well. This limit was proposed to account for individual differences in fan effects; differences in the amount of activation were suggested, rather than differences in the speed of activation. Understanding the limits in memory activation thus is a basic goal awaiting further research.

It is also unclear just how many phenomena finally will be subsumed under the heading of activation. Many of the phenomena that piqued the field's interest in short-term memory in the first place have been shown to be independent of the concept of temporary memory activation. For example, recency and modality effects occur with extended lists in which the items are separated by distracting periods (e.g., Bjork & Whitten, 1974; Glenberg & Swanson, 1986). It is difficult to distinguish between effects of temporary activation and effects of context on access to items that are no longer active. Whereas the physiologists are busy working on activation directly (e.g., Lü et al., 1992*a*, 1992*b*), it is likely to be years before the physiological indications of contextual effects in long-term memory will be known. Until that occurs, one must wonder if the two are easily separable on physiological grounds or not.

8.1.2 Effects of memory on attention

The relation between memory and attention is not a one-way street. Having a repeating pattern of stimulation in memory appears to allow the observer to ignore that pattern of stimulation (i.e., the orienting response to the stimuli habituates), which frees up attention to be directed voluntarily (Sokolov, 1963; Waters et al., 1977; Kraut & Smothergill, 1978; Cowan, 1988). Conversely, a change in the physical properties of the unattended stimulus recruits attention (Cherry, 1953).

What still is not clear is how much attention must be used to encode the items in memory in the first place, in a way that allows the continued habituation of orienting to occur. If the subject concentrates very hard on an attended channel, can attention completely eliminate orienting to physically new stimuli in an unattended channel? To the extent that the initial orienting is weakened, is the formation of a neural model commensurately weakened? These questions have not been addressed in much detail, but they could be.

Even in the early-filter theory of attention, Broadbent (1958) assumed that a rudimentary physical analysis of the stimulus took place automatically. This automatic analysis may recruit attention to physical changes in the stimuli. Näätänen (1990) assumed that a complete physical analysis takes place automatically. Näätänen's evidence was that the mismatch negativity response to a change in auditory stimuli occurs when the auditory stimuli are unattended. However, that evidence has been questioned by the finding of a large effect of attention on the mismatch negativity in at least some circumstances (Woldorff et al., 1991). Even if it can be shown that there is a truly automatic component to the mismatch negativity (e.g., see Alho et al., 1992), it has not been proven that the mismatch negativity consistently recruits an attentional response (see Lyytinen et al., 1992; Näätänen, 1992). Thus, though we are closer to answering the question of how much memory is formed through automatic analysis, in that we have more specific mechanisms to look for, the question has not been answered satisfactorily.

The research questions that have been highlighted so far involve memory storage: is there a limit to the amount of concurrent activation, and is attention needed to permit a neural model of the stimulus to form? There also are important questions remaining regarding the focus of attention. The previous chapter suggests that the unitary nature of attention and awareness, and therefore the basic validity of the attentional construct, has not yet been proven beyond a reasonable doubt.

Even assuming, as I do, that attention is a valid construct and that the focus of attention is unitary in the neurologically normal adult human, there are questions about what the focus of attention does. What happens when one concentrates more intensely? One possibility is that it increases the total size of the focus of attention, allowing more to be taken in. This type of function would be useful in a divided attention task. However, a far more common function of concentration might be the opposite; to more completely shut out external stimuli that are exerting a force on the attentional system with a risk that attention could be recruited away from the topic of voluntary interest.

The observation that the attentional focus involves the inhibition of irrelevant stimuli and irrelevant concepts (e.g., Walley & Weiden, 1973; Tipper et al., 1988; Carr & Dagenbach, 1990; Neumann & DeSchepper, 1991) seems clear. However, given a field of multiple relevant objects and multiple irrelevant ones, it is not yet possible to develop a metric for determining the difficulty of an attentional task, with any confidence. The metric may be straightforward; for example, effort might be reasonably estimated by the number of relevant items kept in mind plus the number of irrelevant items kept out. On the other hand, more complex interactions between the mind and stimulus field might occur. Why do some people like to study to music? Perhaps they are not very highly motivated or are distracted by unsettling thoughts. Without the music, internal thoughts may intrude and may be difficult to shut out. Perhaps the act of shutting out external stimuli places enough of a load on the attentional system that the activation on irrelevant internal thoughts decreases substantially. Again research is needed.

8.2 Some directions for further work

Cowan (1988) proposed a model, depicted in Fig. 1.5 of this book, that is quite general. The research discussed in this book strengthens the evidence for this model. Nevertheless, it might be improved in various ways. In this section, several fundamental directions for improvement will be considered. To anticipate, increases in the amount of detail and in the explicitness of assumptions are possible; but with the presently available evidence, additional progress could be made simply by correlating behavioral and psychophysiological levels of analysis more closely.

8.2.1 Amount of detail

The model might be improved by becoming more detailed. The model proposed by Schneider and Detweiler (1987), for example, is analogous to Cowan (1988) except that it provides a great deal more detail. The added detail is from two sources: articulation of a modular structure of memory, and explicit detail as to the mathematical way in which operations take place.

Regarding the modular structure of memory, the long-term memory system was divided by Schneider and Detweiler (1987) into modality modules, specifically: visual, auditory, speech, lexical, semantic, motor, mood, and context modules. These modules were connected by an intercommunicating neural loop. However, as I have already mentioned, I have doubts about the extent to which these modules should be considered as fundamentally different or separate. If there are strong similarities in the neural and computational manner in which they operate, then it may not be essential to include the modular structure. The risk of including it is that it may lump together some functions that are equally separate, and there is no explicitly stated criterion for determining what is considered a module. I say this despite the intuitive feeling that the modular organization decided upon by Schneider and Detweiler is a reasonable one.

Regarding the mathematically explicit nature of processing operations in the model; again, it is useful in examining the ramifications of what may be true, but it does not define the core of what must be true. Models that set out what may be true in considerable detail rest upon many untested assumptions. They are highly testable, but are likely to require one modification after another for years on end.

8.2.2 Explicitness of assumptions

Another way that the model could be improved is to become more explicit about its fundamental assumptions. For example, is activation limited or unlimited? Is it discrete or continuous with inactivation? Is the focus of attention discrete or continuous? Is it qualitatively different, or only quantitatively different, from activation? Although it would indeed be an improvement if these questions were answered, they cannot yet be answered on the basis of the available evidence.

8.2.3 Level of analysis

There is one final way to improve the model that may be more tenable at present. The model was stated at only one level of analysis, that of the general cognitive structure. It may now be possible to examine the same processes at a lower level of analysis. In the last few years, new technology has added more and more detail to our knowledge of the functioning of the human brain. (Some of this information already has been included in the previous chapters of this book.) Initially, cognitive psychology avoided theorization at the level of brain structure, because not enough was known. Also, largely inspired by the work of Lashley (1929, 1950), it generally has been assumed that any one function might be mediated by an assembly of cells so scattered throughout the brain that it might be practically impossible to identify specifically. However, this no longer appears to be the case. Specific areas of the brain, or at least manageable ensembles of specific areas, do seem to be identifiable with particular, definable cognitive functions.

Because of this change in the status of neuroscience, it is possible to engage reasonably in a type of speculation that before would have been regarded as naive. That is the direction that the present discussion will go. Summarizing across various recent types of physiological evidence, I will attempt to identify (in an approximate fashion) some of the most important neural structures and processes corresponding to the cognitive system sketched by Cowan (1988).

The speculation will not stop short of the Holy Grail of cognitive science, namely conscious awareness. Some would warn that no one area of the brain can mediate consciousness, that it must be mediated by many areas of the brain working together. That is indeed likely to be true in some sense, but it is too conservative a pronouncement. Neuroscience has progressed to the point that there are at least restrictions on the theory of the neural mediation even of consciousness. Some of these will be reviewed.

Before delving into neuroscience, it may be worthwhile to contemplate where the neuroscientific method stands in relation to the information processing approach. In their explanations of the information processing approach, Palmer and Kimchi (1986) and Massaro and Cowan (1993) noted that an important property of the approach is "recursive decomposition," the ability to break down one stage of processing into substages. Recursive decomposition is what one gets in an information processing model by shifting to a lower level of analysis. For example, a stimulus encoding process might be broken down further into feature-encoding and feature-combination processes. Within the model of Cowan (1988), memory activation might be separated into visual activation, auditory activation, semantic activation, and so on. However, staying within a recursive decomposition approach is not the only way to shift levels of analysis; searching for a neural model that will parallel the cognitive model is another way. Strictly speaking, a one-to-one mapping between cognitive and neural constructs might not even seem to be a change in the level of analysis at all; but switching to neural terms allows easier access to the level of interacting neural centers, which does represent a lower level of analysis than is likely to be attained with behavioral methods alone.

8.3 Toward a neuroscience of memory and attention

8.3.1 What are we looking for?

Neuropsychology has vacillated between the view that various areas of the brain are equipotential for a particular higher mental function or representation (Lashley, 1929, 1950) and the currently predominant view (e.g., Fodor, 1983) that mental functions, even higher ones, are localized in particular brain regions. An understanding of how such opposing views may have arisen from the same set of observations comes from the recent work of Farah (1994). She proposes that the brain consists of various areas that have different functions, but that work in a highly interactive fashion. This is essentially an intermediate view.

Take, for example, the observation that some brain lesions result in the loss of the ability to identify from memory particular living things, with the identification of nonliving things spared or, in other patients, the reverse, selective sparing of the memory of living things only (Warrington & McCarthy, 1987). Militating against the most straightforward interpretation (i.e., that there are separate brain areas mediating knowledge in these domains), there were exceptions to the rule. Patients with deficiencies in knowledge of living things also had impaired knowledge of gemstones and fabrics, and patients with deficiencies in knowledge of nonliving things retained knowledge of large, outdoor objects such as bridges and windmills.

An alternative hypothesis that has been considered is that there are separate areas for processing and retaining sensory vs. functional information. Living things can be grouped primarily according to the sensory impressions that they leave (e.g., in their visual forms), whereas nonliving things can be grouped primarily according to their functions. This fits the data better, but Farah points out remaining problems with this simple hypothesis. For example, patients who lose knowledge of living things lose even their functional knowledge of living things (e.g., that parrots are kept as pets and can talk).

Farah and McClelland (1991) were able to model semantic memory impairment with a more interactive version of the sensory/functional distinction. With the sensory module impaired, for example, knowledge of living things suffers more than knowledge of nonliving things. However, retrieval is interactive between these two modules. Without input from the sensory module to support knowledge of living things, the retrieval of even the functional knowledge of those living things is impaired.

However, this type of example cannot actually prove that the connectionist account is correct. A nonconnectionist view, in particular the "fuzzy logical" view, would lead to the suggestion that knowledge of a particular category is formed from a weighted average of sensory and functional features (cf. Massaro, 1988; Massaro & Friedman, 1991). Although the fuzzy logical view may not have been used previously to reason about neural modules, it could be applied here with the assumption that the sensory and functional modules do not interact after all, but feed their output to a third, higher-level module responsible for integrating the results.

This, then, provides a little insight into what we are looking for. Various modules that carry out distinctly separate operations are, to some extent, spatially separate in the brain. In order to account for how the entire system works, we either should expect that the modules are highly interactive or should expect that there is at least one separate area of the brain responsible for integrating the output of lower-level processing modules. Either of these possibilities still could turn out to be correct, or both could be correct in different instances.

8.3.2 Mapping brain processes onto the model of Cowan (1988)

In Fig. 8.1, all of the salient components of the model of Cowan (1988), whether structures or processes, are tentatively mapped onto what seem to be the best candidates for neural representation. The features of the model that are labeled in the figure are described in more detail below.

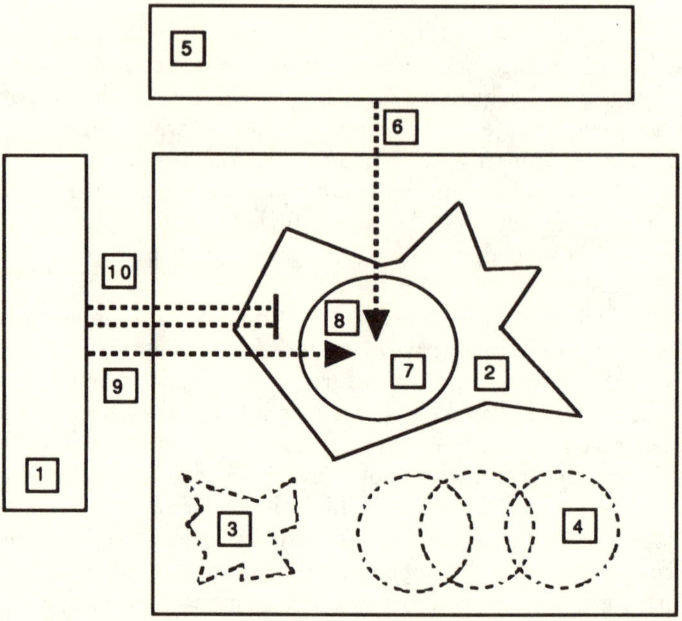

	Cognitive Component	Likely Neural	Possible Neural
1	Brief sensory store	Sensory cortex	Cell assembl. activ.
2	Memory activation	Association cortex	Synaptic plasticity
3	Automatic storage	Diffuse cortical	Hebbian circuits
4	Storage with attention	Hippocampus	Septum, Frontal lobes
5	Central executive	Prefrontal cortex	
6	Attentional innervation	Thalamus/ARAS Support	
7	Focus of attention	Parietal lobes	Frontal lobes/Thalamus
8	Entry into focus	Thalamus	Synch. Oscillations
9	Orienting of Attention	Locus C./Hippoc./Parietal	Frontal lobes
10	Habituation of Orienting	Hippocampus	Frontal lobes

Fig. 8.1 Neural counterparts of the psychological components of Cowan's (1988) model.

(1) A brief, literal sensory store

Cowan (1988), and Chapter 2 of this book, reviewed considerable evidence for the existence of a sensory storage process in all modalities lasting up to several hundred milliseconds (for brief stimuli, at least), and containing literal, unanalyzed information about a stimulus. It is not yet at all clear how this type of sensory storage is neurally mediated, but several points do seem clear. First, the "store" is a process that is time-locked to the onset rather than the offset of the stimulus (e.g., Efron, 1970*a*, 1970*b*, 1970*c*). Second, the neural signal reaches the cortex quickly, within about the first 30 ms or so. Third, there are electrical events observable at the scalp within roughly the same time period as the proposed duration of the literal sensory store (several hundred milliseconds), reflecting cortical activity that could underlie this sensory storage process (e.g., see Hari et al., 1982; Näätänen, 1992). Fourth, this electrical activity is greatest in the modality-specific cortical areas corresponding to the stimulus in question. Recordings of magnetoencephalography have verified this locus of activity in modality-specific cortex (Hari et al., 1984; Näätänen, 1992).

There has been work at a cellular level that could eventually provide a basis for understanding evoked potentials that follow the stimulus onset. Chemical events at the synapse following cell firing leave behind an environment in which the same cell is temporarily more likely to fire again (or in some cases less likely), a situation that has been termed "short-term synaptic plasticity" (Zucker, 1989). It has been suggested that one function of this plasticity is to preserve temporarily memories of an event until a more permanent coding can set in (Magleby, 1987; Crick & Koch, 1990).

There are various distinguishable components of temporary synaptic change, but among them is a component that is very short, declining to about 37% of its initial magnitude in about 50 ms, at least in frog tissue (see Magleby, 1987). A related process, involving temporary desensitization of the receptor for GABA, a main inhibitory neurotransmitter, has been observed in rat brain receptors *in vitro* with a time constant very similar to that of the aforementioned temporary synaptic change (Cash & Subbarao, 1987). Thus, there are grounds for expecting that the brief, literal phase of sensory storage may be accounted for by the ordinary properties of neurons in modality-specific cortical areas.

(2) Memory activation

Cowan (1988) proposed that the temporary neural activation corresponding to sensory and nonsensory (abstract) types of memory is similar in principle, although the two types of activated elements might well occupy different locations in the cerebral cortex. Both types of activation presumably decay markedly across about 30 seconds, in roughly an exponential fashion. Activation generated by stimuli and by mental processes should be similar, although there would be limits to how well the sensory properties of stimuli could be imagined.

As we already have discussed, there is evidence in the auditory modality that components of the event-related potential, including N1 and mismatch negativity components, reflect the retention of information for a number of seconds. In the case of the N1, the response is diminished if similar stimuli are presented closer together than a few seconds (Hari et al., 1982; Lü et al., 1992*b*). In the case of the mismatch negativity, there is no response if the stimuli are farther apart than about 10 seconds, although there is some debate about the exact amount of time (Näätänen, 1992; Sams et al., 1993).

There also are marked changes in synaptic responding within a similar time period. Magleby (1987) identified a number of components of short-term synaptic changes in the frog with time constants ranging from fairly short durations up to 20 seconds or more. Cash and Subbarao (1987) found a second mechanism of GABA receptor desensitization with a half-life of 533 ms, which was described in practical terms as a total duration of "a few seconds." (Even if the same neural activity is indexed by all methods, it is likely that the exact time constant observed would vary depending upon the sensitivity of the measure.)

As for the proposed similarity (but not identity) of activation generated through stimuli vs. mental events, the recent behavioral evidence, though indirect, is fairly convincing. Crowder (1989*b*), for example, presented subjects with a pitch via a pure tone and another via a musical instrument. Reaction times in comparing the pitches of the tone and the musical note were reduced when the subject had been instructed to imagine a note the same as the actual first tone, but in the instrument that was to be used to produce the second note. There also is good neuropsychological evidence that some similar areas of the brain are used for vision and visual imagery, and that lesioning these areas affects both functions in similar ways (Farah, 1988).

(3) Automatic long-term storage

It is unclear just what neural mechanisms are responsible for the storage of knowledge in the brain; one possibility is that the long-term potentiation of synapses is involved (e.g., Brown, Ganong, Kairiss, Keenan, & Kelso, 1989), and the end result could be the formation of modulated circuits as discussed by Hebb (1949) and explored further by the recent PDP work (McClelland & Rumelhart, 1986).

It is clear that the representation of knowledge is somewhat diffuse across the cortex. There are modular structures involved in storing knowledge, but they are organized according to particular types of knowledge features, not according to events. For example, a localized brain damage will never make one forget specifically everything one learned in a particular time period (e.g., 15 May to 3 August, 1989). Instead, the brain damage might allow one to recall some aspects but make one forget others. One might recall the events but forget what various objects are called, or one might be unable to recognize objects on the basis of their visual shapes (e.g., see Shallice, 1988). Because there are many brain areas involved with different types of processing, many of them operating concurrently, the representation of any one piece of real-world knowledge is likely to involve a diffuse network of specific areas across the brain. This diffuseness can account for the earlier view (Lashley, 1929, 1950) that there is no localization of memory storage in the brain. There is localization, but the representation of most events is spread out across many localized featural traces.

It has been suggested, according to a "proceduralist" view, that information is stored in the same sets and assemblies of nerve cells that were responsible for processing the information in the first place (e.g., Crowder, 1989*a*). This would mean that the primary projection areas and most immediately surrounding association areas would contain sensory memories: the occipital cortex for visual memories, the temporal cortex for auditory memories, and the parietally located sensory strip for tactile memories. This can account for, among other things, the finding that neural activity in the auditory cortex lasts for about as long as the tolerable delay between two acoustic stimuli to be compared to one another (Lü et al., 1992*b*). However, the storage of more abstract information, such as lexical information that can arrive through various senses, presumably would be stored in higher-level association areas of the cortex that receive input not from the primary projection areas, but from other association areas. The parietal and frontal lobes appear to contain areas of that nature (Schacter, 1989; Posner & Peterson, 1990).

(4) Attention-related long-term storage

In Fig. 8.1, long-term memory with the involvement of attention is indicated with dashed circles to represent the areas of the long-term memory network where attention has been. Neurally, this presumably corresponds to various diffuse association areas in the brain.

The additional neural loci needed to retain memories of events in a way that makes them available for recall in a direct memory task (presumably conscious, explicit recall) are, as we have discussed, much more restricted. Specifically, normal explicit recall requires, in addition to the diffuse network of areas used for indirect forms of memory tasks, intact areas within the frontal lobe and the hippocampus and surrounding cortical areas (Squire, 1987; Shallice, 1988; Zola-Morgan, Squire, Amaral, & Suzuki, 1989; Petri & Mishkin, 1994; Eichenbaum, Otto, & Cohen, in press).

In Chapter 6, I summarized evidence that material must be stored and retrieved with the aid of attention if it is to be available in direct memory tests (see also Schacter, 1989; Jacoby and Kelly, 1992). As we shall discuss later, the frontal lobe controls that attention, so it is not surprising that memory can be thrown off when attentional control is impaired through frontal damage.

What might appear less consistent with this view is the fact that an intact hippocampus, and some surrounding areas, is essential for the storage of information for later conscious recall (e.g., Squire, 1987). By all accounts, subjects with hippocampal damage have normal attentional capacities, so why is their recall affected? The assumption here, following Schacter (1989), is that the link between memory storage processes and conscious awareness is partly or totally disconnected when the hippocampal connection is damaged.

Zola-Morgan and Squire (1990) provided more detail concerning the involvement of the hippocampal areas in memory. In their experiment, monkeys learned to discriminate 100 pairs of objects and then some of the monkeys underwent hippocampectomies at variable times after learning. Normal monkeys performed quite well (about 80% correct) if tested soon after learning, but forgot much of what they learned (declining to 70% correct) over 16 weeks. The monkeys with hippocampal areas removed were severely deficient (60% correct) in their recall of recently learned discriminations, whereas they did better, in fact as well as the normal control monkeys, on discriminations that had been learned 16 weeks ago. The results suggest that recent memories can be retrieved only with the involvement of hippocampal areas, but become more independent of hippocampal areas as time passes.

We might speculate that, during this time, the memory representation of the relevant semantic information (e.g., in Zola-Morgan & Squire's study, the answers to the discrimination problems) become independent of any representation of the specific context in which that information was acquired. The hippocampus could be needed to associate semantic learning to the original episodic context that went with the learning.

Farah (1994) offered a conflicting interpretation of the difference between explicit and implicit knowledge, using as a test case visual face recognition. Farah, O'Reilly, and Vecera (1993) found that the difference between memory types could be modeled by lesioning an artificial neural network that represented the relevant information. The damaged network lost explicit information (e.g., could not recognize previously learned faces) although implicit information was preserved (e.g., there were savings in relearning faces). This seemed to imply that there was no need for a separate area to represent the conscious experience that is assumed to go along with explicit recall. Consequently, their model differed from the type of model discussed by Schacter (1989), in which various processing modules report their output to a common module that represents the subject's conscious knowledge. Extrapolating from Farah's approach, one might wonder if explicit memory and consciousness in general, like visual face recognition in particular, resides in the network in which the specific processing occurs.

What this approach in itself may not account for is that various types of conscious knowledge can be related to one another in what appears to be a global workspace (Baars, 1988) or, in present terms, the focus of attention. The network model of visual processing may well be correct, but according to the present approach the output of the module still would have to be interpreted and related to other types of information by the more global processor. The residual information in a damaged module might be used beneficially in implicit tasks, even though the output coming from the module would not be strong or precise enough to indicate to the global workspace that explicit knowledge was present. Thus, there need be no contradiction between Farah's conception of processing modules and the general architecture proposed by Schacter (1989) and others.

(5) A central executive

It seems clear from years of research on brain-damaged patients that, if any one general area of the brain is to be associated with the control of attention and cognition, it is the frontal lobes. Fuster (1989, Chapter 6) summarized the often-found symptoms of frontal cortical damage as including disorders of attention and perception (including lowering of general awareness, sensory neglect, distractibility, disorders of visual search or gaze control, and difficulties in concentration), as well as disorders of motility (hypo- or hyperkinesis and a paucity of deliberate actions), disorders of temporal integration (defective memory, defective planning, and defective control of interference), and disorders of affect and emotion (apathy or, more rarely, euphoria).

Most or all of these problems can be viewed as the result of damage to a central executive, conceived as a mechanism that is critical in controlling, regulating, and coordinating other cognitive functions. The affective symptoms probably are related to the strong connections to the limbic system and make sense in that cognitive functions should be affectively motivated. The memory-loss symptoms probably are related to the strong connections between the frontal lobes and hippocampal areas. As discussed previously, it seem highly plausible that signals from the frontal lobes may help to determine which memories are recorded for conscious recall with the actions of the hippocampus (Posner, 1984).

If it were possible to have only one, logically indivisible type of central executive, then one might not be able to account for all of the individual differences in cognitive style. Some suggestions might be made to begin to subdivide the central executive. For example, Iversen (1984, p. 238) reviewed evidence from monkeys that, within the frontal lobe, "lesions confined to the sulcus principalis and the immediately surrounding dorsolateral cortex" produce spatial memory deficit with delayed response (presumably a working-memory function of the focus of attention), whereas "damage focused on the orbital cortex" produces response disinhibition. It is not yet clear how the different central executive functions would be integrated with one another.

The implication that the frontal lobes have an essential role in controlling attention receives additional, experimental support from studies of positron emission tomography (see Posner & Rothbart, 1991). However, this evidence will be discussed under item 7 (the focus of attention) because there are complex issues regarding the roles of three separate attentional systems that Posner and Rothbart identify, and these issues are more directly relevant to the focus of attention.

(6) The sources of arousal

The classic studies involving the electrical stimulation of the ascending reticular activating system (ARAS) in animals make it clear that this system is especially important in determining the overall state of arousal of the organism (Moruzzi & Magoun, 1949). Stimulation in different areas of the ARAS can result in states ranging from hyperarousal to sleep. The ARAS scatters innervation (in the form of higher concentrations of certain neural transmitters, including norepinephrine) diffusely across the cerebral cortex.

On the other hand, the ARAS does not appear to be implicated in the differential arousal that seems to favor some areas over others in selective attention; it is too diffuse. Cell assemblies that receive other input conceivably might benefit to a special degree from the increased signal-to-noise ratio possible in a higher-arousal state, but there must be some kind of special input to attended items making the distinction between merely activated items and those that are attended; that is, between conscious and unconscious processing. The role of the ARAS in this is unclear, although one ARAS center is especially involved in the orienting of attention (see below).

The finding that attentional resources must be shared between hemispheres in split-brain patients even though specific information is not shared (Holzman & Gazzaniga, 1982) suggests that the resource that is shared has a subcortical locus. However, it need not be the ARAS. Other connections, such as via the anterior commissure, and numerous subcortical areas, remain present (Gazzaniga, 1985). Attention appears to be shared between hemispheres through a subcortical route that has not yet been clearly identified.

The thalamus and related subcortical areas have been implicated as a gating mechanism in selective attention. In research with cats, Skinner and Yingling (1977) showed that one brain area, the mesencephalic reticular formation, mediates a general arousal of various cortical regions. A thalamic region that was termed the mediothalamic-frontocortical system produces inhibition in various brain locations. Both of these regions appear to work together in selective attention by converging upon another thalamic area, the reticular nucleus, which may serve as an attentional gate.

Interest in thalamic mechanisms in selective attention has been revived recently (LaBerge, 1990). LaBerge and Buchsbaum (1990) used positron emission tomography (PET) recording techniques to demonstrate that, in humans, an area of the thalamus involved in visual processing (the pulvinar) is more active in a visual selective attention task (recognizing the middle letter in an array) than in a nonselective task (recognizing an isolated letter). This effect was asymmetrical: when the left hemisphere received the array, the left hemisphere's portion of the pulvinar was more active than the right, but when the right hemisphere received the array, there was no laterality effect in the pulvinar. This suggests a left-hemisphere dominance for this attentional control that seems to be in keeping with the evidence reviewed by Gazzaniga (1985).

(7) The focus of attention

On a priori grounds it would be possible to argue that there is no special focus of attention, but that activities of the brain that are "attended" are enhanced in some way, and thus made more efficient. However, this view would not appear to be adequate to describe behavior. We have seen that many activities can be accomplished efficiently outside of awareness. The automatization of a task, which allows it to be accomplished more efficiently but sometimes results in the automatized schema being inappropriately "activated" and thereby overapplied (e.g., driving home when one had intended to drive elsewhere), is accompanied by reduced awareness and memory of the activity. It thus seems likely that attention is a change in the kind or locus of neural activity, and not just an extreme degree of the same mental activity that occurs for unattended information. This separate process or locus of activity is what I have called the focus of attention.

There is good empirical support for the idea of a focus of attention, but one may debate whether it should be equated with one neural entity or several. Posner and Peterson (1990) described evidence from PET research that clearly distinguishes multiple brain areas involved in attention. The research, which proceeded by comparing the distribution of brain metabolism in experimental and control situations, has identified two anterior centers and one posterior center involved in attention. (Other neuroanatomical work that they reviewed confirms that the three areas are closely interconnected.)

The findings of such studies are summarized in Fig. 8.2, reproduced from Posner and Rothbart (1991). Basically, an anterior system centered medially in the cingulate gyrus was found to be active whenever the task required effortful attending on the part of the subject. Another anterior system, centered laterally in the right frontal lobe, was found to be active in vigilance tasks; but vigilance is beyond the scope of this book and will not be considered further. Finally, a posterior attention system, centered laterally in the posterior parietal lobes, was found to be active when the subject oriented to a location in space, no matter whether that orienting occurred as the result of input from the environment (i.e., involuntary

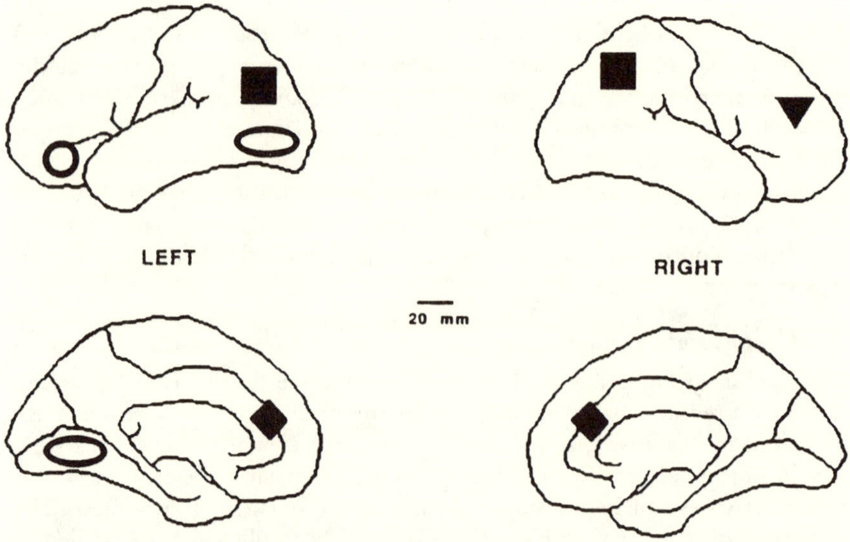

Fig. 8.2 Brain areas revealed in PET studies. Top, lateral view; bottom, medial view. Squares, posterior attention system (parietal lobes); diamonds, anterior attentional control system (anterior cingulate); triangle, vigilance network (right frontal); open shapes, word form (ellipse) and semantic association (circle) areas. (From M. Posner and M. Rothbart, 1991, Attentional mechanisms and conscious experience. In A. D. Milner & M. D. Rugg, Eds., *The neuropsychology of consciousness,* p. 92, Fig. 5.1. Reprinted by permission of Academic Press Ltd.)

attentional recruitment) or input from the anterior attentional system (i.e., voluntary attending).

These research findings seem clear; but where is the focus of attention and awareness? The answer to that question is not transparent. Posner and Rothbart (1991, p. 97) stated that "there is little reason to connect closely the operation of the posterior network in itself to awareness." The type of evidence that they cited is that it seems possible to orient to stimuli automatically, while maintaining an attentional focus on other ideas. They noted that, in blindsight, a type of orienting to the signal is possible without conscious awareness of the signal. For Posner and Rothbart, conscious awareness resides primarily with the anterior attention system.

However, Schacter (1989) offered a different view, on the basis of data from cases of brain damage. He noted that damage to the parietal lobe areas often results in impairments of consciousness. Reviewing the literature, he noted (pp. 371–372) that:

> . . . confusional states have been reported in right parietal patients . . . Second, the syndrome of anosognosia—unawareness and denial of a neuropsychological

deficit—is often associated with parietal damage ... Further relevant evidence is provided by the phenomenon of unilateral neglect [that occurs with] unilateral damage to the inferior parietal lobe.

Similar deficits of awareness apparently can occur with frontal damage, but they are more characteristic of parietal damage (Heilman, Watson, & Valenstein, 1985; Schacter, 1989). Frontal damage more typically results in apathy and lack of initiative, control, organization, and planfulness, but not unawareness *per se*.

One reason to favor parietal regions as the focus of attention is that these regions subserve not only orienting, but also the integration of data from all of the senses. The involvement of the posterior parietal region as an integrative mechanism, and therefore a "palette" of attention, is an idea that can be traced back to Luria (1966), through Dimond (1976), Mountcastle (1978), Heilman, Watson, and Valenstein (1985), and Schacter (1989). More recent evidence provides additional specificity for that idea. Reinoso-Suärez (1984) and Heilman, Watson, & Valenstein (1985) suggested that association areas surrounding the various primary projection areas of the brain, in turn project to a more distal association area, in particular an area of the parietal lobe referred to as "Area 7" (approximately marked with squares in Fig. 8.2). This same part of the parietal lobe is thought to be most involved in attentive behavior (Robinson & Peterson, 1984). Area 7 cells respond to both visual and tactile stimulation. They may not respond to auditory stimulation, but an adjacent and cytoarchitecturally similar region in the parietal lobe, Area Tpt, responds to both auditory and visual stimulation and its location (see Hyvärinen, 1982), so it may be functionally related to Area 7.

Most of the work on the parietal lobes and attention has focused on visual input, but there is evidence from patients with parietal lesions for the involvement of these areas in spatial attention from auditory as well as visual cues (Farah, Wong, Monheit, & Morrow, 1989). Electrophysiological data also are consistent with some sort of cross-modal agency of attention. Hillyard, Simpson, Woods, Van Voorhis, and Münte (1984) found that attention to visual stimuli in one of several spatial locations enhanced event-related potentials to auditory, as well as visual, stimuli in the same location, and analogous findings were obtained with attention to auditory stimuli in one of several spatial locations. Related findings were summarized by Posner and Peterson (1990).

The arguments put forward by Posner and Rothbart (1991) suggesting that the anterior attentional system itself is the seat of awareness were not terribly convincing. For example, although it is possible to search the environment visually and orient to various objects (presumably using the posterior attention system) while concentrating on something else (presumably using the anterior attention system), there is no evidence that orienting to visual objects does not interfere with the ongoing thoughts or that the objects oriented upon are less available to awareness than the competing material. It may be a split-attention situation. Also, notice that it is not relevant if the eye movements themselves enter awareness; what is relevant is the conditions under which the objects focused upon, through those eye movements, enter awareness.

Posner and Rothbart (1991) further support their view of consciousness with a recent study by Bullemer and Nissen (1990). Subjects learned to respond to a sequence of lights. They often decreased their reaction times without becoming explicitly aware of the sequence; it was procedural learning. However, the response to a deviant position within a learned sequence resulted in a slower mean reaction time than was obtained in a control sequence that had not been learned. Posner and Rothbart took this as evidence of inhibition and therefore attention, even though there was lack of awareness of the sequence in many of the subjects who showed the inhibitory increase. Thus, there appeared to be a dissociation between attention and awareness. However, it seems possible that the increase in reaction times in this situation does not reflect inhibitory attention after all; a different possibility is that motor planning that was conducted automatically had to be aborted, which could account for the slowing of reaction times compared to the control situation.

So far, we have debated about whether consciousness is focused with the special involvement of tissue in the anterior or posterior systems. A third possibility is that consciousness resides in the modules where processing takes place originally; a view compatible with the philosophical arguments of Dennett (1991), discussed (and rebutted) in the previous chapter. Farah (1994) implied that such a view may be correct.

The biggest uncertainty about the view of processing modules as the seat of consciousness is how the various pieces would be integrated to form a global workspace. In Farah's type of view, the highly interactive nature of the various processing modules could cause them to act together as a global workspace. An alternative view, more consistent with the approach of Massaro (1988), would be that the modules would not interact but would be fed to a higher-level integrator responsible for combining the inputs of the specific processing modules. In neural terms, should such an integrator exist?

To clarify that question, consider another example discussed by Farah (1994). Patients with a unilateral lesion in the parietal lobe often appear to have difficulty disengaging attention from the side of the visual field ipsilateral to the lesion in order to shift attention to the contralateral side (Posner, Walker, Friedrich, & Rafal, 1984). Posner et al. inferred that there is a component of the visual system in the parietal cortex that is specialized for disengaging attention. However, Cohen, Romero, and Farah (in press) proposed an alternative model involving only attentional engagement components in both hemispheres. The components inhibit one another, so failure of one component would result in a locking-in of attention by the intact hemisphere.

The nonconnectionist model based on Massaro's work presumably would have to propose that a third area serves as an arbiter between the left and right parietal modules and channels attention to the hemisphere providing the strongest input. For voluntary attention it could in fact be that the frontal areas serve as such an arbiter, but that would not make sense for involuntary orienting of attention, which seems to involve the parietal areas without apparent direction from the frontal lobes (Posner & Peterson, 1990). However, parts of the thalamus could serve such a function; for example, the pulvinar area of the thalamus is strongly interconnected to the attention centers in the parietal lobe. Farah could be right that there is no "disengage" module but, at the same time, the thalamus could coordinate the activities of attention centers in the left and right parietal lobes rather than them competing directly in a connectionist network.

One recent study appears to favor the latter view. Failure to disengage attention, a "locking-in" of attention similar to what one sees in unilateral parietal lobe patients, has been observed in autistic children who have parietal lobe damage, and not in other autistic children with intact parietal lobes (Townsend & Courchesne, in press.) Yet, in these children the parietal damage is bilateral, so the locking in of attention cannot as easily be attributed to a balance between the hemispheres. Other examples of bilateral parietal damage also were reviewed and suggested a similar conclusion; for example, see Verfaellie, Rapcsak, & Heilman, 1990.

Although there are at least three hypotheses about the location of the focus of attention that probably still remain viable (that it is located primarily in the anterior attention system, posterior attention system, or neither), my favored hypothesis thus is that the focus of attention is primarily in the posterior attention system of the parietal lobe, in conjunction with information from diffuse areas of the cortex. As noted above, much of the parietal lobes receive input primarily from other association areas and therefore appear to be higher-order association areas cutting across modalities. The way that this presumably would work, metaphorically, is that the anterior attention system and external stimuli together would act to control the direction of an attentional spotlight that is shined on areas in the posterior attentional system. Whether or not this is correct, it is satisfying at least that the candidates for anatomical correlates of consciousness may be tangible.

(8) Entry of information into the focus of attention

Let us assume for the sake of argument that, as suggested above, there is an anatomical locus of the focus of attention (e.g., the posterior attention system). This still leaves unresolved the difficult work of determining how information gets in and out of the focus of attention. Is information that is represented elsewhere in the brain replicated somewhere in the areas that make up the focus of attention? Is there in effect an index in the posterior attention system, with pointers to all currently attended information? Is the form of that information altered? These are important unknowns.

No matter how information enters the focus of attention, it is possible to reassure Dennett (1991) that it may not be wasteful for the brain to "reprocess" information once it has been processed in disparate locations within the brain. This reprocessing, which would take place for attended items only, would serve the purpose of binding features together into coherent objects (Treisman, 1992*a*) or perhaps, more broadly, a coherent scene.

It would be reassuring to cognitive theory, though, if there were some idea as to how this binding together of attended features might occur. On the basis of animal electrophysiological data, Stryker (1989) and Crick and Koch (1990) suggested a mechanism whereby information carried by various locations on the cortex could enter awareness. There is a cyclic type of neural activity at about 40 Hz that appears to occur for the various attended features of stimuli. When several types of feature are activated simultaneously, the cyclic activity occurs for all of the corresponding regions. It was suggested that this could be the neural basis of the features being bound together with the assistance of attention.

One of the most compelling findings was that of Gray, König, Engel, and Singer (1989). They stimulated two columns of cells that responded maximally to the same angle of stimulation, but for stimuli in different parts of the visual field. In one condition they were stimulated concurrently by short lines moving together, but in another condition they were stimulated by a long line that cut across both receptive fields. The cyclic activity was correlated across the two columns of cells only when they both were stimulated by the single, long line. This evidence suggests that synchrony of cyclic neural responding might signal the combination of features into a single object (for a more complete account of how this might occur physiologically, see Lopes da Silva, 1991).

The role of cyclic activity and object perception in itself might not appear to be a link to attention, especially since the cyclic activity can occur in lightly anesthetized animals as well as awake animals (Stryker, 1989). However, other research suggests that attention operates by opening "object files" and keeping track of the characteristics of each object (Kahneman, Treisman, & Gibbs, 1992; Kanwisher & Driver, 1992; Treisman, 1992*b*). In this type of cognitive research, investigators have elicited attention to an object at a particular spatial location in an array of objects, and then have moved the objects in the visual field. The general finding from this type of manipulation has been that attention typically stays with the moving object, not with its original spatial location. The strongest type of evidence for the object-centered nature of attention is that both priming effects and inhibition of return (the difficulty of attending to the same thing a second time if attention proved to be misguided the first time) also stay with the moving object rather than the original spatial location.

Analogous to Treisman's hypothesis that attention is needed to bind features of an object when the field contains multiple objects, perhaps the synchrony of cyclic responding observed among cells representing different features of a single object (Gray et al., 1989) breaks down when more than one object is presented at a time, except for objects that are in the focus of attention.

The role of a coherence between the firing of different neural populations as a mechanism of attention is not an isolated one; it has been raised many times before on the basis of various sources of evidence. For example, Thatcher and John (1977) suggested it and illustrated (p. 95) that the enhancement in the average evoked potential in a cat (recorded from the middle sylvian gyrus) when a signal was made meaningful through its association with foot shock depended not only on an increase in the amplitude of the individual-trial responses, but also on the decreased variance in the latency of these individual responses.

Lopes da Silva, Wadman, Arnolds, Veeken, and Holsheimer (1984) described an oscillatory mechanism that could help to explain why attended information is recorded for explicit recall. Rhythmic slow or "theta" activity in the hippocampus is generated by signals from the nearby septal area when it receives certain signals from the brainstem reticular formation. The cause of this activity still is uncertain but the authors propose that it occurs basically "when the awake animal is exploring and scanning the environment" (p. 166).

The oscillation theory might be combined with the propositions that the anterior attentional system controls attention through the thalamus (although with interruptions from involuntary orienting of attention) and that the parietal lobe contains the integrated contents. In some sense, the parietal lobe may be the long-missing Cartesian theater that Dennett (1991) discussed and rejected. The 40-Hz neural cyclicity defines the players and may occur in synchrony for all neural elements in the focus of attention. The role of the focus of attention would be as a mechanism for those, and only those, concurrent events to be coordinated into a privileged, attended perceptual draft. This is not the same as conceiving of the Cartesian theater as something to be viewed by a little man in the head; it is a "theater" defined as a place where something dramatic happens.

Tiitinen et al. (1993) studied the 40-Hz neural activity in event-related potentials within humans. Some subjects were to listen for a deviant tone within a series of tones presented to one ear, ignoring tones in the other ear. Other subjects were to ignore all of the tones and read a book silently. Attended tones produced a higher level of repetitive electrical activity, specific to a 40-Hz repetition rate, for attended tones as compared to either tones presented in the unattended ear or tones presented while the subject read. The 40-Hz activity was seen over frontal and central locations and thus is consistent with a conjoint frontal-parietal system of attentional focus.

(9 & 10) Habituation and dishabituation of orienting

Some thought about how habituation and dishabituation of orienting must occur leads to insight about where it may occur. I have suggested (Chapter 5) that habituated sensory input continues to make contact with features stored in long-term memory, and continues to be processed at least in some of its physical features, but no longer attracts attention. In terms of the brain model developed here, this suggests that the input may become impotent in its effect on the hippocampal system.

Presumably, then, the neural model of the stimulus that permits habituation would heavily involve the hippocampal system. Given the present framework in which the hippocampal system works selectively for attended stimuli, this also suggests that a stimulus must first be attended in order to become habituated; logically speaking, unattended stimuli in a multiple-channel situation should not have much of an effect on the hippocampus and therefore should not develop a neural model sufficient to permit habituation to the stimulus, unless these stimuli first recruited attention. The likely scenario is that, in fact, novel stimuli cannot be completely ignored at first and can be ignored only after the neural model is sufficiently developed. This suggestion is consistent with Öhman (1992) and counter to an offhand speculation by Cowan (1988) that a neural model might be built up automatically. Provided that the neural model can develop quickly, though, a channel might become unattended so quickly that its attended period is easily overlooked.

The little evidence that we have on the neural mechanisms of habituation is consistent with this view. Sokolov (1975) summarized evidence from a systematic program of Russian neurophysiological research on the issue. He concluded that novelty-detecting cells are absent from the primary processing system in vision including the visual cortex, but present in the hippocampus. He suggested that the sensory systems analyze the features of the stimulus and send the results of this analysis to the hippocampus for comparison with the current neural model, resulting in a response only for results that violate the neural model. This theory might have to be modified to take into consideration the role of significance in orienting (e.g., Gati & Ben-Shakhar, 1990), but the anatomical locus still may be correct. (More evidence on the role of the hippocampus will be presented below.)

On the other hand, the theory may also have to be modified in that a comparison of models in the cortical regions themselves, in the form of a mismatch negativity (Näätänen, 1992) already may be forwarded to the hippocampal regions. The mismatch negativity reflects a neural process that is likely to trigger an orienting response, but it also may be possible to have a mismatch negativity without orienting.

Some support for the role of the hippocampus in the habituation of orienting comes from the work of Teyler, Chiaia, DiScenna, and Roemer (1984). They took slices of the rat brain and examined habituation of responding to repeated electrical stimulation *in vitro*. The optic tectum of goldfish also was examined. The areas in the rat examined included portions of the neocortex (dorsomedial parietal and occipital lobes) and allocortex (hippocampal slices). Out of all of these areas, it was found that only the dentate gyrus of the hippocampal formation responded in a manner consistent with the notion of habituation as traditionally defined (Thompson & Spencer, 1966). Among other properties it was found that, in the dentate gyrus, repeated stimulation resulted in a response that decreased according to a negative exponential function; the response recovered spontaneously over time if the stimulation was withheld; the rate of habituation increased across a repeating series of alternating habituation and recovery stimulation; a faster rate of stimulation resulted in faster habituation; and weaker stimulation resulted in faster habituation. The last property is critical because it is the opposite of what is expected from a fatigue process.

One way to test Sokolov's theory in humans would be to test habituation of orienting in patients with hippocampectomies, such as H.M. They should not reveal normal habituation of orienting. I have not been able to locate any studies of this sort, even though a wide variety of tests have been administered to these patients.

There are, however, relevant data in animals. Isaacson (1982) reviewed evidence that lesions of the hippocampus in rats and monkeys result in the decrease or even abolishment of habituation of orienting and an increase in the tendency for irrelevant stimuli to distract the animal from the rewarded task. Douglas and Pribram (1969) obtained especially clear results in rhesus monkeys who were lesioned bilaterally in the hippocampus or amygdala or were sham-operated. The monkeys learned a simple task in which two different digits appeared, the first in the lower right-hand panel of a 4 × 4 array, and the second in the upper left. Monkeys were rewarded for pressing the two relevant panels in turn, and the inter-response times were recorded. The hippocampally lesioned subjects surprisingly learned the task somewhat more quickly than the other two groups, which did not differ; but this was not the result of primary interest.

When the task was learned, a distracting digit was introduced on some trials (4 of 50 trials in each session), simultaneous with the second relevant digit but at a different spatial location. For the normal, sham-operated monkeys, distractions slowed responding, but the effect of distractors wore off (i.e., habituated) across 10 daily sessions. In the hippocampal-lesioned group, there was an equally large distraction effect in the first session, but very little, if any, habituation to the distractors across sessions.

In the amygdala-lesioned group, there was at first almost twice as much distraction as in the other two groups, but this effect habituated rapidly, so that this group resembled the normal monkeys by the third session. However, the interpretation of lesions of the amygdala is tempered by the consideration that it plays a large role in the emotional system (Heilman, Bowers, & Valenstein, 1985). The greater orienting to an unfamiliar stimulus could have resulted from a larger than normal fear response.

Following the tenth session, evidence on dishabituation also was collected. The distractors that had been used were replaced by distractors that consisted of the same digits in a new distracting location in the array, or of new distracting digits but in the same distracting location. The hippocampal-lesioned monkeys failed to dishabituate to any appreciable degree, presumably because they never habituated to the distractors in the first place. The other two groups dishabituated and then habituated again rapidly across trials. Other evidence reviewed by Gray (1982, pp. 151–152) indicates that lesions of either the hippocampus or the nearby septal areas interfere with habituation of learned responding, no matter whether the response involves motor activity or inhibition of it.

Unlike most of the relevant animal studies, which focused on behavioral responding, Sanwald, Porzio, Deane, and Donovick (1970) studied the effect of dorsal hippocampal and septal lesions on the cardiac deceleration that occurs as part of the orienting response. This study observed normal cardiac deceleration in both lesioned groups in the early trials, but a deficiency in the rate at which cardiac deceleration habituated across trials. Thus, it seems clear that the hippocampal system plays an important role in the habituation of orienting. Electrophysiological evidence in humans also supports a central role of the hippocampus in orienting of attention. Kissin (1986, pp. 115–116) reviewed evidence from studies on conscious epileptic patients with deep intracerebral electrodes, indicating that the P300 component (which may be the first step in orienting; see Näätänen, 1992) begins in or near the hippocampus and traverses up through the parietal lobe and adjacent association areas (e.g., Halgren et al., 1980). More recent work by that laboratory (Smith, Stapleton, & Halgren, 1986) suggests that later electrical components related to recognition memory also may originate in these medial temporal lobe areas.

Not every study of habituation has implicated the diencephalon alone. Butter (1964) linked habituation to the orbital-frontal cortex in monkeys. The subjects with orbital-frontal lesions, lateral frontal lesions, or no lesion pressed a bar for food on a variable-interval schedule, with an average of 50 seconds between food rewards. For 20-second periods during some of the response periods, a novel stimulus that included drum beats and flashing colored lights was presented. This novel stimulus severely disrupted bar-pressing in all groups, but the recovery of responding across presentations was considerably slower in the orbital-frontal group than in the other two groups.

It seems possible, though, that this study by Butter did not actually reflect the habituation of orienting. Orienting responses (as would be indexed, for example, by heart rate deceleration; see, for example, Graham, 1979) never fully habituated throughout the session. The role of the orbital frontal area might instead have been to inhibit responding to the novel stimuli, and thereby to permit continued bar-pressing despite the orienting responses. This interpretation would be more consistent with the previously discussed functions of the frontal lobe (e.g., Fuster, 1989; Posner & Peterson, 1990). On the other hand, there appears to be a frontal component of the mismatch negativity (Giard, Perrin, Pernier, & Bouchet, 1990), and it may be that the frontal lobes are involved in interpreting these signals and contributing to the triggering of the full-fledged orienting response.

One of the first steps in the neural processes in dishabituation of the orienting response would be the same as in habituation of orienting (i.e., the hippocampal areas might bear a special responsibility in the comparison of the neural model to the current stimulus input). However, the process of orienting itself must involve other areas. According to the theory of Cowan (1988), orienting results in the involuntary entry of the stimulus into the focus of attention. If the focus of attention is primarily in the parietal lobes of the brain, as we have speculated above, then the hippocampus somehow would have to open up (acting directly or indirectly) a channel between the cortical areas responsible for providing the sensory analysis of the novel or significant input, and the parietal areas involved in the focus of attention. The P300 results of Halgren et al. (1980) and others reviewed by Kissin (1986) appear to support this conjecture.

There also is evidence suggesting that one of the reticular centers, the locus coeruleus, plays a special role in the orienting of attention (Foote, Berridge, Adams, & Pineda, 1991; Harley, 1991). That center transmits noradrenergic innervation broadly throughout the thalamus, hippocampus, and cortex. Activation of the locus coeruleus appears to produce the cortical desynchronization and hippocampal theta rhythm found with orienting and attentional alerting. However, it is still unclear how these mechanisms work and what makes the locus coeruleus respond. The same neural signs of cortical or hippocampal activation can be observed without locus coeruleus activity, in rapid eye-movement sleep and at certain other times (see Foote et al., 1991, p. 530). The locus coeruleus appears to be innervated only by lower centers; recurrent innervation from the cortex, thalamus, or other higher centers so far have not been reliably observed (Aston-Jones et al., 1991). It seems unlikely, therefore, that the locus coeruleus participates in a neural model comparison process. Other possibilities are that it carries out a quite basic comparison of new stimuli with recent sensory pathway stimulation, or that it receives indirect, perhaps neurochemical, direction from higher brain centers.

8.3.3 Summary of neural hypotheses

It may be useful to restate the core of the neural hypotheses that have been suggested together, as shown in Fig. 8.1: (1) the brief sensory afterimage may arise in modality-specific cortical areas and may be reflected in long-latency event-related potentials; (2) short-term synaptic changes in the same or closely allied regions of the cortex may mediate temporary memory activation, which may be observed in the form of refractory N1 and change-dependent mismatch negativity responses in event-related potentials; (3) automatic long-term storage is reflected in changes in diffuse areas of the brain; (4) attention-related long-term memory is stored with the involvement of the hippocampus; (5) the central executive functions involved in determining the direction of attention and in planning and carrying out voluntary actions is located primarily in the frontal lobes; (6) the level of arousal is determined by innervation from the reticular activating system, whereas a selective modulation of the attentional system occurs through the thalamus, which itself may be controlled by frontal lobe input; (7) the focus of attention itself may be located in the parietal lobe, perhaps with the necessary input of the thalamus, frontal lobes, or diverse sensory areas; (8) entry of an item into the focus of attention may be mediated by synchronized oscillations of the neural detectors of separate features of the object, which in a complex stimulus field may be dependent upon synchronizing input from the thalamus; (9) habituation of orienting to habitual stimuli depends upon comparisons taking place first in the sensory cortex, then in the hippocampus with possible input from the frontal lobes; and (10) dishabituation of orienting to novel or significant stimuli depends upon the same comparisons, with signals sent to the frontal or parietal regions allowing the entry of the changed or significant signals to enter the focus of attention.

8.3.4 Consciousness in a wider context

The current zeitgeist in the examination of conscious processes follows the latest technology, such as PET recording (e.g., Posner & Rothbart, 1991) and magnetoencephalography (e.g., Näätänen, 1992), which allows anatomically specific observations of on-line neural functioning in normal humans. This work, though indeed exciting, should not overshadow the much wider-ranging body of evidence from older sources, such as anatomical lesions and electrophysiological recording, which can lead to a broader understanding of the mechanisms involved in conscious thought. The best integration of the older research that I have seen is to be found in a book by Kissin (1986).

Kissin defined three levels of neural mediation of consciousness, with each level hierarchically dependent on the previous levels being intact. The lowest level is that of basic alertness and is mediated by signals showering the entire cortex from the reticular activating system. With damage to that system, a persistent vegetative state or coma can result.

Provided that the signals from this first level are intact, neural circuits involving the diencephalon, particularly the thalamus and basal ganglia, produce a general awareness. Damage to this system can result in syndromes such as "akinetic mutism," described by Girvin (1975, cited by Kissin, 1986, p. 92) as follows:

> Akinetic mutism is a peculiar alteration in consciousness characterized by the appearance of seeming wakefulness but the absence of any evidence of the expected human content of consciousness; there is absence of any but rudimentary movement, emotional expression, response to commands, or other evidence of mental activity.

The third level of awareness is that of focused self-awareness. It was said to depend on the neural integration of signals from various association areas to form a consistent, multimodal map of the self in relation to the environment, precisely the function of the posterior inferior parietal lobes (Areas 7 & Tpt; see Hyvärinen, 1982) along with the connecting fibers between left and right (in the corpus collosum and to some extent, possibly, in the cingulate gyrus; see Dimond, 1976), provided that they are energized by the appropriate lower centers. It was stressed by Kissin (1986) that the implications of this "self-awareness" system are broader than they might seem, because the interpretation and significance of environmental stimuli can be judged only in relation to the self. The hemispatial neglect syndrome and related symptoms, which occur most frequently with posterior parietal lesions (Heilman, Watson, & Valenstein, 1985), were said to result from damage to this self-awareness system.

Considerable processing of the information that is ignored in unilateral neglect can occur. Berti and Rizzolatti (1992) had neglect patients quickly categorize target pictures presented in the normal visual field according to their semantic categories, using a two-choice button press. Reaction times were faster for all neglect patients when the target stimulus was immediately preceded by the same stimulus in the neglected field (which most of the patients never reported). There also was a priming advantage when the preceding stimulus in the neglected field differed from the target but was a member of the same semantic category.

Moreover, an inspection of the individual subject means for Berti and Rizolatti's semantic priming condition reveals something else interesting. The locus of brain damage, observed with MRI (magnetic resonance imaging) scans, included the parietal lobe in all patients except one, and that one patient was the only one who did not display a semantic priming effect with non-identical target and prime pictures. It appears tentatively as if unilateral neglect involving parietal lobe damage does not imply impairment of semantic processing, though semantic processing can be impaired with nonparietal bases of neglect. Awareness clearly can be dissociated from processing.

The tendency for neglect symptoms to be more common with right-hemisphere damage (Heilman, Watson & Valenstein, 1985) also was interpreted by Kissin. He noted, first, that right-field (left-hemisphere) neglect can be obscured by aphasic symptoms. Additionally, the right hemisphere appears to operate more holistically and less analytically than the left, at least when acting alone (on this point, see also Lamb, Robertson, & Knight, 1990; Kosslyn, Chabris, Marsolek, & Koenig, 1992; Hellige, 1993), which may make it more suitable as a medium for a holistic concept of the self in relation to its environment.

In Kissin's view, the frontal lobe structures are not central to the experience of self-consciousness, although they are critical for the voluntary control of that consciousness. Frontal lobe damage does not characteristically result in neglect (although it can occur), but more characteristically results in loss of voluntary control and planfulness (Fuster, 1989). Perhaps planfulness should be viewed as a fourth level of awareness dependent on the other three.

A theme of this book has been that memory and attention are closely interrelated. The evidence reviewed by Kissin, and also by Miller (1991), certainly reinforces that view. We already have noted that the hippocampus and related structures, which are essential for explicit long-term memory of particular episodes, are heavily involved also in the orienting of attention and its habituation. Kissin and Miller cite further evidence from animal research that the theta rhythm of the hippocampus signifies attentive processing of elements in the environment. This theta rhythm is triggered by the septum, which in turn may be driven by its strong input from the frontal lobe. Thus, the evidence supports the notion of hippocampal involvement in both voluntary and automatic attention shifts. The mechanism for preserving episodic memories thus is included in the attentional loop.

One simplified version of the neural system of consciousness, modeled after the ideas of Kissin (1986), is illustrated in Fig. 8.3. Not every route of transmission shown in the figure is certain, and there may be other routes. However, it does point out that a theory of the brain functioning underlying memory and attention is not beyond hoping for.

Three particular aspects of the model are specified by number (see Fig. 8.3). First (1), the thalamus and related structures act as a switching device that directly determines the focus of attention. It does this presumably both by attenuating the neural activation from irrelevant incoming sensory processes (Treisman, 1964*b*; Cowan, 1988; Hackley, 1993) and by controlling the admission of data into the integration center in the posterior parietal lobes.

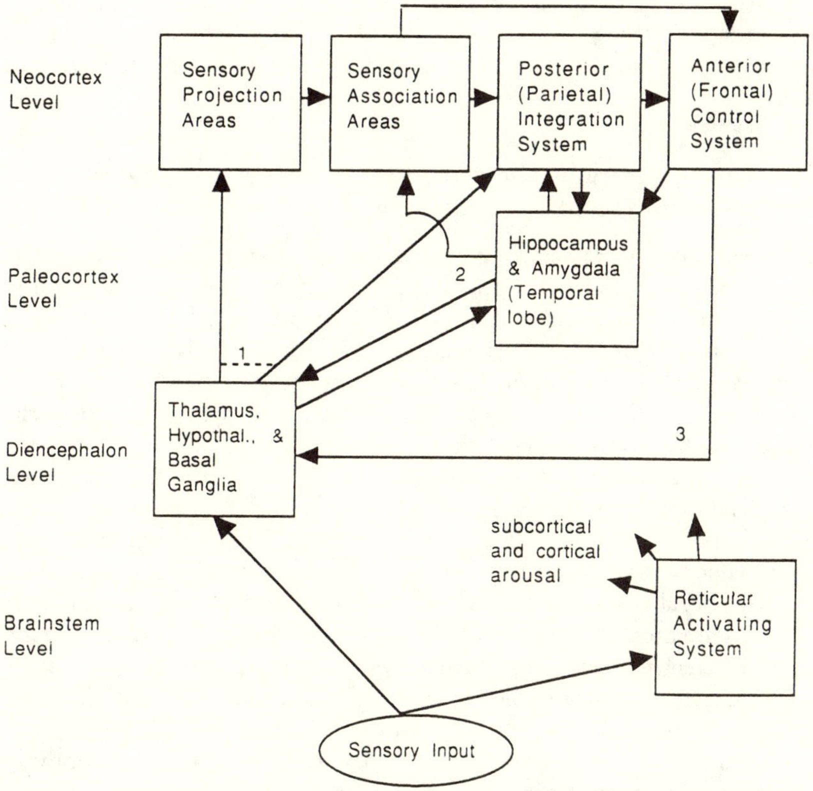

Fig. 8.3 A speculative model of the role of brain centers in conscious awareness.

Second (2), the hippocampus and related structures help to keep track of the current neural model of the environment and to detect a change from that neural model. When a change is detected, or when a match to a significant target template is detected (Gati & Ben-Shakhar, 1990), an interrupt signal is sent out to the relevant areas. Orienting is completed when attention-controlling areas of the anterior control system receive this message and switch the voluntary attentional control setting to match the new information.

It is unclear if the interrupt action of the hippocampus occurs through its direct links to the cortex, or through its links to the thalamus and related structures. However, given that attentive behavior is possible even following hippocampectomy, it seems likely that at least voluntary attention is routed through the thalamus, which is essential for conscious awareness (as shown by Fig. 8.3), and not only through the hippocampus.

Thus, we have the basis of a neural representation of the concepts of activation, voluntary attentional direction, and orienting and habituation processes that make up the psychological processing model described by Cowan (1988). It is just one possible representation, but something like it appears to be supported by a considerable amount of physiological evidence.

8.4 Some observations about the future: on the changing relation between brain research and cognition

One possibility that mainstream cognitive psychologists have not been quick to recognize and acknowledge is that the role between behavioral cognitive research and neuroscience research is changing as the neuroscientific methods quickly improve. Posner and Carr (1992) did explain ways in which recent research on the brain has a bearing on theories of lexical access, imposing restrictions on theorizing. However, one might even go further and assert that some of the behavioral methods that have been the best available to examine certain problems may no longer be the best. For example, psychophysiological methods may be better for identifying the points in processing where attention plays a role (see Hackley, 1993).

This is not to say that purely behavioral research is no longer needed; just that behavioral researchers would do well to define for themselves which problems are most useful to attack with purely behavioral methods. First of all, neuroscientific methods still are time-consuming and expensive. It makes sense for certain issues to be examined, first behaviorally, and then with psychophysiological research to follow the interesting behavioral leads. Second, there still are areas of behavior that are unclear, and psychophysiological research cannot explain behavior until it knows what behavior to explain. To say the very least, psychophysiologists must find out as much as they can about the cognitive literature; to say more, they should be intensely interested in seeing more progress in behavioral research on cognition, as some are. In my own recent research (e.g., Cowan, 1992), I have gravitated toward behaviors that are simple enough to be investigated with behavioral methods, but temporally complex enough to be beyond what psychophysiology currently can address.

Cognitive researchers must learn neuroscience, but it also is important for neuroscientists to realize (as some now do) the importance of cognitive research for their own research. A good example of its importance is finding that some well-known illusions of shape and contour disappear when the stimuli are formed from equiluminant colors, which has driven the neural research indicating that form and color perception follow separate pathways (see Livingstone & Hubel, 1988).

So far, there has been some interaction between fields, but elsewhere there has been mutual neglect bordering on denigration between some of the members of distinguishable professional groups involved in cognitive and physiological research: medical doctors, biological physicists, cognitive psychologists, and psychophysiologists trained primarily as psychologists. Even among physiologists there have been methodological boundaries. One finds books on "biological psychology" that cover only animal lesion and single-cell methods, books on "neuropsychology" that cover only human lesion methods, and so on. In the end, all available findings that bear on a particular theoretical problem must be considered. It seems to me that, for maximal progress to be made, researchers in every field should spend more time in the library than in the past and should resist specializing arbitrarily.

There are some real differences in the world views of researchers using different types of research methods, and more mutual understanding seems imperative. Many psychophysiological researchers talk as if scientific understanding amounts to reducing the level of analysis as much as possible. By this standard, much of behavioral research is at a more holistic level of analysis than is desirable. In response, cognitive psychologists will point out that much of what is to be understood is in the organization of the organism, not in the individual neurons. One learns little about how computers work by studying the exact method by which a digital bit switches on and off, and the same might be said about the brain. In turn, one group of cognitive psychologists, the connectionists, might side with the psychophysiologists and assert that the organization itself is an outgrowth of the basic connectivity properties of the cellular units. In truth, it appears most useful to work at more than one level of analysis concurrently. Thus, in this book, basic components of the memory and attention systems have been examined from the point of view of the mind, on the basis of behavioral data; and from the point of view of the brain, on the basis of physiological data.

The physiological evidence has been limited to findings that appear to be of direct relevance to the concepts constructed on a cognitive level of analysis. Because neurological constructions might be found corresponding to each component of the cognitive model, one might wish to do away with the cognitive model and replace it with a neural one. That, in fact, is the sentiment of Edelman (1989), who claims in his introduction that he wants to do away with information processing models. However, it would be a mistake to do so, at least at present. The neural mechanism proposed to underlie a particular component of the cognitive model may be incomplete or imprecisely defined, whereas the cognitive concept can be defined to indicate exactly a specific function. Even when the diagram of neural processes corresponding to the functional component eventually is complete, it may be so complicated as to defy human understanding. Information processing models can help.

Finally, behavioral and physiological investigators alike could question the usefulness of the present approach because of what often has been called the homunculus problem; that is, the explaining of a mental function merely by attributing it to a cognitive or neural component that is, in itself, an agent that acts in an unknown manner. In the *reductio-ad-absurdum*, classical argument, it is said that a human can see only because there is a little man inside the head who examines the sensory input. This little man then needs a little man inside his head, and so on *ad infinitum*, so that the nature of the causative agent never gets resolved. Critics might compare this to the present suggestion that attention is controlled by a "central executive" or by "frontal lobe structures," or that memory is signalled for conscious recollection by the "hippocampus," or that the substance of consciousness may be assembled in the "focus of attention," possibly with special help from "parietal lobe structures." Postulating neural loci for mysterious cognitive entities would not seem to solve the homunculus problem, any more than Descartes solved the problem of the relation between the body and soul by suggesting that they interact through the pineal gland (see Boring, 1957).

On my reasons for permitting "homunculoid" concepts, I quote from a philosophically minded investigator (Lycan, 1991, pp. 259–260):

> Too often in philosophy and in the history of psychology, purported answers to questions [about brain mechanisms] have only put the problem off, by, in effect, positing an internal homunculus whose job it is to accomplish the task in question, and letting it go at that. 'How does one recognize a person one has not seen in a long time?'—'One forms a mental image of that person and compares the physical person to the image.' (That is, one has an internal device or functionary capable of recognizing the person, and the device does its job, so there . . .). Such answers to psychological 'how'-questions were rightly derided by Ryle (1949), Skinner (1964), and others as pseudo-explanatory and empty; accordingly, homunculi—internal devices characterized by job description—have had very bad press.

However, Lycan goes on to note:

> It was Attneave's [1960] insight that homunculi can after all be useful posits, so long as their appointed functions do not simply parrot the intelligent capacities being explained. For a subject's intelligent performance can be explained as being the joint product of several constituent performances, individually less demanding, by subagencies of the subject acting in concert. We account for the subject's intelligent activity . . . by reference to a collaborative team of homunculi, whose members are individually more specialized and less talented. The team members' own functions are specified first, and then the explanation details the ways in which the members cooperate in producing the more intelligent corporate explanandum activity.

I believe that, through this type of theoretical framework, an individual researcher can work on philosophical problems about the mind that have been perplexing for centuries and yet reach some kind of partial solution that can overcome the countervailing thought that the work was in vain.

References

Adams, J. A., & Dijkstra, S. (1966). Short-term memory for motor responses. *Journal of Experimental Psychology*, **71**, 314–318.

Adey, W. R., & Noda, H. (1973). Influence of eye movements on geniculo-striate excitability in the cat. *Journal of Physiology*, **235**, 805–821.

Alho, K., Woods, D. L., Algazi, A., & Näätänen, R. (1992). Intermodal selective attention. II. Effects of attentional load on processing of auditory and visual stimuli in central space. *Electroencephalography & Clinical Neurophysiology*, **82**, 356–368.

Allport, D. A. (1968). Phenomenal simultaneity and the perceptual moment hypothesis. *British Journal of Psychology*, **59**, 395–406.

—— (1980). Attention and performance. In G. Claxton (Ed.), *Cognitive psychology: New directions*. London: Routledge & Kegan Paul.

—— (1988). What concept of consciousness? In A. J. Marcel & E. Bisiach (Eds.), *Consciousness in contemporary science*. Oxford: Clarendon Press.

——, Antonis, B., & Reynolds, P. (1972). On the division of attention: A disproof of the single channel hypothesis. *Quarterly Journal of Experimental Psychology*, **24**, 225–235.

——, Tipper, S.P. & Chmiel, N. R. J. (1985). Perceptual integration and post-categorical filtering. In M. I. Posner & O. S. M. Marin (Eds.), *Attention & performance XI* (pp. 107–132). Hillsdale, NJ: Erlbaum.

Anderson, J. R. (1974). Retrieval of propositional information from long-term memory. *Cognitive Psychology*, **6**, 451–474.

——, (1983). *The architecture of cognition*. Cambridge, MA: Harvard University Press.

——, & Pirolli, P. L. (1984). Spread of activation. *Journal of Experimental Psychology: Learning, Memory, & Cognition*, **10**, 791–798.

Arnheim, R. (1971). Art in bits and chunks. *Contemporary Psychology*, **16**, 459–461.

Asimov, I., & Shulman, J. A. (1988). *Isaac Asimov's book of science and nature quotations*. New York: Weidenfeld & Nicolson.

Aston-Jones, G., Shipley, M. T., Chovret, G., Ennis, M., Van Bockstaele, E., Pieribone, V., Shiekhattar, R., Akaoka, H., Drolet, G., Astier, B., Charléty, P., Valentino, R. J. & Williams, J. T. (1991). Afferent regulation of locus coeruleus neurons: Anatomy, physiology, and pharmacology. In C. D. Barnes & O. Pompeiano (Eds.), *Progress in brain research* (Vol. 88, pp. 47–75). Amsterdam: Elsevier.

Atkinson, R. C., & Shiffrin, R. M. (1968). Human memory: A proposed system and its control processes. In K. W. Spence & J. T. Spence (Eds.), *The psychology of learning & motivation: Advances in research & theory* (Vol. 2, pp. 89–195). New York: Academic Press.

Attneave, F. (1960). In defense of homunculi. In W. Rosenblith (Ed.), *Sensory communication* (pp. 777–782). Cambridge, MA: MIT Press.

Averbach, E., & Coriell, A. S. (1961). Short-term memory in vision. *Bell System Technical Journal*, **40**, 309–328.

Ayres, T. J., Jonides, J., Reitman, J. S., Egan, J. C., & Howard, D. A. (1979). Differing suffix effects for the same physical suffix. *Journal of Experimental Psychology: Human Learning & Memory*, **5**, 315–321.

Baars, B. J. (1987). Biological implications of a global-workspace theory of consciousness: Evidence, theory, and some phylogenetic speculations. In G. Greenberg & E. Tobach (Eds.), *Cognition, language, and consciousness: Integrative levels*. Hillsdale, NJ: Erlbaum.

—— (1988). *A cognitive theory of consciousness*. London: Cambridge University Press.

—— (1992). Divided consciousness or divided self? *Consciousness & Cognition*, **1**, 59–60.

Baddeley, A., Lewis, V., & Vallar, G. (1984). Exploring the articulatory loop. *The Quarterly Journal of Experimental Psychology*, **36A**, 233–252.

——, Papagno, C., & Vallar, G. (1988). When long-term learning depends on short-term storage. *Journal of Memory and Language*, **27**, 586–595.

Baddeley, A. D., (1966). The influence of acoustic and semantic similarity on long-term memory for word sequences. *Quarterly Journal of Experimental Psychology*, **18**, 302–309.

—— (1986). *Working memory*. Oxford: Clarendon Press.

——, & Scott, D. (1971). Short-term forgetting in the absence of proactive inhibition. *Quarterly Journal of Experimental Psychology*, **23**, 275–283.

——, Thomson, N., & Buchanan, M. (1975). Word length and the structure of short-term memory. *Journal of Verbal Learning & Verbal Behavior*, **14**, 575–589.

Balota, D. A. (1983). Automatic semantic activation and episodic memory encoding. *Journal of Verbal Learning & Verbal Behavior*, **22**, 88–104.

——, & Duchek, J. M. (1986). Voice-specific information and the 20-second delayed suffix effect. *Journal of Experimental Psychology: Learning, Memory, & Cognition*, **12**, 509–516.

——, Pollatsek, A., & Rayner, K. (1985). The interaction of contextual constraints and parafoveal visual information in reading. *Cognitive Psychology*, **17**, 384–390.

Beatty, J. (1982). Task-evoked pupillary responses, processing load, and the structure of processing resources. *Psychological Bulletin*, **91**, 276–292.

Berry, D. C., & Broadbent, D. E. (1988). Interactive tasks and the implicit–explicit distinction. *British Journal of Psychology*, **79**, 251–272.

Berti, A., & Rizzolatti, G. (1992). Visual processing without awareness: Evidence from unilateral neglect. *Journal of Cognitive Neuroscience*, **4**, 343–351.

Binet, A. (1889–1890). *On double consciousness*. Chicago: Open Court. (Reprinted as new edition, 1896).

Bisiach, E. (1988). The (haunted) brain and consciousness. In A. J. Marcel & E. Bisiach (Eds.), *Consciousness in contemporary science*. Oxford: Clarendon Press.

—— (1992). Understanding consciousness: Clues from unilateral neglect and related disorders. In A. D. Milner & M. D. Rugg (Eds.), *The neuropsychology of consciousness* (pp. 113–137). London: Academic Press.

Bjork, R. A., & Whitten, W. B. (1974). Recency-sensitive retrieval processes in long-term free recall. *Cognitive Psychology*, **6**, 173–189.

Blakemore, C. (1977). *Mechanics of the mind.* Cambridge: Cambridge University Press.

Borges, J. L. (1984). *Seven nights.* London: Faber & Faber. (Originally in Spanish, 1980, by Fondo de Cultura Economica, Mexico; translated by Eliot Weinberger)

Boring, E. G. (1957). *A history of experimental psychology* (2nd ed.). Englewood Cliffs, NJ: Prentice-Hall.

Bower, G. H., & Hilgard, E.R. (1981). *Theories of learning* (5th ed.). Englewood Cliffs, NJ: Prentice-Hall.

Bowers, J. S., & Schacter, D. L. (1990). Implicity memory and test awareness. *Journal of Experimental Psychology: Learning, Memory, & Cognition*, **16**, 404–416.

Bowers, K. S. (1991). Dissociation in hypnosis and multiple personality disorder. *International Journal of Clinical & Experimental Hypnosis*, **39**, 155–176.

Brainerd, C. J., & Kingma, J. (1985). On the independence of short-term memory and working memory in cognitive development. *Cognitive Psychology*, **17**, 210–247.

Bransford, J. D., & Franks, J. J. (1971). The abstraction of linguistic ideas. *Cognitive Psychology*, **2**, 331–350.

Broadbent, D. (1982). Task combination and the selective intake of information. *Acta Psychologica*, **50**, 253–290.

Broadbent, D. E. (1952). Failures of attention in selective listening. *Journal of Experimental Psychology*, **44**, 428–433.

—— (1957). Immediate memory and simultaneous stimuli. *Quarterly Journal of Experimental Psychology*, **9**, 1–11.

—— (1958). *Perception & communication.* New York: Pergamon Press.

—— (1971). *Decision and stress.* London: Academic Press.

—— (1984). The Maltese Cross: A new simplistic model for memory. *The Behavioral & Brain Sciences*, **7**, 55–94.

Brown, A. (1991). A review of the tip-of-the-tongue experience. *Psychological Bulletin*, **109**, 204–223.

Brown, G. D. A., & Hulme, C. (1993). Connectionist models of human short-term memory. In O. Omidvar (Ed.), *Progress in neural networks* (Vol. 3). Norwood, NJ: Ablex.

Brown, H. L., & Kirsner, K. (1980). A within-subjects analysis of the relationship between memory span and processing rate in short-term memory. *Cognitive Psychology*, **12**, 177–187.

Brown, J. (1958). Some tests of the decay theory of immediate memory. *Quarterly Journal of Experimental Psychology*, **10**, 12–21.

Brown, T. H., Ganong, A. H., Kairiss, E. W., Keenan, C. L., & Kelso, S. R. (1989). Long-term potentiation in two synaptic systems of the hippocampal brain slice. In J. H. Byrne & W. O. Berry (Eds.), *Neural models of plasticity.* New York: Academic Press.

Bullemer, P., & Nissen, M. J. (1990, November). Attentional orienting in the expression of procedural knowledge. Paper presented to the Psychonomic Society, New Orleans.

Burgess, N., & Hitch, G. (1992). Towards a network model of the articulatory loop. *Journal of Memory & Language*, **31**, 429–460.

Butter, C. M. (1964). Habituation of responses to novel stimuli in monkeys with selective frontal lesions. *Science*, **144**, 313–315.

Butters, N., & Miliotis, P. (1985). Amnesic disorders. In K. M. Heilman & E. Valenstein (Eds.), *Clinical neuropsychology* (2nd ed., pp. 403–451). New York: Oxford University Press.

Cantor, J., & Engle, R. W. (1993). Working memory capacity as long-term memory activation: An individual differences approach. *Journal of Experimental Psychology: Learning, Memory, & Cognition*, **19**, 1101–1114.

——, ——, & Hamilton, G. (1991). Short-term memory, working memory, and verbal abilities: How do they relate? *Intelligence*, **15**, 229–246.

Caplan, D., Rochon, E., & Waters, G. S. (1992). Articulatory and phonological determinants of word length effects in span tasks. *Quarterly Journal of Experimental Psychology*, **45A**, 177–192.

Carlson, R. A., & Detweiler, M. (1992). A unified theory for psychologists? *Behavioral & Brain Sciences*, **15**, 440.

Carr, T. H., & Dagenbach, D. (1990). Semantic priming and repetition priming from masked words: Evidence for a center-surround attentional mechanism in perceptual recognition. *Journal of Experimental Psychology: Learning, Memory, & Cognition*, **16**, 341–350.

Carrier, M., & Pashler, H. (1992). The attention demands of memory retrieval. (Unpublished manuscript.)

Carroll, J. B. (1988). Individual differences in cognitive functioning. In R. C. Atkinson, R. J. Herrnstein, G. Lindzey, & R. D. Luce (Eds.), *Stevens' handbook of experimental psychology.* (2nd ed., Vol. 2). New York: Wiley.

Case, R., Kurland, D. M., & Goldberg, J. (1982). Operational efficiency and the growth of short-term memory span. *Journal of Experimental Child Psychology*, **33**, 386–404.

Cash, D. J., & Subbarao, K. (1987). Desensitization of γ-aminobutyric acid receptor from rat brain: Two distinguishable receptors on the same membrane. *Biochemistry*, **26**, 7556–7562.

Cavanagh, J. P. (1972). Relation between the immediate memory span and the memory search rate. *Psychological Review*, **79**, 525–530.

Cermak, L. S., Talbot, N., Chandler, K., & Wolbarst, L. R. (1985). The perceptual priming phenomenon in amnesia. *Neuropsychologia*, **23**, 615–622.

Chase, W. G. (1977). Does memory scanning involve implicit speech? In S. Dornic (Ed.), *Attention and performance VI.* Hillsdale, NJ: Erlbaum. (pp. 607–628)

Cheng, C. (1974). Different roles of acoustic and articulatory information in short-term memory. *Journal of Experimental Psychology*, **103**, 614–618.

Cherry, E. C. (1953). Some experiments on the recognition of speech, with one and with two ears. *The Journal of the Acoustical Society of America*, **25**(5), 975–979.

Cherry, C., & Bowles, J. A. (1960). Contribution to a study of the "cocktail party problem." *Journal of the Acoustical Society of America*, **32**, 884.

Chipman, S. F. (1992). Re-membering cognition. *Behavioral & Brain Sciences*, **15**, 441–442.

Clifton, C., & Tash, J. (1973). Effect of syllabic word length on memory-search rate. *Journal of Experimental Psychology*, **99**, 231–235.

Cohen, J. D., Romero, R. D., & Farah, M. J. (in press). Disengaging from the disengage function: The relation of macrostructure to microstructure in parietal attention deficits. *Journal of Cogntive Neuroscience*.

Cohen, N. J., & Corkin, S. (1981). The amnesic patient H.M.: Learning and retention of a cognitive skill. *Neuroscience Abstracts*, **7**, 235.
Colombo, M., D'Amato, M. R., Rodman, H. R., & Gross, C. G. (1990). Auditory association cortex lesions impair auditory short-term memory in monkeys. *Science*, **246**, 336–338.
Conrad, R. (1957). Decay theory of immediate memory. *Nature*, **179**, 831–832.
—— (1964). Acoustic confusion in immediate memory. *British Journal of Psychology*, **55**, 75–84.
—— (1967). Interference or decay over short retention intervals? *Journal of Verbal Learning and Verbal Behavior*, **6**, 49–54.
Consumer Reports (1993). High anxiety. *Consumer Reports*, **58**, 19–24.
Cowan, N. (1984). On short and long auditory stores. *Psychological Bulletin*, **96**, 341–370.
—— (1987). Auditory sensory storage in relation to the growth of sensation and acoustic information extraction. *Journal of Experimental Psychology: Human Perception and Performance*, **13**, 204–215.
—— (1988). Evolving conceptions of memory storage, selective attention, and their mutual constraints within the human information processing system. *Psychological Bulletin*, **104**, 163–191.
—— (1989). The reality of cross-modal Stroop effects. *Perception & Psychophysics*, **45**, 87–88.
—— (1992). Verbal memory span and the timing of spoken recall. *Journal of Memory & Language*, **31**, 668–684.
—— (1993). Activation, attention, and short-term memory. *Memory & Cognition*, **21**, 162–167.
——, & Barron, A. (1987). Cross-modal, auditory-visual Stroop interference and possible implications for speech memory. *Perception & Psychophysics*, **41**, 393–401.
——, Cartwright, C., Winterowd, C., & Sherk, M. (1987). An adult model of preschool children's speech memory. *Memory and Cognition*, **15**, 511–517.
——, Day, L., Saults, J. S., Keller, T. A., Johnson, T., & Flores, L. (1992). The role of verbal output time in the effects of word length on immediate memory. *Journal of Memory & Language*, **31**, 1–17.
——, Hosmer, J., Elder, C., Reeves, A., Jennings, S., & Kaye, L. (in prep). *Two mechanisms of cross-modal interference in a color-naming task: memory contamination and distraction.* (Manuscript in preparation).
——, Keller, T., Hulme, C., Roodenrys, S., McDougall, S., & Rack, J. (1994). Verbal memory span in children: Speech timing clues to the mechanisms underlying age and word length effects. *Journal of Memory & Language*, **33**, 234–250.
——, Lichty, W., & Grove, T. R. (1990). Properties of memory for unattended spoken syllables. *Journal of Experimental Psychology: Learning, Memory, & Cognition*, **16**, 258–269.
——, & Stadler, M. (in prep.). *Estimating unconscious processes: Benefits of considering some general constraints on process dissociation models.*
——, Winkler, I., Teder, W., & Näätänen, R. (1993). Memory prerequisites of the mismatch negativity in the auditory event-related potential (ERP). *Journal of Experimental Psychology: Learning, Memory, & Cognition*, **19**, 909–921.
——, Wood, N. L., & Borne, D. N. (1994). Reconfirmation of the short-term storage

concept. *Psychological Science*, **5**, 103–106.

Creel, W., Boomsliter, P. C., & Powers, S. R., Jr. (1970). Sensations of tones as perceptual forms. *Psychological Review*, **77**, 534–545.

Crick, F., & Koch, C. (1990). Towards a neurobiological theory of consciousness. *Seminars in the Neurosciences*, **2**, 263–275.

——, & —— (1992, September). The problem of consciousness. *Scientific American*, pp. 153–159.

Crosson, B. (1992). *Subcortical functions in language and memory.* New York: Guilford Press.

Crowder, R. G. (1969). Behavioral strategies in immediate memory. *Journal of Verbal Learning and Verbal Behavior*, **8**, 524–528.

—— (1971). The sound of vowels and consonants in immediate memory. *Journal of Verbal Learning and Verbal Behavior*, **10**, 587–596.

—— (1976). *Principles of learning & memory.* Hillsdale, NJ: Erlbaum.

—— (1982). Decay of auditory memory in vowel discr(AD)imination. *Journal of Experimental Psychology: Learning, Memory, & Cognition*, **8**, 153–162.

—— (1983). The purity of auditory memory. *Philosophical Transactions of the Royal Society of London*, *B302*, 251–265.

—— (1989*a*). Modularity and dissociations in memory systems. In H. L. Roediger & F. I. M. Craik (Eds.), *Varieties of memory and consciousness: Essays in Honor of Endel Tulving*. Hillsdale, NJ: Erlbaum.

—— (1989*b*). Imagery for musical timbre. *Journal of Experimental Psychology: Human Perception & Performance*, **15**, 472–478.

—— (1993). Short-term memory: Where do we stand? *Memory & Cognition*, **21**, 142–145.

——, & Morton, J. (1969). Precategorical acoustic storage. *Perception & Psychophysics*, **5**, 365—373.

Cunningham, T. F., Healy, A. F., Till, R. E., Fendrich, D. W., & Dimitry, C. Z. (1993). Is there really very rapid forgetting from primary memory? The role of expectancy and item importance in short-term recall. *Memory & Cognition*, **21**, 671–688.

Curran, T., & Keele, S. W. (1993). Attentional and nonattentional forms of sequence learning. *Journal of Experimental Psychology: Learning, Memory, & Cognition*, **19**, 189–202.

Dagenbach, D., Carr, T. H., & Barnhardt, T. M. (1990). Inhibitory semantic priming of lexical decisions due to failure to retrieve weakly activated codes. *Journal of Experimental Psychology: Learning, Memory, & Cognition*, **16**, 238–240.

Dalezman, J. J. (1976). Effects of output order on immediate, delayed, and final recall performance. *Journal of Experimental Psychology: Human Learning & Memory*, **2**, 597–608.

Daneman, M., & Carpenter, P. A. (1980). Individual differences in working memory and reading. *Journal of Verbal Learning & Verbal Behavior*, **19**, 450–466.

Darwin, C. J. (1976). The perception of speech. In E. C. Carterette & M. P. Friedman (Eds.), *Handbook of perception, Volume VII*. NY: Academic Press.

——, Turvey, M. T., & Crowder, R. G. (1972). An auditory analogue of the Sperling partial report procedure: Evidence for brief auditory storage. *Cognitive Psychology*, **3**, 255–267.

Dawson, M. E., Filion, D. L., & Schell, A. M. (1989). Is elicitation of the autonomic orienting response associated with allocation of processing resources? *Psychophy-*

siology, **26**, 560–572.

——, & Schell, A. M. (1982). Electrodermal responses to attended and unattended significant stimuli during dichotic listening. *Journal of Experimental Psychology: Human Perception & Performance*, **8**, 315–324.

Deacon, D., Breton, F., Ritter, W., & Vaughan, H. G., Jr. (1991). The relationship between N2 and N400: Scalp distribution, stimulus probability, and task relevance. *Psychophysiology*, **28**, 185–200.

Debner, J. A., & Jacoby, L. L. (1994). Unconscious perception: Attention, awareness, and control. *Journal of Experimental Psychology: Learning, Memory, & Cognition*, **20**, 304–317.

Dell, G. S. (1986). A spreading-activation theory of retrieval in sentence production. *Psychological Review*, **93**, 283–321.

Dennett, D. C. (1991). *Consciousness explained*. Boston: Little, Brown & Co.

——, & Kinsbourne, M. (1992). Time and the observer: The where and when of consciousness. *Behavioral & Brain Sciences*, **15**, 183–247.

Deutsch, D. (1975). The organization of short-term memory for a single acoustic attribute. In D. Deutsch & J. A. Deutsch (Eds.), *Short-term memory* (pp. 107–151). New York: Academic Press.

Deutsch, J. A., & Deutsch, D. (1963). Attention: Some theoretical considerations. *Psychological Review*, **70**(1), 80–90.

Di Lollo, V., & Dixon, P. (1988). Two forms of persistence in visual information processing. *Journal of Experimental Psychology: Human Perception & Performance*, **14**, 671–681.

Dimond, S. J. (1976). Brain circuits for consciousness. *Brain, Behavior & Evolution*, **13**, 376–395.

Dosher, B., & Ma, J-J. (1992, November). Relation of recall output time and accuracy in STM. Paper presented at the annual convention of the Psychonomic Society, St. Louis, MO.

Dostoevsky, F. (1960). *'Notes from underground' and 'The grand inquisitor'*. New York: E. P. Dutton & Co. (Translated by R. E. Matlaw; *Notes from underground*, originally published 1864.)

Douglas, R. J., & Pribram, K. H. (1969). Distraction and habituation in monkeys with limbic lesions. *Journal of Comparative & Physiological Psychology*, **69**, 473–480.

Drewnowski, A., & Murdock, A. B., Jr. (1980). The role of auditory featues in memory span for words. *Journal of Experimental Psychology: Human Learning and Memory*, **6**, 319–332.

Driver, J., & Baylis, G. C. (1993). Cross-modal negative priming and interference in selective attention. *Bulletin of the Psychonomic Society*, **31**, 45–48.

Duncan, J. (1980). The locus of interference in the perception of simultaneous stimuli. *Psychological Review*, **87**(3), 272–300.

——, & Humphreys, G. W. (1989). A resemblance theory of visual search. *Psychological Review*, **96**, 433–458.

——, & —— (1992). Beyond the search surface: Visual search and attentional engagement. *Journal of Experimental Psychology: Human Perception & Performance*, **18**, 578–588.

Dyer, F. N. (1973). The Stroop phenomenon and its use in the study of perceptual, cognitive, and response processes. *Memory & Cognition*, **1**, 106–120.

Edelman, G. M. (1989). *The remembered present: A biological theory of consciousness.* New York: Basic Books.

Efron, R. (1970*a*). The relationship between the duration of a stimulus and the duration of a perception. *Neuropsychologia*, **8**, 37–55.

—— (1970*b*). The minimum duration of a perception. *Neuropsychologia*, **8**, 57–63.

—— (1970*c*). Effects of stimulus duration on perceptual onset and offset latencies. *Perception & Psychophysics*, **8**, 231–234.

Eich, E. (1984). Memory for unattended events: Remembering with and without awareness. *Memory & Cognition*, **12**, 105–111.

Eichenbaum, H., Otto, T., & Cohen, N.J. (in press). Two component functions of the hippocampal memory system. *Behavioral & Brain Sciences.*

Elmasian, R., & Galambos, R. (1975). Loudness enhancement: Monaural, binaural, and dichotic. *Journal of the Acoustical Society of America*, **58**, 229–234.

——, ——, & Bernheim, A. (1980). Loudness enhancement and decrement in four paradigms. *Journal of the Acoustical Society of America*, **67**, 601–607.

Engle, R. W., Cantor, J., & Carullo, J. J. (1992). Individual differences in working memory and comprehension: A test of four hypotheses. *Journal of Experimental Psychology: Learning, Memory, & Cognition*, **18**, 972–992.

Eriksen, C. W., & Collins, J. F. (1967). Some temporal characteristics of visual pattern perception. *Journal of Experimental Psychology*, **74**, 476–484.

——, & —— (1968). Sensory traces versus the psychological moment in the temporal organization of form. *Journal of Experimental Psychology*, **77**, 376–382.

——, & Johnson, H. J. (1964). Storage and decay characteristics of nonattended auditory stimuli. *Journal of Experimental Psychology*, **68**, 28–36.

Estes, W. K. (1972). An associative basis for coding and organization in memory. In A. W. Martin & E. Martin (Eds.), *Coding processes in human memory* (pp. 161–190). Washington, DC: Winston.

Fanselow, M. S. (1993). Associations and memories: The role of NMDA receptors and long-term potentiation. *Current Directions in Psychological Science*, **2**, 152–156.

Farah, M. J. (1988). Is visual imagery really visual? Overlooked evidence from neuropsychology. *Psychological Review*, **95**, 307–317.

—— (1994). Neuropsychological inference with an interactive brain: A critique of the locality assumption. *Behavioral & Brain Sciences*, **17**, 43–104.

——, & McClelland, J. L. (1991). A computational model of semantic memory impairment: Modality-specificity and emergent category-specificity. *Journal of Experimental Psychology: General*, **120**, 339–357.

——, O'Reilly, R. C., & Vecera, S. P. (1993). Dissociated overt and covert recognition as an emergent property of lesioned neural networks. *Psychological Review*, **100**, 571–588.

——, Wong, A. B., Monheit, M. A., & Morrow, L. A. (1989). Parietal lobe mechanisms of spatial attention: Modality-specific or supramodal? *Neuropsychologia*, **27**, 461–470.

Fendrich, D. W., Healy, A. F., & Bourne, L. E., Jr. (1991). Long-term repetition effects for motoric and perceptual procedures. *Journal of Experimental Psychology: Learning, Memory, & Cognition*, **17**, 137–151.

Fendrich, R., Wessinger, C. M., & Gazzaniga, M. S. (1992). Residual vision in a scotoma: Implications for blindsight. *Science*, **258**, 1489–1491.

Filion, D. L., Dawson, M. E., Schell, A. M., & Hazlett, E. A. (1991). The relationship between skin conductance orienting and the allocation of processing resources. *Psychophysiology*, **28**, 410–424.

Fisher, D. L., Duffy, S. A., Young, C., & Pollatsek, A. (1988). Understanding the central processing limit in consistent-mapping visual search tasks. *Journal of Experimental Psychology: Human Perception & Performance*, **14**, 253–266.

Fisk, A. D., & Schneider, W. (1984). Memory as a function of attention, level of processing, and automatization. *Journal of Experimental Psychology: Learning, Memory, & Cognition*, **10**, 181–197.

Fodor, J. A. (1983). *The modularity of mind: An essay on faculty psychology.* Cambridge, MA: MIT Press.

Foote, S. L., Berridge, C. W., Adams, L. M., & Pineda, J. A. (1991). Electrophysiological evidence for the involvement of the locus coeruleus in alerting, orienting, and attending. In C. D. Barnes & O. Pompeiano (Eds.), *Progress in brain research* (Vol. 88, pp. 521–532). Amsterdam: Elsevier.

Frankish, C. (1989). Perceptual organization and precategorical acoustic storage. *Journal of Experimental Psychology: Learning, Memory, & Cognition*, **15**, 469–479.

Frensch, P. A., & Miner, C. S. (1994). Effects of presentation rate and individual differences in short-term memory capacity on an indirect measure of serial learning. *Memory & Cognition*, **22**, 95–110.

Friedman, A., Polson, M. C., & Dafoe, C. G, & Gaskill, S. (1982). Dividing attention within and between hemispheres: Testing a multiple resources approach to limited-capacity information processing. *Journal of Experimental Psychology*, **8**, 625–650.

——, ——, & —— (1989). Dividing attention between the hands and the head: Performance trade-offs between rapid finger tapping and verbal memory. *Journal of Experimental Psychology: Human Perception & Performance*, **14**, 60–68.

Fuster, J. M. (1989). *The prefrontal cortex: Anatomy, physiology, and neuropsychology of the frontal lobe*. New York: Raven Press.

Gardiner, J. M., & Gregg, V. H. (1979). When auditory memory is not overwritten. *Journal of Verbal Learning & Verbal Behavior*, **18**, 705–719.

Garrett, H. E. (1941). *Great experiments in psychology* (rev. & enlarged ed.). New York: Appleton-Century-Crofts.

Gathercole, S. E., & Baddeley, A. D. (1989). Evaluation fo the role of phonological STM in the development of vocabulary in children: A longitudinal study. *Journal of Memory and Language*, **28**, 200–213.

——, & —— (1990). Phonological memory deficits in language disordered children: Is there a causal connection? *Journal of Memory and Language*, **29**, 336–360.

Gati, I., & Ben-Shakhar, G. (1990). Novelty and significance in orientation and habituation: A feature-matching approach. *Journal of Experimental Psychology: General*, **119**, 251–263.

Gazzaniga, M. S. (1985). *The social brain: Discovering the networks of the mind.* New York: Basic Books.

—— (1988). Brain modularity: towards a philosophy of conscious experience. In A. J. Marcel & E. Bisiach (Eds.), *Consciousness in contemporary science*. Oxford, UK: Clarendon Press.

——, Bogen, J. E., & Sperry, R. W. (1965). Observations of visual perception after disconnection of the cerebral hemispheres in man. *Brain*, **88**, 221.

——, Holtzman, J. D., & Smylie, C. S. (1987). Speech without conscious awareness. *Neurology*, **37**, 682–685.

Geary, D. C., & Burlingham-Dubree, M. (1989). External validation of the strategy choice model for addition. *Journal of Experimental Child Psychology*, **47**, 175–192.

——, & Widaman, K. F. (1992). Numerical cognition: On the convergence of componential and psychometric models. *Intelligence*, **16**, 47–80.

Gersuni, G. V. (1971). Temporal organization of the auditory function. In G. V. Gersuni (Ed.), *Sensory processes at the neuronal and behavioral levels* (pp. 85–114). New York: Academic Press.

Giard, M.-H., Collet, L., Bouchet, P., & Pernier, J. (1994). Auditory selective attention in the human cochlea. *Brain Research*, **633**, 353–356.

——, Perrin, F., Pernier, J., & Bouchet, P. (1990). Brain generators implicated in processing of auditory stimulus deviance: A topographic event-related potential study. *Psychophysiology*, **27**, 627–640.

Girvin, J. P. (1975). Clinical correlates of hypothalamic and limbic system function. In G. J. Mogenson & F. R. Calaresu (Eds.), *Neural integration of physiological mechanisms and behavior* (pp. 412–434). Toronto: University of Toronto Press.

Glanzer, M., & Cunitz, A. R. (1966). Two storage mechanisms in free recall. *Journal of Verbal Learning & Verbal Behavior*, **5**, 351–360.

——, & Razel, M. (1974). The size of the unit in short-term storage. *Journal of Verbal Learning & Verbal Behavior*, **13**, 114–131.

Glenberg, A. M. (1984). A retrieval account of the long-term modality effect. *Journal of Experimental Psychology: Learning, Memory, & Cognition*, **10**, 16–31.

——, & Jona, M. (1991). Temporal coding in rhythm tasks revealed by modality effects. *Memory & Cognition*, **19**, 514–522.

——, & Swanson, N. C. (1986). A temporal distinctiveness theory of recency and modality effects. *Journal of Experimental Psychology: Learning, Memory, & Cognition*, **12**, 3–15.

Glucksberg, S., & Cowen, G. N., Jr. (1970). Memory for nonattended auditory material. *Cognitive Psychology*, **1**, 149–156.

Goldman-Rakic, P. S. (1992, September). Working memory and the mind. *Scientific American*, 111–117.

Goodman, N. (1978). *Ways of worldmaking*. Sussex, England: Harvester.

Gopher, D., & Donchin, E. (1986). Workload—An examination of the concept. In K. R. Boff, L. Kaufman, & J. P. Thomas, (Eds.), *Handbook of perception and human performance* (Vol. 2). New York: Wiley.

Graf, P., & Komatsu, S. (in press). Process dissociation procedure: Handle with caution! *European Journal of Cognitive Psychology.*

——, Mandler, G., & Haden, P. (1982). Simulating amnesic symptoms in normal subjects. *Science*, **218**, 1243–1244.

——, Squire, L. R., & Mandler, G. (1984). The information that amnesic patients do not forget. *Journal of Experimental Psychology: Learning, Memory, & Cognition*, **10**, 164–178.

Graham, F. K. (1979). Distinguishing among orienting, defense, and startle reflexes. In H. D. Kimmel, E. H. van Olst, & J. F. Orlebeke (Eds.), *The oreinting reflex in humans* (pp. 137–167). Hillsdale, NJ: Erlbaum.

Grand, S., & Segal, S. J. (1966). Recovery in the absence of recall: An investigation of color-word interference. *Journal of Experimental Psychology*, **72**, 138–144.

Gray, C. M., König, P., Engel, A. K., & Singer, W. (1989). Oscillatory responses in cat visual cortex exhibit inter-columnar synchronization which reflects global stimulus properties. *Nature*, **338**, 334–337.

Gray, J. A. (1982). *The neuropsychology of anxiety: An enquiry into the functions of the septo-hippocampal system.* Oxford: Clarendon Press.

——, & Wedderburn, A. A. I. (1960). Grouping strategies with simultaneous stimuli. *Quarterly Journal of Experimental Psychology*, **12**, 180–184.

Greenberg, S. N., & Engle, R. W. (1983). Voice changes in the stimulus suffix effect: Are the effects structural or strategic? *Memory & Cognition*, **11**, 551–556.

Greene, R. L. (1986). A common basis for recency effects in immediate and delayed recall. *Journal of Experimental Psychology: Learning, Memory, & Cognition*, **12**, 413–418.

——, & Samuel, A. G. (1986). Recency and suffix effects in serial recall of musical stimuli. *Journal of Experimental Psychology: Learning, Memory, & Cognition*, **12**, 517–524.

Greenwald, A. G. (1972). Evidence of both perceptual filtering and response suppression for rejected messages in selective attention. *Journal of Experimental Psychology*, **94**, 58–67.

Gregg, V. H., & Gardiner, J. M. (1984). Phonological similarity and enhanced auditory recency in longer-term free recall. *Quarterly Journal of Experimental Psychology*, **36A**, 13–27.

Gronlund, S. D., & Ratcliff, R. (1989). Time course of item and associative information: Implications for global memory models. *Journal of Experimental Psychology: Learning, Memory, & Cognition*, **15**, 846–858.

Gross, E. G., Vaughan, H. G., Jr., & Valenstein, E. (1967). *Electroencephalography and Clinical Neurophysiology*, **22**, 204–209.

Guilford, J. P. (1967). *The nature of human intelligence*. New York: McGraw-Hill.

Gustafsson, J.-E. (1984). A unifying model for the structure of intellectual abilities. *Intelligence*, **8**, 179–203.

Guttentag, R. E. (1984). The mental effort requirement of cumulative rehearsal: A developmental study. *Journal of Experimental Child Psychology*, **37**, 92–106.

Guttman, N., & Julesz, B. (1963). Lower limits of auditory periodicity analysis. *Journal of the Acoustical Society of America*, **35**, 610.

Haber, R. N. (1983). The impending demise of the icon: A critique of the concept of iconic storage in visual information processing. *Behavioral & Brain Sciences*, **6**, 1–54.

——, & Standing, L. G. (1969). Direct measures of short-term visual storage. *Quarterly Journal of Experimental Psychology*, **21**, 43–54.

——, & —— (1970). Direct estimates of the apparent duration of a flash. *Canadian Journal of Psychology*, **24**, 216–229.

Hackley, S. (1993). An evaluation of the automaticity of sensory processing using event-related potentials and brainstem reflexes. *Psychophysiology*, **30**, 415–428.

Hale, S. (1990). A global developmental trend in cognitive processing speed. *Child Development*, **61**, 653–663.

Halgren, E., Squires, N. K., Wilson, C. L., Rohrbaugh, J. W., Babb, T. L., & Crandall, P. H. (1980). Endogenous potentials generated in the human hippocampal formation and amygdala by infrequent events. *Science*, **210**, 803–805.

Hari, R., Aittoniemi, K., Järvinen, M.-L., Katila, T., & Varpula, T. (1980). Auditory-evoked transient and sustained magnetic fields of the human brain: Localization of neural generators. *Experimental Brain Research*, **40**, 237–240.

——, Hämäläinen, M., Ilmoniemi, R., Kaukoranta, E., Reinikainen, K., Salminen, J., Alho, K., Näätanen, R., & Sams, M. (1984). Responses of the primary auditory cortex to pitch changes in a sequence of tone pips: Neuromagnetic recordings in man. *Neuroscience Letters*, **50**, 127–132.

——, Kaila, K., Katila, T., Tuomisto, T., & Varpula, T. (1982). Interstimulus interval dependence of the auditory vertex response and its magnetic counterpart: Implications for their neural generation. *Electroencephalography & Clinical Neurophysiology*, **54**, 561–569.

Harley, C. (1991). Noradrenergic and locus coeruleus modulation of the perforant path-evoked potential in rat dentate gyrus supports a role for the locus coeruleus in attentional and memorial processes. In C. D. Barnes & O. Pompeiano (Eds.), *Progress in brain research* (vol. 88) (pp. 307–321). Amsterdam: Elsevier.

Hasher, L., Stolzfus, E. R., Zacks, R. T., & Rypma, B. (1991). Age and inhibition. *Journal of Experimental Psychology: Learning, Memory, & Cognition*, **17**, 163–169.

——, & Zacks, R. T. (1979). Automatic and effortful processes in memory. *Journal of Experimental Psychology: General*, **108**, 356–388.

Hawkins, H. L., & Presson, J. C. (1977). Masking and preperceptual selectivity in auditory recognition. In S. Dornic (Ed.), *Attention & Performance VI*. Hillsdale, NJ: Erlbaum.

Hawley, K. J., & Johnston, W. A. (1991). Long-term perceptual memory for briefly exposed words as a function of awareness and attention. *Journal of Experimental Psychology: Human Perception & Performance*, **17**, 807–815.

Hayes, N. A., & Broadbent, D. E. (1989). Two modes of learning for interactive tasks. *Cognition*, **28**, 249–276.

Hebb, D. O. (1949). *Organization of behavior*. New York: Wiley.

—— (1961). Distinctive features of learning in the higher animal. In J. F. Delafresnaye (Ed.), *Brain mechanisms and learning* (pp. 37–46). London: Oxford University Press.

Heilman, K. M., Bowers, D., & Valenstein, E. (1985). Emotional disorders associated with neurological diseases. In K. M. Heilman & E. Valenstein (Eds.), *Clinical neuropsychology* (2nd, ed., pp. 377–402). New York: Oxford University Press.

——, Watson, R. T., & Valenstein, E. (1985). Neglect and related disorders. In K. M. Heilman & E. Valenstein (Eds.), *Clinical neuropsychology* (2nd ed., pp. 243–293) New York: Oxford University Press.

Held, R., & Hein, A. (1963). Movement-produced stimulation in the development of visually guided behavior. *Journal of Comparative & Physiological Psychology*, **56**, 872–876.

Hellige, J. B. (1993). Unity of thought and action: Varieties of interaction between the left and right cerebral hemispheres. *Current Directions in Psychological Science*, **2**, 21–25.

Hellström, Å. (1985). The time-order error and its relatives: Mirrors of cognitive processes in comparing. *Psychological Bulletin*, **97**, 35–61.

Henry, L. A. (1991). The effects of word length and phonemic similarity in young children's short-term memory. *Quarterly Journal of Experimental Psychology,* **43A**, 35–52.

Herdman, C. M., & Friedman, A. (1985). Multiple resources in divided attention: A cross-modal test of the independence of hemispheric resources. *Journal of Experimental Psychology: Human Perception & Performance*, **11**, 40–49.

Hilgard, E. R. (1986). *Divided consciousness: Multiple controls in human thought and action* (expanded ed.). New York: Wiley.

—— (1992). Divided consciousness and dissociation. *Consciousness & Cognition*, **1**, 16–31.

Hillyard, S. A., Simpson, G. V., Woods, D. L., Van Voorhis, S., & Münte, T. (1984). Event-related brain potentials and selective attention to different modalities. In F. Reinoso-Suarez & C. Ajmone-Marsan (Eds.), *Cortical integration*. New York: Raven Press.

Hinton, G. (1979). Some demonstrations of the effects of structural descriptions in mental imagery. *Cognitive Science*, **3**, 231.

Hirsh, I. J. (1959). Auditory perception of temporal order. *Journal of the Acoustical Society of America*, **31**, 759–767.

Hirst, W., & Kalmar, D. (1987). Characterizing attentional resources. *Journal of Experimental Psychology: General*, **116**, 68–81.

——, Spelke, E. S., Reaves, C. C., Caharack, G., & Neisser, U. (1980). Dividing attention without alternation or automaticity. *Journal of Experimental Psychology: General*, **109**, 98–117.

Hockley, W. E. (1984). Analysis of response time distributions in the study of cognitive processes. *Journal of Experimental Psychology: Learning, Memory, & Cognition*, **10**, 598–615.

Holender, D. (1986). Semantic activation without conscious identification in dichotic listening, parafoveal vision, and visual masking: A survey and appraisal. *Behavioral & Brain Sciences*, **9**, 1–66.

Holtzman, J. D., & Gazzaniga, M. S. (1982). Dual task interactions due exclusively to limits in processing resources. *Science*, **218**, 1325–1327.

——, Volpe, B. T., & Gazzaniga, M. S. (1984). Spatial orientation following commissural section. In R. Parasuraman & R. Davies (Eds.), *Varieties of attention* (pp. 375–394). Orlando, FL: Academic Press.

Hubel, D. H., & Wiesel, T. N. (1963). Shape and arrangement of columns in the cat's visual cortex. *Journal of Physiology*, **165**, 559–568.

Hulme, C., Maughan, S., & Brown, G. D. A. (1991). Memory for familiar and unfamiliar words: Evidence for a long-term memory contribution to short-term memory span. *Journal of Memory & Language*, **30**, 685–701.

——, Thomson, N., Muir, C., & Lawrence, A. (1984). Speech rate and the development of short-term memory span. *Journal of Experimental Child Psychology*, **38**, 241–253.

——, & Tordoff, V. (1989). Working memory development: The effects of speech rate, word length, and acoustic similarity on serial recall. *Journal of Experimental Child Psychology*, **47**, 72–87.

Hulstijn, W. (1979). Selective attention and the orienting response. In H. D. Kimmel, E. H. Van Olst, & J. F. Orlebeke (Eds.), *The orienting reflex in humans* (pp. 557–566). New York: Erlbaum.

Humphreys, M. S., Bain, J. D., & Pike, R. (1989). Different ways to cue a coherent memory system: A theory for episodic, semantic, and procedural tasks. *Psychological Review*, **96**, 208–233.

Hunt, E., & Luce, D. (1992). SOAR as a world view, not a theory. *Behavioral & Brain Sciences*, **15**, 447–448.

Hyvärinen, J. (1982). *The parietal cortex of monkey and man*. Berlin: Springer-Verlag.

Inhoff, A. W., & Rayner, K. (1980). Parafoveal word perception: A case against semantic preprocessing. *Perception & Psychophysics*, **27**, 457–464.

Irwin, D. E. (1991). Information integration across saccadic eye movements. *Cognitive Psychology*, **23**, 420–456.

——, & Yeomans, J. M. (1986). Sensory registration and informational persistence. *Journal of Experimental Psychology: Human Perception & Performance*, **12**, 343–360.

——, & Zwislocki, J. J. (1971). Loudness effects in pairs of tone bursts. *Perception & Psychophysics*, **10**, 189–192.

Isaacson, R. L. (1982). *The limbic system* (2nd ed). New York: Plenum Press.

Iversen, S. D. (1984). Behavioral aspects of the corticosubcortical interaction with special reference to frontostriatal relations. In F. Reinoso-Suärez & C. Ajmone-Marsan (Eds.), *Cortical integration: Basic, archicortical, and cortical association levels of neural integration* (pp. 237–254). New York: Raven Press.

Jacoby, L. L. (1983). Remembering the data: Analyzing interactive processses in reading. *Journal of Verbal Learning & Verbal Behavior*, **22**, 485–508.

—— (1991). A process dissociation framework: Separating automatic from intentional uses of memory. *Journal of Memory & Language*, **30**, 513–541.

——, Allan, L. G., Collins, J. C., & Larwill, L. K. (1988). Memory influences subjective experience: Noise judgments. *Journal of Experimental Psychology: Learning, Memory, & Cognition*, **14**, 240–247.

——, & Kelly, C. M. (1992). A process-dissociation framework for investigating unconscious influences: Freudian slips, projective tests, subliminal perception, and signal detection theory. *Current Directions in Psychological Science*, **1**, 174–179.

——, Toth, J. P., & Yonelinas, A. P. (1993). Separating conscious and unconscious influences of memory: Measuring recollection. *Journal of Experimental Psychology: General*, **122**, 139–154.

——, & Whitehouse, K. (1989). An illusion of memory: False recognition influenced by unconscious perception. *Journal of Experimental Psychology: General*, **118**, 126–135.

——, Woloshyn, V., & Kelly, C. (1989). Becoming famous without being recognized: Unconscious influences of memory produced by divided attention. *Journal of Experimental Psychology: General*, **118**, 115–125.

Jakimik, J., & Glenberg, A. (1990). Verbal learning meets psycholinguistics: Modality effects in the comprehension of anaphora. *Journal of Memory and Language*, **29**, 582–590.

James, W. (1890). *The principles of psychology*. NY: Henry Holt.

—— (1892/1961). *Psychology: The briefer course*. New York: Henry Holt & Co., (Reprinted by Harper & Brothers).

Johnston, W. A. (1978). The intrusiveness of familiar nontarget information. *Memory & Cognition*, **6**, 38–42.

——, & Dark, V. J. (1982). In defense of intraperceptual theories of attention. *Journal of Experimental Psychology: Human Perception & Performance*, **8**(3), 407-421.

——, Hawley, K. J., Plewe, S. H., Elliott, J. M. G., & DeWitt, M. J. (1990). Attention capture by novel stimuli. *Journal of Experimental Psychology: General*, **119**, 397–411.

——, & Heinz, S. P. (1978). Flexibility and capacity demands of attention. *Journal of Experimental Psychology: General*, **107**(4), 420–435.

Jones, D. M., & Macken, W. J. (1993). Irrelevant tones produce an 'irrelevant speech effect': Implications for phonological coding in working memory. *Journal of Experimental Psychology: Learning, Memory, & Cognition*, **19**, 369–381.

——, & —— (in press). Phonological similarity in the irrelevant speech effect: Within- or between-stream similarity? *Journal of Experimental Psychology: Learning, Memory, & Cognition.*

——, Madden, C., & Miles, C. (1992). Privileged access by irrelevant speech to short-term memory: The role of changing state. *Quarterly Journal of Experimental Psychology*, **44A**, 645–669.

Jones, G. V. (1989). Back to Woodworth: Role of interlopers in the tip-of-the-tongue phenomenon. *Memory & Cognition*, **17**, 69–79.

Jonides, J., & Yantis, S. (1988). Uniqueness of abrupt visual onset in capturing attention. *Perception & Psychophysics*, **43**, 346–354.

Joordens, S., & Merikle, P. M. (1993). Independence or redundancy? Two models of conscious and unconscious influences. *Journal of Experimental Psychology: General*, **122**, 462–467.

Joynt, R. J., & Shoulson, I. (1985). Dementia. In K.–M. Heilman & E. Valenstein (Eds.), *Clinical neuropsychology* (2nd ed., pp. 453–479). New York: Oxford University Press.

Just, M., & Carpenter, P. A. (1992). A capacity theory of comprehension: Individual differences in working memory. *Psychological Review*, **99**, 122–149.

Kahneman, D. (1973). *Attention and effort.* Englewood Cliffs, NJ: Prentice-Hall.

——, Treisman, A., & Gibbs, B. J. (1992). The reviewing of object files: Object-specific integration of information. *Cognitive Psychology*, **24**, 175–219.

Kail, R. (1992). Processing speed, speech rate, and memory. *Developmental Psychology*, **28**, 899–904.

Kallman, H. J., & Massaro, D. W. (1979). Similarity effects in backward recognition masking. *Journal of Experimental Psychology: Human Perception and Performance*, **5**, 110–128.

——, & Morris, M. E. (1984). Backward recognition masking as a function of ear of mask presentation. *Perception and Psychophysics*, **35**, 379–384.

Kanwisher, N., & Driver, J. (1992). Objects, attributes, and visual attention: Which, what, and where. *Current Directions in Psychological Science*, **1**, 26–31.

Kanwisher, N. G. (1987). Repetition blindness: Type recognition without token individuation. *Cognition*, **27**, 117–143.

——, & Potter, M. C. (1990). Repetition blindness: Levels of processing. *Journal of Experimental Psychology: Human Perception & Performance*, **16**, 30–47.

Keller, T. A., Cowan, N., & Saults, J. S. (in press). Can auditory memory for tone pitch be rehearsed? *Journal of Experimental Psychology: Learning, Memory, & Cognition.*

Kelly, D. D. (1985). Sleep and dreaming. In E. R. Kandel & J. H. Schwartz (Eds.), *Principles of neural science* (2nd ed.). New York: Elsevier.

Keppel, G., & Underwood, B. J. (1962). Proactive inhibition in short-term retention of single items. *Journal of Verbal Learning and Verbal Behavior*, **1**, 153–161.

Kidd, G. R., & Greenwald, A. G. (1988). Attention, rehearsal, and memory for serial order. *Americal Journal of Psychology*, **101**, 259–279.

Kihlstrom, J. F. (1987). The cognitive unconscious. *Science*, **237**, 1445–1452.

—— (1992). Dissociation and dissociations: A comment on consciousness and cognition. *Consciousness & Cognition*, **1**, 47–53.

Kim, J. J., Fanselow, M. S., DeCola, J. P., & Landeira-Fernandez, J. (1992). Selective impairment of long-term but not short-term conditional fear by the N-Methyl-D-Aspartate antagonist APV. *Behavioral Neuroscience*, **106**, 591–596.

Kimmel, H. D., van Olst, E. H., & Orlebeke, J. F. (1979). *The orienting reflex in humans*. Hillsdale, NJ: Erlbaum.

Kissin, B. (1986). *Conscious and unconscious programs in the brain*. New York: Plenum.

Klapp, S. T., Marshburn, E. A., & Lester, P. T. (1983). Short-term memory does not involve the "working memory" of information processing: The demise of a common assumption. *Journal of Experimental Psychology: General*, **112**, 240–264.

Knox, V. J., Crutchfield, L., & Hilgard, E. R. (1975). The nature of task interference in hypnotic dissociation: An investigation of hypnotic behavior. *International Journal of Clinical & Experimental Hypnosis*, **23**, 305–323.

Koffka, K. (1935/1963). *Principles of Gestalt psychology*. New York: Harcourt, Brace, & World.

Köhler, W. (1947). *Gestalt psychology*. New York: Liveright Publishing.

Kolers, P. A., & von Grünau, M. (1976). Shape and color in apparent motion. *Vision Research*, **16**, 329–335.

Koppenaal, L., & Glanzer, M. (1990). An examination of the continuous distractor task and the "long-term recency effect". *Memory & Cognition*, **18**, 183–195.

Koriat, A., & Feuerstein, N. (1976). The recovery of incidentally acquired information. *Acta Psychologica*, **40**, 463–474.

Kosslyn, S. M., Chabris, C. F., Marsolek, C. J., & Koenig, O. (1992). Categorical versus coordinate spatial relations: Computational analyses and computer simulations. *Journal of Experimental Psychology: Human Perception & Performance*, **18**, 562–577.

Kraut, A. G. (1976). Effects of familiarization on alertness and encoding in children. *Developmental Psychology*, **12**, 491–496.

——, & Smothergill, D. W. (1978). A two-factor theory of stimulus-repetition effects. *Journal of Experimental Psychology: Human Perception & Performance*, **4**(1), 191–197.

——, ——, & Farkas, M. S. (1981). Stimulus repetition effects on attention to words and colors. *Journal of Experimental Psychology: Human Perception & Performance*, **7**, 1303–1311.

Kristofferson, M. W. (1972). Effects of practice on character-classification performance. *Canadian Journal of Psychology*, **26**, 54–60.

Kutas, M., & Hillyard, S. A. (1980). Reading senseless sentences: Brain potentials reflect semantic incongruity. *Science*, **207**, 203–205.

Kyllonen, P. C., & Christal, R. E. (1990). Reasoning ability is (little more than) working-memory capacity?! *Intelligence*, **14**, 389–433.

LaBerge, D. (1990). Thalamic and cortical mechanisms of attention suggested by recent positron emission tomographic experiments. *Journal of Cognitive Neuroscience*, **2**, 358–372.

——, & Buchsbaum, M. S. (1990). Positron emission tomographic measurements of pulvinar activity during an attention task. *The Journal of Neuroscience*, **10**, 613–619.

Lachman, R., Lachman, J. L., & Butterfield, E. C. (1979). *Psychology and information processing*. Hillsdale, NJ: Erlbaum.

Laird, J., Rosenbloom, P., & Newell, A. (1986). *Universal subgoaling and chunking: The automatic generation and learning of goal hiererarchies*. Boston: Kluwer Academic.

Lamb, M. R., Robertson, L. C., & Knight, R. T. (1990). Component mechanisms underlying the processing of hierarchically organized patterns: Inferences from patients with unilateral cortical lesions. *Journal of Experimental Psychology: Learning, Memory, & Cognition*, **16**, 471–483.

Lambert, A. J. (1993). Attentional interaction in the split-brain: Evidence from negative priming. *Neuropsychologia*, **31**, 313–324.

Landauer, T. K. (1962). Rate of implicit speech. *Perceptual & Motor Skills*, **15**, 646.

La Pointe, L. B., & Engle, R. W. (1990). Simple and complex word spans as measures of working memory capacity. *Journal of Experimental Psychology: Learning, Memory, & Cognition*, **16**, 1118–1133.

Lashley, K. S. (1929). *Brain mechanisms and intelligence: A quantitative study of injuries to the brain*. Chicago: University of Chicago Press.

—— (1950). In search of the engram. *Proceedings from Social Experimental Biology*, **4**, 454–482.

Lee, C. L., & Estes, W. K. (1981). Item and order information in short-term memory: Evidence for multilevel perturbation processes. *Journal of Experimental Psychology: Human Learning and Memory*, **7**, 149–169.

Lewandowsky, S., & Murdock, B. B., Jr. (1989). Memory for serial order. *Psychological Review*, **96**, 25–57.

Lewis, J. L. (1972). Semantic processing with bisensory stimulation. *Journal of Experimental Psychology*, **96**, 455–457.

Libet, B., Pearl, D. K., Morledge, D. E., Gleason, C. A., Hosobuchi, Y., & Barbaro, N. M. (1991). Control of the transition from sensory detection to sensory awareness in man by the duration of a thalamic stimulus. *Brain*, **114**, 1731–1757.

Lichtenstein, M. (1961). Phenomenal simultaneity with irregular timing components of the visual stimulus. *Perceptual & Motor Skills*, **12**, 47–60.

Livingstone, M., & Hubel, D. (1988). Segregation of form, color, movement, and depth: Anatomy, physiology, and perception. *Science*, **240**, 740–749.

Logan, G. D. (1983). On the ability to inhibit simple thoughts and actions: I. Stop-signal studies of decision and memory. *Journal of Experimental Psychology: Learning, Memory, & Cognition*, **9**, 585–606.

—— (1985). On the ability to inhibit simple thoughts and actions: II. Stop-signal studies of repetition priming. *Journal of Experimental Psychology: Learning, Memory, & Cognition*, **11**, 675–691.

—— (1988*a*). Toward an instance theory of automatization. *Psychological Review*,

95, 492–527.
—— (1988*b*). Automaticity, resources, and memory: Theoretical controversies and pratical implications. *Human Factors*, **30**, 583–598.
—— (1989). Automaticity and cognitive control. In J. S. Uleman & J. A. Bargh (Eds.), *Unintended thought*. New York: Guilford Press.
—— (1990). Repetition priming and automaticity: Common underlying mechanisms? *Cognitive Psychology*, **22**, 1–35.
——, & Stadler, M. A. (1991). Mechanisms of performance improvement in consistent mapping memory search: Automaticity or strategy shift? *Journal of Experimental Psychology: Learning, Memory, & Cognition*, **17**, 478–496.
Lopes da Silva, F. (1991). Neural mechanisms underlying brain waves: From neural membranes to networks. *Electroencephalography & Clinical Neurophysiology*, **79**, 81–93.
Lopes da Silva, F. H., Wadman, W. J., Arnolds, D. E. A. T., Veekan, C., & Holsheimer, J. (1984). Hippocampus: Behavior and modulation of local circuits. In F. Reinoso-Suärez & C. Ajmone-Marsan (Eds.), *Cortical integration: Basic, archicortical, and cortical association levels of neural integration* (pp. 147–170). New York: Raven Press.
Lorch, E. P., Anderson, D. R., & Well, A. D. (1984). Effects of irrelevant information on speeded classification tasks: Interference is reduced by habituation. *Journal of Experimental Psychology: Human Perception & Performance*, **10**(6), 850–864.
——, & Horn, D. G. (1986). Habituation of attention to irrelevant stimuli in elementary school children. *Journal of Experimental Child Psychology*, **41**, 184–197.
Loveless, N. E., Hari, R., Hämäläinin, M., & Tiihonen, J. (1989). Evoked responses of human auditory cortex may be enhanced by preceding stimuli. *Electroencephalography & Clinical Neurophysiology*, **74**, 217–227.
Lü, Z.-L., Williamson, S. J. & Kaufman, L. (1992*a*). Human auditory primary and association cortex have differing lifetimes for activation traces. *Brain Research*, **572**, 236–241.
——, ——, & —— (1992*b*). Physiological measures predict behavioral lifetime of human auditory sensory memory. *Science*, **258**, 1668–1670.
Luck, S. J., Hillyard, S. A., Mangun, G. R., & Gazzaniga, M. S. (1994). Independent attentional scanning in the separated hemispheres of split-brain patients. *Journal of Cognitive Neuroscience*, **6**, 84–91.
Luria, A. R. (1966). *The higher cortical functions in man*. New York: Basic Books.
Lycan, W. G. (1991). Homuncular functionalism meets PDP. In W. Ramsey, S. P. Stich, & D. E. Rumelhart (Eds.), *Philosophy and connectionist theory* (pp. 259–286). Hillsdale, NJ: Erlbaum.
Lyytinen, H., Blomberg, A. P., & Näätänen, R. (1992). Event-related potentials and autonomic responses to a change in unattended auditory stimuli. *Psychophysiology*, **29**, 523–534.
Mackworth, J. F. (1963). The duration of the visual image. *Canadian Journal of Psychology*, **17**, 62–81.
—— (1964). Auditory short-term memory. *Canadian Journal of Psychology*, **18**, 292–303.
—— (1969). *Vigilance and habituation: A neuropsychological approach*. Middlesex, UK: Penguin Books.

Magleby, K. L. (1987). Short-term changes in synaptic efficacy. In G. M. Edelman, W. E. Gall, & W. M. Cowan (Eds.), *Synaptic function*. New York: Wiley.

Malone, J. C. Jr. (1990). William James and habit: A century later. In M. G. Johnson & T. B. Henley (Eds.), *Reflections on "The Principles of Psychology": William James after a century.* Hillsdale, NJ: Erlbaum.

Mandler, G. (1980). Recognizing: The judgment of previous occurrence. *Psychological Review*, **87**, 252–271.

Mäntysalo, S. & Näätänen, R. (1987). The duration of a neuronal trace of an auditory stimulus as indicated by event-related potentials. *Biological Psychology*, **24**, 183–195.

Marcel, A. J. (1983). Conscious and unconscious perception: Experiments on visual masking and word recognition. *Cognitive Psychology*, **15**, 197–237.

Martin, J. H. (1985). Cortical neurons, the EEG, and the mechanisms of epilepsy. In E. R. Kandel & J. H. Schwartz (Eds.), *Principles of neural science* (2nd ed.). New York: Elsevier.

Martin, R. C. (1993). Short-term memory and sentence processing: Evidence from neuropsychology. *Memory & Cognition*, **21**, 176–183.

Massaro, D. W. (1970*a*). Retroactive interference in short-term recognition memory for pitch. *Journal of Experimental Psychology*, **83**, 32–39.

—— (1970*b*). Perceptual processes and forgetting in memory tasks. *Psychological Review*, **85**, 411–417.

—— (1972). Preperceptual images, processing time, and perceptual units in auditory perception. *Psychological Review*, **79**, 124–145.

—— (1973). A comparison of forward versus backward recognition masking. *Journal of Experimental Psychology*, **100**, 434–436.

—— (1975*a*). *Experimental psychology and information processing*. Chicago: Rand McNally.

—— (1975*b*). Backward recognition masking. *Journal of the Acoustical Society of America*, **58**, 1059–1065.

—— (1976). Perceptual processing in dichotic listening. *Journal of Experimental Psychology: Human Learning & Memory*, **2**, 33–339.

—— (1987). *Speech perception by ear and eye: A paradigm for psychological inquiry.* Hillsdale, NJ: Erlbaum.

—— (1988). Some criticisms of connectionist models of human performance. *Journal of Memory & Language*, **27**, 213–234.

——, & Cohen, M. M. (1991). Integration versus interactive activation: The joint influence of sensory information and context in perception. *Cognitive Psychology*, **23**, 558–614.

——, & Cowan, N. (1993). Information processing models: Microscopes of the mind. *Annual Review of Psychology*, **44**, 383–425.

——, & Friedman, D. (1991). Models of integration given multiple sources of information. *Psychological Review*, **97**, 225–252.

McCall, R. B., & Carriger, M. S. (1993). A meta-analysis of infant habituation and recognition memory performance as predictors of later IQ. *Child Development*, **64**, 57–79.

McCauley, C., Kellas, G., Dugas, J., & De Vellis, R. F. (1976). Effects of serial rehearsal training on memory search. *Journal of Educational Psychology*, **68**, 474–481.

McClelland, J. L. (1979). On the time relations of mental processes: An examination of systems of processes in cascade. *Psychological Review*, **86**, 287–330.

——, & Elman, J. L. (1986). The TRACE model of speech perception. *Cognitive Psychology*, **18**, 1–86.

——, & Rumelhart, D. E. (Eds.). (1986). *Parallel distributed processing: explorations in the microstructure of cognition.* (2 Vol.) Cambridge, MA: MIT Press.

——, Rumelhart, D. E., & Hinton, G. E. (1986). The appeal of parallel distributed processing. In D. E. Rumelhart & J. L. McClelland (Eds.), *Parallel distributed processing: Explorations in the microstructure of cognition* (Vol. 1), pp. 3–44.

McCloskey, M., & Watkins, M. J. (1978). The seeing-more-than-is-there phenomenon: Implications for the locus of iconic storage. *Journal of Experimental Psychology: Human Perception & Performance*, **4**, 553–564.

McGeoch, J. A. (1932). Forgetting and the law of disuse. *Psychological Review*, **39**, 352–370.

McKoon, G., & Ratcliff, R. (1979). Priming in episodic and semantic memory. *Journal of Verbal Learning & Verbal Behavior*, **18**, 463–480.

Meck, W. H., Church, R. M., Wenk, G. L., & Olton, D. S. (1987). Nucleus basilis magnocellularis and medial septal area lesions differentially impair temporal memory. *Journal of Neuroscience*, **7**, 3505–3511.

Melton, A. W. (1963). Implications of short-term memory for a general theory of memory. *Journal of Verbal Learning and Verbal Behavior*, **2**, 1–21.

Merikle, P. M. (1980). Selection from visual persistence by perceptual groups and category membership. *Journal of Experimental Psychology: General*, **109**, 279–295.

——, & Reingold, E. M. (1990). Recognition and lexical decision without detection: Unconscious perception? *Journal of Experimental Psychology: Human Perception & Performance*, **16**, 574–583.

——, & —— (1991). Comparing direct (explicit) and indirect (implicit) measures to study unconscious memory. *Journal of Experimental Psychology: Learning, Memory, & Cognition*, **17**, 224–233.

Mewhort, D. J. K., Campbell, A. J., Marchetti, F. M., & Campbell, J. I. D. (1981). Identification, localization, and "iconic memory": An evaluation of the bar-probe task. *Memory & Cognition*, **9**, 50–67.

Meyer, D. E., Osman, A. M., Irwin, D. E., & Yantis, S. (1988). Modern mental chronometry. *Biological Psychology*, **26**, 3–67.

Miles, C., & Jones, D. M. (1989). The fallacy of the cross-modal Stroop effect: A rejoinder to Cowan (1989). *Perception & Psychophysics*, **45**, 85–86.

Miller, G. A. (1956). The magical number seven, plus or minus two: some limits on our capacity for processing information. *Psychological Review*, **63**, 81–97.

—— (1987). *Psychology: The science of mental life*. New York: Penguin.

Miller, J. (1989). The control of attention by abrupt visual onsets and offsets. *Perception & Psychophysics*, **45**, 567–571.

Miller, R. (1991). *Cortico-hippocampal interplay and the representation of contexts in the brain*. Berlin: Springer-Verlag.

Moray, N. (1959). Attention in dichotic listening: Affective cues and the influence of instructions. *Quarterly Journal of Experimental Psychology*, **11**, 56–60.

——, Bates, A., & Barnett, T. (1965). Experiments on the four-eared man. *Journal of the Acoustical Society of America*, **38**, 196–201.

——, & O'Brien, T. (1967). Signal-detection theory applied to selective listening. *Journal of the Acoustical Society of America*, **42**, 765–772.

Morris, N., & Jones, D. M. (1990). Habituation to irrelevant speech: Effects on a visual short-term memory task. *Perception & Psychophysics*, **47**, 291–297.

Morris, W. (Ed.). (1976). *The American Heritage Dictionary.* Boston: Houghton-Mifflin.

Morton, J. (1969). Categories of interference: Verbal mediation and conflict in card sorting. *British Journal of Psychology*, **60**, 329–346.

——, Crowder, R. G., & Prussin, H. A. (1971). Experiments with the stimulus suffix effect. *Journal of Experimental Psychology*, **91**, 169–190.

Moruzzi, G., & Magoun, H. (1949). Brain stem reticular formation and activation of the EEG. *Electroencephalography and Clinical Neurophysiology*, **1**, 455–473.

Mountcastle, V. B. (1978). Some neural mechanisms for directed attention. In P. A. Buser & A. Rougent-Buser (Eds.), *Cerebral correlates of conscious experience* (pp. 37–52). Amsterdam: Elsevier/North Holland.

Murdock, B. B., Jr. (1961). The retention of individual items. *Journal of Experimental Psychology*, **62**, 618–625.

Muter, P. (1980). Very rapid forgetting. *Memory & Cognition*, **8**, 174–179.

Näätänen, R. (1990). The role of attention in auditory information processing as revealed by event-related potentials and other brain measures of cognitive function. *Behavioral & Brain Sciences*, **13**, 201–288.

——. (1991). Mismatch and processing negativities in auditory stimulus processing and selection. *Behavioral & Brain Sciences*, **14**, 764–768.

—— (1992). *Attention and brain function.* Hillsdale, NJ: Erlbaum.

——,, & Picton, T. W. (1987). The NI wave of the human electric and magnetic response to sound: A review and an analysis of the component structure. *Psychophysiology*, **24**, 375–425.

Nairne, J. S. (1990). A feature model of immediate memory. *Memory & Cognition*, **18**, 251–269.

—— (1992). The loss of positional certainty in long-term memory. *Psychological Science*, **3**, 199–202.

——, & Walters, V. L. (1983). Silent mouthing produces modality- and suffix-like effects. *Journal of Verbal Learning & Verbal Behavior*, **22**, 475–483.

Naveh-Benjamin, M., & Ayres, T. J. (1986). Digit span, reading rate, and linguistic relativity. *Quarterly Journal of Experimental Psychology*, **38A**, 739–751.

Navon, D. (1977). Forest before trees: The precedence of global features in perception. *Cognitive Psychology*, **9**, 353–383.

—— (1984). Resources—A theoretical soup stone? *Psychological Review*, **91**, 216–234.

—— (1985). Attention division or attention sharing? In M. I. Posner & O. S. M. Marin (eds.), *Attention and Performance XI*. Hillsdale, NJ: Erlbaum.

——, & Gopher, D. (1979). On the economy of the human-processing system. *Psychological Review*, **86**, 214–255.

Neath, I., & Crowder, R. G. (1990). Schedules of presentation and temporal distinctiveness in human memory. *Journal of Experimental Psychology: Learning, Memory, & Cognition*, **16**, 316–327.

——, Surprenant, A. M., & Crowder, R. G. (1993). The context-dependent stimulus suffix effect. *Journal of Experimental Psychology: Learning, Memory, & Cognition*,

19, 698–703.
Neely, J. H. (1977). Semantic priming and retrieval from lexical memory: Roles of inhibitionless spreading activation and limited-capacity attention. *Journal of Experimental Psychology: General*, **106**, 226–254.
Neill, W. T. (1977). Inhibitory and facilitatory processes in selective attention. *Journal of Experimental Psychology: Human Perception & Performance*, **3**(3), 444–450.
——, Lissner, L. S., & Beck, J. L. (1990). Negative priming in *same-different* matching: Further evidence for a central locus of inhibition. *Perception & Psychophysics*, **48**, 398–400.
——, & Valdes, L. A. (1992). Persistence of negative priming: Steady state or decay? *Journal of Experimental Psychology: Learning, Memory, & Cognition*, **18**, 565–576.
——, ——, Terry, K. M., & Gorfein, D. S. (1992). Persistence in negative priming: II. Evidence for episodic trace retrieval. *Journal of Experimental Psychology: Learning, Memory, & Cognition*, **18**, 993–1000.
Neisser, U. (1967). *Cognitive psychology.* New York: Appleton-Century-Crofts.
——, & Becklen, R. (1975). Selective looking: Attending to visually specified events. *Cognitive Psychology*, **7**, 480–494.
Neumann, E., & DeSchepper, B. G. (1991). Costs and benefits of target activation and distractor inhibition in selective attention. *Journal of Experimental Psychology: Learning, Memory, & Cognition*, **17**, 1136–1145.
Neumann, O. (1990). Visual attention and action. In O. Neumann & W. Prinz (Eds.), *Relationships between perception and action.* Berlin: Springer-Verlag.
Newell, A. (1973). You can't play 20 questions with nature and win: Projective comments on the papers of this symposium. In W. G. Chase (Ed.), *Visual information processing* (pp. 283–308). New York: Academic Press.
——. (1990). *Unified theories of cognition.* Cambridge, MA: Harvard University Press.
——. (1992). Précis of *Unified theories of cognition. Behavioral & Brain Sciences*, **15**, 425–492.
——, & Simon, H. A. (1972). *Human problem-solving.* Englewood Cliffs, NJ: Prentice-Hall.
Nicolson, R. (1981). The relationship between memory span and processing speed. In M. Friedman, J. P. Das, & N. O'Connor (Eds.), *Intelligence and learning.* (pp. 179–184) New York: Plenum Press.
Nielsen, L. L., & Sarason, I. G. (1981). Emotion, personality, and selective attention. *Journal of Personality & Social Psychology*, **41**, 945–960.
Nisbett, R. E., & Wilson, T. D. (1977). Telling more than we can know: Verbal reports on mental processes. *Psychological Review*, **84**, 231–259.
Nissen, M. J., & Bullemer, P. (1987). Attentional requirements of learning: Evidence from performance measures. *Cognitive Psychology*, **19**, 1–32.
——, Ross, J. L., Willingham, D. B., Mackenzie, T. B., & Schacter, D. L. (1988). Memory and awareness in a patient with multiple personality disorder. *Brain & Cognition*, **8**, 117–134.
Norman, D. A. (1968). Toward a theory of memory and attention. *Psychological Review*, **75**(6), 522–536.
—— (1969). Memory while shadowing. *Quarterly Journal of Experimental*

Psychology, **21**, 85–93.

——, & Bobrow, D. G. (1975). On data-limited and resource-limited processes. *Cognitive Psychology*, **7**, 44–64.

——, & Shallice, T. (1985). Attention to action. In T. Shallice (Ed.), *Consciousness and self-regulation, Vol. 4*. New York: Plenum Press.

Öhman, A. (1979). The orienting response, attention, and learning: An information-processing perspective. In H. K. Kimmel, E. H. Van Olst, & J. F. Orlebeke (Eds.), *The orienting reflex in humans* (pp. 443–471). Hillsdale, NJ: Erlbaum.

—— (1992). Orienting and attention: Preferred preattentive processing of potentially phobic stimuli. In B. A. Campbell, R. Richardson, & H. Hayne (Eds.), *Attention and information processing in infants and adults: Perspectives from human and animal research*. Hillsdale, NJ: Erlbaum.

Olton (1989). Inferring psychological dissociations from experimental dissociations: The temporal context of episodic memory. In H. L. Roediger & F. I. M. Craik (Eds.), *Varieties of memory and consciousness*. Hillsdale, NJ: Erlbaum.

Palmer, S. E., & Kimchi, R. (1986). The information processing approach to cognition. In T. J. Knapp & L. C. Robertson (Eds.), *Approaches to cognition: Contrasts and controversies*. Hillsdale, NJ: Erlbaum.

Parkin, A. J., & Russo, R. (1990). Implicit and explicit memory and the automatic/effortful distinction. *European Journal of Psychology*, **2**, 71–80.

Pashler, H. (1984). Evidence against late selection: Stimulus quality effects in previewed displays. *Journal of Experimental Psychology: Human Perception & Performance*, **10**, 429–448.

—— (1990). Do response modality effects support multiprocessor models of divided attention? *Journal of Experimental Psychology: Human Perception & Performance*, **16**, 826–842.

—— (1991). Shifting visual attention and selecting motor responses: Distinct attentional mechanisms. *Journal of Experimental Psychology: Human Perception & Performance*, **17**, 1023–1040.

—— (1993). Dual-task interference and elementary mental mechanisms. In D. E. Meyer & S. Kornblum (Eds.), *Attention and performance XIV: Synergies in experimental psychology, artificial intelligence, and cognitive neuroscience*. (pp. 245–264). Cambridge, MA: MIT Press.

Peak, H. (1940). The time order error in successive judgments and in reflexes: II. As a function of the first stimulus of a pair. *Journal of Experimental Psychology*, **26**, 103–115.

Pechmann, T., & Mohr, G. (1992). Interference in memory for tonal pitch: Implications for a working-memory model. *Memory & Cognition*, **20**, 314–320.

Penner, M. J. (1977). Detection of temporal gaps in noise as a measure of the decay of auditory sensation. *Journal of the Acoustical Society of America*, **61**, 552–557.

Penney, C. G. (1975). Modality effects in short-term verbal memory. *Psychological Bulletin*, **82**, 68–84.

—— (1989). Modality effects and the structure of short-term verbal memory. *Memory & Cognition*, **17**, 398–422.

Penrose, R. (1989). *The emperor's new mind*. Oxford, England: Oxford University Press.

Peterson, L. R., & Johnson, S. T. (1971). Some effects of minimizing articulation on short-term retention. *Journal of Verbal Learning and Verbal Behavior*, **10**,

346–354.
——, & Peterson, M. J. (1959). Short-term retention of individual verbal items. *Journal of Experimental Psychology*, **58**, 193–198.
Petri, H. L., & Mishkin, M. (1994). Behaviorism, cognitivism and the neuropsychology of memory. *American Scientist*, **82**, 30–37.
Phillips, W. A. (1974). On the distinction between sensory storage and short-term visual memory. *Perception & Psychophysics*, **16**, 283–290.
——, & Christie, F. M. (1977). Interference with visualization. *Quarterly Journal of Experimental Psychology*, **29**, 637–650.
Piaget, J. (1954). *The construction of reality in the child*. New York: Basic Books (Margaret Cook, translator; originally published in 1937).
Picton, T. W. (1992, June). Auditory evoked potentials and the human auditory cortex. Paper presented at the 10th International Conference on Event-related Potentials of the Brain (EPIC X), Eger, Hungary.
Pike, R. (1986). Comparison of convolution and matrix distributed memory systems for associative recall and recognition. *Psychological Review*, **91**, 281–293.
Pisoni, D. B. (1973). Auditory and phonetic memory codes in the discrimination of consonants and vowels. *Perception & Psychophysics*, **13**, 253–260.
Platt, J. R. (1964). Strong inference. *Science*, **146**, 347–353.
Pollack, I., Johnson, I. B., & Knaff, P. R. (1959). Running memory span. *Journal of Experimental Psychology*, **57**, 137–146.
Polson, M. C., & Friedman, A. (1988). Task-sharing within and between hemispheres: A multiple-resource approach. *Human Factors*, **30**, 633–643.
Port, R. F. (1991). Can complex temporal patterns be automatized? *Behavioral & Brain Sciences*, **14**, 762–764.
Posner, M. I. (1978). *Chronometric explorations of mind*. Hillsdale, NJ: Erlbaum.
—— (1980). Orienting of attention. *Quarterly Journal of Experimental Psychology*, **32**, 3–25.
—— (1984). Selective attention and the storage of information. In G. Lynch, J. L. McGaugh, & N. M. Weinberger (Eds.), *Neurobiology of learning and memory*. New York: Guilford Press.
——, & Carr, T. H. (1992). Lexical access and the brain: anatomical constraints on cognitive models of word recognition. *American Journal of Psychology*, **105**, 1–26.
——, Cohen, Y., Choate, L.S., Hockey, R., & Maylor, E. (1984). Sustained concentration: Passive filtering or active orienting? In S. Kornblum & J. Requin (Eds.), *Preparatory states and processes* (pp. 49–65). Hillsdale, NJ: Erlbaum.
——, & Klein, R. M. (1973). On the functions of consciousness. In S. Kornblum (Ed.), *Attention and performance IV*. New York: Academic Press.
——, & Peterson, S. E. (1990). The attention system of the human brain. *Annual Review of Neuroscience*, **13**, 25–42.
——, & Rothbart, M. K. (1991). Attentional mechanisms and conscious experience. In A. D. Milner & M. D. Rugg (Eds.), *The neuropsychology of consciousness* (pp. 91–111). London: Academic Press.
——, Sandson, J., Dhawan, M., & Shulman, G. L. (1989). Is word recognition automatic? A cognitive anatomical approach. *Journal of Cognitive Neuroscience*, **1**, 50–60.
——, & Snyder, C. R. R. (1975*a*). Facilitation and inhibition in the processing of

signals. In P. M. A. Rabbitt & S. Dornic (Eds.), *Attention & performance V.* New York: Academic Press.

——, & —— (1975*b*). Attention and cognitive control. In R. L. Solso (Ed.), *Information processing and cognition*. Hillsdale, NJ: Erlbaum.

——, Walker, J. A., Friedrich, F. J., & Rafal, R. D. (1984). Effects of parietal lobe injury on covert orienting of visual attention. *Journal of Neuroscience*, **4**, 1863–1874.

Postman, L. (1961). The present status of interference theory. In C. N. Cofer (Ed.), *Verbal learning and verbal behavior.* New York: McGraw-Hill.

Ptito, A., Lepore, M., Ptito, M., & Lassonde, M. (1991). Target detection and movement discrimination in the blind field of hemispherectomized patients. *Brain*, **114**, 497.

Puckett, J. M., & Kausler, D. H. (1984). Individual differences and models of memory span: A role for memory search rate? *Journal of Experimental Psychology: Learning, Memory, & Cognition*, **10**, 72–82.

Ramachandran V. S. (1992). Filling in gaps in perception: Part 1. *Current Directions in Psychological Science*, **1**, 199–205.

Rayner, K., Inhoff, A. W., Morrison, R., Slowiaczek, M. L., & Bertera, J. H. (1981). Masking of foveal and parafoveal vision during eye fixations in reading. *Journal of Experimental Psychology: Human Perception & Performance*, **7**, 167–179.

Reinitz, M. T., Lammers, W. J., & Cochran, B. P. (1992). Memory-conjunction errors: Miscombinations of stored stimulus features can produce illusions in memory. *Memory & Cognition*, **20**, 1–11.

Reinoso-Suärez, F. (1984). Connectional patterns in parietotemporooccipital association cortex of the feline cerebral cortex. In F. Reinoso-Suärez & C. Ajmone-Marsan (Eds.), *Cortical integration: Basic, archicortical, and cortical association levels of neural integration* (pp. 255–278). New York: Raven Press.

Reisberg, D., Baron, J., & Kemler, D. G. (1980). Overcoming Stroop interference: The effects of practice on distractor potency. *Journal of Experimental Psychology: Human Perception & Performance*, **6**, 140–150.

——, Rappaport, I., & O'Shaughnessy, M. (1984). Limits of working memory: The digit-digit span. *Journal of Experimental Psychology: Learning, Memory, & Cognition*, **10**, 203–221.

Reuter-Lorenz, P. A., Kinsbourne, M., & Moscovitch, M. (1990). Hemispheric control of spatial attention. *Brain & Cognition*, **12**, 240–266.

Richardson, J. T. E. (1979). Precategorical acoustic storage and postcategorical lexical storage. *Cognitive Psychology*, **11**, 265–286.

Richardson-Klavehn, A., & Bjork, R. A. (1988). Measures of memory. *Annual Review of Psychology*, **39**, 475–543.

Ritter, W., Paavilainen, P., Lavikainen, J., Reinkainen, K., Alho, K., Sams, M., & Näätänen, R. (1992). Event-related potentials to repetition and change of auditory stimuli. *Electroencephalography & Clinical Neurophysiology*, **83**, 306-321.

——, Simson, R., Vaughan, H. G., Jr., & Macht, M. (1982). Manipulation of event-related potential manifestations of information processing stages. *Science*, **218**, 909–910.

Robinson, C. E., & Pollack, I. (1971). Forward and backward masking: Testing a discrete perceptual-moment hypothesis in audition. *Journal of the Acoustical Society of America*, **50**, 1512–1519.

Robinson, D. L., & Peterson, S. E. (1984). Posterior parietal cortex of the awake monkey: Visual responses and their modulation by behavior. In F. Reinoso-Suärez & C. Ajmone-Marsan (Eds.), *Cortical integration: Basic, archicortical, and cortical association levels of neural integration* (pp. 279–290). New York: Raven Press.

Roediger III, H. L., Weldon, M. S., & Challis, B. H. (1989). Explaining dissociations between implicit and explicit measures of retention: A processing account. In H. L. Roediger & F. I. M. Craik (Eds.), *Varieties of memory and consciousness: Essays in Honor of Endel Tulving*. Hillsdale, NJ: Erlbaum.

Rosenbaum, D. A. (1991). *Human motor control* (pp. 110–112). San Diego: Academic Press.

Rostron, A. B. (1974). Brief auditory storage: Some further observations. *Acta Psychologica*, **38**, 471–482.

Ryle, G. (1949). *The concept of mind.* San Francisco, C A: Hutchinson.

Sachs, J. S. (1967). Recognition memory for syntactic and semantic aspects of connected discourse. *Perception & Psychophysics*, **2**, 437–442.

Salamé, P., & Baddeley, A. (1982). Disruption of short-term memory by unattended speech: Implications for the structure of working memory. *Journal of Verbal Learning and Verbal Behavior*, **21**, 150–164.

Sams, M., Hari, R., Rif, J., & Knuutila, J. (1993). The human auditory sensory memory trace persists about 10 s: Neuromagnetic evidence. *Journal of Cognitive Neuroscience*, **5**, 363–370.

——, Kaukoranta, E., Hämäläinen, M., & Näätänen, R. (1991). Cortical activity elicited by changes in auditory stimuli: Different sources for the magnetic N100m and mismatch responses. *Psychophysiology*, **28**, 21–29.

Sanders, A. F. (1990). Issues and trends in the debate on discrete vs. continuous processing of information. *Acta Psychologica*, **74**, 123–167.

Sanwald, J. C., Porzio, N. R., Deane, G. E., & Donovick, P. J. (1970). The effects of septal and dorsal hippocampal lesions on the cardiac component of the orienting response. *Physiology & Behavior*, **5**, 883–888.

Sarbin, T. R. (1992). Accounting for "dissociative" actions without invoking mentalistic constructs. *Consciousness & Cognition*, **1**, 54–58.

Scarborough, D. L. (1972). Stimulus modality effects on forgetting in short-term memory. *Journal of Experimental Psychology*, **95**, 285–289.

Schacter, D. L. (1987). Implicit memory: History and current status. *Journal of Experimental Psychology: Learning, Memory, & Cognition*, **13**, 501–518.

—— (1989). On the relation between memory and consciousness: Dissociable interactions and conscious experience. In H. L. Roediger & F. I. M. Craik (Eds.), *Varieties of memory and consciousness: Essays in honor of Endel Tulving*. Hillsdale, NJ: Erlbaum.

——, & Graf, P. (1986). Preserved learning in amnesia patients: Perspectives from research on direct priming. *Journal of Clinical & Experimental Neurophysiology*, **8**, 727–743.

Scherg, M., Vajsar, J., & Picton, T. W. (1989). A source analysis of the late human auditory evoked potentials. *Journal of Cognitive Neuroscience*, 1, 336–355.

Schmidt, R. A. (1988). *Motor control and learning* (2nd ed.). Champaign, Illinois: Human Kinetics Publishers.

Schneider, W. (1985). Toward a model of attention and the development of automatic processing. In M. I. Posner & O. S. Marin (Eds.), *Attention & performance XI* (pp. 475–492). Hillsdale, NJ: Erlbaum.

—— (1987). Connectionism: Is it a paradigm shift for psychology? *Behavior Research Methods, Instruments, & Computers*, **19**, 73–83.

——, & Detweiler, M. (1987). A connectionist/control architecture for working memory. In G. H. Bower (Ed.), *The psychology of learning and motivation* (Vol. 21). New York: Academic Press.

——, & —— (1988). The role of practice in dual-task performance: Towards workload modeling in a connectionist/control architecture. *Human Factors*, **30**, 539–566.

Schweickert, R. (1993). Information, time, and the structure of mental events: A twenty-five year review. In D. E. Meyer & S. Kornblum (Eds.), *Attention and performance XIV: Synergies in experimental psychology, artificial intelligence, and cognitive neuroscience*. (pp. 535–566) Cambridge, MA: MIT Press.

——, & Boruff, B. (1986). Short-term memory capacity: Magic number or magic spell? *Journal of Experimental Psychology: Learning, Memory, and Cognition*, **12**, 419–425.

Scoville, W. B., & Milner, B. (1957). Loss of recent memory after bilateral hippocampal lesions. *Journal of Neurology, Neurosurgery and Psychiatry*, **20**, 11–21.

Searle, J. (1984). Panel discussion: Has artificial intelligence research illuminated human thinking? In H. R. Pagels (Ed.), *Computer culture: the scientific, intellictual, and social impact of the computer.* New York: Annals of the New York Academy of Sciences (vol. 426).

Shallice, T. (1988). From neuropsychology to mental structure. Cambridge, UK: Cambridge University Press.

—— (1991). Précis of *From neuropsychology to mental structure. Behavioral & Brain Sciences*, **14**, 429–469.

——, & Vallar, G. (1990). The impairment of auditory-verbal short-term storage. In G. Vallar & T. Shallice (Eds.), *Neuropsychological impairments of short-term memory* (pp. 11–53). Cambridge, UK: Cambridge University Press.

——, & Warrington, E. K. (1970). Independent functioning of verbal memory stores: A neuropsychological study. *Quarterly Journal of Experimental Psychology*, **22**, 261–273.

Shiffrin, R. M. (1988). Attention. In R. C. Atkinson, R. J. Herrnstein, G. Lindzey, & R. D. Luce (Eds.), *Stevens' handbook of experimental psychology.* (2nd ed., Vol. 2). New York: Wiley.

——, & Schneider, W. (1977). Controlled and automatic human information processing: II. Perceptual learning, automatic attending, and a general theory. *Psychological Review*, **84**, 127–190.

Shimamura, A. P. (1986). Priming effects in amnesia: Evidence for a dissociable memory function. *Quarterly Journal of Experimental Psychology*, **38A**, 619–644.

——, & Squire, L. (1989). Impaired priming of new associations in amnesia. *Journal of Experimental Psychology: Learning, Memory, & Cognition*, **15**, 721–728.

Siddle, D. A. T. (1991). Orienting, habituation, and resource allocation: An associative analysis. *Psychophysiology*, **28**, 245–259.

——, & Spinks, J. A. (1979). Orienting response and information-processing: Some theoretical and empirical problems. In H. K. Kimmel, E. H. Van Olst, & J. F. Orlebeke (Eds.), *The orienting reflex in humans* (pp. 473–497). Hillsdale, NJ:

Erlbaum.

——, & —— (1992). Orienting, habituation, and the allocation of processing resources. In B. Campbell, R. Richardson, & H. Hayne (Eds.), *Attention and information processing in infants and adults: Perspectives from human and animal research*. Hillsdale, NJ: Erlbaum.

Siegler, R. S. (1986). Unities across domains in children's strategy choices. In M. Perlmutter (Ed.), *Perspectives for intellectual development: Minnesota symposia on child psychology, Vol. 19*, (pp. 1–48). Hillsdale, NJ: Erlbaum.

Sininger, Y. S., Klatzky, R. L., & Kirchner, D. M. (1989). Memory scanning speed in language-disordered children. *Journal of Speech & Hearing Research*, **32**, 289–297.

Skinner, B. F. (1964). Behaviorism at fifty. In T.W. Wann (ed.), *Behaviorism and phenomenology* (pp. 79–108). Chicago: University of Chicago Press.

Skinner, J. E., & Yingling, C. D. (1977). Central gating mechanisms that regulate event-related potentials and behavior. In J. E. Desmedt (Ed.), *Attention, voluntary contraction and event-related cerebral potentials*. Basel: S. Karger.

Smith, L., & Klein, R. (1990). Evidence for semantic satiation: Repeating a category slows subsequent semantic processing. *Journal of Experimental Psychology: Learning, Memory, & Cognition*, **16**, 852–861.

Smith, L. C. (1984). Semantic satiation affects category membership decision time but not lexical priming. *Memory & Cognition*, **12**, 483–488.

Smith, M. E., & Oscar-Berman, M. (1990). Repetition priming of words and pseudowords in divided attention and amnesia. *Journal of Experimental Psychology: Learning, Memory, & Cognition*, **16**, 1033–1042.

——, Stapleton, J. M., & Halgren, E. (1986). Human medial temporal lobe potentials evoked in memory and language tasks. *Encephalography & Clinical Neurophysiology*, **63**, 145–159.

Smyth, M. M., & Scholey, K. A. (1992). Determining spatial span: The role of movement time and articulatory rate. *Quarterly Journal of Experimental Psychology*, **45A**, 479–501.

Sokolov, E. N. (1963). *Perception and the conditioned reflex*. NY: Pergamon Press.

—— (1975). The neuronal mechanisms of the orienting reflex. In E. N. Sokolov & O. S. Vinogradova (Eds.), *Neuronal mechanisms of the orienting reflex* (pp. 217–235). Hillsdale, NJ: Erlbaum.

Spearman, C. (1904). General intelligence objectively determined and measured. *American Journal of Psychology*, **15**, 201–293.

—— (1927). *The abilities of man*. London: MacMillan.

Spelke, E. S., Hirst, W. C., & Neisser, U. (1976). Skills of divided attention. *Cognition*, **4**, 215–230.

Sperling, G. (1960). The information available in brief visual presentations. *Psychological Monographs*, **74** (whole no. 498).

—— (1967). Successive approximations to a model for short-term memory. *Acta Psychologica*, **27**, 285–292.

Spoehr, K. T., & Corin, W. J. (1978). The stimulus suffix effect as a memory coding phenomenon. *Memory & Cognition*, **6**, 583–589.

Squire, L. R. (1987). *Memory and brain*. New York: Oxford University Press.

——, Shimamura, A. P., & Graf, P. (1985). Independence of recognition memory and priming effects: A neuropsychological analysis. *Journal of Experimental Psychol-*

ogy: Learning, Memory, & Cognition, **11**, 37–44.

Stadler, M. (1989). On learning complex procedural knowledge. *Journal of Experimental Psychology: Learning, Memory, & Cognition*, **15**, 1061–1069.

—— (1992, May). Attention and implicit serial learning. Paper presented at the annual convention of the Midwestern Psychological Association, Chicago.

Standing, L., Bond, B., Smith, P., & Isely, C. (1980). Is the immediate memory span determined by subvocalization rate? *British Journal of Psychology*, **71**, 525–539.

Sternberg, S. (1966). High-speed scanning in human memory. *Science*, **153**, 652–654.

—— (1969). The discovery of processing stages: Extensions of Donders' Method. *Acta Psychologica*, **30**, 276–315.

—— (1975). Memory scanning: New findings and current controversies. *Quarterly Journal of Experimental Psychology*, **27**, 1–32.

——, Monsell, S., Knoll, R. L., & Wright, C. E. (1978). The latency and duration of rapid movement sequences: comparisons of speech and typewriting. In G. E. Stelmach (Ed.), *Information processing in motor control and learning*. NY: Academic Press.

——, Wright, C. E., Knoll, R. L., & Monsell, S. (1980). Motor programs in rapid speech: Additional evidence. In R. A. Cole (Ed.), *Perception and production of fluent speech*. Hillsdale, NJ: Erlbaum.

Stevenson, J. H. (1976). Effect of posthypnotic dissociation on the performance of interfering tasks. *Journal of Abnormal Psychology*, **85**, 398–407.

Stigler, J. W., Lee, S.-Y., & Stevenson, H. W. (1986). Digit memory in Chinese and English: Evidence for a temporally limited store. *Cognition*, **23**, 1–20.

Strayer, D. L., & Kramer, A. F. (1990). An analysis of memory-based theories of automaticity. *Journal of Experimental Psychology: Learning, Memory, & Cognition*, **16**, 291–304.

Stroop, J. R. (1935). Studies of interference in serial verbal reactions. *Journal of Experimental Psychology*, **18**, 643–662.

Stroud, J. M. (1955). The fine structure of psychological time. In H. Quastler (Ed.), *Information theory in psychology*. Glencoe, IL: The Free Press.

Stryker, M. P. (1989). Is grandmother an oscillation? *Nature*, **338**, 297–298.

Teyler, T. J., Chiaia, N., DiScenna, P., & Roemer, R. A. (1984). Habituation of central nervous system evoked potentials: Intrinsic habituation examined in neocortex, allocortex, and mesencephalon. In H. V. S. Peeke & L. Petrinovich (Eds.), *Habituation, sensitization, and behavior* (pp. 251–285). Orlando, FL: Academic Press.

Thackray, R. I., & Jones, K. N. (1971). Level of arousal during Stroop performance: Effects of speed stress and "distraction." *Psychonomic Science*, **23**, 133–135.

Thapar, A., & Greene, R. L. (1993). Evidence against a short-term-store account of long-term recency effects. *Memory & Cognition*, **21**, 329–337.

Thatcher, R. W., & John, E. R. (1977). *Foundations of cognitive processes*. Hillsdale, NJ: Erlbaum.

Thompson, R. F., & Spencer, W. A. (1966). Habituation: A model phenomenon for the study of neuronal substrates of behavior. *Psychological Review*, **73**, 16–43.

Thorndike, E. L. (1914). *The psychology of learning*. NY: Teachers College.

Thurstone, L.L., & Thurstone, T. G. (1941). Factorial studies of intelligence. *Psychometric Monographs*, No. 2.

Tiitinen, H., Sinkkonen, J., Reinikainen, K., Alho, K., Lavikainen, J., & Näätänen, R. (1993). Selective attention enhances the auditory 40-Hz transient response in humans. *Nature*, **364**, 59–60.

Tipper, S. P. (1992). Selection for action: The role of inhibitory mechanisms. *Current Directions in Psychological Science*, **1**, 105–109.

——, Bourque, T. A., Anderson, S. H., & Brehaut, J. C. (1989). Mechanisms of attention: A developmental study. *Journal of Experimental Child Psychology*, **48**, 353–378.

——, & Driver, J. (1988). Negative priming between pictures and words in a selective attention task: Evidence for semantic processing of ignored stimuli. *Memory & Cognition*, **16**, 64–70.

——, MacQueen, G. M., & Brehaut, J. C. (1988). Negative priming between response modalities: Evidence for the central locus of inhibition in selective attention. *Perception & Psychophysics*, **43**, 45–52.

Townsend, J., & Courchesne, E. (in press). Parietal damage and narrow "spotlight" spatial attention. *Journal of Cognitive Neuroscience*.

Townsend, V. M. (1973). Loss of spatial and identity information following a tachistoscopic exposure. *Journal of Experimental Psychology*, **98**, 113–118.

Treisman, A., Squire, R., & Green, J. (1974). Semantic processing in dichotic listening? A replication. *Memory & Cognition*, **2**, 641–646.

Treisman, A. M. (1960). Contextual cues in selective listening. *Quarterly Journal of Experimental Psychology*, **12**, 242–248.

—— (1964*a*). The effect of irrelevant material on the efficiency of selective listening. *The American Journal of Psychology*, **77**(4), 533–546.

—— (1964*b*). Selective attention in man. *British Medical Bulletin*, **20**, 12–16.

—— (1964*c*). Monitoring and storage of irrelevant messages in selective listening. *Journal of Verbal Learning and Verbal Behavior*, **3**, 449–459.

—— (1992*a*). Spreading suppression or feature integration? A reply to Duncan and Humphreys (1992). *Journal of Experimental Psychology: Human Perception & Performance*, **18**, 589–593.

—— (1992*b*). Perceiving and re-perceiving objects. *American Psychologist*, **47**, 862–875.

——, & Geffen, G. (1967). Selective attention: perception or response? *Quarterly Journal of Experimental Psychology*, **19**, 1–17.

——, & Gelade, G. (1980). A feature integration theory of attention. *Cognitive Psychology*, **12**, 97–136.

——, & Schmidt, N. (1982). Illusory conjunctions in the perception of objects. *Cognitive Psychology*, **14**, 107–141.

Treisman, M., & Rostron, A. B. (1972). Brief auditory storage: A modification of Sperling's paradigm. *Acta Psychologica*, **36**, 161–170.

Trejo, L. J., Ryan-Jones, D., & Kramer, A. F. (1992, October). Attentional modulation of the pitch-change mismatch negativity. Paper presented to the Annual Meeting of the Society for Psychophysiological Research, San Diego, CA.

Tulving, E. (1983). *Elements of episodic memory*. New York: Oxford University Press.

—— (1985). How many memory systems are there? *American Psychologist*, **40**, 385–398.

——, & Patkau, J. E. (1962). Concurrent effects of contextual constraint and word frequency on immediate recall and learning of verbal material. *Canadian Journal of Psychology*, **16**, 83–95.

Turner, M. L., LaPointe, L. B., Cantor, J., Reeves, C. H., Griffeth, R. H., & Engle, R. W. (1987). Recency and suffix effects found with auditory presentation and with mouthed visual presentation: They're not the same thing. *Journal of Memory & Language*, **26**, 138–164.

Turvey, M. T. (1973). On peripheral and central processes in vision: Inferences from an information processing analysis of masking with patterned stimuli. *Psychological Review*, **80**, 1–52.

Tzeng, O. J. L. (1973). Positive recency effect in a delayed free recall. *Journal of Verbal Learning & Verbal Behavior*, **12**, 436–439.

Underwood, B. J. (1957). Interference and forgetting. *Psychological Review*, **64**, 49–60.

Vallar, G., & Baddeley, A. D. (1982). Short-term forgetting and the articulatory loop. *Quarterly Journal of Experimental Psychology*, **34**, 53–60.

——, & Shallice, T. (1990). *Neuropsychological impairments of short-term memory.* Cambridge, UK: Cambridge University Press.

Van Dusen, L. M., Britton, B. K., & Glynn, S. M. (1992). Memory transfer process: An extension of the Sternberg paradigm. *American Journal of Psychology*, **105**, 59–73.

Velmans, M. (1991). Is human information processing conscious? *Behavioral & Brain Sciences*, **14**, 651–726.

Verfaellie, M., Rapcsak, S. Z., & Heilman, K. M. (1990). Impaired shifting of attention in Balint's Syndrome. *Brain & Cognition*, **12**, 195–204.

Vince, M. (1949). Rapid response sequences and the psychological refractory period. *British Journal of Psychology*, **40**, 23–40.

Von Wright, J. M., Anderson, K., & Stenman, U. (1975). Generalization of conditioned GSRs in dichotic listening. In. P. M. A. Rabbitt & S. Dornic (Eds.), *Attention & performance V* (pp. 194–204). New York: Academic Press.

Walley, R. E., & Weiden, T. D. (1973). Lateral inhibition and cognitive masking: A neuropsychological theory of attention. *Psychological Review*, **80**, 284–302.

Warrington, E. K., & McCarthy, R. (1987). Categories of knowledge: Further fractionation and an attempted integration. *Brain*, **110**, 1273–1296.

——, & Shallice, T. (1972). Neuropsychological evidence of visual storage in short-term memory tasks. *Quarterly Journal of Experimental Psychology*, **24**, 30–40.

——, & Weiskrantz, L. (1970). Amnesic syndrome: Consolidation or retrieval? *Nature*, **228**, 629–630.

Waters, W. F., McDonald, D. G., & Koresko, R. L. (1977). Habituation of the orienting response: A gating mechanism subserving selective attention. *Psychophysiology*, **14**(3), 228–236.

Watkins, M. J. (1974). Concept and measurement of primary memory. *Psychological Bulletin*, **81**, 695–711.

——, LeCompte, D. C., Elliott, M. N., & Fish, S. B. (1992). Short-term memory for the timing of auditory and visual signals. *Journal of Experimental Psychology: Learning, Memory, & Cognition*, **18**, 931–937.

——, & Sechler, E. S. (1989). Adapting to an irrelevant item in an immediate recall task. *Memory & Cognition*, **17**, 682–692.

——, & Todres, A. K. (1980). Suffix effects manifest and concealed: Further evidence for a 20-second echo. *Journal of Verbal Learning & Verbal Behavior*, **19**, 46–53. 251–278.

——, Watkins, O. C., & Crowder, R. G. (1974). The modality effect in free and serial recall as a function of phonological similarity. *Journal of Verbal Learning & Verbal Behavior*, **13**, 430–447.

Watkins, O. C., & Watkins, M. J. (1980). The modality effect and echoic persistence. *Journal of Experimental Psychology: General*, **109**.

Watson, J. B. (1919). *Psychology from the standpoint of a behaviorist*. Philadelphia: J. B. Lippincott.

—— (1924). *Behaviorism*. New York: Norton.

Waugh, N. C. (1970). Retrieval time in short-term memory. *British Journal of Psychology*, **61**, 1–12.

——, & Norman, D. A. (1965). Primary memory. *Psychological Review*, **72**, 89–104.

Weiskrantz, L. (1988). Some contributions of neuropsychology of vision and memory to the problem of consciousness. In A. J. Marcel & E. Bisiach (Eds.), *Consciousness in contemporary science*. Oxford, UK: Clarendon Press.

Welford, A.T. (1952). The "psychological refractory period" and the timing of high speed performance—A review and a theory. *British Journal of Psychology*, **43**, 2–19.

—— (1967). Single-channel operation in the brain. *Acta Psychologica*, **27**, 5–22.

Welsh, M. C., Pennington, B. F., & Groisser, D. B. (1991). A normative-developmental study of executive functioning: A window on prefrontal function in children. *Developmental Neuropsychology*, **7**, 131–149.

Werker, J. F., & Tees, R. C. (1984). Cross-language speech perception: Evidence for perceptual reorganization during the first year of life. *Infant Behavior & Development*, **7**, 49–63.

Whitten II, W. B. (1978). Output interference and long-term serial position effects. *Journal of Experimental Psychology: Human Learning & Memory*, **4**, 685–692.

Wickelgren, W. A. (1965). Short-term memory for phonemically similar lists. *American Journal of Psychology*, **78**, 567–574.

—— (1975). More on the long and short of memory. In D. Deutsch & J. A. Deutsch (Eds.), *Short-term memory*. New York: Academic Press.

Wickens, C. D. (1980). The structure of attentional resources. In R. S. Nickerson (Ed.), *Attention and performance VIII* (pp. 239–257). Hillsdale, NJ: Erlbaum.

—— (1984). Processing resources in attention. In R. Parasuraman & R. Davies (Eds.), *Varieties of attention* (pp. 63–101). Orlando, FL: Academic Press.

Wickens, D. D. (1972). Characteristics of word encoding. In A. Melton & E. Martin (Eds.), *Coding processes in human memory* (pp. 191–215). Washington, DC: Winston.

——, Moody, M. J., & Dow, R. (1981). The nature and timing of the retrieval process and of interference effects. *Journal of Experimental Psychology: General*, **110**, 1–20.

——, ——, & Vidulich, M. (1985). Retrieval time as a function of memory set size, type of probes, and interference in recognition memory. *Journal of Experimental Psychology: Learning, Memory, & Cognition*, **11**, 154–164.

Willingham, D. B., Nissen, M. J., & Bullemer, P. (1989). On the development of procedural knowledge. *Journal of Experimental Psychology: Learning, Memory, & Cognition*, **15**, 1047–1060.

Winkler, I. & Näätänen, R. (1992). Event-related brain potentials to infrequent partial omissions in series of auditory stimuli. In H-J. Heinze, G. R. Mangun, & T. F. Münte (Eds.), *Perspectives in cognitive neurophysiology.* Boston: Birkhauser.

——, Paavilainen, P., Alho, K., Reinikainen, K., Sams, M., & Näätänen, R. (1990). The effect of small variation of the frequent auditory stimulus on the event-related brain potential to the infrequent stimulus. *Psychophysiology*, **27**, 228–235.

——, Reinikainen, K., & Näätänen, R. (1993). Event-related brain potentials reflect traces of echoic memory in humans. *Perception & Psychophysics*, **4**, 443–449.

Woldorff, M. G., Gallen, C. C., Hampson, S. A., Hillyard, S. A., Pantev, C., Sobel, D., & Bloom, F. E. (1993). Modulation of early sensory processing in human auditory cortex. *Proceedings of the National Academy of Science*, **90**, 8722–8726.

——, Hackley, S. A., & Hillyard, S. A. (1991). The effects of channel-selective attention on the mismatch negativity wave elicited by deviant tones. *Psychophysiology*, **28**, 30–42.

——, & Hillyard, S. A. (1991). Modulation of early auditory processing during selective listening to rapidly presented tones. *Electroencephalography and Clinical Neurophysiology*, **79**, 170–191.

Wood, N., & Cowan, N. (in press). The cocktail party phenomenon revisited: How frequent are attention shifts to one's name in an irrelevant auditory channel? *Journal of Experimental Psychology: Learning, Memory, & Cognition.*

Woods, D. L. (1990). The physiological basis of selective attention: Implications of event-related potential studies. In J. W. Rohrbaugh, R. Parasuraman, & R. Johnson (Eds.), *Event-related brain potentials: Basic issues and applications.* New York: Oxford University Press.

Yantis, S. (1993). Stimulus-driven attentional capture. *Current Directions in Psychological Science*, **2**, 156–161.

——, & Hillstrom, A. P. (1992, November). Stimulus-driven attentional capture. Paper presented at the annual meeting of the Psychonomic Society.

——, & Johnson, D. N. (1990). Mechanisms of attentional priority. *Journal of Experimental Psychology: Human Perception & Performance*, **16**, 812–825.

——, & Jonides, J. (1984). Abrupt visual onsets and selective attention: Evidence from visual search. *Journal of Experimental Psychology: Human Perception & Performance*, **10**, 601–621.

——, & —— (1990). Abrupt visual onsets and selective attention: Voluntary versus automatic allocation. *Journal of Experimental Psychology: Human Perception & Performance*, **16**, 121–134.

Yates, J., & Thul, N. (1979). Perceiving surprising words in an unattended auditory channel. *Quarterly Journal of Experimental Psychology*, **31**, 281–286.

Zacks, R. T., Hasher, L., & Sanft, H. (1982). Automatic encoding of event frequency: Further findings. *Journal of Experimental Psychology: Learning, Memory, & Cognition*, **8**, 106–116.

Zbrodoff, N. J., & Logan, G. D. (1986). On the autonomy of mental processes: A case study of arithmetic. *Journal of Experimental Psychology: General*, **115**, 118–130.

Zhang, G., & Simon, H. A. (1985). STM capacity for Chinese words and idioms: Chunking and the acoustical loop hypothesis. *Memory & Cognition*, **13**, 193–201.

Zihl, J., von Cramon, D., & Mai, N. (1983). Selective disturbance of movement vision after bilateral brain damage. *Brain*, **106**, 313–340.

Zola-Morgan, S., Squire, L. R., Amaral, D. G., & Suzuki, W. A. (1989). Lesions of perirhinal and parahippocampal cortex that spare the amygdala and hippocampal formation produce severe memory impairment. *Journal of Neuroscience*, **9**, 4355–4370.

Zola-Morgan, S. M., & Squire, L. R. (1990). The primate hippocampal formation: Evidence for a time-limited role in memory storage. *Science*, **250**, 288–290.

Zucker, R. S. (1989). Short-term synaptic plasticity. *Annual Review of Neuroscience*, **12**, 13–31.

Author index

Subject index